58:1 · April 2020

ENGLISH LANGUAGE NOTES

Indigenous Narratives of Territory and Creation: Hemispheric Perspectives

LEILA GÓMEZ, Special Issue Editor

Introduction

LEILA GÓMEZ

In addressing Indigenous American languages in a transhemispheric context, this issue of *ELN* opens up conversations across disciplines and regions of the Americas. Failure to cross the North-South boundary constitutes a long-standing geographic blind spot in the field of Indigenous studies, one that this special issue encourages scholars to examine meaningfully. This issue brings together fruitful comparisons of theoretical frameworks and case studies across regions to find commonalities and specificities that shed light on hemispheric Indigenous studies in North and South America today.

This special issue is devoted to studying narratives of creation and territorial origin as they are told and transmitted in Indigenous languages and conflictive settings of the Americas. This emphasis on tribal language, long the target of colonial policies of eradication, constitutes the editor's endeavor to engage Linda Tuhiwai Smith's framework of "decolonizing methodologies": the central anticolonial strategies for which Smith advocates are the revitalization and revaluation of Indigenous languages, not merely for linguistic purposes but also because these languages are vehicles of non-Western worldviews and forms of knowledge for epistemological and political purposes.[1] For this reason, this special issue includes studies across the broader sweep of the Americas with a focus on interdisciplinary work (anthropology, film studies, literature, linguistics, and so on) and on the theme of origin and territory narratives (i.e., the Theft of the Sun, Fallen Star, Isko Bird, and others) that often share transhemispheric commonalities and have the capacity to provide narratological, cosmological, and mythopoetic bases for transgeographic, transhistorical, and transdisciplinary discursive analyses.

This issue also invokes Emil Keme's proposal of Abiayala as a transhemispheric Indigenous bridge. This category could "potentially lead us to develop political alliances in the formation of a new Indigenous and non-Indigenous historical bloc that opposes Eurocentric concepts and projects like 'Latin America,' 'Latinity,' or 'Americas,' as well as extractive economies based on capitalism and socialism at national, continental, and intercontinental levels."[2]

Following Aníbal Quijano's critique of the coloniality of power as the system that imposed the devaluing of certain cultural knowledge, including that of Native Americans, to enforce Western racial, cultural, and male superiority, this issue

ENGLISH LANGUAGE NOTES

58:1, April 2020 DOI 10.1215/00138282-8237366
© 2020 Regents of the University of Colorado

investigates Indigenous narratives of the hemisphere depicting visions of territorial origin that claim the land as their own.[3] Symbolic territory and land reclamation are the focus of much Indigenous activism in the Americas. This issue explores Native narratives that provide legitimacy and a foundation for this political practice and, at the same time, finds ways in which they are spread continentally in specific contexts and beyond national histories. Furthermore, through these narratives this issue explores a system of knowledge that contradicts discourses of the conquest of empire and modern nations, discourses imposed by the coloniality of power; moreover, these discursive formations are authored by settler colonialism, a process-based structure that Patrick Wolfe informs us insists on "the elimination of the Native,"[4] an observation with particular prescience in the context of Latin America and a pivot around which Latinidad is often leveraged, as Keme argues. Specifically, Keme contends that Latinidad must be removed from scholarly discussions to allow the indigene, and presumably Indigenous thought, to emerge in Latinx contexts. Our contributors' reliance on language as a methodology seeks to disrupt and intervene in the totalizing force of Latinity in the cultural imaginary and illustrate the creation of indigenx models in Central and South American Indigenous studies as defined by Penelope Kelsey.[5] Kelsey's concept of indigenx praxis gestures to the choices that Latinx/Chicanx scholars must make about how to engage indigeneity within Latin American and Chicanx texts and cultural production. Specifically, indigenx theory implies the structures of analysis a scholar crafts that may address these intersections specifically and in a thoroughgoing way, situate oneself along the borders of these two streams of identity, or amplify the presence and epistemologies of one in preference to the others. Indigenx methodologies always acknowledge the presence of Indigenous peoples and Indigenous ancestry, but whether and how those theoretical practices are engaged is a matter of informed choice, of strategic maneuvering, and of an awareness of the implications of the choice to identify cultural expressions as Latinx or Indigenous.

This issue comparatively studies narratives of territory and creation of Native communities that were and are today constantly displaced and seeks to understand the diasporic meaning of these narratives in the context of the struggle for land. As LeAnne Howe writes in "Tribalography": "Native stories are power. They create people. They author tribes. America is a tribal creation story. Creation stories, as numerous as Indian tribes, gave birth to our people. It is with absolute certainty that I tell you now—our stories also created the immigrants who landed on our shores."[6] Thus "Native people created narratives that were histories and stories with the power to transform," and the contributors in this special issue analyze the power of these stories.[7]

Although all the authors in this special issue engage—to a different extent—in discussions around all the above-mentioned problematics in the Indigenous studies of Abiayala, they are divided into groups conforming to the main topics they address: land and language.

The Land Question

In 1928, in his influential essay "The Question of the Land," José Carlos Mariátegui clarified for his fellow Peruvians as well as Latin Americans in general that "the problem of the Indian" is not their culture, their language, or their beliefs—it is their land itself.[8] Although his essay additionally addresses the problems resulting from the Peruvian bourgeoisie's flawed mechanisms of land exploitation, Mariátegui inaugurated a way of thinking about a situation that has persisted since the conquest and colonization of the Abiayala peoples: the dispossession, forced displacement, and subsequent criminalization and marginalization of the original inhabitants and their descendants. Thus the articles in this group study narratives of origin or belonging that address the relationships of different Indigenous peoples of the Abiayala to their land. In this sense these narratives function as foundational tales that configure not only social and cultural spaces but also their intricate relationship with their surroundings and the natural world. The authors included in this group do so by approaching diverse aspects of this relationship: they explore linguistic loss and recovery, ancestral memory, land expropriation, and the restitution of human remains, as well as political and economic struggles against the colonial legacy of national states and new imperial oppression.

This critical lens foregrounds these narratives of origin as intimately linked to what Winona LaDuke has termed "struggles for the land," which, in Latin America, have expanded over centuries and in alliance with non-Indigenous popular sectors, similarly "deterritorialized" or marginalized struggles in which Indigenous peoples were in conflict with not only the republican states but also industrial expropriation.[9] These narratives of origin in connection with territory are a fundamental part of the activism that today occupies the Indigenous struggle.

In "The Chamorro Creation Story, Guam Land Struggles, and Contemporary Poetry," Craig Santos Perez explores how narratives of Chamorro creation have historically performed as a source of Indigenous values and ethics until settlers attempted to supplant them during the colonization of Guam's land and waters. He then recounts the history of Guam's occupation and resistance to militarization of the Mariana Islands and examines recent efforts to reclaim the Chamorro creation story as a vehicle for cultural revitalization. Specifically, he analyzes Jay Baza Pascua's "Chachalåni," a Chamorro-language chant-poem, which has been made into a film. Perez's translation and close reading of the poem illustrates how Baza not only subverts Christian narratives of creation but also expresses Chamorro beliefs and values as central to the ecological health of the land and people.

The Abenaki poet Cheryl Savageau's essay "Listening to the Land" contemplates Abenaki Territory of the Dawn Land through the lens of geography and the story of Ktsi Amiskw (Beaver). Savageau frames the Abenaki creation story as a "conversation" among various Abenaki writers, including the historian Lisa Brooks, the anthropologist Marge Bruchac, and her, establishing how the land carries knowledges that "speaks" and asserting that Abenaki people hold a responsibility to be present, listen, and help recover those stories. She then exemplifies this process by recounting the story of Ktsi Amiskw and providing specific examples of where one can find particular geographic features that correspond to this story's record of the land's formation.

In "Borders Be Damned!" Geary Hobson examines the origins of the Native Writers' Circle of the Americas and its associated Returning the Gift conference and places it in the longer history of border-crossing narratives from 1492 to the present. Pointing to examples like Chief Clinton Rickard and Returning the Gift's own extensive experience in bridging the US-Canadian border and bringing First Nations and Native American authors together, Hobson issues a call for an ongoing effort among Indigenous authors to traverse colonial boundaries throughout North and South America. He models the gains of such Indigenous collaboration by offering a bibliography of Indigenous authors from throughout the Américas, Arctic region, and Sámiland.

In "Restitution of Human Remains and Landscape Resignification: The Case of Chapal-có Hill (La Pampa, Argentina) and the Rankülche Nation," Rafael Pedro Curtoni, Guillermo Heider, María Gabriela Chaparro, and Ángel T. Tuninetti explore the restitution process of human remains in twenty-first-century Argentina in relation to the appearance of new actors, the reconfiguration of public policies, and various academic approaches to land restitution and resignification. The authors point out that in the case studies involving the Rankülche Nation, there was a clear resignification of territory after the discovery of ancestral remains in the region. The subsequent restitution process deepened the roots of the Rankülche people in this territory, which have long been an object of dispute in modern Argentina.

Javier Alonso Muñoz-Diaz's "Indigenous-Inspired Authorial Figures and Networks of Rural-Urban Migrants in *The Fox from Up Above and the Fox from Down Below* (1971), by José María Arguedas," discusses the representation of Indigenous-inspired authorial figures in Arguedas's novel about the highland rural migrants in the coastal city of Chimbote, Peru. A bicultural and bilingual writer (Quechua and Spanish), Arguedas explores the complexity of the experience of Andean contemporary migration and how narratives of origin and mythical characters are reconfigured in urban settings. The Quechua population of Chimbote evinces an incredible capability to create networks of rural-urban migrants that speak to the vitality of their narratives of origins and their cultural practices.

Alexandre Belmonte's article "The Past Embedded in Everyday Life: The Meseta del Collao as an Illustrative Case" describes how, to attain financial success, people in the Andes look to the assistance of *yatiris* (symbolic miniatures found in local markets), which were considered heretical and therefore were severely repressed by Spanish priests in the colonial period but which constitute part of an important tradition in myth and rituals today. Belmonte's article highlights the importance of the *yatiris* in a practice that connects past and present in Andean culture and ties people to the social space they inhabit.

Leila Gómez's article "Narrative of Origin and Utopia in Lucrecia Martel's *New Argirópolis*" analyzes how both Domingo F. Sarmiento's essay *Argirópolis* and Martel's film address the question of landownership and river navigation in Argentina. In Martel's *New Argirópolis* in particular, an eight-minute film that presents a multilingual plot and multilingual characters, the Qom people's fight for their land is placed in the sphere of science fiction and foundational narrative. The inability of Argentine officials to understand Indigenous languages leads to their insurrectional plans of land recovery. Martel's story is that of the land question itself, precisely what Mariátegui in 1928 asserted to be "the problem of the Indian." In her film Martel recovers the history of over five centuries of colonization that continued with the Argentine nation and persists today.

Language and Epistemologies

The careful application of language-based methodologies in Indigenous studies acts as an irreplaceable ameliorative for addressing the absences of Native thought in the academy throughout the Americas. One could argue that only through the careful study of language can scholars identify and outline the parameters of Indigenous epistemology; further, these languages serve as generative loci of Indigenous thought and theory in ways in which few other sources (e.g., story, land) are capable. In Native American and Indigenous studies (NAIS), a new generation of Indigenous linguists is emerging (e.g., Jenny Davis, Margaret Noodin, Frederick White) whose scholarship exerts pressure on how linguists engage with Native peoples and languages. Rather than limit its scope to the discipline of linguistics, this special issue endeavors to illustrate the *transdisciplinary* gains made possible by applying knowledges and methods based in Indigenous languages to environmental studies, film, history, literature, religious studies, and NAIS texts. The issue works to expand the scope of the journal itself by engaging scholars with expertise across a range of Anglophone and Hispanophone contexts and regions. The essays in this section are meant to provide models for understanding how Indigenous languages refuse confinement to the territory of linguistics and instead far exceed the boundaries established by the Western academy and insist that we engage with them on their own terms, in their own ways, and across a range of academic fields.

Indigenous languages are arguably the catalyst that can make indigenizing the academy a challenge, which Devon Mihesuah, Linda Tuhiwai Smith, Robert Warrior, and many others have written about. However, this movement toward a new academy can happen only when Indigenous studies scholars hold themselves responsible for studying the languages of the peoples whose cultural, history, literature, and religions they research and write about. This shift begins as simply as no longer issuing master's and doctoral degrees to candidates who do not speak an Indigenous language; this is notably a simple change, but it is one that would require many institutions to change the nature of graduate study. Those of us in the previous generation need to acknowledge this oversight in our own training and find the resources to study Indigenous languages germane to our area of expertise. For some, this adaptation means convincing our institutions to commit to offering courses in languages indigenous to the territory in which they are located; in other cases, pursuing online classes is sometimes the best way to appropriately expand our knowledge base. By taking these courses ourselves, we model for our graduate students the approaches they need to take to perform responsible—and thorough—scholarship.

The essays in this group evince a heartfelt appreciation for what Indigenous languages can teach us and how their closer examination reveals worlds of knowledge that would otherwise remain hidden. In essence, by reclaiming the epistemologies housed in languages in the service of Indigenous studies scholarship, these essays work to undo damage and loss caused by colonial education and showcase the revelatory insights made possible by reading texts and cultural expressions through the lens of language. Ultimately, by using language-based approaches to Indigenous hemispheric narratives, these scholars engage and model *tribal theory* as a method derived from Indigenous language and worldview, and they leave a body of work that will stand for generations of Indigenous studies scholars to follow and expand on.

Amber Meadow Adams's "Yotsi'tishon and the Language of the Seed in the Haudenosaunee Story of Earth's Creation" invites us to consider the creation story as recounted by John Arthur Gibson (Onondaga) to the ethnologist J. N. B. Hewitt (Tuscarora) in 1888, the longest extant version of Iroquois creation and easily the richest in ethnobotanical knowledge. Couching her analysis in an exhaustive knowledge of the extant print versions of Haudenosaunee origins, Adams builds an insightful linguistically based argument for why we should read language surrounding Sky Woman through the lens of seeds and generation and focus on the sequential emergence of plant species of the Carolinian biome in both the Hewitt-Gibson and Dayodekane Seth Newhouse's versions as a principal interpretive frame for the narrative. Adams uses Kanien'keha concepts such as *yoti'nikòn:ra* (the collective's "mind," or thought, will, and decision), *'nihstenh* (to mother someone), and *ka'shatstenhsera* (power, potential) to aptly demonstrate how language performs as a necessary key to understanding many early ethnological texts.

In "A Central Sierra Miwok Origins Story: The Theft of the Sun," Andrew Cowell turns our attention to a Sierra Miwok creation story, "Coyote Steals the Sun." Examining the story in the original language, Cowell's line-by-line translation functions as a centralizing methodology in his "ethnopoetical" reading of Lena Cox's recounting of the narrative to the non-Native linguist Lucy Freeland in the 1930s. Cowell's attention to word, imagery, and structure highlight how Cox's version confirms Sierra Miwok knowledge of their origins in the Great Basin and their arrival in the California woodland as simultaneous with the arrival of the Sun.

Christopher Vecsey takes readers into early contact between Native Americans and missionaries in "American Indians Encounter the Bible: Reception, Resistance, and Reinterpretation" and examines how Indigenous peoples understood and deployed the Christian Bible within their own discursive and rhetorical frames regardless of the intended meaning of the non-Natives disseminating it. While principles of the Doctrine of Discovery envision Indigenous peoples of the Americas as without writing, culture, or civilization, Vecsey details how early explorers and missionaries confronted the presence of pictography and various forms of Native record keeping (such as birchbark scrolls, wampum) and how Native peoples often used the Bible for their own purposes and not those intended by their would-be evangelists.

Sarah Hernandez's essay "Translating and Retranslating 'Fallen Star': An *Ohų'kaką* Tale" focuses on a Dakota creation story that literary critics have ignored. Hernandez considers both Stephen Riggs and Ella Deloria's renditions of this story. Hernandez contends that Deloria's English-language version of Fallen Star decolonizes the Dakota storytelling tradition, asserting the primacy of Dakota language, literature, and lifeways through the medium of print culture.

In "Tales of (De)colonization in the Peruvian Amazon: The Case of the Isko-nawa," José Antonio Mazzotti presents some of the results of a long-term research project on the Iskonawa, one of the endangered communities in the Peruvian Amazon. Since 2010 Mazzotti and a team of researchers have been collecting Iskonawa oral tradition. In this article he analyzes two narratives of origin and survival that explain the Iskonawa's relationship with nature and its fundamental role in shaping their social rules and cultural practices. Their alternative views of nature challenge the Western, neoliberal approach to the Amazonian Basin that has brought defor-estation, contamination, crime, and drug trafficking. The article also traces the way these narratives of origin have been incorporated into the literature of decolonial Peruvian writers such as Arguedas and César Calvo.

Enrique Bernales Albites's "Indigenous Narratives of Creation and Origin in *Embrace of the Serpent*, by Ciro Guerra" explores how narratives on the cura-tive power of plants such as Ayahuasca are valuable for understanding Indigenous rationality in relation to Western science and how the knowledge of these plants enriches the communities and histories of Indigenous cultures of the Amazon. The same can be said for the soundscapes in Guerra's film, which shows both the interaction of Indigenous and non-Indigenous languages in the contact zone of the Amazon and the conflictive power-knowledge relationship among those who are multilingual: diverse groups of Indigenous people, priests, anthropologists, and businesspeople and their conflictive perceptions and uses of natural resources.

In "World(build)ing in Mohawk- and Seneca-Language Films," Penelope Kel-sey examines recent Indigenous-language films produced in Hodínöhšö:ni:h lan-guages, focusing on environmental and ethical concerns within digital media. Her essay illustrates how these films articulate "ecologies of expression," as defined by Zayin Cabot, which simultaneously regard all epistemologies as equal *and* seek to confirm Iroquois conceptions of the natural world. Through these filmmakers' focus on Iroquois languages in the film, Kelsey reads their works as expressive of a collective agency that reflects and extends Cabot's theorization of Indigenous ontologies.

This special issue, in sum, links narratives of creation/origin to land strug-gle from transdisciplinary and hemispheric perspectives and Native people's narra-tives of their kinship and responsibilities to the land. The issue includes contribu-tions on origins and diaspora, land reclamation and Indigenous activism, territorial struggle and environmentalism, Indigenous resistance to state and neoliberal poli-cies of land expropriation, alliances between academic and Indigenous knowledges and activisms, non-Western epistemologies and territory, and films on land claims and Indigenous languages and epistemes.

LEILA GÓMEZ is associate professor of Spanish and director of the Latin American Studies Center at the University of Colorado Boulder. Among her books are *Iluminados y tránsfugas: Relatos de viajeros y ficciones fundacionales en Argentina, Paraguay y Perú* (2009) and the edited collection *Darwin in Argentina (Major Texts, 1845–1909)* (2011). She is also coeditor of *Entre Borges y Conrad: Estética y territorio en W. H. Hudson* (2012) and *Teaching Gender through Latin American, Spanish, and Latino Literature and Culture* (2015). Gómez is writing a book about the mythical image of Mexico in travel writing of the nineteenth to the twenty-first centuries. For this book project she was awarded the Alexander von Humboldt Fellowship for Advanced Researchers in Germany.

Notes

1   Smith, *Decolonizing Methodologies.*
2   Keme and Coon, "For Abiayala to Live," 42.
3   Quijano, "Colonialidad del poder."
4   Wolfe, "Settler Colonialism."
5   *Indigenx* here is used to refer to Indigenous studies models applied in Latin American and Chicana/o/x contexts. The *x* invokes the crosscurrents of Latinity and indigeneity that inform these methods and also acknowledge the intersection that *must* be navigated—whether removed, as Keme suggests; obviated temporarily; or delved into and meditated on as part of one's theoretical praxis.
6   Howe, "Tribalography," 118.
7   Howe, "Tribalography," 118.
8   Mariátegui, *Seven Interpretative Essays of Peruvian Reality.*
9   LaDuke, *All Our Relations.*

Works Cited

Howe, LeAnne. "Tribalography: The Power of Native Stories." *Journal of Dramatic Theory and Criticism* 14, no. 1 (1999): 117–25.

Keme, Emil, and Adam Coon. "For Abiayala to Live, the Americas Must Die: Toward a Transhemispheric Indigeneity." *Native American and Indigenous Studies* 5, no. 1 (2018): 42–68.

LaDuke, Winona. *All Our Relations: Native Struggles for Land and Life.* Chicago: Haymarket, 2016.

Mariátegui, José Carlos. *Seven Interpretative Essays of Peruvian Reality.* Austin: University of Texas Press, 1971.

Mohawk, John. *Thinking in Indian: A John Mohawk Reader,* edited by Jose Barreiro. Golden, CO: Fulcrum, 2010.

Quijano, Aníbal. "Colonialidad del poder: Eurocentrismo y América Latina." In *Cuestiones y horizontes: De la dependencia histórico-estructural a la colonialidad/ descolonialidad del poder,* 201–46. Buenos Aires: CLACSO, 2014.

Smith, Linda Tuhiwai. *Decolonizing Methodologies: Research and Indigenous Peoples.* London: Zed, 2012.

Wolfe, Patrick. "Settler Colonialism and the Elimination of the Native." *Journal of Genocide Research* 8, no. 4 (2006): 387–409.

The Chamorro Creation Story, Guam Land Struggles, and Contemporary Poetry

CRAIG SANTOS PEREZ

Abstract   This essay focuses on the creation story of the Indigenous Chamorro people from the western Pacific Island of Guam. The essay presents and analyzes the deeper meaning of the story of Puntan and Fu'una as they birth the island of Guam and the Chamorro people. Moreover, it maps the history of Catholic missionization that displaced and replaced the Chamorro creation story. The essay covers the related issue of how colonization removed Chamorros from their ancestral lands and appropriated these lands for imperial, military, tourism, and urban development. Then it highlights the decades-long struggle of Chamorro activists to reclaim the land. Lastly, it turns to contemporary Chamorro poetry to illustrate how authors have revitalized and retold the story of Puntan and Fu'una to critique and protest the degradation of Chamorro lands and to advocate for the protection and return of the land.
Keywords   Indigenous literature, Pacific literature, Chamorro literature, creation stories, ecopoetics

In this essay I focus on the creation story of my people, the Chamorro, who are the Indigenous islanders from the Mariana archipelago in the western Pacific Ocean region known as Micronesia.[1] First, I show how the Chamorro creation story was an important source of Indigenous values and ethics in regard to spiritual, ecological, cultural, gender, familial, and social relationships. I then outline how Spanish, American, and Japanese imperialism, missionization, and militarism displaced the Chamorro creation story and spiritual beliefs, changed traditional land tenure systems, removed the Native people from customary land habitation, and desecrated the lands and waters. Next I highlight recent decolonial acts to revitalize the Chamorro creation story, reenact Chamorro spiritual practices tied to the land, and inspire Indigenous cultural revitalization. Furthermore, I illustrate how the Chamorro creation story has formed the spiritual foundation of Indigenous land struggles against US militarism. Lastly, I analyze a contemporary Chamorro-language poem that shows how the Chamorro creation story continues to inspire us to remain

ENGLISH LANGUAGE NOTES
58:1, April 2020   DOI 10.1215/00138282-8237377
© 2020 Regents of the University of Colorado

rooted in our culture and live harmoniously with the natural world as well as guide us toward a decolonized, sustainable future. For the limited scope of this essay, I focus on my ancestral home island of Guam, the most populated and militarized island of the Mariana archipelago.[2]

"Puntan and Fu'una": The Chamorro Creation Story and Its Meanings

The Chamorro creation story has been passed down for thousands of years, and while there are multiple versions with slight variations, this is the most common narrative: In the beginning, Fu'una and her brother Puntan decided to sacrifice their lives to create our islands. Fu'una transformed Puntan's back into the land, his chest into the sky, and his eyebrows into rainbows. She transformed one of his eyes into the sun and the other into the moon. Fu'una then breathed life into the sun so that it would shine, into the soil so that it would blossom, and into the waters so that they would flow. Then she transformed herself into a large stone and birthed Chamorros from her body and the surrounding sands.[3]

In the Chamorro language, Fu'una's name translates as "first" and Puntan's name translates as "coconut tree sapling." The large stone is known as "Lasso' Fu'a," or Fouha Rock, which is located in the bay of Humåtak, known as Fouha Bay and the "Cradle of Creation," on the southwestern coast of the island of Guam. Ancient Chamorros went on an annual pilgrimage, known as *lukao* (procession), to Fouha Rock, sang songs and recited chants, made offerings, and sought blessings for their seeds, crops, and fishing implements in the hope of bountiful harvests.[4]

The Chamorro creation story was an important source of Indigenous values, wisdom, and knowledge. Because the land was created from the bodies of Puntan and Fu'una, Chamorros view the land itself as an ancestor; thus land, genealogy, and spirituality are interconnected. Chamorros refer to themselves as *i taotao tano*, or "the people of the land," and several villages on Guam are named after body parts, such as Barrigada (flank), Tiyan (stomach), Hagatna (blood), and Mongmong (heartbeat). In Chamorro epistemology, the spirits of the dead continue to dwell on and in the land.

Called *taotaomo'na* (people of before), the spirits were "treated as members of the family and referred to by name or through terms of endearment."[5] The powerful *taotaomo'na* had "a district to guard and were worshipped in rituals by the living. Many of the spirits had individual names and histories fixed by myths."[6] When Chamorros died, they were often buried in the earth beneath the family home so that their spirits could continue to support and protect the family. When entering certain lands guarded by *taotaomo'na*, Chamorros would first ask *petmisu*, or permission, to enter (failure to observe protocol could result in sickness or misfortune). The Chamorros invoked and prayed to *taotaomo'na* when planting and fishing. They also offered them drinks and a part of the catch or harvest. In Chamorro epistemology, "all that is, all that exists, is a testament to the cooperation between the ancestral spirits of Chamorros and those currently living."[7] This belief in interconnection is further embodied in the most important Chamorro cultural value, *inafa'maolek*, or the interdependence between nature, man and woman, and relatives.[8] Because the land was viewed as the literal bodies of Puntan's and Fu'una's bodies and spirits, as the dwelling place of *taotaomo'na*, and as the source of nourishment and protection, it followed that the land was sacred and must be treated with reverence and reciprocity.

The Chamorro creation story also teaches us about proper kinship practices, gender relations, and land customs. The relationship between Puntan and Fu'una shows that the sibling relationship was paramount and that men and women were respected as contributing members of a society in which "gender roles were balanced equitably so that men and women shared power and responsibility."[9] In the Chamorro land tenure system, families controlled land tenure and usage rights, and both men and women had various obligations to sustainably care for the land and its resources. However, land was inherited through the women's lineage, reflecting the matrilineal aspects of Chamorro society.[10] Overall, the profound story of Puntan and Fu'una transmitted core Chamorro values, wisdom, and knowledge through the generations.

Reducción: Colonizing Creation and Desecrating the Land

In 1521 Magellan made landfall on Guam, which became "the first inhabited island in the Pacific Ocean known to Europeans."[11] Spain nominally claimed Guam in 1564, establishing its first colony in the Pacific. The first cargo of products from Asia was delivered to Mexico that year via the Acapulco–Guam–Manila trade route. In the following decades galleons loaded with silver from Mexico (along with soldiers, merchants, missionaries, government officials, mail, and supplies) set sail from Acapulco and reprovisioned off Guam before arriving in the Philippines to trade with Chinese merchants. When the galleons returned to Acapulco, the products made their way across the New World and the Atlantic Ocean to European markets. The Spanish Empire mapped "a great circular loop around the Pacific north of the equator [with Guam as] a sure and useful landmark and stopover on the trans-Pacific trade route."[12]

Spanish authorities officially colonized the island in 1668 and shortly thereafter initiated the Christian conquest of the Pacific by establishing a mission on Guam, as well as the first European educational institution in the Pacific, the Colegio de San Juan de Letrán, a seminary. The Catholic authorities renamed the archipelago Islas de Marianas to honor the queen of Spain, Maria Ana de Austria, who funded the mission. Many Chamorros resisted the conversion efforts, which led to the "Spanish-Chamorro Wars" (1668–95). By the end of the wars the violence associated with Christian conversion, military conquest, and foreign disease had led to massive Chamorro depopulation. Through the policy of *reducción*, the colonial authorities destroyed about 180 Chamorro settlements and forcibly relocated the surviving Chamorro population into a few large villages centered on a church and guarded by a garrison.[13] Spanish missionization suppressed and replaced Chamorro spiritual beliefs with Christianity and replaced the Chamorro creation story with the Christian one.

Spanish control of the Marianas ended as a result of the Spanish-American War of 1898. In defeat Spain sold the fourteen Northern Mariana Islands to Germany, and Guam became a territory of the United States. The Spanish "crown lands" (nearly a third of the island), as well as all fortifications and public buildings, were ceded to the US government. A series of landmark Supreme Court cases, collectively known as the Insular Cases (1901–22), created a new political category, "unincorporated territory," which meant that a territory could be a possession of the United Sates without becoming a fully incorporated part of the nation.[14] From 1898 to 1941 the US Navy administered Guam and established schools, hospitals, businesses, and roads as part of their "civilizing" and "militarizing" mission. In addition to appropriating land, the US naval government began construction throughout the island, creating drainage systems, new government buildings, a water distillation plant, water storage plants, outhouses, a telephone station, a military commissary, a post exchange, hospitals, and roads.[15] Just as Guam was strategic to Spain's trans-Pacific trade route, Guam became a strategic location for US military transports traveling between San Francisco, Hawai'i, and the Philippines.

Colonial power in the Marianas shifted in 1914 when Japan seized the Northern Mariana Islands from Germany. In December 1941 Japan invaded Guam and defeated the US forces there, uniting the archipelago under Japanese rule. Guam was renamed Omiya Jima, or "Great Shrine Island," and Japanese authorities initiated several militarizing and civilizing projects to transform Guam into a strategic base for Japan's vision of a "Coprosperity Sphere of Greater East Asia." From 1941 to 1944 the Japanese authorities focused on increasing agricultural production and military fortification. One of the most urgent priorities was the production of rice. Ignoring private land titles, the Japanese authorities appropriated and deforested land to create rice paddies; more than a dozen rice farms were established throughout the island. As the war progressed, the Chamorros were compelled to support the Japanese war effort with their agricultural labor. Alongside increasing agricultural production, the Japanese authorities initiated mining and logging efforts to create lumber for military construction, firewood, and charcoal. Japanese industrialization also focused on the militarization of the island. Forced Chamorro labor was used to construct several airfields, munitions storage, pillboxes, real and dummy cannons, man-made caves, and tank traps. Like the Spanish and American colonizers, the Japanese imperialists desecrated the islands through colonial agriculture, industrialization, and militarization.[16]

Bombing and fighting during the three-week battle between the United States and Japan in 1944 devastated the Mariana archipelago. After the war the fourteen Northern Mariana Islands became part of the United Nations Trust Territory of the Pacific Islands, administered by the United States until the 1970s, at which point the political status of the islands changed to the "Commonwealth of the Northern Mariana Islands." Guam, on the other hand, once again became an "unincorporated territory" (a status that continues to this day), and its residents were granted US citizenship in 1950. After the war land that had been taken by the Japanese military became US military farms and eventually fell under the jurisdiction of the US Department of Agriculture. In the following years the US military took nearly 50 percent of Guam's landmass (about seventy-five thousand acres) through purchase, lease, or condemnation (most of which was coercive and extralegal) to build bases and other installations. The United States aimed to develop Guam into a substantial military base, second only to Pearl Harbor in the Pacific. The decades-long US military presence has caused severe environmental devastation. Eighty contaminated military dump sites exist on the island. The now-civilian Ordot landfill (a former military dump site) contains seventeen toxic chemicals. The same seventeen pollutants are also found in the landfills located over the island's aquifer at Andersen Air Force Base. In the 1970s the military used the waters around Guam as a decontamination site during its nuclear testing in the Pacific, which resulted in massive radiation and strontium-90 exposure. During the Vietnam War, Agent Orange and Agent Purple, both used as defoliants, were stored on Guam in drums. Military dumping and nuclear testing also contaminated the Pacific with PCBs and radiation, polluting the largest barrier reef system of Guam and poisoning fish and fishing grounds. Today the territory of Guam and the Commonwealth of the Northern Mariana Islands are among the most militarized and contaminated places in the world.[17]

One irreversible effect of ecological imperialism in Guam has been the extinction and endangerment of native and endemic species of more than two dozen birds, mammals, reptiles, mollusks, and plants. This species loss has been caused by habitat destruction, environmental pollution, and the introduction of invasive species. After World War II brown tree snakes arrived in Guam as stowaways on US military ships or aircraft. Having no natural predators, the snakes quickly multiplied and colonized the island. In just a few decades nearly eight hundred thousand native birds were killed and most species became extinct, while a few were taken into captivity and are now bred in US zoos. The loss of birds in Guam is reverberating through the island's ecology; because there are no birds to spread and germinate seeds, many native trees may become extinct and the tropical forests may soon experience desertification.[18]

Once a lush tropical archipelago with abundant biodiversity, the Mariana Islands are now a site of environmental precarity. Spanish imperialism first suppressed the Chamorro creation story and displaced Chamorros from their land, thus asserting that the land is under the Spanish crown and the dominion of the Christian god. Since the twentieth century American imperialism has militarized, desecrated, and contaminated the land, asserting that it is simply territory for American military basing, betraying the belief that land is sacred and should be treated with reverence and respect.

"Our Islands are Sacred": The Chamorro Creation Story and Guam Land Struggles

During the last seventy-five years the struggle over land and land rights has been a central component of the Chamorro decolonization movement. After World War II many Chamorros resisted and protested military land appropriation on Guam.[19] In the 1970s Chamorro legal and political activism focused on the return of land occupied by the federal government and the military to the original landowners and other landless Chamorros. In the 1980s and 1990s Chamorro activists protested the desecration of ancient Chamorro burial grounds.[20] Several Chamorro rights groups emerged during those decades, including I Nasion Chamorro and the

Organization of People for Indigenous Rights, and framed the struggle over land within the context of Indigenous rights. The activism of the period successfully advocated for the creation of the Chamorro Land Trust Act and the establishment of the Chamorro Land Trust Commission, which has issued deeds to more than twenty-five hundred acres of land to Chamorros. In 1994 the Guam Excess Lands Act was passed, and the Guam Ancestral Lands Commission was later established to facilitate the transfer of unused federal property to the Government of Guam.[21] The importance of this activism and legal acts speaks to the significance of land in Chamorro culture: "The role native ownership of land plays in the preservation of Chamorro culture and social stability cannot be underestimated. Land is the only significant asset of the Chamorro, and it is the basis of family organization. It traditionally passes from generation to generation, creating family identity and contributing to the economic well-being of family members."[22] Because land is a key site, symbol, and marker of Chamorro cultural identity, "the issue of land persists as an essential component to the survival of the Chamorro people, especially in the face of persistent exploitation of land."[23]

Chamorro land struggles in the twenty-first century have focused on protesting an ongoing and massive military buildup on Guam and the Northern Marianas. In 2006 the US and Japan announced a major realignment of US military forces and operations in the Asia-Pacific region. This new arrangement would include one of the largest buildups and relocations in US history. Described as a "mega-buildup," it would include the construction of facilities to house and support eighty-six hundred marines, transferred with their nine thousand dependents from Okinawa, as well as seven thousand transient navy personnel, six hundred to one thousand army personnel, and twenty thousand foreign workers. Additionally, the buildup would establish an Air and Missile Defense Task Force.[24]

An especially controversial aspect of the buildup was a proposal to transform an area around the jungles of Pågat, the site of an ancestral Chamorro village where many ancient artifacts and remains are found, into a live firing-range complex, thus restricting access to Pågat. In a letter addressed to the Department of Defense, a coalition of University of Guam faculty addressed the religious significance of the site: "[The *taotaomo'na*] dwelling places can be found everywhere in Guam . . . but are known to have an especially strong presence in Pågat. . . . As [it is] a place of religious significance, Chamorros treat Pågat with great respect, and our generation's responsibility is to protect and nurture the site so that it is treated with the respect paid to the world's great cathedrals and temples."[25] Additionally, two new activist groups formed during this time, We Are Guahan and Our Islands Are Sacred, which emphasized the sacredness and biodiversity of the land. They highlighted the fact that Pågat was home to several endangered species, particularly the Mariana eight-spot butterfly. They also spearheaded campaigns that involved demonstrations during Department of Defense public meetings, as well as at rallies in Guam, Hawai'i, and the continental United States.[26] One of their actions was for participants to create protest signs about why the islands are sacred to them and then to post photos of them online using the hashtag #OurIslandsAreSacred. By articulating land as a sacred dwelling place of Chamorro spirits, contemporary

Chamorros are articulating an ecological identity tied to genealogy and spirituality. Furthermore, this rhetorical strategy has become a powerful statement against the idea that land is simply a base for military testing and operations.

A poignant cultural revitalization project known as Lukao Fuha, or "A Procession to Fuha," also emerged during this time. Religious colonialism had suppressed this tradition for centuries. However, on February 1, 2014, Our Islands Are Sacred and another Chamorro cultural group, Hinasso, revived this ancient spiritual practice. According to the ancestral thirteen-month Chamorro calendar, the first day of February marks the Chamorro new year. As the Chamorro genealogist Bernard Punzalan wrote, the Lukao Fuha celebrated not only the new year but also "the birth of life emanating from the stories of Fo'na (Fu'una) yan Pontan (Puntan)."[27] The Chamorro creation story, having survived centuries of narrative repression, has birthed a Chamorro identity reconnected to the *taotaomo'na* and the sacredness of the land. In turn, belief in the sacredness of the land has formed the foundation of anti-military environmental activism.

"Chachalåni": The Chamorro Creation Story in Contemporary Chamorro Poetry

While the Chamorro creation story has formed the spiritual and cultural foundation of land struggles on Guam, it has also inspired new Chamorro poetry that renarrates the land as a sacred space. The Chamorro chanter, storyteller, writer, and actor Jay Baza Pascua offers a poignant example. Pascua has worked in Guam's media industry as a news anchor and reporter, as an editor for a business journal, and as a contributor to both of Guam's newspapers. After a cultural and spiritual awakening, he began composing stories and chants about Chamorro culture. Some of his chants have been made into films and featured at several film festivals. His twenty-three-line chant-poem, "Chachalåni," published in 2011, directly speaks to the Chamorro creation story. Before analyzing the poem, I quote it in full, first in the Chamorro language and then in Pascua's own English translation:

Chachalåni

Fa'uma yan Pontan hu gagaogao hamyo chachalåni i famaguon-miyu!
Ginen Pontan na gaige ham guini gi tano-ta. Ma nåhi ham i tataotao-niha!
Fa'uma yan Pontan hu gagaogao hamyo chachalåni i famaguon-miyu!
Ginen Fa'uma na gaige ham guine gi tano-ta. Ma nåhi ham i lina'lå-ta!
Fa'uma yan Pontan hu gagaogao hamyo chachalåni i famaguon-miyu!
Puengi yan ha'åni annok i famaguon Pontan yan i che'lu-nihan
    Fa'uma.
Fa'uma yan Pontan hu gagaogao hamyo chachalåni i famaguon-miyu!
Gi puengi i pilan i attadok-nihan Pontan . . . ha li'e i famaguon-niha.
Fa'uma yan Pontan hu gagaogao hamyo chachalåni i famaguon-miyu!
Gi ha'åni i atdao i attadok-nihan Pontan . . . ha li'e i famaguon-niha.
Fa'uma yan Pontan hu gagaogao hamyo chachalåni i famaguon-miyu!

Yanggen gaige i Chamoli Matao taifinakpo i lina'lan Fa'uma.
Fa'uma yan Pontan hu gagaogao hamyo chachalåni i famaguon-miyu!
Yanggen gaige i tano taifinakpo i lina'lan Pontan.
Fa'uma yan Pontan hu gagaogao hamyo chachalåni i famaguon-miyu!
Gaige i fegge-ta gi tatalo-nihan Pontan. Na adahi hamyo.
Fa'uma yan Pontan hu gagaogao hamyo chachalåni i famaguon-miyu!
Munga piniti i tano sa puputi nu Pontan. Na adahi hamyo.
Fa'uma yan Pontan hu gagaogao hamyo chachalåni i famaguon-miyu!
Munga piniti i taotao-miyu sa puputi nu Fa'uma. Na adahi hamyo.
Fa'uma yan Pontan hu gagaogao hamyo chachalåni i famaguon-miyu!
Tattiyi Fa'uma yan Pontan sa ginen siha na gaige ham guine gi tano-ta.
Fa'uma yan Pontan hu gagaogao hamyo chachalåni i famaguon-miyu!

[I humbly ask you Fu'una and Puntan to guide your children!
Through Puntan we are here on our land. He gave us his body!
I humbly ask you Fu'una and Puntan to guide your children!
Through Fu'una we are here on our land. She gave us our lives!
I humbly ask you Fu'una and Puntan to guide your children!
The children of Puntan and Fu'una can be seen night and day.
I humbly ask you Fu'una and Puntan to guide your children!
The moon, during the evening, is the eye of Puntan . . . able to see his
    children.
I humbly ask you Fu'una and Puntan to guide your children!
The sun, during the day, is the eye of Puntan . . . able to see his children.
I humbly ask you Fu'una and Puntan to guide your children!
Fu'una's life is eternal as long as there are Chamorros.
I humbly ask you Fu'una and Puntan to guide your children!
Puntan's life is eternal as long as the land remains.
I humbly ask you Fu'una and Puntan to guide your children!
Our footprints are on Puntan's back. Be careful all of you.
I humbly ask you Fu'una and Puntan to guide your children!
Do not hurt the land because you are hurting Puntan. This is a
    warning to all of you.
I humbly ask you Fu'una and Puntan to guide your children!
Do not hurt your people because you are hurting Fu'una. This is a
    warning to all of you.
I humbly ask you Fu'una and Puntan to guide your children!
Follow Fu'una and Puntan for it is because of them that we are here
    on our land.
I humbly ask you Fu'una and Puntan to guide your children!][28]

"Chachalåni," translates as "the journey, the path, or to guide and to lead." In the Chamorro version of the poem, the first and every other line begins with "Fa'uma yan Pontan," the Chamorro spelling for Fu'una and Puntan, thus invoking and calling forth the Chamorro creators. Pascua embodies the humility one should show to the ancestors, which reflects the Chamorro value of *respetu*, or respect. Throughout the poem Pascua asks for guidance, recognizing the wisdom inherent in the Chamorro creation story. Moreover, he refers to the Chamorro as *i famaguon-miyu*, or "your children," to acknowledge that they are born from Fu'una and Puntan. Formally, the repetition of the same verse in every other line embodies the chantlike structure found in many oral chants—a mnemonic device to aid in recitation. I suggest that the repetition has another effect: it continuously evokes Fu'una and Puntan to echo across the centuries of silence in which they were not invoked.

The first half of the alternating, even lines of the poem retell the Chamorro creation story. Lines 2 and 4 speak to the sacrifice that Fu'una and Puntan made to create the Chamorro. It is *ginen*, or "through" and "from," their bodies that they have their land, *gi i tano-ta*, and their lives, *i lina'lå-ta*. While these lines are straightforward, they take on a more profound meaning when we consider the long history of religious colonialism on Guam. These few lines subvert the Christian creation story and renarrate the Chamorro creation story as the islanders' true origin story. Lines 6, 8, and 10 remind us that the sun, *i atdao*, and the moon, *i pilan*, are the eyes of Puntan, which not only asserts that the natural environment is connected to the Chamorro genealogically but also speaks to the Chamorro belief in how *taotao-mo'na* exist all around and, more important, are watching over the islanders to protect or to punish them. While the previous lines show how Chamorro lives come from and are dependent on the Puntan and Fu'una embodied by the land, sun, and moon, lines 12 and 14 show how the lives of Puntan and Fu'una in turn depend on the continued survival of Chamorros and the continued health and biodiversity of the land. These lines allude to the Chamorro value of *inafa'maolek*, in which humans and nature, the living and the dead, are all interconnected and interdependent. In lines 16, 18, and 20 Pascua then warns the Chamorro to avoid hurting the land and the people not only because it will harm their creators but because it will harm themselves, as they depend on the land for sustenance. The penultimate line expresses a crucial message of the poem: "Tattiyi Fa'uma yan Pontan sa ginen siha na gaige ham guine gi tano-ta" (Follow Fu'una and Puntan for it is because of them that we are here on our land). As Pascua powerfully asserts throughout the poem, it is important for the Chamorro to remember and reconnect with Puntan and Fu'una, because they are the creators who, through their story, teach the people to care for and respect the land through *inafa'moalek* and sustainability ethics.

Conclusion

The Chamorro creation story was silenced by religious imperialism and replaced by the Christian creation story. For centuries Spanish, American, and Japanese colonialisms displaced Chamorros from their land to appropriate it for military, touristic, agricultural, and urban development. The destructive impacts of these changes included the contamination of the environment and the loss of native wildlife. Another impact is symbolic: colonialism renarrated the land as nothing more than a territory, a military base, a tourist destination, an exploitable asset. Centuries of desecration have left Guam, the Mariana archipelago, and Chamorros in a state of ecological and cultural precarity.

Yet the Chamorro creation story survived through oral inheritance and, later, written accounts—a testament to the resiliency of Native narratives. Puntan and Fu'una taught the Chamorros about their origins and their most important cultural, familial, and environmental values. The Chamorro land struggles of the twentieth and twenty-first centuries were empowered by the Chamorro creation story and the wisdom that the land is sacred and the dwelling place of our ancestors; thus the land must be revered and protected from desecration. Moreover, the story of Puntan and Fu'una has inspired contemporary Chamorro poetry as another venue through which to aesthetically express the values embodied in our creation story: *inafa'maolek*. With the revitalization of the Lukao Fuha, Puntan and Fu'una will continue to inspire the Chamorros' cultural lives and decolonial struggles and teach them about their legendary origins *and* sustainable futures.

....

CRAIG SANTOS PEREZ is associate professor of creative writing at the University of Hawai'i, Mānoa. He is an Indigenous Chamorro poet and scholar.

Notes

1   *Chamorro* is also spelled *Chamoru* and *CHamoru*. One theory is that it derives from the Indigenous word *chamorri*, the name of the highest-ranking members of ancient Chamorro society. *Chamorro* is also a word in Spanish that means "bald" or "shorn," and because ancient Chamorro men shaved their heads, leaving only a topknot, the Spanish called them *Chamorro*. See Taitano, "Origin of Chamorro as an Ethnic Identifier."

2   The Mariana archipelago comprises fifteen islands: Guam (the largest and southernmost island in the chain), Rota, Aguijan, Tinian, Saipan, Farallon de Medinilla, Anatahan, Sarigan, Guguan, Alamagan, Pagan, Agrihan, Asuncion, Maug, and Farallon de Pajaros. Guam is an unincorporated territory of the United States, while the fourteen northern islands are a separate political entity known as the Commonwealth of the Northern Mariana Islands (CNMI). For a history of the CNMI, see Willens, *Honorable Accord*; and Farrell, "Partition of the Marianas."

3   Hattori, "Folktale."

4   Perez, "Fu'una."

5   Bevacqua, "Taotaomo'na."

6   Soker, "Taotaomona Stories of Guam," 156.

7   Bevacqua, "Chamorro World View."

8   Perez-Iyechad, "Inafa'maolek."

9   Bevacqua, "Chamorro World View." In the scholarship on the Chamorro creation story, there is no mention of nonbinary gender relations. For a discussion of nonbinary and queer identities within Chamorro culture, see Camacho, "Homomilitarism."

10   Tolentina, "Ancient Chamorro Kinship and Land Tenure."

11   Rogers, *Destiny's Landfall*, 1.

12   Rogers, *Destiny's Landfall*, 15.

13   See Buschmann, Slack, and Tueller, *Navigating the Spanish Lake*; Hezel, "From Conversion to Conquest"; and Hezel, "From Conquest to Colonization."

14   See Leibowitz, *Defining Status*; Raustiala, *Does the Constitution Follow the Flag?*; and Lai, "Discontiguous States of America."

15   See Hattori, *Colonial Dis-ease*; Underwood, "American Education and the Acculturation of the Chamorros of Guam"; DeLisle, "Navy Wives/Native Lives"; and Diaz, "Paved with Good Intentions . . . ."

16   See Peattie, *Nan'yō*, 16; Higuchi, "Japan's Industrial Development of a U.S. Territory"; and Higuchi, "Japanisation Policy for the Chamorros of Guam."

17   See Natividad and Kirk, "Fortress Guam"; Camacho, "Enframing 'I TaoTao Tano'"; Clement, "Sella Bay Ammunition Wharf Controversy"; and Viernes, "Fanhasso I Taotao Sumay."

18   Nilsson, *Endangered Species Handbook*.

19   See Hattori, "Guardians of Our Soil."

20   See Perez, "Contested Sites."

21   See Aguon, "Update."

22   Phillips, "Land Ownership on Guam."

23   Phillips, "Land."

24   Natividad and Kirk, "Fortress Guam."

25   Bevacqua, "Pågat"; Bevacqua, "Pågat Protest Today."
26   We Are Guahan, "About."
27   Punzalan, "Lukao Fuha yan i Pina'ok Tumaiguini."
28   Pascua, "Chachalåni."

Works Cited

Aguon, Julian. "Update: Land Ownership on Guam." *Guampedia.* Last modified June 28, 2018. www.guampedia.com/update-land-ownership-on-guam.

Bevacqua, Michael Lujan. "Chamorro World View." *Guampedia.* Last modified June 29, 2018. www.guampedia.com/chamorro-world-view.

Bevacqua, Michael Lujan. "Pågat." *Minagahet Blog.* Last modified May 16, 2010. minagahet.blogspot.com/2010/05/pagat.html.

Bevacqua, Michael Lujan. "Pågat Protest Today." *Magahet Blog.* Last modified July 23, 2010. minagahet.blogspot.com/2010/07/pagat-protest-today.html.

Bevacqua, Michael Lujan. "Taotaomo'na." *Guampedia.* Last modified June 21, 2018. www.guampedia.com/taotaomona-taotaomona.

Buschmann, Rainer F., Edward R. Slack Jr., and James B. Tueller, eds. *Navigating the Spanish Lake: The Pacific in the Iberian World, 1521–1898.* Honolulu: University of Hawai'i Press, 2014.

Camacho, Keith L. "Enframing 'I TaoTao Tano': Colonialism, Militarism, and Tourism in Twentieth Century Guam." MA thesis, University of Hawai'i, Mānoa, 1998.

Camacho, Keith L. "Homomilitarism: The Same-Sex Erotics of the US Empire in Guam and Hawai'i." *Radical History Review,* no. 123 (2015): 144–75.

Clement, Michael, Jr. "The Sella Bay Ammunition Wharf Controversy: Economic Development, Indigenous Rights, and Colonialism in Guam." MA thesis, University of Guam, 2002.

DeLisle, Christine Taitano. "Navy Wives/Native Lives: The Cultural and Historical Relations between Naval Wives and Chamorro Women in Guam, 1898–1945." PhD diss., University of Michigan, 2008.

Diaz, Vicente M. "Paved with Good Intentions . . . Roads, Citizenship, and a Century of American Colonialism in Guam." Paper presented at the Centennial of the Spanish American War Summer Seminar, Obermann Center for Advanced Study, University of Iowa, 1998.

Farrell, Don A. "The Partition of the Marianas: A Diplomatic History, 1898–1919." *ISLA: A Journal of Micronesian Studies* 2, no. 2 (1994): 273–301.

Hattori, Anne Perez. *Colonial Dis-ease: US Navy Health Policies and the Chamorros of Guam, 1898–1941.* Honolulu: University of Hawai'i Press, 2004.

Hattori, Anne Perez. "Folktale: Puntan and Fu'una; Gods of Creation." *Guampedia.* Last modified June 20, 2018. www.guampedia.com/puntan-and-fuuna-gods-of-creation.

Hattori, Anne Perez. "Guardians of Our Soil: Indigenous Responses to Post–World War II Land Appropriation on Guam." In *Farms, Firms, and Runways: Perspectives on U.S. Military Bases in the Western Pacific,* edited by L. Eve Armentrout, 186–202. Chicago: Imprint Publications, 2001.

Hezel, Francis X., S.J. "From Conquest to Colonization: Spain in the Marianas, 1690–1740." *Journal of Pacific History,* no. 23 (1988): 137–55.

Hezel, Francis X., S.J. "From Conversion to Conquest: The Early Spanish Mission in the Marianas." *Journal of Pacific History,* no. 17 (1982): 115–20.

Higuchi, Wakako. "Japanisation Policy for the Chamorros of Guam, 1941–1944." *Journal of Pacific History* 36.1 (2001): 19–35.

Higuchi, Wakako. "Japan's Industrial Development of a U.S. Territory: Guam, 1941–1944." *Pacific Studies* 31, no. 1 (2008): 55–104.

Lai, Paul. "Discontiguous States of America: The Paradox of Unincorporation in Craig Santos Perez's Poetics of Chamorro Guam." *Journal of Transnational American Studies* 3, no. 2 (2011). escholarship.org/uc/item/02f4v8m3.

Leibowitz, Arnold H. *Defining Status: A Comprehensive Analysis of United States Territorial Relations.* Dordrecht: Nijhoff, 1989.

Natividad, LisaLinda, and Gwyn Kirk. "Fortress Guam: Resistance to US Military Mega-buildup." *Asia-Pacific Journal* 8, no. 19 (2010): 1–17. apjjf.org/-Gwyn-Kirk--LisaLinda-Natividad/3356/article.pdf.

Nilsson, Greta. *Endangered Species Handbook.* Washington, DC: Animal Welfare Institute, 2005.

Pascua, Jay Baza. "Chachalåni." *Platte Valley Review* 33 (2011–12). www.plattevalleyreview.org/Webpages/2011%20start/Short%20Fiction%20A-K/Perez.html.

Peattie, Mark R. *Nan'yō: The Rise and Fall of the Japanese in Micronesia, 1885–1945.* Honolulu: University of Hawai'i Press, 1988.

Perez, Celeste. "Fu'una." *Guampedia.* Last modified June 20, 2018. www.guampedia.com/fuuna.

Perez, Michael. "Contested Sites: Pacific Resistance in Guam to U.S. Empire." *Amerasia Journal* 27, no. 1 (2001): 97–115.

Perez-Iyechad, Lilli. "Inafa'maolek: Striving for Harmony." *Guampedia*. Last modified June 27, 2018. www.guampedia.com/inafamaolek.

Phillips, Michael F. "Land." In *Kinalamten Pulitikat: Sinenten I Chamorro, Issues in Guam's Political Development; The Chamorro Perspective, 3.* Agana, Guam: Political Status Education Coordinating Commission, 1996.

Phillips, Michael F. "Land Ownership on Guam." *Guampedia*. Last modified June 28, 2018. www.guampedia.com/land-ownership-on-guam.

Punzalan, Bernard. "Lukao Fuha yan i Pina'ok Tumaiguini." *Chamorro Roots Genealogy Project*, February 5, 2014. www.chamorroroots.com/v7/index.php/pubs-projects/49-taotao-tano/history/337-lukao-fuha.

Raustiala, Kal. *Does the Constitution Follow the Flag? The Evolution of Territoriality in American Law.* New York: Oxford University Press, 2009.

Rogers, Robert F. *Destiny's Landfall: A History of Guam.* Honolulu: University of Hawai'i Press, 1995.

Soker, Donald. "The Taotaomona Stories of Guam." *Western Folklore* 31, no. 3 (1972): 153–67.

Taitano, Gina E. "Origin of Chamorro as an Ethnic Identifier." *Guampedia*. Last modified October 14, 2019. www.guampedia.com/origin-of-chamorro-as-an-ethnic-identifier.

Tolentina, Dominica. "Ancient Chamorro Kinship and Land Tenure." *Guampedia*. Last modified July 2, 2018. www.guampedia.com/ancient-chamorro-kinship-and-land-tenure.

Underwood, Robert. "American Education and the Acculturation of the Chamorros of Guam." PhD diss., University of Southern California, 1987.

Viernes, James Perez. "Fanhasso I Taotao Sumay: Displacement, Dispossession, and Survival in Guam." MA thesis, University of Hawai'i, Mānoa, 2008.

We Are Guahan. "About." We Are Guahan. Last modified March 20, 2015. www.weareguahan.com/about-weareguahan.

Willens, Howard P. *An Honorable Accord: The Covenant between the Northern Mariana Islands and the United States.* Honolulu: University of Hawai'i Press, 2002.

Stories, Language, and the Land

CHERYL SAVAGEAU

Abstract When I listen to the old stories, I am struck by the attention the Ancestors gave to the world around them, and how that informs the old stories, how the Ancestors were reading the Land. The Land, for us, is epistemologically and ontologically primary. That is to say, we know what we know and we know who we are through the Land. We know what we know because the Ancestors paid attention and put it into stories. And through that attention to the Land, we know who we are because we recognize that our life is the life of the Land, the Forest—the lakes, rivers, swamps, ocean, and further, that they are all alive, all persons. I am Alnôbak, an Abenaki woman—Aben-aki, Dawn Land. Our name describes us as the Land we are part of.
Keywords Abenaki, creation stories, land, poetry

During the Q&A period of a recent reading, a student asked, "What's the difference between creating a book of poetry that becomes a set form, and doing what you're doing now—a kind of storytelling?" I loved the question because it acknowledges the choices that were made in a collection of poetry, as a particular moment, and a reading of poetry as another moment, in which poems will be read in a different order, in which there are stories around words, stories around the poems, stories around the stories, and stories that come from the interaction between us all in a room together, the reciprocal relationship between storyteller and listeners—all participants in the telling of stories. So that's what I want to do here, to approach this essay as I would a reading or storytelling session.

I didn't set off to be a poet, didn't begin writing until my late twenties, majored in biology, not English, and in fact taught biology and earth science in high school for a short time before working as a writer-in-the-schools. People often react as if it's a huge jump from one "discipline" to another, but that's not true. Science and poetry both begin in observation of the world. I tell my writing students a Zen story about a man who traveled far and climbed a mountain to ask a wise man how to find enlightenment. "Attention," he was told. So he left and traveled for a year with no luck, and finally climbed back up the mountain, and asked again. "Attention. Attention," the master told him. Finally, after another year, he climbed the mountain yet

ENGLISH LANGUAGE NOTES
58:1, April 2020 DOI 10.1215/00138282-8237388
© 2020 Regents of the University of Colorado

again, and asked for the third time. "There must be something else, some secret. Tell me, what do I have to do to become enlightened?" "Attention. Attention. Attention."

It is the same with poetry, I tell them. It all starts with Attention. If this were a Native story, the man would most likely travel back one more time, because the number four is our number of completion. "Attention. Attention. Attention. Attention." It becomes a ceremony. It sets things in motion.

When I listen to the old stories, I am struck by the attention the Ancestors gave to the world around them, and how that informs the old stories, how the Ancestors were reading the Land. The Land, for us, is epistemologically and ontologically primary. That is to say, we know what we know and we know who we are through the Land. We know what we know because the Ancestors paid attention and put it into stories. And through that attention to the Land, we know who we are because we recognize that our life is the life of the Land, the forest, the lakes, rivers, swamps, ocean—and further, that they are all alive, all persons. I am *Alnôbak*, an Abenaki woman—*Aben-aki*, Dawn Land. Our name describes us as the Land we are part of.

Ktsi Amiskw

We are standing in a cornfield in a western Massachusetts town on the Connecticut River. From here, if we look to the south, we can see the Holyoke Range—the only east-west mountain range in the Appalachians. If we look north, we can see three hills. It is easy to see that we are in a basin, a place that used to be a lake. It's easy to see that the Holyoke Range is the dam of the Great Beaver, Ktsi Amiskw, who makes up the hills now called Sugarloaf.

We do this now by reading or hearing the story and then looking around us. But I would argue that the story arises from the Land. Stories are alive. And in fact, this story, about the Great Beaver, forgotten for a long time, reemerged when two Abenaki women, Marge Bruchac and I, were living in the Valley in the 1990s doing graduate work at UMass, Amherst. We were unaware of each other's having "found" the story. I wrote the story into a poem, then discovered that Marge was telling the story at gatherings and performances. When the poem was published, I dedicated it to Marge.

> **At Sugarloaf, 1996**
> . . . *for Marge*
> **i. Ktsi Amiskw**
>
> *In the big pond, Ktsi Amiskw, the Beaver, is swimming. He has built a dam.*
> *The water in his pond grows deeper. He patrols the edges, chasing everyone*
> *away. This is all mine, he says. The people and animals grow thirsty.*
> *Cut it out, Creator says. And turns Ktsi Amiskw to stone. The pond is*
> *drained. There is water and food for everyone. See those hills, Ktsi Amiskw's*
> *head, body, and tail? He's lying there still, this valley his empty pond.*[1]

Since then, two other Abenaki women, Lisa Brooks, historian, and Judy Dow, educator, artist, and keeper of Traditional Ecological Knowledge, have become involved in understanding and retelling this story. The awakening of this story has resulted in an ongoing conversation, which has brought the knowledge of Ktsi Amiskw and of the Kwinitekw (Connecticut) River Valley as Indigenous space into the larger conversation of the Northeast.

A crucial component in recovering this story is that when the Land speaks, when Story tells itself, we are there to listen. This is part of our responsibility as storytellers—whether poets, historians, novelists, artists—distinctions we do not make in Indian country—to be listening, to pay attention.

The story of Ktsi Amiskw is a very old story, a story that goes back more than ten thousand years, to the time when the melting glaciers flooded the land. The ecology of the Northeast, the Dawn Land, was largely a result of activity by the Beaver. Everywhere water flowed, beavers responded by building dams, and in doing so changed the surrounding land into wetlands, providing habitat for water and wetland plants and animals of all kinds, as well as humans. Eventually, those ponds would become meadows in the process of succession.

In the time when the story of Ktsi Amiskw would have first been told, Indigenous people of the Dawn Land who lived within this ecosystem were well aware of beaver ponds and of the relationships between beavers and the rest of the human and other-than-human community. I can imagine that if they were standing in that great basin between the Holyoke Range and what is now called Sugarloaf, they would see, as we did, that it used to be a large pond or lake. There may have even been tribal memories of that two-hundred-mile-long lake that extended twenty miles to each side of what is now the Connecticut River. There would have to have been a beaver involved who had built that large dam to the south of the pond—a very large beaver by the looks of it. Looking north at the three hills, they saw the beaver's head, body, and tail. But why would the beaver still be there? In the natural succession of pond to meadow, the beavers leave.

Creating habitat that produces food for the community is a generous act. The beavers acted as good relatives, in keeping with the Common Pot, which everyone is part of, everyone contributes to, and everyone benefits from.[2] The Beaver modeled for us what it means to be a good person. Surely there were memories of and remains of bones of the giant Ice Age beavers. Why were they gone? What if this Great Beaver, who was understood through observation of modern beavers, acted in a very un-Beaver-like way, by refusing to share the gifts of the pond?

As a poet, I looked at the Land, and listened to other old stories. What I saw was a Great Beaver, who had been turned to stone. In places, as you climb or drive up to the summit, you can see the sandstone, with just a thin layer of soil and green plants—moss, trees, and other forest plants. The Great Beaver is stone, but is also a living presence in the valley. I can feel his presence. Imposing. But not threatening. Asleep.

I remembered that in another of our stories, there are also beings who were stone, and who were put to sleep. Those were the first human beings, the ones Gluscabe created from stone, so they would be strong. Unfortunately, their hearts were cold and without compassion, and they stomped on everything around them—uprooting trees, killing animals, unwilling or unable to listen when confronted with their unbalanced behavior. Like the Beaver who would not share his pond, the Stone people did not know how to be good relatives. So Gluscabe put them to sleep. You can still see them asleep in the forests and fields of the Northeast. Glacial erratics from the last Ice Age, we are told in another story, the scientific story. I hold both in my mind with no contradiction. Because that is how the world is. Many worlds operating at once, as the poet Joy Harjo says.[3] And so in my telling, the Great Beaver does not die. He is put to sleep.

But the Beaver story does not end there. The Land was invaded, and the invaders did not see beavers as generous contributors to the Common Pot, did not see them as persons or relatives, but only as the fur they wanted for themselves. The trade in beaver pelts extended into hundreds of years of overhunting that almost wiped out the beavers. In writing the poem, I could not leave this part of the story out.

> *For living out of balance, Ktsi Amiskw lies still, while for centuries his descendants are trapped in every stream, caught in every river, killed by the millions for fur-lust from across the sea. Their pelts buy blankets, cloth, weapons, knives.*[4]

In speaking of the tribal voice, Anna Lee Walters talks about how we receive it through stories, through the world around us, our families and communities. Then we add our own stories, the stories of our time, and those stories become part of the tribal voice going forward. "Out of the desires to express memory and experience individually in each generation, another voice is given to it, a voice both inclusive and exclusive of oral tradition, one that picks up *after* the pause of oral tradition and carries on the story of particular tribes and what life is in that generation."[5] I ask, How does this story live now? How does it take us into the future? Creation stories are ongoing; they do not take place in some long-ago time as static artifacts. They are not simply how and why stories. They live. And of course, they reflect cultural values. Why did this story wake up now, at the same time when the Language is reawakening, and during a great gathering-in of the People? How does it help us in this particular time? What is it we need to know? The poem continues:

> *In this world out of balance, Ktsi Amiskw dreams a hard dream: a world without beavers. Then, far away, like the promise of a winter dawn, he dreams the rivers back, young mothers building, secure in their skins, and a pond full of the slapping tails of children.*[6]

Stories make things happen, and dreams are stories. Beavers barely escaped extinction and have recovered—so well that sometimes passing by on a highway, I catch sight of a beaver dam. The story is also about us, about our own "not vanishing," and the nature of our dreams. What are we dreaming for the children of our grandchildren? How do we ensure that there will be "ponds full of the slapping tails of children"?

First Woman

Our story of First Woman says that she was born of dew in the early-morning sun on a leaf of a beautiful plant. The story is very short, but profound. The life of First

Woman comes from the meeting of sun and water with a green leaf. What is described is the moment of photosynthesis, when a green plant uses water and sunlight to create food. This is the basis of all life on earth, the basis of our atmosphere made of oxygen.

In this story about the birth of First Woman, there is profound knowledge, what is now called Traditional Ecological Knowledge, of our ancestors here in the Northeast. There was no way for them to have observed carbon dioxide, an important component of photosynthesis, but they paid such close attention to the green world that they understood not only that sunshine and water were required for plants to make food, but that this moment of transformation is the basis of all plant and animal life. No animals could exist without the generosity of plants in providing food, not only for themselves, but for all of us. Good relatives, contributing to the Common Pot.

The word *generosity* could be seen as overstatement—that the plant doesn't wish to be eaten—but that is wrong. Plants wrap their seeds in sweet fruit that is meant to be eaten so that the seeds will be dispersed. Some seeds cannot germinate without passing through a bird's digestive system. If you cut off a leaf or stem, the plant will grow two new ones. From recent experiments by Robin Wall Kimmerer, with her ethnobotany students, sweetgrass grows better the more it is eaten or harvested by humans.[7]

All of this is contained mythopoetically in the simple lines of this creation story. It could have been said in a much more prosaic lesson-story, but it would not have the same power. Even now, if I say, "All life on earth relies on the photosynthesis of green plants," people look at me blankly, or nod, maybe giving it a moment's thought, maybe not. They do not feel it as magical—that plants can make food from water and sunshine.

The question of how we give weight to information, to facts that can change the way people see the world, is an important one, and the answer is in the stories. First Woman is born from the magic of that moment when water catches the sunlight on a green leaf. There is the power of poetry in this, the power of the sacred. It creates a feeling of awe and a matrix within which the world, and all other stories, can be understood. Finally, ultimately, it is this moment that is the beginning of all life—not just human life but all life on the planet. I always imagine First Woman leaping forth, almost dancing—for the leaf is described as being "on her heel"—into life. It is an image full of exuberance.

This same attention to the green world is apparent also in our language, where "leaf" is *wanabagw*. What's extraordinary about this word is its use of the suffix *bagw*, which means stillness and is most often used in words like "lake" or "pond" or "ocean," as opposed to *tekw*, which means movement, used for rivers and waves. When I learned this word, I wondered, Why would a leaf be perceived as still?

You wouldn't think leaves and stillness, just looking at a tree, how the leaves move in the slightest breeze, how they rustle against each other in the wind. But a deeper look into the tree, into the movement within the tree, and you see the tree as part of the circle of water, and the leaves as places of stillness. The sap, the blood of the tree, runs in rivers up to the branches and twigs,

*then finds a resting place in the leaves, as brooks flow into a pond. The leaf
is the place that holds water and sunshine and air for the great
transformation to occur. Where water and carbon dioxide become sweet
food and oxygen.*[8]

The biologist in me kicked in, and I wondered, Is there knowledge of the water
cycle in this word? Did our ancestors understand this so long ago that it's embedded
in the language? When I spoke to an elder who is a language keeper, he said, Yes. It
is exactly so. Science would continue the story by saying that trees release that water
into the air, where it eventually gathers into clouds and falls as rain. I don't know
enough language to know if there's another word that contains this process, but I
wouldn't be surprised to find it.

In a Land in which water is so prevalent—a Land of rivers and streams, ponds
and rivers, swamps and bogs and ocean—it's not surprising that *bagw* and *tekw* are
such important concepts. In fact, they become another way we know ourselves. In
Out of the Crazywoods, my memoir about manic-depressive/bipolar illness, I consider the illness not in terms of up and down, but of movement and stillness:

*Bagw and Tekw, stillness and movement. I want to learn from this. I want
to find the calm stillness of a pond, and the clear flow of running water. We,
like the trees who are our ancestors, are beings of water. My rivers run high,
with rapids and whirlpools the stories say were created by the impetuous
twin. The ponds have stagnated, become places with no give and take. The
sunlight hurts, there is no sweetness here. Nothing flows in or out, no breeze
moves the surface.*[9]

Gluscabe and the Creation of Alnôbak—the First Human Beings

A related story is that of Gluscabe, who in some stories is credited with creating a
good part of this world. In one story, Gluscabe is walking through the forest and
mountains and rivers, and it is very beautiful. Yet he feels that it is not finished;
it's missing something. It's *Alnôbak*, human beings, he realizes. He has not created
them yet. He wants the human beings to be strong, so he looks around for something strong to make them from, and decides to make them from stone. These
are the Stone People I spoke of earlier, the ones who stomped on everyone, who
did not know how to be good relatives.

After putting the Stone People to sleep, he looks around for something with a
different kind of strength and sees the trees. In some tellings it's the Ash tree, in
others the Birch. He notices that they are strong in the wind—they bend, but do
not break. They are rooted in the earth. Gluscabe takes his bow and shoots an
arrow into the tree, and from it come the first *Alnôbak*, the first human people. If
you were listening to the old stories on a winter's night, you would be aware of what
is not told in this story, of First Woman, and of life that arises from the green world.

We are children of the forest. In a very real way, our life comes from the forest.
Everything we eat, our medicines, the water we drink, the air we breathe, is part of
the forest. It is not a metaphor to say, "We are the Land up and walking around."[10]
We are the forest, up and walking around.

The mechanism of the story—that there is a spirit-person who creates, who shoots the arrow, who expresses loneliness that can be filled only by human beings—comes, I think, from the People. But the rest of the story is from the Land itself—it is humans reading the Land, listening to the Land, and understanding our place in it. In fact, we become human in this moment of understanding that we are descendants, relatives to the trees, with all the responsibilities that carries. It is also true that we human beings often do not know how to act. We make bad decisions, as Gluscabe does over and over again in other stories, and yet this story affirms that at heart we are the forest; we can learn to be good relatives.

Red

In his new poem
the red autumn woods
are a metaphor
for leftist martyrs
We are traveling east through a maple forest
that blazes the hillsides on both sides of this winding
back-country road Look at the trees I want to tell him
Listen The trees have their own stories to tell
like the story of fire deep within the heart They too
have been martyrs in the long war against the land, a nation
cut down, children denied
A hundred years ago these hills were bare of trees
the stone walls that wind through them
the illusion of ownership Now the hills are red with maples
My heart is leaping out to meet them, my eyes
cannot be full enough Though acid falls from the clouds
maples have gathered on the hillsides
in every direction See how they celebrate
They are wearing their brightest dresses
Come sisters, let me dance with you
I offer you a song
Let me paint
it red with
passion
You are
all the women
I have ever loved
. . . for Chrystos[11]

Not far from Ktsi Amiskw there's a road at the north side of Quabbin Reservoir, based on one of our old trails, as so many roads in New England are. One fall I was driving with another poet from Amherst to Worcester, Massachusetts, on this back road that winds through a maple forest. He saw the red of the trees only in terms of metaphor for human activity. For me, driving through this forest of relatives was a different experience. In fact, as I wrote the poem that would later come from this journey, a tree appeared on the page in that mysterious process of art that is both listening and shaping. (In another poem that also asserted itself on the page as a tree, my mother, who is not Abenaki, becomes a pine tree, a healing tree, part of the forest.)

In the poem I call the trees sisters in a very literal sense. Their history and ours, like the history of the beavers, are the same. What happens to the Land happens to the People. Even now, acid rain falls from the clouds, threatening the life of our forest. Yet the maples are gathered in every direction—as the Abenaki people have been gathering in over the past fifty years. We celebrate, wearing our brightest dresses. It is so necessary to remember to celebrate that we are here, all our relatives; it is our strength. And finally, "Red" is a love song—our connection to the Land, this particular Land of which we are a part, is a passionate love, not an abstract principle, but a deep and passionate love—physical, emotional, spiritual.

Even if we are not living in the old traditional way of hunting, gathering, fishing, and farming—even if we live in a city, we still live under the canopy here in New England; our very air comes from the breathing of the trees. My son remembers the day I took him to Worcester Airport and we looked down at the city—the second largest in New England. All we could see were trees, with only the tops of buildings here and there. Here in the city it is not the complex ecosystem it should be, but it is here and could take back the cities in a matter of years. Our yards here go quickly to meadow, and from meadow to small trees, within a span of five to ten years if we leave them be. All the Dawn Land is Forest waiting to return.

Gluscabe and the Game Bag

When I was in fifth grade, a teacher said, in a very patronizing way, that while the Mayans had invented the wheel, they used it only in toys. It "never occurred to them," he said, that this was a tool they could use. I raised my hand and asked, "What if they decided not to use it? What if they could see that it might bring bad things? Maybe they decided not to." He laughed. "That's not possible," he said. "Progress is its own imperative. You can't say no to progress. If you invent something, it will be used." I knew he was wrong.

Years later I heard the story of Gluscabe and the Game Bag: how he has the idea to trick all the animals in the world to go inside his game bag so he won't have to hunt anymore.

Game Bag

Grandmother Woodchuck

This grandson of mine always has a better idea. Why not capture all the animals in one huge bag, he thinks to himself. Why not tie up the eagle who creates the wind? And no sooner does he think it, than he does it. Still, that is the way he learns. Someday he will grow up. People will speak well of him. Doesn't he always listen to his grandmother in the end?

Gluscabe is young in this story—impatient, disrespectful, selfish, and lazy. I need a game bag, he tells Grandmother Woodchuck.

Grandmother Woodchuck makes him beautiful game bags—of deer and caribou and moose hair. He rejects them all, throws them on the floor. Grandmother Woodchuck is incredibly patient. She asks him what kind of game bag he wants. In doing so, she shows us that children may be rude because they don't know how to ask for what they want or need. It turns out that this is the right question. He wants one made of Woodchuck fur, he tells her.

Gifts

Grandmother Woodchuck pulls the hair from her belly, from the tender place. Each pull stings, but she will do this for the grandson who will bring tobacco back for her in her old age. She weaves the hair into a game bag, one that will stretch big enough to hold all the animals in the world. It is a woman's strength that will hold them, and a woman's strength that will set them free.

"The World is ending," Gluscabe tells the animals. "But I know a safe place," he says, and opens the game bag.

Inside

We are a million eyes open in the dark. We are chipmunk and mole, rabbit and squirrel. We are musk and fur and claw and feathers. We are fox, raccoon, mink, and fisher. We are chickadees, blue jays, owls, and turkeys. We are hooves and hide, deer and elk, moose and caribou, lynx and bear, cougar and wolf. We are all listening in the dark for the sound of the world ending.

He proudly takes the game bag full of animals back to Grandmother Woodchuck. "Whenever we're hungry," he tells Grandmother Woodchuck, "we can just open the game bag and take out what we want." Grandmother Woodchuck is not impressed.

The Conversation

— Why are you always doing things like this?
— It seemed like a good idea at the time.

She asks Gluscabe, "What are they going to eat? What's it going to smell like in there in a few days? What happens when all these animals die? You will get lazy and fat," she tells him. Finally, she asks him, "What are your grandchildren going to eat?" And so Gluscabe listens to his Grandmother, and sets the animals free. And the world is put back into balance.

The World Is Restored

When he finally let us out, I thought there'd be nothing left. But here it is,
just as before, only more beautiful. Trees, air, water, and the sound of all
of us breathing in the dark woods.[12]

So here it is. A cultural decision not to domesticate animals. A story that says clearly, we have thought about this, but the costs outweigh the benefits, so we will not do it. Not only that, but we'll tell this story over the generations, so people will remember why we made this decision. And the decision is made over and over again.

When the invaders come, they have a different story. One that gives them dominion over the Land. They do not belong to the Land; they think they own it. They bring their domesticated animals who tear up oyster beds and drop seeds from foreign ecosystems; they plow and plant in ways that deplete the soil. They destroy habitat. They hunt so many deer that they have to enact laws to limit the number that can be hunted. And so the cities are built; the animals have fewer and fewer places to live. Some of them, like Beaver and Wolf, are hunted almost to extinction—the beavers for their fur, the wolves out of pure hatred and fear.

So how does this story go into the future? One of the most important things it tells us is that we can say No. We are not at the mercy of some "imperative," we are sovereign, we can say No even when people call it "progress." It is a way of being good relatives, good ancestors—that we weigh very carefully what it will mean for the Land, the other-than-human people, for our children and grandchildren, as we make decisions.

Although the Gamebag story is from Deep Time, it is not static, not stuck in the past. There is more to this story that comes into the poem—that of the other-than-human people. They have written their way back into the Gamebag story. I began hearing reports—from friends, relatives, on local tv, and newspapers.

Gamebag Dream

Grey Fox in the snow beneath my window. Wolves in the towns of
Massachusetts. Eagles in the Quabbin. Black Bears at back-porch
birdfeeders in the Connecticut River Valley. Snow Owls at Logan Airport.
Sea Turtles at Cape Cod. Moose running through the streets of Boston.
Coyotes singing in every wood.
You open the bag and the world is restored.[13]

And so this story returns, in the spiraling way that time moves through the many worlds.

Trees
—for my father, Paul J. Savageau, Sr.

You taught me the land so well
that all through my childhood

I never saw the highway,
the truckstops, lumberyards,
the asphalt works,
but instead saw the hills,
the trees, the ponds on the south end
of Quinsigamond that twined
through the tangled underbrush
where old cars rusted back to earth,
and rubber tires made homes for fish.

Driving down the dirt road home,
it was the trees you saw first,
all New England a forest.
I have seen you get out of a car,
breathe in the sky, the green
of summer maples, listen for the talk
of birds, and squirrels, the murmur
of earthworms beneath your feet.
When you looked toward the house,
you had to shift focus,
as if it were something
difficult to see.[14]

My father taught me his vision—all this man-made stuff is temporary, the Land is primary. He taught us in conversation, as we walked the Land with him, that our people had walked the Land for at least ten thousand years.

I want to be clear here, that I'm not talking about growing up in a rural setting. It is true that I grew up on an island, on a dirt road. But the island was densely populated, the lake, a long, narrow one between Worcester, the second largest city in New England, and Shrewsbury, a suburban town. The Land we were walking was often the dirt roads going down to the water, or the backyard garden, or even the basketball court at the small park across the street from our house. Nevertheless, my father taught me that the Land is the primary reality, the man-made structures only temporary.

When I began writing poetry, and lived in the city, I was challenged by a poet in the workshop I was attending to "write a city poem." And so I wrote "Bones—A City Poem," a poem of loss in which every line begins with *forget*.

forget the great blue heron flying low
over the marsh, its footprints
still fresh in the sand[15]

The Heron showed up in the poem, although there were no herons there when I was growing up. Years later, I read an almost identical line in a poem by Louise Erdrich. We must have written it about the same time. Here's what I think: Just as the Great Beaver woke up and told its story to two Abenaki women at the same time because it was needed in the world, the Heron needed to be called back. The lake where I grew up is full of herons now, they are common birds again—everyone knows what a great blue heron looks like, wings against the sky, long legs flowing behind, or standing tall in a swamp or pond. I realize this might sound grandiose, as if I were responsible for bringing the Heron back, single-handedly. No. But I was responsible; that is, I had to be responsible to the voice of the Heron who entered my poem. I could have chosen to edit the Heron out, because after all, it was not there when I was growing up. But it left its footprints in the sand in my poem, and I chose to record that. Stories have power. In some mysterious way, Erdrich's poem and mine are tied to the return of the Heron as part of that intricate web of relations that exists through the many worlds.

Poison in the Pond
i.

the skin on my arms burns
It is hot today and sticky
and poison is flowing
out of orange barrels
into the waters of the pond

My eyes burn my lips burn
my tongue is thick
I cannot swallow
my throat is
sore as strep

the fish are dying
turtles wash up on shore
the lilies shrivel
sweetflag blackens

cattails are ragged sticks
the floating island
has stopped wandering

but it is for our own good
they tell us and no one
leaves, we tough it out

those orange barrels
the bans on swimming
on eating fish

our lungs burn
the air is hot and thick
this pond used to want
to be a river

now it wants to be
a meadow

these orange barrels
will teach it whose boss[16]

When we read the Land, we have to witness and grieve the losses that have occurred. This story of poisoning the water comes from this particular time, from my own childhood—it's a story that has to be added to those other stories. The animacy, the personhood, the sovereignty of the Lake is acknowledged—"this pond used to want / to be a river / now it wants to be / a meadow"—as well as its colonization by those who "will teach it whose [*sic*] boss." If we are lucky, maybe this will be a Deep Time story someday, another cautionary tale. Wouldn't Gluscabe be upset that the vegetation is clogging up the engine on his boat? Wouldn't Gluscabe want to change the pond to suit himself? Maybe it is Gluscabe who places those orange barrels full of poison. Gluscabe, who always has a better idea, usually based on greed or laziness.

We don't have the end of this story yet. Where is the balance? Where is Grandmother Woodchuck, who is the voice of the Land, to tell us to stop—to explain that there is a decision we need to make here, not once, but over and over again? Do not poison the Land. To poison the Land is to poison the People. "The baby is born wrong." Everyone is sick. The false remedy comes from "little orange pills"— I imagine them long and barrel-shaped, though I didn't write that into the poem. It is part of the role of poets and storytellers in this generation to speak for the Land, to listen for the voice of Grandmother Woodchuck, to tell those stories that make clear the consequences of being out of balance.

Home Country

A friend from New Mexico once asked me, "How do you know where your Land is?" I didn't understand his question. He continued, "Without a Rez—how do you know what's Indian Land?" All of this, I told him, all of this is our Land.

One night
my father brings in a book.
See, he says, Abenaki,
and shows me the map
here and here and here
he says, all this
is Abenaki country.[17]

When my brother and his wife inherited a trailer in the White Mountains, those walks on the Land extended through the woods and down to the river—the Pemigewasset, the river that springs from the source, the emergence place in the White Mountains. There was an old, decaying railroad bridge that crossed the river just upstream of our swimming place. That old bridge didn't matter to us as we swam and hung out on the rocks. One of my favorite photos is of my father sitting on a boulder in the river, his dog next to him. Years later, I said to my sister, "It was lucky John got that trailer so we could get to know the Whites like we did." She looked at me like I'd missed something. "You think that was by accident?" she said. *We were supposed to be there*, is what she was saying. The Land called us back.

Pemigewasset

*we are at the source
the place where the Pemi
streams out of the lake
over the granite
in cascades
and whirlpools*

*tourists
rush past us
two Abenaki women
gazing silently
into water*

*I feel like a ghost
she says
they can't even see
us*

*tourists follow the signs
to the next attraction
they don't
want to miss
anything*

*below us
around us
water is
flowing*

*that's because
they are in a state park
I say
and we are at
the center
of the world*

*the rocks
are full of
water
everywhere
water
is moving*[18]

Our mountains, the Whites, *Wôbiadenak*, are not the imposing Rockies. They are old mountains, ancient, worn down to the mother's bones. They are much more intimate—mostly forest, except for the granite at the top, and exposed in cliffs, white in the sunlight, which gives them their name. Two rivers run through the Whites—rivers I keep coming back to, the rivers that run through my dreams, that are home.

The Land is primary here, and we see what the tourists do not. We are at the source, the emergence place, and surrounded by water, by life: "the rocks / are full of / water / everywhere / water / is moving." This story is one of both creation and survivance. It acknowledges our invisibility and also our presence, our continuous emergence and movement—that we are, in fact, still here in this Land where the dominant narrative is one of disappearance. In the companion poem, "Swift River," we sit on a boulder in the middle of the River:

> . . . *where in summer swimmers*
> *loll on the rocks*
> *like otters*
> *grandmothers*
> *and grandbabies*
> *wade in the icy*
> *shallows where*
> *sand has been pounded*
> *soft and teenagers*
> *dive into deeper*
> *pools and come*
> *out shining*
> *beaded with water*
>
> . . . *someday someone will*
> *find two women in rock*
> *back to back*
> *on this mountain*
> *facing sunset, facing dawn*[19]

Here the women turn to stone, not because of a punishment, but because of the permanency of their relationship to this River, the fact of their identity with the Land, and the assertion of survivance into the future.

Nebi/Nebizon

What I Save

Like my grandmother now, I save teabags for a second cup. String, stamps
without postmarks, aluminum foil. Wrapping paper, paper bags, bags of
scrap fabric, blue rubber bands, clothes hangers. I save newspaper clippings,
recipes, bits of yarn, photographs in shoeboxes, tins of buttons. I save

cancelled checks, instruction manuals, warranties for appliances long since
thrown away. Feathers, shells, pebbles, acorns. I save faces, phrases,
bits of melody, the light on the trees from a late autumn day. I save my
grandmother's hair, carefully braided and coiled in tissue paper. I save the
moment my infant son nuzzled my breast and began to suck. I save my
lover's hands touching me. I save his tongue, his teeth. I save the strong
smell of sex. I save the rhythm. I save the sound of geese flying overhead, the
smooth young bark against my cheek, the white dust of birch on my hands.
I save the water flowing through me that cannot be contained.[20]

One of the first words I learned in Abenaki was water, *Nebi*. Of course. Water is life. We are a land of rivers, lakes, and ponds, bordering the ocean. *Nebi*. And *Nebizon*, which means medicine water. But it also means all those streams of experience that make up our own *Nebizon*, our personal power. Here in one word was what it had taken me an entire poem to express. The poem began, very consciously, as a list of physical things, but by the end revealed itself as a stream of experience that flows through me like water—that is *Nebizon*. But how did this memory, this concept, come down to me? This "thinking in Indian" that looks for a way to say it in English. Poetry, the most malleable form of language, is a way many of us have found to "talk Indian" in the languages of the colonizers.

The Dawn Land is a world of movement. "Everywhere water is moving." And not only water—the seasons change; the weather changes so quickly that people joke about it. "All four seasons in a week, brought to you by Mother Nature," which was a recent meme on social media, or the favorite phrase "Don't like the weather? Stick around for an hour" that people take such glee in repeating to each other. As a child, I understood the alternating days of rain and sun, the changing seasons, as "taking turns." Today it is the Rain's turn; tomorrow, or in a few days, it will be the Sun's turn. It is Winter's turn now, but soon it will be Spring's turn. It followed an ethical model of egalitarian participation and balance—because we all know what happens if it rains too long or not enough.

Our language reflects this constant movement. What English would express as nouns are often verbs—a river is "rivering"—and so much more. Speaking in English, but using an Abenaki construction in this poem evokes the passionate, erotic (in the sense of empowering life force) connection to the River, not as an amorphous idea, but as a person. The poem invites the action of the river, in a reciprocal relationship, not as a human being viewing a landscape.

Nebi

. . . this is the river
I belong to . . . Polin, Abenaki leader 1739

We breathe
the traveling clouds
and drink what falls
glistening from cliffs

and into whirlpool
basins carved in granite
on its way back to sky

water me
glisten me
carve and
whirlpool me
cascade me
white water me
sing me babble me
pool me pond me
swamp me
bog me
trout and salmon me
frog and dragonfly me
loon and otter me

breathe me
the humid sky
while leaves
gather pools
of summer air

Nebi we say
wligonebi
the water is good[21]

I Know I'm Home

My son and I had a conversation this morning. It was about the ways Native people introduce themselves when we meet at conferences or writers' festivals. The first question we ask is, where are you from? And we all understand what that means. Not where are you living, though it might be that, but where is Home for you?

My son grew up in a city. We talk about Home, what it means when you grow up away from the Homeland, in an urban environment. We are less than two hundred miles from the White Mountains, the heart of the Homeland, and we both have to get up to the Whites from time to time, to get centered, to connect and be nourished.

"I know I'm home," he told me, "because I can feel it."

And that's it: how your body relaxes, how you are at the same time more alert, more in tune, more alive. But that does not begin to describe or explain it, how you are part of the life around you, the movement of air and water and trees and birds and insects. The moose who might show themselves to you at dusk by the river, the black bears you know are there, the cougars who were there, whose spirits still inhabit these mountains. The red and gray squirrels, the blue jays, hawks, the little upside-down birds.

Survivance

We are here, we are told in other stories, to take care of the Land. Wabanaki people in Maine are doing that every day in their struggles to maintain the water as part of their Land, and their roles as keepers of those waters, in the face of the state's attempts to steal what they want for "development"—in an artificial separation of Water from Land, as if that were possible.

In *Red on Red*, Craig Womack suggests an "alternative definition of traditionalism as anything that is useful to Indian people in retaining their values and worldviews, no matter how much it deviates from what people did one or two hundred years ago."[22] Adaptation and change are an essential part of continuing as living cultures, of our survivance as Indian people.

Knitting is not traditional, in the sense that it's not something we did before the European invasion. Just as we didn't have glass beads, we didn't have wool, but we did intricate designs in porcupine quills, and made warm winter clothing from fur. I chose knitting in this poem because it is not "traditional," yet it is entirely traditional. In the poem, Grandmother—is this Grandmother Woodchuck?—knits, not from wool, but from the Land itself. Knowledge, healing, all we are is in the Land. She is the artist, storyteller, and knowledge keeper. She is the Grandmother who will become the Ancestor. She is doing the work of survivance. She is all of us.

from **Grandmother Knits**

> . . . *I will knit a vest of feathers*
> *a house of pine cones*
> *a shawl of maple leaves*
> *Here is a cape of birch bark*
> *hats of ghost elms*
> *moccasins of pine needles*
>
> *I will knit a dress of fall grass*
> *a coat of loon calls*
> *I will knit a nightgown of lichens*
> *gathered from fallen logs*
> *I will knit lace of maple syrup*
> *I will knit a shield of raspberry canes*
> *though my fingers will bleed*
>
> *I will knit a spider web beaded with*
> *blueberries I will knit a bed of corn silk*
> *I will knit prayers of smoke I will knit coverlets of*
> *cricket song pillows of milkweed down*
> *scarves from the long howls of coyotes*
> *I will knit embraces of warm spring rains*
> *sweaters of squash blossoms I will knit*
> *whatever we need my fingers*
> *will never be still*[23]

CHERYL SAVAGEAU teaches at Bread Loaf School of English at Middlebury College. She is a French/Abenaki poet and writer. She has received Fellowships in Poetry from the National Endowment for the Arts and the Massachusetts Artists Foundation. Her most recent book is *Mother/Land* (2006). Her memoir, *Out of the Crazywoods*, is forthcoming from the University of Nebraska Press, Spring 2020.

Notes

1   Savageau, *Mother/Land*, 15.
2   *Ktsi wliwni*, great thanks, to Lisa Brooks, for her insights and extensive discussion of Ktsi Amiskw in *The Common Pot*, 13–24. See also Brooks, "Ktsi Amiskw, the Great Beaver."
3   Harjo appears in Bill Moyers's *Power of the Word Series: Ancestral Voices*, PBS, 1989. billmoyers .com/content/ancestral-voices-2.
4   Savageau, *Mother/Land*, 15.
5   Walters, *Talking Indian*, 100.
6   Savageau, *Mother/Land*, 15.
7   *Wliwni* to Robin Wall Kimmerer, who has a long discussion about this in *Braiding Sweetgrass*, 156–66. An ethnobotanist and keeper of traditional knowledge, Kimmerer's vision and use of language is that of a poet and storyteller, blurring the supposed boundaries between disciplines.
8   Savageau, "Bagw and Tekw," in *Out of the Crazywoods*, 2.
9   Savageau, "Bagw and Tekw," in *Out of the Crazywoods*, 3.
10 This quote has been attributed to Wendy Rose, but she has not confirmed it.
11 Savageau, *Mother/Land*, 26.
12 Savageau, *Mother/Land*, 9–10. With thanks to Joseph Bruchac for his telling of this story.
13 Savageau, *Mother/Land*, 134.
14 Savageau, *Dirt Road Home*, 5–6.
15 Savageau, *Dirt Road Home*, 55.
16 Savageau, *Mother/Land*, 63–64.
17 Savageau, "Looking for Indians," in *Dirt Road Home*, 8.
18 Savageau, *Mother/Land*, 84–85.
19 Savageau, *Mother/Land*, 24–25.
20 Savageau, *Dirt Road Home*, 49.
21 Savageau, "Nebi" as "Water/Nebi."
22 Womack, *Red on Red*, 42.
23 Savageau, *Mother/Land*, 137–38.

Works Cited

Brooks, Lisa. *The Common Pot*. Minneapolis: University of Minnesota Press, 2008.

Brooks, Lisa. "Ktsi Amiskw, the Great Beaver." *Our Beloved Kin: Remapping a New History of King Philip's War*. Last updated May 31, 2019. www .ourbelovedkin.com/awikhigan/ktsi-amiskw.

Kimmerer, Robin Wall. *Braiding Sweetgrass*. milkweed.org/book/braiding-sweetgrass.

Savageau, Cheryl. *Dirt Road Home*. Willimantic, CT: Curbstone, 1995.

Savageau, Cheryl. *Mother/Land*. Cambridge: Salt, 2006.

Savageau, Cheryl. *Out of the Crazywoods*. Lincoln: University of Nebraska Press, 2020.

Savageau, Cheryl. "Water/Nebi." *Yellow Medicine Review*, Fall 2012, 84.

Walters, Anna Lee. *Talking Indian: Reflections on Survival and Writing*. Ithaca, NY: Firebrand, 1992.

Womack, Craig. *Red on Red*. Minneapolis: University of Minnesota Press, 1999.

Borders Be Damned!

GEARY HOBSON

Abstract   This article provides a summary of Canadian First Nations writing and publishing within the context of Native American literature, with references to the entire area
of Western Hemisphere Native writing. Admittedly, some readers and scholars will notice
the omission of certain writers and their works, but it is maintained that this is somewhat
the essence of the article: Native writing in the Western Hemisphere is still in the process of
being identified, read, and recognized as such. Thus this article underpins the notion that
the work of recognizing and categorizing such work is a continuing, necessary, and won-
derful endeavor.
Keywords   borders, border theory, Indigenous, Native America

As I was talking to J_____ about seeing the film *Borders* and the ironies it raises, he said "Borders Be Damned!" At first I thought that he was criticizing the film (which he had already said he had not seen), but no, it was the concept embedded in the title—which Tom King presents so admirably—in both the published short story and the subsequent film script adapted from the story.[1] Why the hell borders anyway? Good question. Well, consult Chief Clinton Rickard, late of the New York Tuscaroras, in his book *Fighting Tuscarora*, as well as King himself, and you will likely get a response that will answer the question so demonstrably that it ought to make border officials on both sides hang their heads in shame.[2]

In this discourse I am seeking to apprise one and all of what I perceive to be some issues relative to the 2019 Returning the Gift (RTG) (and Native Writers' Circle of the Americas [NWCA]) literary festival, slated for the summer and hosted by the University of Calgary, in Alberta, Canada.[3] It will be, in effect, a compendium of nearly two years gone by since the last RTG gathering in Norman, Oklahoma, in October 2017. Over the years I have noticed, with dismay, a growing distance between US and Canadian Native writers and scholars, and so, like the family in *Borders*, I want to break down some fences that I feel are separating us. Allow me to say, as I proceed, that I feel the major flaws relative to the barrier are more attributable to those of us southward than our northward brothers and sisters. As a consequence, to state it more plainly: Canadian (or First Nations) literati know more about universal Native writing than do us southward. Hence, to hopefully rectify matters,

ENGLISH LANGUAGE NOTES
58:1, April 2020   DOI 10.1215/00138282-8237399
© 2020 Regents of the University of Colorado

I want herewith to name-drop enough Canadian Native (or First Nations) writers that should make those of us south of the border lift our eyebrows in amazement, quite simply for not knowing them.[4] However, before we get under way, I have several words of caution. While this brief manifesto will parade itself as a portion of that subject called literary criticism, it is really not that at all. Rather, it is hopefully a fence buster of sorts, or a border breaker. I have no interest in parading forth assessments of writers as a presumptive last word on the topic—or, as is so blithely done these days, the assessment of writers-about-writers. Thus no mentions—after this sentence—will be made of Lacan or Derrida or Muggy-muggs as they all too often profess to assess (how about that for a rhyme!) the literary offerings of N. Scott Momaday or Richard Van Camp or James Welch or Jeannette Armstrong or Craig Womack or Cheryl Suzack and so forth. Darn it, boys and girls, there are just too many fine Louise Erdrich novels and Marilyn Dumont poems to read for us to waste our time trying to keep up with every new overly vaunted critical theory of the month!

Rather, what I will do here, in my own pseudocritical fashion, is set up some four areas to keep in mind as we examine just what 'Skin literature has been/is about. To wit:

1. Pre-Columbian to the 1770s. The days of the oral tradition.
2. 1772 to 1968. Early groundbreaking works by Natives in European languages.
3. 1968 to 1992. The Native American Renaissance, beginning with *House Made of Dawn* and surfacing in the quincentennial RTG Festival, in which approximately three hundred Native American writers took part, surprising in their numbers not only all outside interests but even Native writers themselves.
4. The results, or aftereffects, of the festival. The writing continues, with that three hundred number being represented by perhaps three times or more today, depending on who's counting and how they are doing it.

And this last phrase, "depending on who's counting and how they are doing it," is the key to what I go on about here. How are Indians (i.e., Native Americans, American Indians, First Nations, aborigines, etc.) to be described and identified? Some will say that only the genetic counts (how much one is by blood); some will maintain the cultural (how much does one know of one's culture); some, the social (how one interacts—or doesn't—with others of the race); and others, only the legal matters (whether the federal powers within which the Native peoples reside are respected or not by these outside interests). I have expatiated on this matter before.[5] These categories or stipulations apply to all Native peoples, not only in the United States but in other nations within the Western Hemisphere.

Personally, I have always maintained that the cultural realm is the most significant in recognizing or maintaining "Indianism," nationhood, or, call it, if you will, tribe. Culture is what we are always learning, from 4/4ths blood quantum folks to, say, the 1/64ths one being introduced into the tribal or national fabric through personal interaction—for example, education, of all kinds, either at one's parents' or other elders' sides, or in all types of formal classroom tutelage, or of one's private readings and observations. Learning is what makes us.

However, let's move on past the Indian identity issue and look a bit more closely at these four stages of Native American literary expression:

1. The first stage, not only in the United States but hemispheric, is the now-labeled oral tradition—the stories, songs, philosophies, and even neighborly gossiping—indeed, all forms of verbal expression arguably fall into the broad category of literature. In 1492 and thereafter any examination of aboriginal expression of all sorts is illustrated through verbal rendition. The first literary publications dealing with Native American expression, as thus rendered in Spanish, French, and English, are generally regarded as literary works about aborigines and thus slighted as Native literature per se. But is this wholly valid? Such renditions, often designated as "as told to" and "as told by" works—in which the actual writing was done by a non-Native writing in European languages—and "voices" are thus dismissed as if they had not been involved in the creation of the work in question. However, later on, the assumed autobiographies of, say, Geronimo, Black Hawk, Black Elk, etc., are, to Native American people and their non-Native friends, very definite contributions to Native American literature.

2. As is illustrated in the groundbreaking volumes *A Biobibliography of Native American Writers, 1772–1924*, by Daniel F. Littlefield and James W. Parins, the earliest known work by a Native American in English in the United States is a Christian sermon of the Reverend Samson Occam (Mohegan) in 1772.[6] This, and other such works, in English and additionally in Spanish and French, by Native authors writing in these European languages, constitutes the second stage, the natural progression of the oral tradition. The phase continues to the mid-twentieth century. How much of a ghostwriter, or a heavy-handed critic, is involved, is continually debated. Here's my answer: if Francis LaFlesche hadn't written his chronicle of a few years in a Presbyterian school in the English that he was still learning, while being heavily edited by his mentor, Alice Cunningham Fletcher, then we wouldn't have the work. As I was always in the habit of telling my students, everyone can use an editor. Like, for example, the arguably greatest "autobiography" by a Native American, *Black Elk Speaks*. Although John G. Neihardt engineered the work to happen, encouraging Black Elk to tell his story in the only language he knew—Lakota—with the narrative then being rendered into a pidgin English by Lakota translators, then Neihardt's daughter putting it into workable English, stenographer-wise, and then Neihardt refurbishing it all into the beautifully expressed English of which he as a poet was eminently capable, the story, if not the book itself—even with Neihardt's name on the cover as

the author—is now considered Black Elk's. Neihardt wouldn't have had a book if Black Elk hadn't told his story. Other third- or fourth-hand accounts of this era are those by/about Geronimo, Black Hawk, Lame Deer, and the list goes on.[7]

In the last few years of my teaching career, I sometimes had students who insisted that Black Elk couldn't be an author, since he didn't do any writing by hand, yet maintained that Sarah Palin, narrating her life story to a "ghostwriter," was an actual author. (I suppose that the same thing can be said these days for Donald Trump, hmm?)

And while many "as-told-to" works were produced in English during this nearly two-hundred-year period, works actually written in English by Native American people began to appear. As Littlefield and Parins show in their work, the Reverend Samson Occam (Mohegan) wrote and published a Christian sermon in 1772 in the English that he had learned as an adult. This is likely the first such work to appear. Others in this multiple-stage era include many Cherokees, Chippewas/Ojibways, and other tribal representatives writing from either a political or an artistic framework, such as John Ross, Elias Boudinot, John Rollin Ridge, DeWitt Clinton Duncan, John M. Oskison, Will Rogers, Lynn Riggs, Muriel H. Wright, D'Arcy McNickle, John Joseph Mathews, Alexander L. Posey, Dan Madrano, etc., as well as other Christian convert writers, such as the aforementioned Samson Occam and William Apess, and others.

3. The third stage, as I see it, starts with N. Scott Momaday winning the Pulitzer Prize for his novel *House Made of Dawn*, published in 1968. Suddenly, national as well as international attention was turned toward Native American literary expression. Within only a few years, writers such as James Welch, Simon J. Ortiz, Leslie Marmon Silko, Maria Campbell, Jeannette Armstrong, Joy Harjo, Wendy Rose, Joseph Bruchac, Maurice Kenny, Linda Hogan, Harold Cardinal, Gerald Vizenor, Carroll Arnett/Gogisgi, Vine Deloria Jr., Paula Gunn Allen, and others, burst on the scene. This era is generally called the Native American Renaissance. It culminates in, or rather greatly expands after, the 1992 RTG festival held at the University of Oklahoma in Norman, in which more than three hundred Native American writers (depending on who is doing the counting) were assembled, more than ever before or since.

4. Out of RTG, the number of Native writers has increased tremendously. Certain writers taking part in the 1992 assemblage (and some of the subsequent RTG gatherings), who had published very little, including in most cases their first books, and who have since made themselves the prime forces in the contemporary scene are D. L. Birchfield, Sherman Alexie, Lee Maracle, Jordan Wheeler, Armand Garnet Ruffo, Kimberly Blaeser, Craig S. Womack, Tim Tingle, Robert Warrior, William S. Yellow Robe Jr., Allison Adelle Hedge Coke, and the list will go on and on! These writers, plus now the scores of others, constitute the

contemporary scene, which I call "post-RTG." I don't call it "post-Renaissance," because I feel the Renaissance is still very much with us, at a deeper and more complex stage, and becoming more vital with each passing day.

Native Americanism, as I believe we can all agree on, is definitely international, and so are all the forms of literary expression found therein. Thus the RTG festival was certainly groundbreaking. A listing of 241 attendees can be found in the last pages of Joseph Bruchac's anthology, *Returning the Gift: Poetry and Prose from the First North American Native Writers' Festival* (1994), a volume that commemorates the event. However, even this listing is incomplete, because a number of writers were left off. Throughout the twenty-five-year aftermath, I, as a scholar of Native American literature and one of the planners of the original RTG, have run across various writers who had been in attendance at the festival and who are not listed therein. My count now—and this is ever-changeable, based on new discoveries of hitherto unknown attendees—is approximately three hundred. And there were probably more, not even counting the numerous non-Native critics and scholars who were present. Furthermore, a tremendous aspect of the first RTG was the significant number of Canadian Native writers who came to participate. Not only that, but nations and regions such as Guatemala, Mexico, Peru, Cuba, and, arguably, Siberia, were represented by Native writers from those places.

At this point I would like to become more oriented to First Nations writers. As mentioned, the 2019 RTG festival is slated to take place in Calgary, Alberta, in June of that year and will include aspects of the 2018 nonmeeting, in which awards for this year will be bestowed then. William S. Yellow Robe Jr., the 2018 Lifetime Achievement Award winner, will be honored, along with the winners of the 2018 First Book competition (to be announced on July 1 of this year). Hopefully, these three writers will be in attendance in Calgary, along with the 2019 Lifetime Achievement Award winner and the First Books winners for the same year. And this leads to my main purpose in drafting this harangue.[8]

In twenty-six years of the awarding of the Lifetime Achievement Award, there has not been a Canadian First Nations writer to win it. Unfortunately, word seemed to have circulated in Canada that the award is a "States thing," that it didn't (doesn't) apply to First Nations people, and that First Nations writers shouldn't bother with it, in terms of voting. Consequently, fewer First Nations writers submitted their votes each year, so that in effect it *has*, unfortunately, become something of a "States thing." Well, boys and girls, as the project historian of the NWCA, I am here to tell you *that not only will the voting for the 2019 Lifetime Achievement Award winner be directed toward a First Nations writer (or writers, since on two occasions in the past there have been dual winners of the award), but that the only writers who can be voted on for 2019 will be First Nations writers.* And this is the reason for the forthcoming listing and name-dropping of First Nation writers, including some brief assessments of some of them as definitely worthy recipients of the award.

The following is a list of Canadian First Nations writers and some of their works. I apologize for not being more thorough in listing all of a particular writer's work, in terms of published books, plays, or articles, but since this is an essay professing to be a manifesto—or vice versa—I hope that the reader will spare me opprobrium and see fit to indulge me for my attempt to be as inclusive as possible in the time and space allowed. As well, please excuse the variations of tribal or national names, such as Anishinaabe, Anishinabe, Ojibway, Ojibwe, Chippewa, Chippeway; Inuit, Inuk, Inuktitut, and (continue to spare me!) Eskimo; Coast Salish, Sto:lo— and on and on. My methodology is simply that I am using the designation accompanying each individual writer, when he or she refers to himself or herself as "Ojibwe" rather than "Chippewa." I consider this natural and in keeping with how various Native tribes view themselves. As a personal example, part of my Native heritage is Cherokee. In Oklahoma most Cherokees refer to themselves in print as "Tsaligi." In Arkansas, where I was born and raised, the label is generally rendered "Jilagi" and often spelled that way in print. Who's right? This applies pretty well all across the map. Therefore I make an effort to use the label that each writer designates for himself or herself. If you find you can't agree with me, then you can report me to the management. . . .

Canadian Native Writers

3—Anne (Carriere) Acco (Cree, SK) RTG 1992 *Ekosi*

4—Janice Acoose (Saulteaux-Metis, SK) *Ishwewak Kah Yaw Ni Wahkomakaanak*

4—Evan Adams (Salish, Sliammon Res., BC) *Dreams of Sheep*; *Snapshots*

3—*Howard J. Adams (Metis, SK) *Prison of Grass*; *The Education of Canadians, 1800–1867*

2—*Edward Ahenakew (Cree, Sandy Lake Res., SK) *Voices of the Plains Cree*

3—*Freda Ahenakaw (Cree, Ahtahakoop Res., SK) *Cree Language Structures*

4—Kateri Akiwenzie-Damm (Ojibway, Cape Croker Res., ON) RTG 1992 *My Heart Is a Stray Bullet*; *Without Reservation: Indigenous Erotica*; *The Stone Collection*

4—*Robert Arthur Alexie (Gwi'chin, NT) *Porcupines and China Dolls*

4—Gerald Taiaiake Alfred (Mohawk, Kahnawake Res., QC) *Being Indigenous*

3—Anahareo (Gertrude Bernard) (Mohawk, ON) *Devil in Deerskins*

3—An Antane-Kapesh (Innu [Montagnais], QC) *Je suis une maudit sauvagesse*; *Qu'as tu fait du mon pays?*

3—*Anne Anderson (Metis-Cree, AB) RTG 1992 *Let's Learn Cree*; *The First Metis: A New Nation*

3—*Mathieu Andre (Innu [Montagnais], QC) *Moi, "Mestenapeu"*

3—Jo-Ann Archibald (Sto:Lo, BC) *Indigenous Storywork*

3—Jeannette Armstrong (Okanagan, Penticton Res., BC) RTG 1992 *Slash; Looking at the Words of Our People; Enwisteethwa (Walk in Water); Neekma and Chemai; Whispering in Shadows; Breath Tracks*

3—Joanne Arnott (Metis, MB) *Wiles of Girlhood; My Grass Cradle*

4—Wayne Arthurson (Metis, MB) *In the Shadows of Our Ancestors; A Killing Winter*

3—*Pitseolak Ashoona (Inuktitut, NU) *Pitseolak: Pictures of My Life*

3—*Bernard Assiniwi (Cree-Algonkin, QC) RTG 1992 *The Beothuk Saga; Survival in the Bush; The Montagnais and Naskapi Indians; La bras coupe; Makwa, the Little Algonquian*

4—Josephine Bacon (Innu [Montagnais], QC) *Message Sticks*

2—Margaret Baikie (Inuit, LB) *Labrador Memories*

3—Marie Annharte Baker (Anishinabe, MB) RTG 1992 *Being on the Moon*

4—James Bartleman (Chippewa, Mujikaning Band, ON) *As Long as the Rivers Flow*

4—Marie Battiste (Mi'kmaq, Potlatch Res., NS) *Reclaiming Indigenous Voices and Vision*

3—Gail Bear (Cree, SK) RTG 1992 *The Indian Family; Learning about the Indian Reserve*

2—*Glecia Bear (Cree, Flying Dust Res., SK) *Our Grandmothers' Lives*

4—Billy-Ray Belcourt (Driftpile Cree Nation, AB) *This Wound Is a World*

4—Shane Belcourt (Metis, ON) *Tkaronto*

4—Donna Beyer (Cree-Ojibway, Peguis Res., MB)

4—Lisa Bird-Wilson (Cree-Metis, SK) *Just Pretending; The Red Files*

3—Sandra Birdsell (Metis, MB) *The Town That Floated Away*

3—*Peter Blue Cloud/Aroniawenrate (Mohawk, Caughnawaga Res., QC) *Elderberry Flute Song*

3—*George Blondin (Dene, NT) *When the World Was New; Trail of the Spirit*

4—Columpa Bobb (Tsliel Waututh Nlaka'pamux, BC) RTG 1992

4—Jennifer Bobiwash (Ojibwe, ON)

4—Tracey Kim Bonneau (Okanagan, BC) RTG 1992 *Wild Food; Occupied Cascadia*

4—David Bouchard (Metis, SK) *If You're Not from the Prairies*; *Aboriginal Carol*

4—Helene Boudreau (Metis, NS) *Real Mermaid* series

3—Ann Brady (Metis) RTG 1992

3—*Beth Brant (Mohawk, Bay of Quinte, ON) RTG 1992 *A Gathering of Spirit*

3—*Eleanor Brass (Cree, Peepeekisis Res., SK) *I Walk in Two Worlds*

4—Alec Butler (Metis, NS) *Black Friday*

4—Frank Christopher Busch (Cree, Nisichawayasiuk Res., MB) *Grey Eyes*

2—Lydia Campbell (Inuit, LB) *Sketches of Labrador Life*

3—Maria Campbell (Metis) *Halfbreed*; *Stories of the Road Allowance People*; *Achimona*

4—Tenille Campbell (Dene-Metis, NU) *Indian Love Poem*

3—Douglas Cardinal (Metis-Blackfoot/Kainai, BC) *The Native Creative Process*; *Of the Spirit*

3—*Harold Cardinal (Cree, Sucker Lake Res.) *The Unjust Society*; *The Rebirth of Canada's Indians*

3—*Joane Cardinal-Schubert (Metis-Blackfoot [Kainai], BC) *J C-S: Aboriginal Woman Artist*

4—David Carpenter (Metis) *The Education of Augie Merasty*

4—Lisa Charleyboy (Tsilhqot'in, BC) *Dreamin' Indian*

3—Paul L. A. H. Chartrand (Metis, MB)

3—Shirley Cheechoo (Cree, QC) *Path with No Moccasins*; *Tangled Sheets*

3—Bruce Chester (Metis-Sokoki, QC) *Paper Radio*

4—Rosie Christie (Cree, Thunderchild Res., SK) *As Tears Go By*

4—Marie Clements (Cree, SK) *The Unnatural and Accidental Woman*

3—Albert Connelly (Innu, QC) *Oti-il-ro-kaepe*

3—Charles Coocoo (Cree, Atikamekw Res., QC) *Broderies sur mocassins*

1—George Copway (Ojibwe, Mississauga Band, ON) *The Life . . . of Kah-ge-ga-gah-bow*

3—Joan Crate (Metis, NT) *Pale as Real Ladies*; *Breathing Water*; *SubUrban Legends*

4—Susan Currie (Cayuga, ON) *Basket of Beethoven*; *The Mask That Sang*

3—Beth Cuthand (Cree, Lac La Ronge Res, SK) *Horse Dance to Emerald Mountain*; *Voices in the Waterfall*.

4—Joseph A. Dandurand (Kwantlen, BC) *Please Don't Touch the Indians*

4—Rosanna Deerchild (Cree, O-Pipon-Na-Pewin Res., MB) *This Is a Small Northern Town*

4—Darrell Dennis (Secwepemc [Shuswap], BC) *Peace Pipe Dreams*: *The Truth about Lies about Indians*

4—Bonnie Devine (Anishinaabe, Serpent River Res., ON) *The Drawings and Paintings of Daphne Odjig*

3—*Olivia Patricia Dickason (Metis, MB) *Canada's First Nations*; *Indian Arts in Canada*

4—Cherie Dimaline (Metis, ON) *The Marrow Thieves*; *A Gentle Habit*

4—*Valerie Dudoward (Tsimshian, BC) *The Land Called Morning*; *Three Plays*

4—Dawn Dumont (Cree, Okanese Res., SK) *Nobody Cries at Bingo*; *Rose's Run*; *Glass Beads*

4—Marilyn Dumont (Cree-Metis, AB) *A Really Good Brown Girl*; *The Pemmican Eaters*

3—Martin F. Dunn (Metis, ON) *Red on White*

4—Jason EagleSpeaker (Blackfoot-Duwamish, AB)

3—Floyd Favel (Cree, Poundmaker Res., SK) *Master of the Dew: A Memorial to Nostalgia and Desire*

4—*Connie Fife (Cree, SK) RTG 1992 *Beneath the Naked Sun*; *Poem for a New World*

4—Julie Flett (Cree-Metis, BC) *Pakwa Che Menisu*

4—Naomi Fontaine (Innu [Montagnais], QC) *Kuessipan: Manikanetish*

4—Natasha Kanape Fontaine (Innu [Montagnais], QC) *Do Not Enter My Soul in Your Shoes*

4—James Forsyth (Cree, Fish River Res., MB)

4—Marie Frawley-Henry (Nipissing, ON) RTG 1992

3—Mini Aodla Freeman (Inuk, Cape Horn Islands, NU) *Life among the Qallunaat*

3—*Alice Masak French (Ninatakmuit Inuit, Baillie Is., NT), *My Name Is Masak*; *The Restless Nomad*

4—Andrew George (Wet'sawet'en, BC) *Feast! Canadian Native Cuisine for All Seasons*

3—*Chief Dan George (Tsleil-waututh [Coast Salish], BC) *My Heart Soars; My Spirit Soars*

3—Pierre Gill (Montagnais, QC) *Les Montagnais: Premiere habitants du Saguenay-Lac-St.-Jean*

3—*Jean Cuthand Goodwill (Cree, Little Pine Res., SK) *John Tootoosis*

3—Richard G. Green (Mohawk, Six Nations Res.,ON) RTG 1992 *The Last Raven and Other Stories*

3—Max Gros-Louis (Wendat [Huron], QC) *First among the Huron*

4—David Groulx (Anishinaabe, ON) *Night in the Exude: Poems; A Difficult Beauty*

4—Louise Bernice Halfe (Cree, Saddle Lake Res., AB) *Bear Bones and Feathers; Blue Marrow*

3—Tomson Highway (Cree, MB) *The Rez Sisters; Dry Lips Oughta Move to Kapuskasing; The Incredible Adventures of Mary Jane Mosquito*

3—Robert Houle (Saulteaux, MB) *The Place Where God Lives*

4—Liz Howard (Anishinaabe, ON) *Infinite Citizen of the Shaking Tent*

3—Beverly Hungry Wolf (Blackfoot, AB) *The Ways of Our Grandmothers*

4—Al Hunter (Anishinaabe, Rainy River Res., ON) RTG 1992 *Spirit Horses; The Recklessness of Love*

3—*Alootook Ipellie (Inuit, Baffin Island, NT) RTG 1992 *Arctic Dreams and Nightmares*

3—*Morris Isaac (Mi'kwaq, NS) RTG 1992 "Funny I'm Still Looking for That Place"

4—Madeline Piujuq Ivalu (Inuk, NU) *Before Tomorrow*

1—*Rev. Peter Jacobs/Pahtahsega (Ojibway, Mississauga, ON) *Journal of . . . Rev. Peter Jacobs . . .*

3—*Rita Joe (Mi'kwaw, NS) *Poems of Rita Joe; Song of Eskasoni*

1—*E. Pauline Johnson (Mohawk, ON) *The White Wampum; Flint and Feather*

2—*Basil H. Johnston (Ojibway, Cape Croker Res., ON) RTG 1992 *Moose Meat and Wild Rice; Indian School Days; Ojibway Ceremonies; Ojibway Heritage; Tales the Elders Told*

4—Aviaq Johnston (Inuk, NU) *Those Who Run in the Sky*

1—*Rev. Peter Jones/Kahkewaquonably (Ojibwe, ON) *A Collection of Chippeway and English Hymns*

2—*Edith Josie (Gwi'chin, YT) *Here Are the News*

4—Daniel Heath Justice (Cherokee from CO, ON); *Our Fire Survives the Storm*; *Kynship*; *Wyrwood*; *Dreyd*

3—Margo Kane (Cree-Saulteaux, AB) *Moonlodge*

3—Lenore Keeshig-Tobias (Chippewa, Nawash, ON) RTG 1992 *Bineshiinh dibaaj mowin: Bird Talk*

3—Orville Keon (Nipissing, ON) *Thunderbirds of the Ottawa*

3—Wayne Keon (Nipissing, ON) RTG 1992 *Thunderbirds of the Ottawa*; *My Sweet Maize*; *Sweetgrass*

3—Thomas King (Cherokee of CA, ON) *Medicine River*; *One Good Story, That One*; *The Truth about Stories*; *Green Grass, Running Water*; *Truth and Bright Water*; *All My Relations*

3—Verna Kirkness (Cree, Fisher River Res., MB) *Wahbung: Our Tomorrows*

4—Jules Koostachin (Cree, Attawapisket Res., ON) *Nii So Te Wak*

3—Michael Arvaarluk Kusugak (Inuit, NU) *Arctic Stories*; *A Promise Is a Promise*

4—Patti LaBoucane-Benson (Metis, AB) *The Outside Circle*

3—Emma LaRocque (Cree-Metis, AB) *Defeathering the Indian*

4—Alice Lee (Metis) RTG 1992

4—Georgia Lightning (Cree, Samson Res., AB) *Older than America*

4—Tracey Lindberg (Cree, Kelly Lake Res., AB) *Birdie*

4—George Littlechild (Cree, Hobbema Res., AB) *This Is My Land*; *We Are All Related*

4—Kevin Loring (Nlaka'pamux [Thompson River Salish], BC) *Where the Blood Mixes*

3—Antoine S. Lussier (Metis, MB) *The Metis: Canada's Forgotten People*

4—Terese Marie Mailhot (Nlaka'pamux [Sto:lo], BC) *Heart Berries*

4—Kanshus Manuel (Secwipewc [Shuswap]-Ktunaxa [Kootenai], BC) "Colonization"

3—George Manuel (Scewipewc [Shuswap], BC) *The Fourth World*

4—*Vera Manuel (Secwipewc [Shuswap]-Ktunaxa [Kootenai], BC) *Two Plays about Residential Schools*

3—Brian Maracle/Owennatekha (Mohawk, Six Nations Res., ON) RTG 1992 *Back on the Rez*; *Crazywater*

3—Lee Maracle (Bobbi Lee) (Coast Salish [Sto:lo], BC) RTG 1992 *Bobbi Lee: Indian Rebel*; *I Am Woman*; *Bent Box*; *Daughters Are Forever*; *Sundogs*; *Ravensong*

3—Duane Marchand (Okanagan, BC) RTG 1992 "Tears from the Earth"

2—Markoosie/Patsaug (Inuktitik, QC) *Harpoon of the Hunter*

4— Keavy Martin (Metis, AB) *Stories in a New Skin*

4—Henry Lorne Masta (Abenaki, QC) *Abenaki Legends, Grammar, and Place Names*

4—Steven Matsheshu (Innu, QC) *Urban Indian Love Songs*

3—Joseph McLellan (b. in US; Nez Perce, MB) *Nanabosho Steals Fire*; *Goose Girl*

3—Gerald McMaster (Plains Cree-Blackfoot, AB) *Reservation X*; *The New Tribe*

4—Billy Merasty (Cree, MB) *Fireweed*

4—Joseph-Auguste Merasty (Cree, Peter Ballantyne Res., SK) *The Education of Augie Merasty*

4—Duncan Mercredi (Cree-Metis, MB) *The Duke of Windsor: Wolf Sings the Blues*

4—Edwin Metatawakin (Cree, Ft. Albany Res., ON) *Up Ghost River*

3—Barry Milliken (Ojibway, Stony Point Res., ON) RTG 1992 *Voices Telling: . . . Stories from . . . Wiikenedong*

3—Muriel Mojica (Cana-Rappannock, Panama/NY/ON) *Princess Pocahontas and the Blue Spots*

3—Joel Monture (Mohawk, Six Nations Res., ON) RTG 1992 *We Share Our Mothers*

4—Patricia A. Monture-Angus (Mohawk, Six Nations Res., ON) *Thunder in My Soul*

4—Rick Monture (Mohawk, Six Nations Res., ON) *We Share Our Matters*

4—Tera Lee Morin (Ojibwe, MB) *As I Remember It*

3—*Norval Morrisseaux (Anishinaabe, Sand Point Res., ON) *Legends of My People, the Great Ojibway*

3—Daniel David Moses (Delaware-Tuscarora, ON) RTG 1992 *Delicate Bodies*

3—Beatrice Culleton Mosionier (Metis, SK) RTG 1992 *In Search of April Raintree*; *In the Shadow of Evil*

3—*Mitiarjuk Nappaaluk (Inuit, BC) *Sanaaq: An Inuit Novel*

3—David Neel (Kwakwaka'wakw, BC) *Our Chiefs and Elders*

4—Michael Noel (Algonkin, QC) *Pien*; *À la recherché du bout du monde*

3—Yvette Nolan (Algonquin, MB) *Blade*; *Annie Mae's Movement*

3—Alanis Obamsawin (Abenaki, Odanak Res, QC) "Incident at Restigouche"

4—Jay Odjick (Anishinaabe, Kitigan Zibi, ON) *Kagag: The Raven*

3—*Daphne Odjig (Odawa-Pottawatomi, ON) *A Paintbrush in My Hand*

3—Delia Opekokew (Cree, Canoe Lake Res., SK) *The Legal and Political Inequalities among Aboriginal Peoples in Canada*

3—*Gilbert Oskaboose (Ojibwe, Serpent Lake Res., ON) *Our Bit of Truth*; "A Dog's Tale"

4—Pamela Palmater (Mi'kwaq, NB) *Beyond Blood*

4—Taqralik Partridge (Inuit, NU) "Fifteen Lakota Visitors"

3—Daniel N. Paul (Mi'kwaq, Indian Brook Res., NS) *Lightning Bolt*

3—Diane Paulette Payment (Metis, SK) "The Free People—Otipemisiwak"

3—*Wilfrid Pelletier (Odawa, Wikwemikong Res., ON) *No Foreign Land*

3—*Henry Pennier (Sto:lo, BC) *Chiefly Indian*; *Call Me Hank*

3—Peter Pitseolak (Inuit, Nottingham Island, NT) *People on Our Side*

4—Margaret Pokiak-Fenton (Inuvialuit, NT) *Fatty Legs*; *Not My Girl*

4—Louise Profeit-LeBlanc (Northern Tuchone, YT) New Media Arts program at Banff, AB

4—*Sharron Proulx-Turner (Metis, AB) *Where the Rivers Join*; *what the auntys say*; *She Is Reading Her Blanket with Her Hands*

4—L. Rain Prudhomme-Cranford (Gomez) (Creek-Choctaw from LA, AB) *Smoked Mullet Cornbread Crawdad Memory*

4—Karyn Pugliese (Algonquin, Pikwaganagan, ON) Aboriginal People's Television Network stories

4—Rachel Qitsualik-Tinsley (Inuktitut, NU) *Skraelings*

4—Sean Qitsualik (Inuktitut, NU) *Skraelings*

3—Duke Redbird (Ojibway, Saugeen Res., ON) *Dance Me Outside; I Am a Canadian*

4—Waubgeshig Rice (Anishinaabe, Wasauksing Res., ON) *Midnight Sweatlodge*

4—Carmen Robertson (Lakota, Fort Qu'Appelle, SK) *Seeing Red: A History of Natives in Canadian Newspapers*

4—Eden Robinson (Haisla-Heiltsuk, BC) *Monkey Beach; Traplines*

3—*Harry Robinson (Okanagan, BC) *Nature Power*

4—Margaret Robinson (Mi'kwaq, Lennox Island, NS) *Two-Spirit and Bisexual People*

4—Janet Rogers (Mohawk-Tuscarora, ON) *Splitting the Heart; Red Erotica; Unearthed*

3—Armand Garnet Ruffo (Ojibwe, ON) RTG 1992 *Grey Owl; Opening in the Sky; Norval Morrisseau*

3—Buffy Ste.-Marie (Cree, Piapot Res., SK) *It's My Way; Loyal till Death*

4—Sylvia McAdam Saysewahum (Cree, SK) *Nationhood Interrupted*

4—Gregory Scofield (Cree-Metis, BC) *The Gathering; Love Medicine and One Song*

3—Murdo Scribe (Swampy Cree, Norway House Res., MB) *Murdo's Story*

3—*D. Bruce Sealey (Metis, MB) *Jerry Potts; The Metis: Canada's Forgotten People*

4—Paul Seeseequasis (Plains Cree, SK) *Tobacco Wars*

4— Bev Sellers (Xat'sull, Soda Creek Res., BC) *They Called Me Number One*

3—*James Sewid (Kwakwaha'wakw [Kwaikiutl], Alert Bay Res., BC) *Guests Never Leave Hungry*

4—Paula Sherman (Algonquin, ON) *Dishonour of the Crown*

4—Alexandra Shimo (Cree, ON) *Up Ghost River; Invisible North*

3—*Angela Sidney (Tagish, YK) *My Stories Are My Wealth*

4—*Lorne Simon (Mi'kwaq, Elispogtok Res., NB) RTG 1992 *Stones and Switches*

3—Glen Simpson (Tahltan-Kaska, BC) RTG 1992 *Art in the Making*

4—Leanne Betasamosake Simpson (Alderville Res., Mississauga Ojibway, ON) *Islands of Decolonial Love*; *Lighting the Eighth Fire*; *Dancing on Our Turtle's Back*; *As We Have Always Done*

4—Christine Sioui-Wawanoloath (Wendat [Huron]-Abenaki, QC) *Beyond Violence*

2—*Eleonore Tecumseh Sioui (Wendat [Huron], QC) RTG 1992 *Andatha*

3—Georges E. Sioui (Wendat [Huron], QC) *For an Amerindian Autohistory*

3—Ruby Slipperjack (Ojibwe, ON) *Weesquachak and the Lost Ones*; *Honour the Sun*

4—Monique Gray Smith (Cree-Lakota) *Tilly: A Story of Hope and Resilience*

3—*Chief John Snow (Stoney [Nakoda/Assiniboine]) *These Mountains Are Our Sacred Places*

3—*Everett Soop (Blood [Kainai], AB) *Soop Take a Bow*; *I See My Tribe Is Still Behind Me*

3—Darlene Speidel (Lakota, SK) RTG 1992 *Eddie the Frog*

4—Blair Stonechild (Cree-Saulteaux, SK) *The Knowledge Seeker*; *The New Buffalo*

4—Madeleine Dion Stout (Cree, Keteskwew Res., AB) *Aboriginal Woman: Women and Health*

4—Smokii Sumac (Ktunaxa [Kootenai], BC)

4—Cheryl Suzack (Batchewana Ojibway, ON) *Indigenous Women's Writing and the Cultural Study of Law*

4—Tanaya Talaga (Ojibwe, ON) *Seven Fallen Feathers*

3—Drew Hayden Taylor (Ojibwe, ON) RTG 1992 *Funny You Don't Look like One*; *Motorcycles and Sweetgrass*; *The Bootlegger Blues*; *The Boy in the Treehouse*; *The Girl Who Loved Her Horses*; *Fearless Warriors*

4—Ningeokuluk Teevee (Inuit, NU) *Alego*

4—Matrine Therriault (Ojibwe, Mishkeegogamavee, ON)

3—Dorothy Thorsen (Metis, YK) RTG 1992

4—Shannon Thunderbird (Coast Tsimshian, BC) *Medicine Wheel and Character Education in the Twenty-First Century*

3—*E. Donald Two-Rivers (Ojibwe, Seine River Res., ON) *Survivor's Medicine*; *A Dozen Cold Ones*; *Briefcase Warriors*

3—*James Tyman (Metis, SK) *Inside Out: An Autobiography of a Native Canadian*

4—Richard Van Camp (Tlicho [Dogrib], NT) *The Lesser Blessed; Angel Wing Splash Pattern; What's the Most Beautiful Thing You Know about Horses?; A Man Called Raven*

4—Katherina Vermette (Cree, MB) *North End Love Songs; The Break*

4—Jan Bourdeau Waboose (Ojibway, ON) *Morning on the Lake; Sky Sisters*

4—*Richard Wagamese (Ojibway, ON) *Keeper 'n Me; Indian Horse*

3—Emma Lee Warrior (Piegan, AB) RTG 1992 "Compatriots" in *All My Relations*

4—Sheila Watt-Cloutier (Inuit, NU) *The Right to Be Cold; Silaturnimut: The Pathway to Wisdom*

3—Cora Weber-Pillwax (Metis, AB) RTG 1992 *Billy's World*; "Orality in Northern Cree Indigenous Worlds"

4—Gloria Cranmer Webster (Kwakwaka'wahw, BC) "The Potlatch: A Strict Law Bids Us Dance"

3—*Bernelda Wheeler (Cree-Assiniboine-Saulteaux, MB) RTG 1992 *A Friend Called Chum; I Can't Have Moccasins but the Beaver Has a Dam*

3—Jordan Wheeler (Cree-Assiniboine-Saulteaux, MB) RTG 1992 *Brothers in Arms; Chuck in the City*

3—Ellen White (Kwalasulwut [Coast Salish], BC) RTG1992 *Storm from the Coast Salish*

4—Frederick H. White (Haida, BC) "Welcome to the City of Rainbows"; *White Feathers*

4—Joshua Whitehead (Ojibwe-Cree, Peguis Res., MB) *Johnny Appleseed; Full-Metal Indigiqueer*

3—*Don Whiteside (Creek from US, ON) RTG 1992

4—Gerry William (Spallumcheen, BC) *Enid Blue Starbreaks*

3—Jane Pachano Willis (Cree, Chisasibi Res., QC) *Geneish: An Indian Girlhood; Waupsh; Chickabash*

4—Leo Yerxa (Saulteaux, Little Eagle Res., ON) *Last Leaf, First Snowflake to Fall*

3—Annie York (Spuzzum, BC) *They Write Their Dreams on the Rock Forever*

3—*Greg Young-Ing (Gregory Younging) (Cree, The Pas, MB) RTG 1992
*Random Flow of Blood and Feathers; (Ad)dressing Our Words beyond
Victimization*

4—Alfred Young Man (Blackfeet, Rocky Boys, MT/AB-SK) *The Buckskin
Ceiling: A Native Perspective on Native Art Politics*

Note: The number preceding each writer's name refers to the particular era that he
or she first began to establish himself or herself as a writer. To wit: 1 refers to the
aforementioned preliterate to first writings period done in non-Native languages
(i.e., English or French); 2, to the period between 1772 and the late 1960s; 3, to the
Native American Renaissance; and 4, to the present-day or post-Renaissance era,
the "now" age, if you will. An asterisk means that the writer indicated is deceased;
RTG 1992, that he or she attended the first RTG festival in July 1992, when the
NWCA began.

As you can see, dear reader, there are hundreds of Native/First Nations/
Indigenous, etc., etc. writers north of that US-Canadian border. I realize as well
that I have possibly made matters a tad difficult for the would-be invited NWCA
writer-scholar in selecting the ones for his or her ballot for the Lifetime Achievement Award. Suffice it to say that I am now providing a brief listing of some of the
more widely acknowledged First Nations writers so as to make the selection process
more easily engage-worthy. Following the format of the Swedish Academy for Nobel
Prize voting, such can be done only for living writers—with the exception of writers
who passed away within the past twelve months. Therefore the voting for writers
is pretty well configured for categories 3 and 4. Here, then, in my opinion and that
of several officials of the NWCA, are suggested awardees, based on our knowledge
of them as outstanding writers. However, please add other names as you see fit.

Category 3 (listed alphabetically): Jeannette Armstrong, Joanne Arnott,
Maria Campbell, Tomson Highway, Thomas King, Lee Maracle, Beatrice
Culleton Mosionier, Armand Garnet Ruffo, Ruby Slipperjack, Buffy
Ste.-Marie, Drew Hayden Taylor, Jordan Wheeler, Leo Yerxa, and Greg
Young Ing (Gregory Younging)

Category 4 (listed alphabetically): Kateri Akiwenzie-Damm, Gerald Taiaiake
Alfred, Dawn Dumont, Marilyn Dumont, Louise Bernice Halfe, Al Hunter,
Jules Koostachin, Terese Marie Mailhot, Eden Robinson, Leanne
Betasamosake Simpson, Cheryl Suzack, Richard Van Camp, and Frederick
H. White

And now, if you feel that we haven't busted borders enough, here are some more for
all to take note of and to consider.

Latin America

These are to be considered in future voting, if you will. However, we encourage you
to begin as soon as possible reading these outstanding carriers of their cultures

through the written and spoken word. A note of thanks to Victor Montejo, whose hard work on the initial planning committee was largely responsible for the attendance at RTG 1992 of some of the below-listed Mayan, Quechua, and Mexican Native writers; also, a strong word for Allison Adelle Hedgecoke, whose remarkable anthology *Sing: Poetry of the Indigenous Americas*, published in 2011, continues to broaden and deepen our knowledge of the rest of the Americas. We might also consider Siberia and Greenland, for aren't there First Nations/Native Americans/Indigenes, etc., etc., in these places, too? We will address this last remark briefly after we examine all "South of the Border" writers coming up in terms of vital voices.[9]

Latin American Native American Authors

> 3—*Humberto Ak'a'bal (K'iche Mayan, Guatemala) RTG 1992 *Poem I Brought Down from the Mountain*

> 3—Ignacio Bizarro Ujpan (Tzutuhil Mayan, Guatemala) *Son of Tecun Uman*; *Campesino: The Diary of a Guatemalan Indian*

> 4—Jose Balvino Camposeco Mateo (Mayan, Guatemala) RTG 1992 *Te'Son, Chinab' o K'ojom/La Marimba de Guatemala*

> 4—Rosa Chavez (K'iche Maya-Kaquiguel, Guatemala)

> 4—Jose Miguel Cocom Pech (Mayan, Mexico)

> 4—Antonio Cota Garcia (Jakaltek, Mayan, Guatemala) RTG 1992

> 4—Maya Cu Choc (Quechua Mayan, Guatemala)

> 3—Gaspar Pedro Gonzalez (Q'anjob'al, Mayan, Guatemala) RTG 1992 *A Mayan Life*

> 4—Emil Kime/Emilio de Valle Escalante (Maya, K'iche)

> 3—Rigoberta Menchú (K'ichi'Mayan, Guatemala) [Nobel Peace Prize in 1992] *I, Rigoberta Menchú*; *Crossing Borders*

> 3—Victor Montejo (Jakatec [Zapotec] Mayan, Guatemala) RTG 1992 *Testimony: Death of a Guatemalan Village*; *The Bird Who Cleans the World*; *Voices from Exile*

> 4—Mario Perfecto Tema Bautista (Mayan, Guatemala) RTG 1992 *Monografia del pueblo sipakapense*

> 3—Jacinto Arias Perez (Jakaltec [Zapotec]-Tzotzil Mayan, Mexico) RTG 1992 *San Pedro Chenalho*

> 3—*Silvester J. Brito (Comanche-Tarascan, Mexico) RTG 1992

> 4—Adela Calva Reyes (Otomi, Mexico) *Ra Hua Ra Hia/A las a la palabra*

4—Luis Carcamo Huechante (Mapuche, Mexico)

4—Sol Ceh Moo (Yucateca, Mexico)

4—Jose Miguel Cocom Pech (Mayan, Mexico) *Muk'ult'an in Nool* (*Grandpa's Secrets*)

3—Elvira Colorado (Chichimec-Otomi, Mexico) RTG 1992 "Letter from Chiapas"; *Blood Speaks*

3—Hortensia Colorado (Chichimec-Otomi, Mexico) RTG 1992 "Letter from Chiapas"; *Blood Speaks*

4—Roberta Cordero (Chumac-Yaqui, Mexico)

4—Briceida Cuevas Cob (Yucateca, Mexico)

3—Jose L. Garza/Blue Heron (Coahuiltecan-Lipan Apache, TX) RTG 1992

4—Gabriela Spears Rio (Purepecha-Matlatzinca, Mexico)

3—*Refugio Savala (Yaqui, Mexico/AZ) *The Autobiography of a Yaqui Poet*

4—Margo Tamez (Lipan Apache-Jumano Apache, TX) *Raven Eye; Naked Wanting; The Daughter of Lightning; Alleys and Allies*

4—Natalia Toledo (Zapateca, Mexico)

3—Jose Barriero/Hatuey (Taino Guajiro-Camaguay, Cuba, NY) RTG 1992

4—Cristina Calderon (Yaghan, Chile) *Hai Kur Mamasu Shis* (*I Want to Tell You a Story*)

4—Jaime Huenun (Mapuche, Chile)

4—Lionel Lienlaf (Mapuche, Chile) *The Bird of My Heart Has Awakened*

2—*Gabriela Mistral (Chile) [Nobel Prize in Literature in 1945] All these many years after her death, Mistral is now recognized as of partial Indigenous background—something that probably couldn't have been done during her lifetime without running the risk of opprobrium and censorship. *Sonetas de la muerte* (*Songs of Death*); *Ternura* (*Tenderness*); *Tala* (*Harvesting*)

2—*Jose Maria Arguedas (Quechua, Peru) *Yawar fiesta*

4—Odilon Ramos Boza (Quechua, Peru)

1—*Garcilaso de la Vega/ El Inca (Quechua, Peru) *Historia de la Florida/ The Florida of the Inca*

1—*Felipe Guaman Poma de Ayala (Quechua, Peru) *Nueva coronica y bien gobierno*

3—Fredy Amilcar Roncalla (Quechua, Peru) RTG 1992

3—Miryam Yataco (Quechua, Peru) RTG 1992

3—Spiderwoman Theater: *Sun Moon and Feather*

3—*Lisa Mayo (Cana-Rappahannock, NY/Panama) RTG 1992

3—Gloria Miguel (Cana-Rappahannock, NY/Panama) RTG 1992

3—Muriel Miguel (Cana/Rappahannock, NY/Panama) RTG 1992

4—Fredy Romiero Campo Chicangana (Yanacona of Cauca, Colombia)

4—Hilario Chacin (Wayua, Colombia) *Los hijos de la lluvia* (*The Children of the Rain*)

4—Hugo Jamioy (Kamentsa, Colombia) *Mi fuego y mi humo, mi tierra y mi sol*

4—Estercilia Simanca Pushaina (Wayuu, Colombia)

4—Lindantonella Solano (Nation not given, Colombia)

4—Ariruma Kowii (Quechua, Ecuador)

4—Fausto Reinaga (Aymara, Bolivia)

"Hispanic," or Chicano, Writers Who Are Indian
In fact, can't an argument be made for Chicanos, Latinos, etc., when we consider the category of blood—as mentioned above—as yet another determinant of Indianism, Indigesma, Native American, etc.? So, now, take a gander at this list:

Jimmy Santiago Baca (Apache, NM) *Immigrants in Our Own Land; A Place to Stand*

Julian Segura Camacho (Mayo-Purepecha, Mexico/CA) *Amexican*

Lorna Dee Cervantes (Chumash, CA) *Emplumada*

Ines M. Talamantez (Mescalero Apache, AZ) *Teaching Religion and Healing*

Margo Tamez (Lipan Apache, TX) *Alleys and Allies*

This list can, of course, be greatly expanded, and possibly will be, if such enormously talented and culturally rich Chicano writers are added to the well of Indigeneity: Ralph M. Flores, Antonio C. Marquez, Leroy Quintana, Leo Romero, Margarita Dalton, Denise Chavez, Richard Griego, etc., etc. Chicanismo, I have always maintained, is another category of Indigeneity.

Now, to bring things back in terms of traditional circularity, let's take a look at Greenland. If you consult Wikipedia, you will learn that Indigenous people there make up 89 percent of the population. And there has always been traditional story-telling and expression in the Native Inuit and nowadays in modern-day Danish. Needless to say, this deserves further exploration by all of us who profess to be scholars in Native American literature. Suffice it to say, for the time being, that I'll make one strong recommendation: take a look at *From the Writings of the Greenlanders: Kalaallit Atuakkiaanit*, compiled, translated, and edited by Michael Fortescue. It includes selections of works by Native storytellers and writings that even predate the beginning of the so-called Native American Renaissance. (And now, how about Iceland? I understand that there are Native people there, too.) Hopefully, these are matters for future scholars in Native American literature.

As we attempt to conclude this document (manifesto? doctrine? invitation?), we might, since we are approaching the Arctic Circle, continue on westward (why always "westward"?) and northward, skirting the already highlighted Alaska, and arrive at the Bering Strait, the islands there, as well as Siberia. Siberia? Yes, there are Yup'ik (Eskimo, etc., etc.) there, too. At the 1992 RTG two writers from Alaska, and natives of St. Lawrence Island, off the coast of both Russia and the United States—Grace K. Slwooko and Helen Slwooko Carius—were in attendance. Truly, then, Native American literature is hemispheric. Slwooko is reported to have said that part of her early years had been spent in the Russian portion of the Bering Sea islands—Siberia—before the structuring of the Soviet-US bloc began in the mid-1920s.

So, if Yup'ik people and culture decide to expand westward, throughout Siberia and on across Russia and on to the Nordic countries, and at the same time the Eskimo, etc., etc., eastward through Iceland and Denmark and on eastward, then truly we could say that these matters are indeed worldwide.

What about the Samis of Finland and the Ainu of Japan? And, how about all the islands throughout the Pacific? Truly, Indigeneity—and its literatures—is still growing and thriving.

Thanks to an anonymous reviewer of this work, I have been able to add some Sami writers—and there are more to come:

4—Lars Magne Andreassen

3—Signe Iversen

4—Amanda Kernell

4—Gunilla Larsson

4—May-Britt Ohman

4—Troy Storfjell

4—Ella-Maija Apiniskim Tailfeathers

1—John Turi

Addendum

Since the initial posting of "Borders Be Damned!," voting for the 2019 Lifetime Achievement Award has been completed, and it is my pleasant task to report that the 2019 winner of the award was Maria Campbell, the widely respected Metis author of such excellent works as *Halfbreed* and *Stories of the Road Allowance People*. Campbell will be honored again at the projected 2020 festival, slated for Calgary, Alberta. The NWCA webpage will post additional information as time goes on.

GEARY HOBSON (Cherokee-Arkansas Quapaw) is a professor emeritus after nearly thirty years at the University of Oklahoma. His recent books are an anthology, *The People Who Stayed: Southeastern Indian Writing after Removal* (2010), edited with Janet McAdams and Kathryn Walkiewicz, and a collection of short fiction, *Plain of Jars and Other Stories* (2011).

Acknowledgment

An earlier version of "Borders Be Damned!" appeared in the Spring 2019 issue of *Yellow Medicine Review*.

Notes

1   In 1993 Canadian television broadcast a half-hour drama titled *Borders*, a teleplay adapted by King from his short story of the same title. In it a widowed First Nations mother and her teenage son drive from their home in Alberta to the US-Canadian border on their way to visit their daughter-sister in Utah. On their way the mother points out various mountains, traditionally special to them as aboriginal people, on both the Canadian and, in the distance, the US side and tells her son that as long as he knows where he is with regard to them, he will always know his home and who he is as a Blackfoot. Then, at the border, when the mother is asked by one of the agents on the Canadian side what her nationality is, she answers, "Blackfoot" instead of "Canadian." After a great deal of hemming and hawing on the part of the officials, the mother and son are allowed to proceed a few feet to the US gates, only to run into the same obstruction when the mother adamantly sticks to her designation of Blackfoot. This happens several times as the mother and her son are sent back and forth from one border gate to the other. When word spreads about what is going on at the border, all sorts of news people with television cameras descend on the scene. Not wishing to make more of an embarrassing predicament, the officials allow the mother and son to go on their way to Utah, as Blackfoot. The short story is in King, *One Good Story, That One*. The film was made shortly afterward.

2   Clinton Rickard was the principal chief of the Tuscarora Nation in Upstate New York and a strong advocate of Native American sovereignty as well as of the rights of Native Americans to come and go across the US-Canadian border without interference. This remains a guaranteed edict in the Jay Treaty of 1795. (A word needs to be said here, in terms of a recommendation on the subject, for Joseph Bruchac's powerful book of poetry, *No Borders*.)

3   See the addendum at the end of this essay.

4   As is well known these days, Canadian Native people generally prefer to be called First Nations people. I can go along with that. However, we need to keep in mind that in earlier literary works such folks are called variously Indian, Native American, Canadian Native, and other terms. I will comply with fashionable tastes and employ, as often as needed, the designation of First Nations.

5   The two works that I make reference to here were written and published several years ago, when the identity question was beginning to raise its head. The first is an essay, "'Skins in Skin Flicks," and the next, a short story, "The Animals' Ballgame." Needless to say, they are both satires.

6   Littlefield and Parins, *Biobibliography of Native American Writers*; Littlefield and Parins, *Supplement*. Unfortunately for our purposes, Littlefield and Parins halt at the borders. Throughout their work there is no mention of the Reverends Copway, Jacobs, and Jones of

the Ojibway/Chippewa, or of the Brants and Johnsons of the Iroquois—all of whom wrote in English and were from Canadian Native nations. Or of Garcilaso de la Vega or Guaman Poma, Natives writing from a Hispanicized format in the seventeenth century.

7   This is covered extremely well in O'Brien, *Plains Indian Autobiographies*.

8   See the addendum at the end of this essay.

9   At this point, I would like to list a number of extremely helpful sources in assembling my listing of Canadian (and other Americas) writers and their work: Hedgecoke, *Sing*; Young-Ing, "Traditional Aboriginal Voice"; Gruber, *Thomas King*; Sarcowsky, "Maps, Borders, and Cultural Citizenship." The following is a list of webpages that proved helpful: Category: 20th Century First Nations Writers; Category: 21st Century First Nations Writers; Category: First Nations Women Writers; Burt Award for First Nations, Metis and Inuit Literature; List of Writers Indigenous to the Americas; List of Mexican-American Writers.

Works Cited

Bruchac, Joseph. *No Borders*. Duluth, MN: Holy Cow! Press, 1999.

Gruber, Eva, ed. *Thomas King: Works and Impact*. Rochester, NY: Camden House, 2012.

Hedgecoke, Allison Adelle, ed. *Sing: Poetry From the Indigenous Americas*. Tucson: University of Arizona Press, 2011.

Hobson, Geary. "The Animals' Ballgame." *Studies in American Indian Literatures* 25, no. 4 (2013): 83–99.

Hobson, Geary. "'Skins in Skin Flicks: A Modest Proposal on the Most Adequate Means for 'Telling' the 'Real' Indians from the 'Reel' Indians in Pornography." *Studies in American Indian Literatures* 25, no. 1 (2013): 69–88.

King, Thomas. *One Good Story, That One*. Toronto: HarperPerennial, 1993.

Littlefield, Daniel F., and James W. Parins. *A Biobibliography of Native American Writers, 1772–1924*. Metuchen, NJ: Scarecrow, 1981.

Littlefield, Daniel F., and James W. Parins. *A Biobibliography of Native American Writers, 1772–1924: A Supplement*. Metuchen, NJ: Scarecrow, 1985.

O'Brien, Lynne Woods. *Plains Indian Autobiographies*. Boise, ID: Boise State College, 1973.

Sarcowsky, Katja. "Maps, Borders, and Cultural Citizenship: Cartographic Negotiations in Thomas King's Work." In *Thomas King: Works and Impact*, edited by Eva Gruber, 210–23. Rochester, NY: Camden House, 2012.

Young-Ing, Greg. "Traditional Aboriginal Voice." *Looking at the Words of Our People: First Nations Analysis of Literature*, edited by Jeannette Armstrong, 179–87. Penticton, BC: Theytus, 1993.

Restitution of Human Remains and Landscape Resignification

The Case of Chapal-có Hill (La Pampa, Argentina) and the Rankülche Nation

RAFAEL PEDRO CURTONI, GUILLERMO HEIDER,
MARÍA GABRIELA CHAPARRO, AND ÁNGEL T. TUNINETTI

Abstract   The restitution of human remains is a process wherein diverse agencies and meanings emerge. In Argentina there has been a significant increase of these processes, as well as claims of human bodies, during the early twenty-first century, allowing the appearance of new actors, the reconfiguration of public policies, and varied academic approaches. This article deals with a seldom-studied phenomenon—resignification of the territory as a consequence of a restitution—focusing on a recent example that involved the Rankülche Nation, an Indigenous nation in central Argentina, and its relationship with the government of La Pampa province, with scientists, and with members of the local community.

Keywords   Rankülche, restitution of remains, landscape, Argentina, Indigenous

The restitution of human remains is a process wherein diverse agencies and meanings emerge. There has been a significant increase of these processes, as well as claims of human bodies, during the early twenty-first century, allowing the appearance of new actors, the reconfiguration of public policies, and varied academic approaches.[1]

This article deals with a seldom-studied phenomenon—resignification of the landscape as a consequence of a restitution—focusing on a recent example that involved the Rankülche Nation, the government of La Pampa province, scientists, and members of the local community. In 2004 remains of at least six individuals were exposed during the archaeological rescue excavation of a local road in the Chapal-có Valley. The job was done in consultation with representatives of the Rankülche Nation, who considered that the remains were from their ancestors, as they were in a territory they regarded as their own. After a long process of negotiation and some specific scientific studies (also negotiated), the remains were reburied where they had been discovered. In this context, we explore three dimensions that

ENGLISH LANGUAGE NOTES

58:1, April 2020 DOI 10.1215/00138282-8237410
© 2020 Regents of the University of Colorado

we view as complementary: (1) the Rankülches, their worldview, and the relationship between sacred spaces and landscape; (2) the changes in the state policies in relationship with the Indigenous nations in general and the restitutions in particular; and (3) the specific reburial that is the object of this study.

The Rankülches, Their Cosmology, and the Relationship between Sacred Spaces and Landscape

The ancestral territory and ethnic origins of the Rankülches are topics of debate.[2] The historical literature gives various references to an origin in the eighteenth century, emerging from an extended process of mixing and replacement between Indigenous groups local to the Chapal-có Valley and others coming from the western side of the Andes.[3] This theory is not supported by the contemporary Rankülche community[4] and is also contradicted by some travel narratives. For example, in his travelogue of 1806 Luis de la Cruz transcribes a response from the *cacique* (chief) Manquel on the occupation of Mamül Mapu: "En estas tierras habitan indios desde tiempos inmemoriales, que así lo oyó á sus antepasados" (Indians have inhabited these lands since time immemorial, that is what he heard from his ancestors).[5] The reported extent of their territorial distribution has changed over time,[6] and contemporary communities claim different areas across La Pampa province. Furthermore, various communities in Buenos Aires, Cordoba, San Luis, and Mendoza provinces, all in central Argentina (fig. 1), self-identify as belonging to the Rankülche Nation.

Whereas the ethnic origins and ancestral territories of the Rankülche appear potentially rather diverse, their cosmology presents greater uniformity. In particular, their creation myth shares many aspects with other Indigenous nations in the Walmapu[7] and is largely centered on the story of a flood caused by a pair of warring brothers: Kai-kai-filú (the snake who ruled the waters in the underworld) and Treng-Tréng (the snake who ruled the land). Kai-kai-filú tries to drown all living beings, moving his tail to raise the waters. To stop this, Treng-Tréng crushes his brother with a boulder that falls from the mountain where humans have taken refuge.[8] This creation tale permeates all the religious beliefs of Mamül Mapu. From it arises the dialectic between good and evil and the importance of water in the Rankülches' sacred world.

The main entities in that dialectic are Chachao, the deity of good, and Gualicho, the deity of evil. As Lucio Victorio Mansilla describes it, "Mientras el uno no piensa en hacerle mal a nadie, el otro anda siempre pensando en el mal del prójimo" (When one of them never thinks about doing evil, the other one is always thinking about doing evil to others).[9] The same duality and the strong relationship with water are expressed by other beings. As an example, Arrüncó, a representation of the toad (*Bufo arenarum*), owns the waterholes and is the protector of the creeks. He is everywhere, from springs and ponds to the homemade *jagüeles* (watering holes for cattle).[10] His presence is a symbol of joy, because it implies rain and life-supporting water.[11] However, if humans offend him, he goes away, drying all sources of water until the offender is punished.[12]

The Rankülches' sacred traditions related to death and burial were described with great detail by Santiago Avendaño in his book *Usos y costumbres de los indios de la pampa* (*Mores and Customs of the La Pampa Indians*).[13] From his descriptions it can be said that both the grave goods (vessels, food, the favorite horse of the deceased,

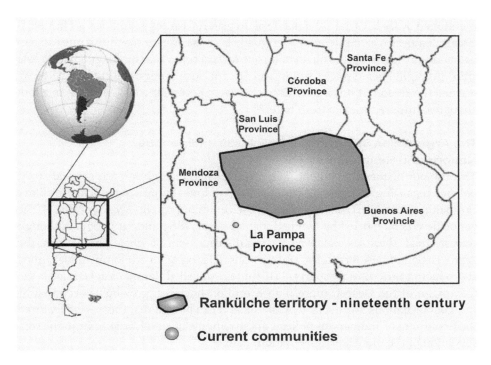

Figure 1. Historical territory of the Rankülche nation and current communities.

etc.) and the position of the corpse correspond with the idea of a resurrection in the Alhué Mapumú. In this sense, a central point for this article is the place in which the burial takes place.[14] Avendaño mentions that the corpse of the Indian Güichal was buried in a place called Gaudá, a big, tall hill with a flat top, where there were many other burials. In the same location, according to Avendaño, the festivities of the devil's witches take place.[15] Mansilla also mentions the importance of the burial site, where the body must rest: "Una sepultura es lo más sagrado. No hay herejía comparable al hecho de desenterrar un cadáver" (A tomb is a most sacred place. There is no heresy comparable to unearthing a corpse).[16]

The selection of elevated sites for burials invites reflection on prominent sites in the landscape, as they are separated from everyday activities and/or offer good visibility.[17] Darwin made similar observations during the first half of the nineteenth century: "Shortly after passing the first spring we came in sight of a famous tree, which the Indians reverence as the altar of Walleechu. It is situated on a high part of the plain; and hence is a landmark visible at a great distance. As soon as a tribe of Indians come in sight of it, they offer their adorations by loud shouts."[18] Another activity that takes place in remote and elevated sites are consultations with Wüekufu, the devil. Regarding that, Avendaño explains that "los lugares destinados para esta consulta, es siempre el lugar más alto, como ser las grandes lomadas y los médanos" (the places devoted to this consultation are always the highest places, such as big hills and dunes).[19]

Finally, the selection of places that are remote from the main dwellings for the performance of religious practices or not suitable for the whole population is also mentioned by De la Cruz: "A la noche oí un griterío, cantos y tambor a las inmedia-ciones de nuestro alojamiento; y averiguada la causa, era un machitún que estaban haciendo con una enferma en un toldo que distará como cosa de dos cuadras de este sitio" (At night I heard voices, songs, and a drum close to our dwelling, and when we learned the reason, it was a machitún they were doing for a sick woman, in a tent about two hundred meters from here).[20]

The Argentinian State and Its Policies on Indigenous Nations and Restitutions

Throughout history the Argentinian state has had changing, even contradictory, policies regarding Indigenous nations. In 1878 and 1879, in a genocidal military campaign, it occupied the territories in the center of present-day Argentina.[21] The genocide was supported by two national laws, 215/1867 and 947/1878. Although controversial, these laws allowed for the displacement of whole populations, the expropriation of new territories, and the consolidation of an economic model aimed at producing agricultural exports.[22] During the so-called Campaña del Desierto, the Campaign of the Desert, more than 8 million hectares, previously occupied by Indigenous nations, were seized by the state. It can be said that this period featured the first group of Indigenous policies at the nation-state level, arising from the con-solidation of the model territory/nation/state.[23]

This was the context of Mansilla's military expedition to Leuvucó.[24] To this day Mansilla's literary work, *Una excursión a los indios ranqueles*, contributes to the agencies of different actors of the Rankülche Nation, local inhabitants, provincial government, and educational institutions.

In the twentieth century, especially before the return to democracy in 1983, regulations on Indigenous nations were erratic and asystematic.[25] During the first half of the century there were no significant changes from the nineteenth century, but the notion of historical reparation and the issue of race were incorporated into public and political discourse.[26] As Diana Lenton explains, a significant change took place in 1946, when Juan Domingo Perón became president. His government created the Dirección de Protección del Aborigen and the Instituto Étnico Nacional and ratified Agreement 169 of the International Labor Organization.[27] Some Indig-enous communities received lands and deeds from the government, and some leaders were incorporated into the public administration, but without specific ethnic recognition.[28] One of the main consequences of this process was the promulgation in 1957 of Law 14932, abolishing forced work, and the First National Indigenous Census in 1965.[29] During that period there was a strong emergence of Indigenous social and political militancy.[30] With the return to democracy in 1983, Law 23.302, Política Indígena y Apoyo a las Comunidades Aborígenes (Indigenous Policies and Support to Indigenous Communities), was approved in 1985 and took effect in 1989. According to Lenton, this law still governs the policies of treatment of Indig-enous nations, regulated by the Instituto Nacional de Asuntos Indígenas.[31] Even with the constitutional reform of 1994 and the adoption of International Labor Organization convention 169, the Indigenous and Tribal Peoples Convention, in 1989, integrationism and subordination of the Indigenous nations still prevail, in contrast with the proclamation of interculturality.

As this brief historical overview shows, the claims for restitution of human remains did not play a role in the agenda of Indigenous nations. This is noteworthy if we remark that the first movements in this direction, as well as the request for no excavation of tombs, took place in the United States and Australia in the 1960s.[32] The Vermillion Accord on Human Remains, adopted in 1989 at the World Archaeological Congress Inter-Congress in Vermillion, South Dakota, marked an inflection point in the scientific world. It established the following: "The express recognition that the concerns of various ethnic groups, as well as those of science, are legitimate and to be respected will permit acceptable agreements to be reached and honored."[33] Years later the International Council of Museums modified its code of ethics to include clauses on research, conservation, and exhibition of sensitive cultural materials.[34] The code establishes that "research on human remains and materials of sacred significance must be accomplished in a manner consistent with professional standards and take into account the interests and beliefs of the community, ethnic or religious groups from whom the objects originated, where these are known."[35]

In Argentina the first claim took place in 1973 and was made informally by a historian from Buenos Aires province. The request was made to the Museo de Ciencias Naturales de La Plata, but its authorities did not consider the request officially. In the claim this historian requested the "custody," not the restitution, of the *caciques* Calfucurá, Manuel Guerra, Gherenal, Indio Brujo, and Chipitruz.[36] The first claims were rejected because it was contended that the remains were part of archaeological collections that were state property, or because of the impossibility of legally proving relationships of consanguinity.[37] The first successful restitutions were treated on a case-by-case basis, usually claiming the remains of chiefs with a renowned trajectory. The restitution of *cacique* Inakayal, a Tehuelche chief whose remains had been in the Museo de la Plata since the beginning of the twentieth century, was ordered under Law 23.940/1991. His remains were finally returned to Tecka, Chubut province, in 1994.[38] The second restitution, by Law 25.276/2001, was the devolution of *cacique* Panghitruz Güor (Mariano Rosas) to the Rankülche Nation; he was buried the same year in Leuvucó, La Pampa province.[39]

Law 25517 from 2001 introduced a change in the policies regarding restitution of human remains, but its implementation was delayed. This law established that museums must put human remains from their collections at the disposition of Indigenous nations.[40] The implementation of the law was achieved thanks to the pressure and mobilization of the Indigenous communities, and the Instituto Nacional de Asuntos Indígenas was designated as the body in charge of following up.[41] Between the approval and the implementation of Law 25517, law 25743 was approved for the "protection of archaeological and paleontological patrimony." This law created controversy at the political and academic levels and among the Indigenous communities because it does not consider the Indigenous communities as subjects of rights.[42]

Along the way, the Indigenous communities became subjects of law, launching broad and specific claims related mostly to their ethnic preexistence. The fundamental claim in this sense was the right to their territories as a constitutive part of their identity and culture.[43] To this basic claim they added the request of political autonomy inside the state, with control of the decision processes and the election of representatives on vital issues (economy, health, housing, culture, cultural patrimony).[44]

Since 2010 the relationship between archaeologists and the Indigenous communities has gone through different stages, always with new and complex challenges. Most restitutions were done under different circumstances and constraints, including the time frame of the claim, the importance and experience of the institution in which the remains were located, the relationship between the claimant and the researchers, the possibility of conducting research on the remains, and the instrumentation of the previous, free, and informed consent. These circumstances create uncertainty among some members of the scientific community, and they are the topic of debates in academic conferences both at the national and the regional level and at the Talleres de Discusión sobre Restitución de Restos Humanos de Interés Arqueológico y Bioantrológico (Workshops of Discussion on the Restitution of Human Remains of Archaeological and Bioanthropological Interest) that have taken place every two years since 2011 with the specific goal of addressing these topics.[45]

Chapal-có Hill

An archaeological site was identified on the shores of the Chapal-có lake, during excavation in the homonymous valley. Dated to the late Holocene, the place was characterized as a site of specific activities.[46] Its location in the valley is shared by most of the archaeological sites in the region. The research indicates a use of space toward the occupation of lowlands, followed by the low slopes and then the medium slopes. In the highest features of the landscape (plateaus and flat tops of the dunes), there were no archaeological remains on the surface.[47] In this context, the identification of human skeletal remains in Chapal-có Hill, located two kilometers from the site above, was an unexpected event. The extraction of rocks next to a local road generated by a widening of the accesses and the removal of a great volume of soil uncovered the burial. A local inhabitant reported this fact to the authorities of La Pampa province in 2004. Given the conditions of the findings and the fact that the human remains were exposed, a rescue was immediately planned. The findings were communicated to representatives of the Willi Kalkin Rankülche community in Toay, La Pampa province. The Rankülche community organized a visit to Chapal-có Hill, where two main issues were discussed: the characterization of the place in the landscape and what to do with the human remains. The community decided to carry out analyses to determine, in the first place, the antiquity of the human remains, to be returned afterward for disposition.[48] After the findings were reported, the local press started to speculate that the remains could belong to missing persons from the last military dictatorship (1976–83). Given this situation, the Toay Rankülche community proposed to do research to date the remains and therefore clarify the issue. The results of the dating were 3090±70 BP, placing the remains in the late Holocene.

It is important to mention that the initial agreement of the 2004 devolution of remains predates the Regulatory Decree 701 of National Law 25.517 from 2010, which regulates the restitution of Indigenous remains that are part of museums and/or public or private collections. Furthermore, this was not a case of restitution, strictly speaking, in the sense of returning something to a previous owner, but an agreed-on devolution that established the reburial of the remains. Another difference with previous restitutions, or at least with the majority of them, is that the human remains in Chapal-có Hill were not part of a museum collection, nor were they the discovery of a planned archaeological excavation. On the contrary, the remains were found by chance, in conditions that significantly damaged the integrity of the burial and made exposed bone fragments vulnerable to the elements. Therefore there was an urgent rescue with the agreement of the Toay Rankülche community.

Restitutions in La Pampa Province and Resignification of the Landscape

Since the end of the twentieth century there have been several initiatives of "historical reparations" related to state policies in the Rankülche ancestral territories. Monuments and commemorative markers were erected as homage and recognition in different places in La Pampa, usually to mark ancestral places.[49] However, the result of those initiatives is a static and patrimonialist view of Rankülche culture that does not take into account their histories, worldview, and contemporary claims.[50] In this context, two of the most significant events in the relationship between the state and the Rankülches involved human remains. The most important one for all involved agents, with national coverage, was the restitution of *cacique* Panguitruz Güor's (Mariano Rosas's) remains in June 2001. As mentioned above, it was the result of a specific law (25.276/2001). The second one, in August 2006, was the claim and reburial of the remains of *capitanejo* Gregorio Yancamil.[51] In both cases, the final resting place of the remains does not coincide with the original burial. Panguitruz Güor's tomb was looted at the end of the nineteenth century, and its original place is not known. His remains were taken to the Museo de la Plata and returned to the shores of Lake Leuvucó. There the Rankülche communities celebrate their Wetripantru in the place where the *cacique* rests.[52] Gregorio Yancamil's remains lie in the central square of the town of Victorica, La Pampa province. Previously he was buried in the municipal cemetery. This reburial was a consequence of a process that involved, seventy years later, the displacement of all the participants in the battle of Cochicó.[53]

The reburial of the remains in Chapal-có Hill represents a new mode of devolution in several aspects. From the beginning the Rankülche Nation was involved in the process and proposed the study of the remains. Afterward it decided on the place for the reburial as well as the date. That decision was taken in a special event, the Vuta Travún.[54] In November 2014, in a meeting attended by one of the authors of this article, there was general consensus on completing the reburial in the same hill where the remains were found, and also on the sacred nature of the place. This last point is crucial, because it gives a new conception of the definition of reburial spaces. Panguitruz Güor and Gregorio Yancamil were reburied in spaces that were significant for many agents (not only the Rankülches), but not in their original burial places. In contraposition, Chapal-có Hill becomes a significant space for the community as a reemergence of an ancestral landscape, because high places were considered sacred.

For the Indigenous communities, the claims go beyond the claimed object or body and the implied action. They are part of the ethnopolitical strategies undertaken in the context of their worldview and own rights.[55] As Daniel Huircapán, Ángela Jar-amillo, and Félix Acuto have written, their ancestors and the burial goods "no perte-necen a cajas en depósitos de museos sino a los procesos activos de autoidentificación y lucha por derechos que los pueblos originarios de la Argentina conducen en la actua-lidad" (do not belong in boxes in museums but to the current processes of self-recognition and the fight for the rights of the Indigenous nations in Argentina).[56]

RAFAEL PEDRO CURTONI is professor of anthropology in the Faculty of Social Sciences, National University of the Center of the Buenos Aires Province, and CONICET researcher.

GUILLERMO HEIDER is visiting associate professor of geology in the Department of Geology, National University of San Luis.

MARÍA GABRIELA CHAPARRO is professor of anthropology in the Faculty of Social Sciences, National University of the Center of the Buenos Aires Province, and CONICET researcher.

ÁNGEL T. TUNINETTI is Armand E. and Mary W. Singer Professor in the Humanities, Eberly College of Arts and Sciences, West Virginia University.

Acknowledgments

To the memory of the *lonkos* (leaders) German Canuhé and Fermín Acuña. This work was possible thanks to the trust of and interactions with the members of the Rankülche Nation through the years. We are grateful to the government of La Pampa province and to Martin Doppelt for editorial assistance.

Notes

1   See, among others, Ametrano, "Historia de una restitución"; Cosmai, Folguera, and Outomuro, "Restitución, repatriación y normativa ética y legal"; Stella, "'Arranqué con esto de transitar, de caminar por este camino . . . '"; and Curtoni and Chaparro, "Políticas de reparación."

2   See, among others, Asociacion Pampeana de Escritores, *Pampas del Sud*; Depetris, *Gente de la tierra*; Fernández, *Historia de los indios ranqueles*; Lazzari, "¡Vivan los indios argentinos!"; Lazzari and Lenton, "Etnología y nación"; Poduje, Garay, and Crochetti, *Narrativa ranquel*; and Salomón Tarquini, "Indígenas y paisanos en La Pampa."

3   See, for example, Canals Frau, "Expansion of the Araucanians in Argentina"; Hux, *Caciques pampa-ranqueles*; Mandrini, *Los araucanos de las pampas en el siglo XIX*; and Tapia, "Fusión y fisión de tolderías ranquelinas."

4   Canuhé, "Historia Rankül (Ranquel)"; Canuhé, "Reseña histórica de la nación Mamülche."

5   Mamül Mapu (*mamül*: "wood"; *mapu*: "land"), or Land of Forests, is the denomination used by the Rankülches for their ancestral territory. All the translations from Spanish are ours.

6   See, among others, Salomón Tarquini, "Estrategias de acceso y conservación"; and Tapia, "Fusión y fisión de tolderías ranquelinas."

7   Wal-mapu has been defined as a very large territory in present-day central Argentina and Chile, from the Atlantic Ocean to the Pacific Ocean, in which there was a permanent movement of populations, goods, and culture, from pre-Hispanic times to the present (see, among others, Bandieri, *Cruzando la cordillera*; Nicoletti and Núñez, "Introducción"; and Berón et al., "Enclaves y espacios internodales").

8   For more details, see Magrassi, *Los aborígenes de la Argentina*; and Canuhé, "Reseña histórica de la nación Mamülche."

9   Mansilla, *Una excursión a los indios ranqueles*, 106. Lucio Victorio Mansilla (Buenos Aires 1831–Paris 1913) was a famous writer, politician, military officer, and socialite. In 1869 he was sent to command a post in southern Córdoba, the northern frontier of Rankülche territory at that time, and in 1870 he led a short trip to visit the Rankülche communities. *Una excursión a*

los indios ranqueles, the book he wrote from that experience, became canonical in Argentine literature, and his views on this ethnic group still loom large in Argentinian culture.

10 Conejeros, "Divinidades en el arte textil del Puel Mapu."

11 Curtoni, "Mapu-kó."

12 Pampas del Sud, *Recopilación de textos*.

13 Avendaño, *Usos y costumbres de los indios de la pampa*. Santiago Avendaño was a captive of the Rankülches for almost nine years, starting in 1842, when he was only seven years old.

14 For theoretical approaches to landscape signification, see Hirsch and O'Hanlon, *Anthropology of Landscape*; Hirsch, "Landscape, Myth, and Time"; Liebmann, "From Landscapes of Meaning to Landscapes of Signification"; and Tilley and Cameron-Daum, *Anthropology of Landscape*.

15 Avendaño, *Usos y costumbres de los indios de la pampa*, 72.

16 Mansilla, *Una excursión a los indios ranqueles*, 106.

17 See, among others, Casamiquela, *Estudio del Ngillatun*; Di Liscia, "Medicina, religión y género"; Llamazares, "Arte chamánico"; and Curtoni, "Mapu-kó."

18 Darwin, *Countries Visited during the Voyage of H.M.S. Beagle*, 68.

19 Avendaño, *Usos y costumbres de los indios de la pampa*, 33.

20 De la Cruz, *Viaje a su costa del alcalde provincial*, 178. A machitún is a ceremony performed by the *machi*, the shaman.

21 See, among many others, Dos Santos Montagne, "'Ni los historiadores'"; and Canuhé, "Reseña histórica de la nación Mamülche."

22 See Lenton, "Política indigenista argentina."

23 See, among others, Delrio, *Memorias de expropiación*; and Lenton, "Política indigenista argentina."

24 Leuvucó (*leuvú*: "stream"; *có*: "water," "spring that runs") is the name of a lake on Ruta Provincial 105, twenty-five kilometers north of Victorica, La Pampa province. It was the center of the Rankülche Nation, at least during the nineteenth century.

25 See, among many others, Lazzari, "Antropología en el estado"; and Lenton, "Política indigenista argentina."

26 Lenton, "Política indigenista argentina."

27 See, among others, Endere and Ayala, "Normativa legal, recaudos éticos y práctica arqueológica"; Lenton, "Política indigenista argentina"; and Slavsky, "Los indígenas y la sociedad nacional."

28 Lenton, "Política indigenista argentina."

29 Endere and Ayala, "Normativa legal, recaudos éticos y práctica arqueológica."

30 Lenton, "Política indigenista argentina."

31 Lenton, "Política indigenista argentina."

32 See, among others, (Deloria, *Custer Died for Your Sins*; Deloria, *Red Earth, White Lies*; Echo-Hawk and Echo-Hawk, *Battlefields and Burial Grounds*; Fay and James, *Rights and Wrongs of Land Restitution*; and West-Newman, "Anger in Legacies of Empire."

33 World Archaelogical Congress, "Vermillion Accord on Human Remains."

34 Endere, "Derechos y reclamos de los pueblos indígenas."

35 International Council of Museums, "Code of Ethics for Museums," 20.

36 Podgorny and Politis, "¿Qué sucedió en la historia?"; Podgorny and Miotti, "El pasado como campo de batalla"; Ametrano, "Los procesos de restitución"; Pepe, Suárez, and Harrison, *Antropología del genocidio*. In 2016 the Museo de La Plata returned to the Indigenous community Cacique Pincén in Trenque Lauquen (Buenos Aires province) the Mapuche-Tehuelche skulls of Manuel Guerra, Gheremal, Indio Brujo, and Gervasio Chipitruz. In a posterior Indigenous parliament it was decided that Guerra and Chipitruz should be buried in Tapalqué (Buenos Aires province) and that Indio Brujo and Gheremal would be returned to Rankülche territory in La Pampa province, since they belonged to that ethnic community.

37 See Endere, "Patrimonios en disputa"; Endere, "Reburial Issue in Argentina"; and Endere and Ayala, "Normativa legal, recaudos éticos y práctica arqueológica."

38 Ametrano, "Los procesos de restitución"; Endere and Ayala, "Normativa legal, recaudos éticos y práctica arqueológica"; Huircapán, Jaramillo, and Acuto, "Reflexiones interculturales."

39 See, among others, Endere and Curtoni, "Entre lonkos y 'ólogos'"; Lazzari, "La restitución de los restos de Mariano Rosas"; and Lazzari, "Reclamos, restituciones y repatriaciones de restos humanos indígenas."

40 See, among others, Cosmai, Folguera, and Outomuro, "Restitución, repatriación y normativa ética y legal"; Endere and Ayala, "Normativa legal, recaudos éticos y práctica arqueológica"; and Ametrano, "Los procesos de restitución."

41 Endere and Ayala, "Normativa legal, recaudos éticos y práctica arqueológica"; Ametrano, "Los procesos de restitución."

42 See, among others, Briones, "Políticas indigenistas en Argentina"; and Endere and Ayala, "Normativa legal, recaudos éticos y práctica arqueológica."

43 Briones, "Formaciones de alteridad"; Briones, "Políticas indigenistas en Argentina"; Lazzari, "Ya no más cuerpos muertos."

44   Canuhé, "Reseña histórica de la nación Mamülche"; Lazzari, "Ya no más cuerpos muertos."

45   Endere et al., "Third Discussion Workshop."

46   Curtoni and Chaparro, "El re-entierro del cacique José Gregorio Yancamil."

47   Curtoni and Chaparro, "El re-entierro del cacique José Gregorio Yancamil."

48   Curtoni and Endere, "Cuando el diálogo facilita el consenso."

49   See, among others, Curtoni, Lazzari, and Lazzari, "Middle of Nowhere"; Curtoni, "La dimensión política de la arqueología"; Lazzari, "Ya no más cuerpos muertos"; and Curtoni and Chaparro, "Políticas de reparación."

50   Curtoni and Chaparro, "Políticas de reparación."

51   Curtoni and Chaparro, "El re-entierro del cacique José Gregorio Yancamil"; Curtoni and Chaparro, "Políticas de reparación."

52   Wetripantu, June 23, is the celebration of the new year for the Rankülche Nation during the winter solstice in the Southern Hemisphere.

53   Curtoni and Chaparro, "Políticas de reparación." The battle of Cochicó occurred in the homonymous place on August 19, 1882. It is considered the last battle between military troops and the Rankülche resistance in La Pampa province (Hux, Caciques pampa-ranqueles).

54   The Rankülche Vuta Travún (big meeting) is an annual event with the goal of promoting social, cultural, and political activities of the Indigenous nations. During these two days representatives from different Indigenous nations of the country exchange ideas.

55   Curtoni and Chaparro, "Políticas de reparación."

56   Huircapán, Jaramillo, and Acuto, "Reflexiones interculturales."

Works Cited

Ametrano, Silvia. "Historia de una restitución." Revista museo, no. 24 (2010): 61–67.

Ametrano, Silvia. "Los procesos de restitución en el Museo de la Plata." Revista argentina de antropología biológica 17, no. 2 (2015): 1–13.

Asociacion Pampeana de Escritores. Pampas del Sud: Recopilación de textos que hacen a las raíces autóctonas de la provincia de La Pampa. Subsecretaría de Cultura, Santa Rosa, La Pampa, 1997.

Avendaño, Santiago. Usos y costumbres de los indios de la pampa. Buenos Aires: El Elefante Blanco, 2012.

Bandieri, Susana. Cruzando la cordillera . . . La frontera argentino-chilena como espacio social. Centro de Estudios de Historia Regional, Facultad de Humanidades, Universidad Nacional del Comahue, República Argentina, 2005.

Berón, Mónica, Ayelen Di Biase, Gabriela Musuabach, and Florencia Páez. "Enclaves y espacios internodales en la dinámica de poblaciones en el Wall-mapu: Aportes desde la arqueología pampeana." Estudios atacameños, no. 56 (2017): 253–72.

Briones, Claudia. "Formaciones de alteridad: Contextos globales, procesos nacionales y provinciales." In Cartografías argentinas: Políticas indígenas y formaciones provinciales de alteridad, 9–40. Buenos Aires: Antropofagia, 2005.

Briones, Claudia. "Políticas indigenistas en Argentina: Entre la hegemonía neoliberal de los años noventa y la 'nacional y popular' de la última década." Antípoda revista de antropología y arqueología, no. 21 (2015): 21–48.

Canals Frau, Salvador. "Expansion of the Araucanians in Argentina." In Handbook of South American Indians, edited by Julian H. Steward, 761–66. Washington, DC: Smithsonian Institution, Bureau of American Ethnology, 1946.

Canuhé, Germán. "Historia Rankül (Ranquel)." faggella.com/histoargenta/Ranqueles.htm (accessed November 18, 2019).

Canuhé, Germán. "Reseña histórica de la nación Mamülche, pueblo rankül (Ranquel), habitante desde siempre del centro de la actual Argentina." Unpublished manuscript, 2003.

Casamiquela, Rodolfo. Estudio del Ngillatun y de la religión araucana. Bahía Blanca: Universidad Nacional del Sur, 1964.

Conejeros, Rut. "Divinidades en el arte textil del Puel Mapu (Tierra del Este)." In El lenguaje de los dioses: Arte Chamanismo y cosmovisión indígena en Sudamérica, edited by Ana Llamazares and Carlos Martínez Sarasola, 199–226. Buenos Aires: Biblos, 2004.

Cosmai, Natalia, Guillermo Folguera, and Delia Outomuro. "Restitución, repatriación y normativa ética y legal en el manejo de restos humanos aborígenes en Argentina." Acta bioethica 19, no. 1 (2013): 19–27.

Curtoni, Rafael. "La dimensión política de la arqueología: El patrimonio indígena y la construcción del pasado." In Aproximaciones contemporáneas a la arqueología pampeana: Perspectivas teóricas, metodológicas, analíticas y casos de estudio, edited by Gustavo Martínez, María Gutiérrez, Rafael Curtoni, Mónica Berón, and Patrica Madrid, 437–49. Olavarría: Facultad de Ciencias Sociales, 2004.

Curtoni, Rafael. "Mapu-kó: El paisaje hecho agua." In Biografías de paisajes y seres: Visiones desde la arqueología sudamericana, edited by Darío Hermo and Laura Miotti, 99–110. Universidad Nacional de Catamarca, Encuentro Grupo Editorial, 2011.

Curtoni, Rafael, and María Gabriela Chaparro. "El re-entierro del *cacique* José Gregorio Yancamil: Patrimonio, política y memoria de piedra en la pampa argentina." *Revista chilena de antropología*, no. 19 (2007–8): 9–36.

Curtoni, Rafael, and María Gabriela Chaparro. "Políticas de reparación: Reclamación y reentierro de restos indígenas; El caso de Gregorio Yancamil." *Archivos virtuales de la alteridad americana* 1, no. 1 (2011): 1–7.

Curtoni, Rafael, and María Luz Endere. "Cuando el diálogo facilita el consenso: Rescate, investigación y re-entierro de restos humanos en la provincia de La Pampa." In *Investigaciones acerca de y con el pueblo ranquel: Pasado, presente y perspectivas; Actas de las Jornadas en Homenaje a Germán Canuhé*, edited by Claudia Salomón Tarquini and Ignacio Roca, 145–58. Santa Rosa: EdUNLPam, 2015.

Curtoni, Rafael, Axel Lazzari, and Marisa Lazzari. "Middle of Nowhere: A Place of War Memories, Commemoration, and Aboriginal Re-emergence (La Pampa, Argentina)." *World Archaeology* 35, no. 1 (2003): 61–78.

Darwin, Charles. *Countries Visited during the Voyage of H.M.S. Beagle round the World*. New York, 1871.

De la Cruz, Luis. *Viaje a su costa del alcalde provincial del muy ilustre Cabildo de la Concepción de Chile: Colección de obras y documentos relativos a la historia antigua y moderna de las provincias de Río de la Plata*. Buenos Aires: Plus Ultra, 1969.

Deloria, Vine. *Custer Died for Your Sins: An Indian Manifesto*. New York: Avon, 1970.

Deloria, Vine. *Red Earth, White Lies: Native Americans and the Myth of Scientific Fact*. New York: Scribner, 1995.

Delrio, Walter. *Memorias de expropiación: Sometimiento e incorporación indígena en la Patagonia, 1872–1943*. Buenos Aires: Ed. de la Universidad Nacional de Quilmes, 2005.

Depetris, José. *Gente de la tierra: Los que sobrevivieron a la conquista, con nombre y apellido; Censo de 1895; Pampa Central*. Santa Rosa: Ediciones de la Travesía, 2003.

Di Liscia, María. "Medicina, religión y género en la relación entre indígenas y blancos (región pampeana y norpatagónica, siglos XVIII y XIX)." In *Historia y género: Seis estudios sobre la condición femenina*, edited by Daniel Villar, María Di Liscia, and María Jorgelina Caviglia, 53–87. Buenos Aires: Biblos, 1999.

Dos Santos Montagne, Antonela. "'Ni los historiadores ni nadie lo tiene en cuenta y, sin embargo, mi abuela me lo contaba . . . ': Narrativas históricas de los ranqueles de La Pampa." *Runa* 35, no. 2 (2014): 89–104.

Echo-Hawk, Roger, and Walter Echo-Hawk. *Battlefields and Burial Grounds: The Indian Struggle to Protect Ancestral Graves in the United States*. Minneapolis: Lerner, 1994.

Endere, María Luz. "Derechos y reclamos de los pueblos indígenas." *Ciencia hoy*, no. 152 (2016): 33–39.

Endere, María Luz. "Patrimonios en disputa: Acervos nacionales, investigación arqueológica y reclamos étnicos sobre restos humanos." *Trabajos de prehistoria* 57, no. 1 (2000): 1–13.

Endere, María Luz. "The Reburial Issue in Argentina: A Growing Conflict." In *The Dead and Their Possessions: Repatriation in Principle, Policy, and Practice*, edited by Cressida Forde, Jane Hubert, and Paul Turnbull, 266–83. London: Routledge, 2002.

Endere, María Luz, and Patricia Ayala. "Normativa legal, recaudos éticos y práctica arqueológica: Un estudio comparativo de Argentina y Chile." *Chungara* 44 (2012): 39–57.

Endere, María Luz, and Rafael Curtoni. "Entre lonkos y 'ólogos': La participación de la comunidad ranquelina en la investigación arqueológica." *Revista de arqueología suramericana* 2 (2006): 72–92.

Endere, María Luz, Gustavo Flesborg, Mariela González, Pablo Bayala, María Gabriela Chaparro, Mónica Berón, and Cristian Favier Dubois. "Third Discussion Workshop on the Return of Human Remains of Archaeological and Bioanthropological Interest." *International Journal of Cultural Property* 21, no. 2 (2014): 231–35.

Fay, Derrick, and Deborah James, eds. *The Rights and Wrongs of Land Restitution*. London: Routledge-Cavendish, 2009.

Fernández, Jorge. *Historia de los indios ranqueles: Origen, elevación y caída del cacicazgo ranquel en la Pampa Central (siglos XVIII y XIX)*. Buenos Aires: Secretaría de Cultura de la Nación, Instituto Nacional de Antropología y Pensamiento Latinoamericano, 1998.

Hirsch, Eric. "Landscape, Myth, and Time." *Journal of Material Culture* 11, nos. 1–2 (2006): 151–65.

Hirsch, Eric, and Michael O'Hanlon, eds. *The Anthropology of Landscape: Perspectives on Place and Space*. Oxford: Clarendon, 1995.

Huircapán, Daniel, Ángela Jaramillo, and Félix Acuto. "Reflexiones interculturales sobre la restitución de restos mortales indígenas." *Cuadernos del Instituto nacional de antropología y pensamiento latinoamericano* 26, no. 1 (2017): 57–75.

Hux, Meinrado. *Caciques pampa-ranqueles*. Buenos Aires: Elefante Blanco, 2003.

International Council of Museums. "Code of Ethics for Museums." icom.museum/en/activities /standards-guidelines/code-of-ethics (accessed November 18, 2019).

Lazzari, Axel. "Antropología en el estado: El Instituto Etnico Nacional (1946–1955)." In *Intelectuales y* expertos: La constitución del conocimiento social en la Argentina, edited by Federico Neiburg and Mariano Plotkin, 203–30. Buenos Aires: Paidós, 2004.

Lazzari, Axel. "La restitución de los restos de Mariano Rosas: Identificación fetichista en torno a la política de reconocimiento de los ranqueles." Estudios en antropología social 1, no. 1 (2008): 35–63.

Lazzari, Axel. "Reclamos, restituciones y repatriaciones de restos humanos indígenas: Cuerpos muertos, identidades, cosmologías, política y justicia." Corpus archivos virtuales de la alteridad americana 1, no. 1 (2011): 1–5.

Lazzari, Axel. "¡Vivan los indios argentinos! Análisis de las estrategias discursivas de etnicización/Nacionalización de los Ranqueles en situación de frontera." MA thesis, Museu Nacional/Universidade Federal do Rio de Janeiro, 1996.

Lazzari, Axel. "Ya no más cuerpos muertos: Mediación e interrupción en el reconocimiento ranquel." E-misférica performance and politics in the Americas 4, no. 2 (2007): 3–9.

Lazzari, Axel, and Diana Lenton. "Etnología y nación: Facetas del concepto de araucanización." Revista avá 1, no. 1 (2000): 125–40.

Lenton, Diana. "Política indigenista argentina: Una construcción inconclusa." Anuário antropológico 1 (2010): 57–97.

Liebmann, Matthew J. "From Landscapes of Meaning to Landscapes of Signification in the American Southwest." American Antiquity 82, no. 4 (2017): 642–61.

Llamazares, Ana. "Arte chamánico: Visiones del universo." In El lenguaje de los dioses: Arte, chamanismo y cosmovisión indígena en Sudamérica, edited by Ana Llamazares and Carlos Martínez Sarasola, 67–125. Buenos Aires: Biblos, 2004.

Magrassi, Guillermo. Los aborígenes de la Argentina. Buenos Aires: Búsqueda Yuchán, 1987.

Mandrini, Raúl. Los araucanos de las pampas en el siglo XIX. Buenos Aires: Centro Editor de América Latina, 1984.

Mansilla, Lucio Victorio. Una excursión a los indios ranqueles. Buenos Aires: Centro Editor de América Latina, 1967.

Nicoletti, María, and Paula Núñez. "Introducción." In Araucanía-Norpatagonia: La territorialidad en debate; Perspectivas ambientales, culturales, sociales, políticas y económicas, edited by María Nicoletti and Paula Núñez, 6–12. Bariloche: Instituto de Investigaciones en Diversidad Cultural y Procesos de Cambio, Universidad Nacional de Río Negro, 2013.

Pampas del Sud. Recopilación de textos que hacen a las raíces autóctonas de la provincia de La Pampa. Subsecretaría de Cultura, Santa Rosa, La Pampa, 1997.

Pepe, Fernando, Miguel Añon Suárez, and Patricio Harrison. Antropología del genocidio: Identificación y restitución; "Colecciones" de restos humanos en el Museo de La Plata. Colectivo GUIAS, edición del autor, La Plata, 2008.

Podgorny, Irina, and Laura Miotti. "El pasado como campo de batalla." Ciencia hoy, no. 25 (1994): 16–19.

Podgorny, Irina, and Gustavo Politis. "¿Qué sucedió en la historia? Los esqueletos araucanos del Museo de La Plata y la conquista del desierto." Arqueología contemporánea 3 (1990): 73–78.

Poduje, María, Ana Fernández Garay, and Silvia Crochetti. Narrativa ranquel: Los cuentos del zorro. Ministerio de Cultura y Educación de la provincia de La Pampa, 1993.

Salomón Tarquini, Claudia. "Estrategias de acceso y conservación de la tierra entre los ranqueles (Colonia Emilio Mitre, La Pampa, primera mitad del siglo XX)." Mundo agrario 11, no. 21 (2010): n.p.

Salomón Tarquini, Claudia. "Indígenas y paisanos en La Pampa: Subalternización, ciclos migratorios, integración urbana (1870–1976)." PhD diss., Universidad Nacional del Centro de la Provincia de Buenos Aires, 2008.

Slavsky, Leonor. "Los indígenas y la sociedad nacional: Apuntes sobre política indigenista en Argentina." In La problemática indígena: Estudios antropológicos sobre pueblos indígenas de Argentina, edited by Juan Carlos Radovich and Alejandro Balazote, 67–79. Buenos Aires: Centro Editor de América, 1992.

Stella, Valentina. "'Arranqué con esto de transitar, de caminar por este camino . . .': Contextos sociales de movilidad en una comunidad urbana." In Parentesco y política: Topologías indígenas en la Patagonia, edited by Claudia Briones and Ana Ramos, 215–35. Viedma: Universidad Nacional de Río Negro, 2016.

Tapia, Alicia. "Fusión y fisión de tolderías ranquelinas como respuesta a las tácticas militares de la conquista del desierto." Cuadernos de antropología, no. 11 (2014): 97–110.

Tilley, Christopher, and Kate Cameron-Daum. An Anthropology of Landscape: The Extraordinary in the Ordinary. London: UCL Press, 2017.

World Archaeological Congress. "The Vermillion Accord on Human Remains." 1989. worldarch.org/code-of-ethics (accessed April 10, 2019).

West-Newman, Catherine Lane. "Anger in Legacies of Empire: Indigenous Peoples and Settler States." European Journal of Social Theory 7, no. 2 (2004): 189–208.

Indigenous-Inspired Authorial Figures and Networks of Rural-Urban Migrants in *The Fox from Up Above and the Fox from Down Below* (1971), by José María Arguedas

JAVIER ALONSO MUÑOZ-DIAZ

Abstract　This article discusses the representation of Indigenous-inspired authorial figures in *The Fox from Up Above and the Fox from Down Below*, by José María Arguedas. In the context of the 1960s Latin American Boom, Arguedas's novel includes a reflection on the professionalization of literary writing, as well as the impact of commodification on Indigenous migrants in Chimbote. This article draws parallels between the diarist Arguedas (who defines himself as a nonprofessional writer attached to Indigenous cultures), the fishing entrepreneur Braschi (a mythical figure and the begetter of Chimbote's industrialization), and the networks of rural-urban migrants (which assimilate the "gringo" Maxwell, performer of Andean folklore). As a model for Indigenous-inspired authorial figures, this article suggests the importance of Arguedas's articles about the mestizo *retablista* Joaquín Lopez Antay, who defended the artistic integrity of his craftwork against economic demands. On that note, the networks of rural-urban migrants negotiate their standing in the modernizing process with a strong and flexible Indigenous identity.
Keywords　José María Arguedas, *Indigenismo*, folklore, migration, authorship

Rural-Urban Migration and Development of Cultural Markets

Deeply influenced by Mariátegui's 1927 thesis about *Indigenismo,* José María Arguedas (1911–69) sought to vindicate Quechua-speaking people in the context of a Peruvian society characterized by white Creole hegemony and systemic marginalization of Indigenous populations. As an *Indigenista* writer, Arguedas had first-hand knowledge of the livelihood and culture of Quechua-speaking rural communities with traditional ways of life. However, since he recognized himself as a bilingual and bicultural subject, he also felt out of place in a literary current char-

ENGLISH LANGUAGE NOTES

58:1, April 2020　DOI 10.1215/00138282-8237421
© 2020 Regents of the University of Colorado

acterized by the non-Indigenous origins of its writers and readership.[1] A white Creole, Arguedas felt a strong identification with Indigenous subjects for specific biographical reasons. Having lost his mother at an early age and with an absent father, Arguedas lived his childhood in the *hacienda* of his hostile stepmother. To cope with his feelings of abandonment, he spent most of his time with the Indigenous servants, learned Quechua, and became familiar with their culture.[2] By the end of his life, Arguedas had famously called himself "a Peruvian who, like a cheerful demon, proudly speaks in Christian and in Indian, in Spanish and in Quechua."[3]

Since modernizing processes in the Andean region speeded up after World War II, Arguedas pushed the limits of *Indigenismo* by becoming more interested in how Indigenous populations were participating in massive rural-urban migrations, industrialization, and market circulation of modern technologies. As an anthropologist, he studied ways in which Andean communities embraced modern technologies (such as concerts in urban settings and radio broadcasting) to produce and distribute their cultural artifacts while maintaining their Quechua language and Indigenous identity. Meanwhile, in his literary writing Arguedas depicted those sociocultural transformations employing experimental devices that reelaborate voices and perspectives from Quechua-speaking people. He worked with both contemporaneous folklore and colonial texts such as the *Huarochirí Manuscript*, which he translated in 1966 with the title *Dioses y hombres de Huarochirí*.[4] Arguedas's remarkable posthumous novel *El zorro de arriba y el zorro de abajo* (*The Fox from Up Above and the Fox from Down Below*) is precisely his major effort to overcome *Indigenismo*'s limitations.[5] By the mid-twentieth century the city and harbor of Chimbote, on the desert coast of Peru, had experienced a massive migration from the Andean hinterland—most of them Quechua-speaking migrants—due to a fishing boom during a time of export-led developmental politics.[6]

At the same time, by the 1960s publishing industries had presented a more consolidated form and had articulated an international network, which gave rise to the Latin American Boom, with full-time writers such as Julio Cortázar (1914–84), Carlos Fuentes (1928–2012), Gabriel García Márquez (1927–2014), and Mario Vargas Llosa (1936). Significantly, the publishing industry was not limited to books but encompassed a broader range of related activities, including advertisement, book fairs, and symposiums. In other words, literary writing became a fully professional activity, one that could provide income as well as a socially recognized and highly regarded identity as literary writers.[7] Within this historical juncture, the "Diaries" of *The Foxes* offer a scathing critique of what Arguedas describes as the "professional writer"—based on the successful Boom writers—who is a specialist in literary techniques but not a rightful authorial figure (*F*, 21–22). In contrast, Arguedas constructs his persona as a truly authorial figure who is attached to Indigenous communal values, ritualizes the creative process, and forecloses commodification.[8]

Likewise, several characters from *The Foxes'* fictional reconstruction of the 1960s Chimbote mirror Arguedas's authorial figure, emphasizing performative and ritual aspects. The roster of characters includes Indigenous migrants such as Esteban de la Cruz and the female prostitutes, as well as the "gringo" Maxwell and the mysterious human-fox Diego, one of the mythical foxes from the *Huarochirí Manuscript*. Notwithstanding their different social origins, all of them participate in networks of rural-urban migrants that, in addition to providing them economic resources, give room to the reformulation of folkloric production and the expression of newer rites/performances of Indigenous inspiration.[9] On the other hand, as a counterpart of the "professional writers," the novel introduces Braschi, the pioneering entrepreneur of fish-meal industries and a sort of "begetter" or "father" of Chimbote's economic boom.

To grasp Arguedas's reflection on the modernization of literary writing and the depiction of newer Indigenous identities, I establish connections between *The Foxes* and contemporaneous essays about the impact of urbanization and commodification on Andean folklore. I argue that the metafictional dimension in Arguedas's novel is the result of a long-term meditation on folklore and craftwork, as is evident in the articles "El arte popular religioso y la cultura mestiza" ("The Religious Popular Art and the *Mestizo* Culture," 1951), "Del retablo mágico al retablo mercantil" ("From the Magical *Retablo* to the Commercial *Retablo*," 1962), and "¿Qué es el folklore?" ("What Is Folklore?," 1964), among others. For instance, in "Del retablo mágico" Arguedas made an explicit reference to the influence of *Indigenista* painters on the craftwork of mestizo *retablista* Joaquín López Antay (1897–1981): "When *Indigenista* painters rediscovered the *retablo*, they suggested to the most inspired of the three sculptors who still practice the craft, Don Joaquín, to change the composition of the 'San Marcos' to a certain degree. And Don Joaquín *dared to do so*."[10] Arguedas highlighted the expression *se atrevió a hacerlo* because it implied that, against any prejudice of cultural conservatism, Lopez Antay's work is experimental.

In this article, I highlight that the interaction between *Indigenista* painters and mestizo/Indigenous artisans is the model for the depiction of Andean folklore and Indigenous-inspired authorial figures in *The Foxes*. Newer artistic manifestation appears as the result of interaction between people of different origins—Indigenous and non-Indigenous—in the context of massive rural-urban migration and the commodification of the cultural sphere. Although these peoples participate in hierarchical power structures,[11] Arguedas celebrates interactions rooted in Andean categories, as is evident in López Antay's boldness and in the networks of rural-urban migrants in *The Foxes*. These interactions do not essentialize Indigenous identities and articulate authorial figures who are, rather than mere "professionals," attached to communal values and resist commodification.

Besides the diarist Arguedas, the nodal points of *The Foxes*' roster of authorial figures are the businessmen Braschi and the "gringo" Maxwell, who actively participates in the networks of rural-urban migrants. To a certain degree, Maxwell's assimilation to Indigenous identities mirrors the case of flesh-and-blood Arguedas, a white Creole who became firmly attached to Quechua-speaking communities. On the other hand, Braschi is not a stranger to those networks, since he also joins them—as a disciple of fishermen Chaucato and Hilario Caullama—to become the "begetter" of Chimbote's industrialization. The following sections analyze the construction of their respective authorial personas.

Braschi, Begetter of Chimbote

As a prominent member of the ruling classes, Braschi is the final iteration of a recurrent character in Arguedas's literature—the *gamonal* (big landowner who exploits Indigenous servants) with a combination of Machiavellian behavior and unrestrained sexuality.[12] Nevertheless, the novelty of Braschi resides in his mythical dimension and his ascription to certain aspects of authorship. On this matter I apply the term *author* to Braschi in a metaphorical sense, since he is neither writer nor musician nor performer—as is the case with other characters, namely, Maxwell and Loco Moncada. In fact, Braschi is a very successful businessman who can manage different interests to maximize his economic profit. As the Aymara-speaker Hilario Caullama says, Braschi is an "Unstoppable Eagle, Eye of Capital" (*F,* 123). Moreover, the mulatto street performer Loco Moncada refers to Braschi as the "begetter" or "father" of Chimbote: "Braschi has made this port grow; he got the sea pregnant; you people are the sons of Braschi" (55). With these metaphors, Loco Moncada is highlighting the businessman's pivotal role in the economic development and social inequality in Chimbote. Ironically, there is no knowledge of Braschi's family members or descendants despite his sexual drive. He also lacks a permanent residence and everyday routines. On the other hand, although Braschi briefly appears in a couple of passages of *The Foxes*, he is constantly mentioned or is the topic of conversations throughout the entire novel. The elusive nature of the businessman throws a veil of mystery over him. As henchman Mantequilla says to Chaucato: "You're right at hand for Braschi. But where are you gonna find him? He's got no house; he's got no family. He lives in a club. There's no way of tellin' when he's in Lima, or in Europe, or behind the Iron Curtain" (197–98).

I propose that Braschi's standing as the "father" or "begetter" of Chimbote must be linked to his mythical status, in particular with his identity as a gifted disciple of the fishermen Chaucato and Hilario Caullama. Accordingly, it is essential to discuss the terms of the mythification of Braschi, notwithstanding the scarcity of biographical background or indices of social class and ethnic heritage. For instance, what is his origin or nationality? It seems a minor detail, but it could provide insight into the nature of his business projects. Identifying Braschi's origin (I propose that the novel inscribes him as a Peruvian with Italian heritage) would prevent overestimating the role of transnational capitalism, as well as give room to the de-essentialization of Indigenous identities in the networks of rural-urban migrants.[13]

Loco Moncada says to Esteban de la Cruz that Braschi is "more of a foreigner [*extranjero*] and a drunkard than you are" (*F,* 149). In this quotation, *foreigner* does not have a strictly literal sense—a person not native to the country, in this case, Peru. For instance, Maxwell and Cardozo, both having been born in the United States, are called "gringos" instead of "foreigners" (33). On the other hand, both Esteban de la Cruz and Gregorio Bazalar, who are Quechua-speakers from the Peruvian highlands, are actually identified as "foreigners" due to the historical marginalization and exploitation of the Indigenous population (148, 227–28). Additionally, it seems that Arguedas sometimes employs *extranjero* or *forastero* as a translation of the Quechua word *wakcha*, which means "orphan" or an unfortunate individual who lacks communal relationships and material goods in his or her current location. Significantly, *wakcha* is also the word used in the *Huarochirí Manuscript* to introduce Huatyacuri, the cultural hero who, after meeting the mythical foxes, becomes the leader of a new community based on the cult of his father, the *huaca* Pariacaca.[14] Since Braschi lacks family ties and a permanent residence, he is also a sort of *wakcha* who becomes the indisputable ruler of Chimbote.[15]

Regarding Braschi's ethnicity, Chaucato identifies him as one of the "white boys" involved in fish-meal business, probably because his Italian last name implies a level of racial whiteness (*F*, 30). In addition, when the factory manager Ángel Rincón Jaramillo speaks to the human-fox Diego about the capitalist investors in Chimbote, Braschi appears next to other non-Spanish or non-Andean last names: "My wife, . . . she knows Braschi, Fullen, and Gildestrer . . . the big fish" (95). Historically, capitalist investors in Peru were foreigners or had foreign ancestry, as seems to be Braschi's case. However, in contrast to those investors, he also spends his formative years in Chimbote: "On that mirror [Chaucato] and from Hilario Caullama, who also came about that time, Braschi learned and grew one of his wings; the other one he grew in the North American and European cosmopolis" (97). Therefore Braschi combines in a sort of balance (the wings of a bird or a ship) what could be considered Native knowledge (Chaucato and Caullama's fishing skills) and cosmopolitan knowledge attached to metropolitan capitalism.

The synthesis represented by Braschi (a *wakcha* turned into a new authority in Chimbote) has as a model the mythical structure and motifs that Arguedas founded in the *Huarochirí Manuscript*. More than a successful Machiavellian entrepreneur or a character dominated by an unrestrained desire for possession, Braschi is a mythical figure who participates in a mythical cycle of creation and renewal of worlds. Importantly, the two masters of Braschi (Chaucato and Hilario Caullama) are an iteration of the dualistic logic expressed in the novel's title: Chaucato is a fisherman from the coast, while Hilario Caullama is a migrant from the Andean mountains (*F*, 55, 98). In this sense, Braschi learns from both sides of the Andean world— the coast and the mountains—and produces a sort of synthesis that is Chimbote's uneven industrialization. On account of these characteristics, I propose that Braschi could be considered an iteration of the cultural hero Huatyacuri: while Huatyacuri becomes the leader of a new community that worships Pariacaca, Braschi becomes the principal authority in the vibrant city of Chimbote. However, the successful businessman Braschi is now in confrontation with his former mentors (the first two sections of the second part make this conflict explicit). In the mythical world recorded in the *Huarochirí Manuscript*, Huatyacuri pays tribute to his father Pariacaca and the mythical foxes who help him; in contrast, in the fictional reconstruction of the 1960s Chimbote, the businessman Braschi is about to commit parricide.

Regarding the intertextuality between Arguedas's novel and the *Huarochirí Manuscript*, Martin Lienhard identifies the other two characters (the diarist Arguedas and the "gringo" Maxwell) as the textual iteration of Huatyacuri.[16] I do not think that my interpretation (Braschi as an iteration of Huatyacuri) contradicts Lienhard's interpretation, but both of them reveal the complexity of *The Foxes*' reelaboration of the *Huarochirí Manuscript* and the importance of the construction of authorial figures. While Braschi is an authorial figure presented in the peak of his potentialities, Maxwell's authorial figure is constructed throughout the narration, which includes several rites of passage, such as his dance in the brothel and his encounter with the human-fox Diego in Cardozo's office, where he receives a *charango* (an Andean guitar). Moreover, while Braschi's businesses bolster the commodification of Andean subjects, Maxwell participates in the networks of rural-urban migrants that resist this same process. In the next section I discuss how *The Foxes* proposes a similarity between the operations of the "Mafia" (an organization that, following Braschi's orders, manages the brothels of Chimbote and attempts to murder Maxwell) and the commodification of Andean folklore.

Commodification and Debasement of Folklore

In chapter 3 of *The Foxes*, Ángel explains to the human-fox Diego an intricate plot in which the brothels in Chimbote are part of an exploitation system: besides under-paying factory workers and fishers, the "big capitalists" cause them to waste their salaries in entertainment venues and on manufactured goods. The mastermind behind this conspiracy is Braschi, who exerts control through the Mafia, encourages overspending, and sows discord. On the other hand, their principal victims are the rural-urban migrants lured to Chimbote by promises of economic prosperity. These migrants indeed experience some economic improvements—compared with the rampant poverty in the highlands—but also new forms of exploitation. Importantly, notwithstanding their economic constraints, the migrants are willing to confront the Mafia and negotiate their standing in this new environment. When it comes to denouncing this exploitation system, *The Foxes* establishes parallelisms between the Mafia's operations and the commodification of Andean folklore.

William Rowe analyzes the above-mentioned conversation between Ángel and Diego as "a hermeneutic debate about the possibility of a true historical discourse," in which "it is sought to clarify who are the protagonists and the antagonists of the history of Chimbote. In the last instance, they are identified as capital and communism."[17] Nevertheless, factories and labor unions only occupy a rather small portion of the represented world. As Ericka Beckman points out, *The Foxes* is not a novel "about factory workers"; rather, it depicts rural-urban migrants who "must find ways to reproduce their daily existence in the city's market stalls, canteens, and brothels."[18] Ángel's narration of the confrontation between factory's managers and labor union's members (such as the general strike and a failed attempt of a bomb attack), notwithstanding the epic tones of the narration, is deprived of effect or resonances in the social milieu of Chimbote.

As Hilario Caullama says, it is more precise to establish Chimbote's history as a confrontation between capital and work (*F*, 108), if we understand this last term beyond factory work to include the array of ritual practices depicted in *The Foxes*. Following José Alberto Portugal, in an environment characterized by degradation and disorientation, the characters continuously perform rites or elaborate mythical explanations of their experiences.[19] For instance, when Braschi inaugurates a grotto with a spurious San Pedro sculpture, the Mafia organizes a feast full of alcohol and prostitution as if the docks have become a subsidiary of the brothels. Shortly after, in a union meeting, Hilario Caullama explicitly accuses the business-man of desecrating a sacred place:

> We've got patron Saint Peter consecrated in the olden days by the Most Holy Roman Catholic Church; he's in the church. The hulk with the great big counterfeit fish, the one the Soperintendent [*sic*] put on the throne in the counterfeit stone-and-cardboard cave in the wharf square, which the hookers have de-baptized—us the workers never asked capital to give it to us. I'm not payin'! If here in the meetin' there's a dopey, skull-numbed fisherman, then let him pay. (108–9)[20]

Significantly, the stance and vocabulary of Hilario Caullama have already appeared in the "First Diary," when Arguedas criticizes a pseudofolk Chilean dance for inter-national audiences. Not unlike the San Pedro statue, the jarring combination of ele-ments and the sexualization of the whole ensemble expresses the trivialization of folklore:

> In the midst of nudes, comics, jazz and long-haired groups, all mediocre, a Chilean "ballet" appeared. Damnit! I'm not saying all that is not Chilean, but for those of us who know the real sound of what the common people do, these mummeries are something that leave us half-angry and half-perplexed. Nor would I say, like others in the know, that it's pure crap. There's *some* Chilean flavor to it. The *huasos* [Chilean cowboys] look all decked out and pansyfied (almost an insult to the *huaso*) and the girls rather tarted up. (15)

Arguedas explains that, in contrast to the pseudofolk Chilean dance degraded by market demands, the originality and strength of the authentic folklore could still be found in both rural and urban settings, as an effect of migration. The debasement of folklore is a consequence not of the urban setting but of the com-modification process (which also reproduces its logic in rural settings). In fact, the urban setting could be an invigorating force: the city provides newer technolo-gies and techniques as well as articulates unprecedented dynamics among people. Nevertheless, the modernization of Andean folklore still takes place in a historical conjuncture characterized by uneven development and the persistence of hierar-chical structures.[21]

In this same passage Arguedas also denies that he is following a narrow nativ-ist perspective as if he were "an *Indigenista* sectarian" (*F*, 16). The decay and travesty of Andean folklore should be evident to anybody (no matter their social class or ethnic heritage) who is not alienated by the commodification process. On the contrary, a pro-fessional writer such as Fuentes (not the flesh-and-blood author but his inscription in the "Diaries" of the novel) would not understand it, because he is already a commod-ity in the literary markets (16).[22] I analyze this link between the commodification of folklore and the professionalization of literary writing in the following section.

Professional Writers, Bricklayers, and Artisans

In the "Diaries" Arguedas explains that, because of their participation in literary markets, professional writers find themselves detached from communal values—that is, the oral expression and mythical thought of historically marginalized communities. Moreover, this detachment from communal values implies the loss of the authorial status, which is replaced by a mere technical skill inserted in the labor division of capitalistic societies. To understand the terms of this disqualification of professional writers, I suggest that it is relevant to review Arguedas's articles about the impact of urbanization and commodification on Andean folklore and craftwork. By establishing these connections, it is clear that the metafictional dimension of *The Foxes* is not a neurotic response to the success of Boom writers but a long-term reflection on the modernization of artistic production.

In his publications during the 1950s and 1960s, Arguedas employed an encompassing sense of artistic creation, which included lettered and prestigious works alongside popular and traditional cultural manifestations. For instance, in 1964 Arguedas edited the magazine *Cultura y pueblo*, in which he published a series of articles about Andean folklore and anthologies of both Quechua and Spanish texts.[23] Additionally, in "¿Qué es el folklore? (III)," he established that the human labor implied in folk production is substantially similar to the human labor invested in literary writing: "The illiterate person who creates a story does so especially to tell it, to transmit it to others in exactly the same way as the novelist and storyteller. Folklore has proved that there's no difference between the creative process of oral literature and written literature."[24] Basically, both creative processes rely on a dynamic interaction between producers and audiences—to think of the audience's characteristics in advance and adjust the work to meet their needs. Also, Arguedas listed a broad range of goals, such as to instruct, to entertain, and "to describe the earthly, celestial, and social work" that folk production and literary writing pursue alike.[25] Significantly, this listing of goals excludes earning money, which is negatively mentioned in the "Diaries" to describe both Boom literary writing and the pseudofolk Chilean dance (*F*, 15, 21).

Literary critics have paid more attention to the debate between Arguedas and Cortázar than to the references to Fuentes in the "Diaries." In his polemic with Cortázar, Arguedas defends the legitimacy of his provincial and national position in contrast to "the high spheres of the supranational" embraced by Cortázar (*F*, 16).[26] On the contrary, I am more interested in discussing the quarrel with Fuentes, who appears as an overrated literary writer (clearly an unjust treatment given his literary production). While Arguedas identifies himself with an authorial persona, the successful Fuentes is a mere professional writer—that is, a specialist in a set of technical devices. Other characteristics of the professional writers (such as being steeped in a lettered culture or being familiar with urban settings) are less important than their status as mere specialists: "The last time I saw Carlos Fuentes I found him writing like *a bricklayer working on a piecework basis.* He had a deadline for handing in the novel. We ate lunch rapidly at his house. He had to get back to the typewriter" (*F*, 178; emphasis added). By means of comparing Fuentes's novelistic writing with the work of a bricklayer, *The Foxes* implies the degradation of literature from the prestigious position acquired in the nineteenth and twentieth centuries. The civic identity of the literary writer was a common feature all along the Romanticism, Spanish American *modernismo*, and high modernism of the Boom generation. From this point of view, these lettered individuals have a high degree of autonomy and invest significant intellectual energy in generating their sophisticated literary works. In contrast, the "Diaries" presents Fuentes as a subordinated worker who is overshadowed by a machine, follows hierarchical orders from the owners of capital, and, in doing so, lacks any sign of autonomy. The creative interaction between producers of folklore/literature and their audiences is reduced to satisfy the consumer's needs.

Although the comparison between professional writers and bricklayers is degrading, such debasement is not caused by the low social status of a manual worker but by its alienation in capitalism. The reference to alienation is essential given that the authorial figures in *The Foxes* are manual workers and hold a low social status: Loco Moncada is a fisherman, Esteban de la Cruz is a shoemaker, and Orfa is a prostitute. Moreover, the rite of passage of Maxwell implies that, in addition to living in a slum and playing Andean music, he starts working as a bricklayer with Cecilio Ramirez (*F*, 205). Although Fuentes is referred to as a bricklayer only in a metaphorical sense, it is necessary to review Arguedas's articles about Andean craftwork and the impact of modernization processes on it. In particular, I pay attention to his articles about the mestizo *retablista* Joaquín López Antay, the foremost exponent of Peruvian popular religious art.

Besides López Antay's artistic sensibility and mastering of craftwork techniques, Arguedas celebrated the *retablista*'s defense of artistic freedom from economic interests: "No popular artist from Huamanga but Don Joaquín has maintained his compromise and cultural integrity against the disturbing influence of the shifting client demand."[27] López Antay even rejected the professionalization of his labor: "A Lima businessman proposed to Don Joaquín Lopez to make his retablos on a larger scale, by dozens. Don Joaquín utterly rejected that proposition. 'I'm not a factory, señor, I'm a *sculptor*,' he said."[28] Like nonprofessional writers in *The Foxes*' "Diaries," López Antay kept his attachment to communal values, which did not imply a paralyzing conservatism or the rejection of innovation. In contrast, the *retablista* always engaged in dynamic interactions with his audiences—both Indigenous agrarian communities and urban lettered groups.

While in Arguedas's article López Antay represented the artist who preserved his or her autonomy and creativity (attached to communal values), Jesús Urbano Rojas (1925–2014) embodies the degraded artist wholly subordinated to the commodification process. Arguedas expressed this hard judgment in the following terms: "Seeing the 'new' *retablos* by Urbano Rojas, it brings us sadness to consider that Don Joaquín is perhaps the last message from the profane *retablo* enlightened by grace, while with Urbano begins the *spectacular retablo*, formless, without internal unity. This is the tame product by a man just merely anxious about succeeding in the market by any means necessary."[29] As is the case with Fuentes in the "Diaries," I am interested not in discussing the *retablos* of Urbano Rojas in themselves (Arguedas's negative judgment seems unfair) but in identifying the construction of a critical discourse about authorship, artistic production, and the effects of the modernization process. Arguedas himself was conscious of the limitations of his judgment but insisted on stressing the pervasive influence of commodification, which even incorporates what seems to be foreign to its domain—namely, the naïveté of Andean craftwork, as Urbano Rojas's *retablos* make evident.[30]

Interestingly, the description of Urbano Rojas's work bears a resemblance to what is known nowadays as kitsch—artistic production of garish nature and bad taste that originates in or is inspired by the culture of marginalized populations. Urbano Rojas's works present a juxtaposition of disparate elements and the absence of a cohesive structure: "Retablo #20 in Urbano's exposition contains a nativity scene. All the figures of saints and animals are painted with a striped pattern and the whole ensemble gives the impression of a picturesque and a bit absurd group of zebras. . . . In the Retablo #3 there are two tuna trees, slightly grotesque, *inside a church*."[31] In fact, the performances of Loco Moncada could be described using similar terms—accumulation, juxtaposition of elements, and flexible structures. For instance, Ángel explains these performances as random and whimsical events: "He [Loco Moncada] will 'prepare' his next speech—nobody knows when or how he will give it. He might dress up like a Turk or an Indian, or like Batman or a gypsy" (*F*, 152). For members of the upper classes of Chimbote (such as Ángel and Braschi), the mad preacher is a picturesque figure and an entertainer. Nevertheless, for the participants of the network of rural-urban migrants (in which Moncada also participates, notwithstanding his *costeño* origin), these performances and ritual events acquire a different meaning—they are tools to negotiate a migrant's standing in a newer sociocultural context such as Chimbote.[32] In the next section I analyze the case of another non-Indigenous man participating in the networks of rural-urban migrants—the "gringo" Maxwell.

Maxwell and the Networks of Rural-Urban Migrants

Maxwell's participation in the networks of rural-urban migrants is a crucial element to overcome *Indigenismo*'s limitations and give an account of the impacts of the modernization process on Andean cultures (which implies a de-essentialization of the notion of Indigenous). Significantly, the novel introduces Maxwell as a disruptive force that challenges the exploitation system organized by Braschi. By dancing to rock 'n' roll with a prostitute, the "gringo" interrupts the sordid routines of brothel life: "In a short time the regular customers—drunk and sober, boat shippers, fishermen, merchants, and onlookers with a yen but no money—were drawing closer to the American and his partner. Some *chola* hookers were staring at Maxwell as if he were a fire" (*F*, 33–34). Right after finishing his alluring dance, the "gringo" escaped from an attempted murder orchestrated by the Mafia, which recognizes the challenges he poses. Chronologically, this episode takes place after Maxwell's trip to Paratía, where he meets one of the mythical foxes and has sex with a woman during an Andean festivity. According to Lienhard, since Maxwell's dance moves are compared with waterfalls, he is an emissary of the upper world (93). The gringo disrupts the brothels through his attachment to Indigenous mythical categories.

The waterfalls also appear in the "First Diary" as an archetype for Arguedas and nonprofessional writers, who reject the commodification process in literary markets by means of embracing communal values. In addition, as was mentioned before, the assumption of those communal values implies the creative incorporation of updated techniques and newer technologies. In the episode in the brothel, notwithstanding Maxwell's assimilation to Andean communities, he is dancing to modern rock 'n' roll—that is, a musical genre that originated in the United States (home country of Maxwell) in the mid-twentieth century and disseminated worldwide through mass media. Certainly, Maxwell is dancing rock 'n' roll as if it were an Andean dance (thus the comparison between his moves and the waterfalls), which implies a process of "transculturation" (in terms of Ángel Rama) or "andinization" (in terms of Lienhard) of dominant genres of mass media.[33] Nevertheless, the first interaction of Maxwell with Andean folklore already implies a degree of modernization—Maxwell meets the Ayarachi, a folk group from Paratía, at a concert in Lima for Westernized audiences. As Maxwell explains to Cardozo in a later episode:

> [The Ayarachi] transform the Municipal Theater of Lima into a fiery furnace rather than a funeral, as if they were some sort of combination of Wagner, Beethoven, Mussorgsky, and Bartok [*sic*], in their roots. "It's funereal, terrible," "It's atrocious and savage," "It's marvelous, strange," "It belongs to another world," exclaimed some people in the audience. I said, "That's what I will be; that's a part of me and to be it wholly, I must go thousands and thousands of kilometers and start forward in time and perhaps even farther—maybe I didn't know it and I don't know it—maybe I have to go backward in time with them, with the ayarachis." And I didn't say this because I had studied musicology.
> (*F*, 229)

Maxwell's praise of Andean folklore is not just aesthetic judgment but also implies a complete transformation of his subjectivity. After listening to the Ayarachi in Lima, Maxwell starts his journey to become an Andean musical performer by learning to play *charango* in the highlands. The gringo passes through the assimilation process—but is it a case of cultural appropriation? It seems not, since Maxwell is not interested in obtaining blatant economic profit, in contrast to the images of Fuentes in *The Foxes*' "Diaries" and Urbano Rojas in "Del retablo mágico."

In addition, Maxwell's whole interaction with Andean folklore has several intermediaries in urban settings, such as state institutions (like the Casa de la Cultura, where Arguedas worked between 1963 and 1964) and the networks created by the rural-urban migrants themselves. For instance, Maxwell spends six months traveling around Lake Titicaca and seeing "thirty different traditional dances, all different as to music, costumes, and choreography" (*F*, 230). Back in the Casa de la Cultura in Lima, he learns musical traditions from other areas of the Andes: "The famous *charanguista* taught me how they play where he comes from—from Huamanga. I spoke to him about some of the towns in his home region and he taught me their 'sad-rapturous' *charango* style; for hours and weeks he taught me" (233).

The training of Maxwell as an Andean musician not only requires his immersion in agrarian communities in Paratía but also relies on the increasing modernization of Andean folklore in urban settings.

According to Javier García Liendo, *The Foxes* presents a negative image of Peruvian uneven modernization because of—among other things—the lack of urban folk-music venues in the fictional reconstruction of 1960s Chimbote. On the contrary, Arguedas's articles about folklore offer a positive perspective about the increasing presence of Andean folklore in folk-music venues, which are settings for the creative interaction of rural-urban migrants with modern technology and capitalism.[34] In fact, García Liendo's assessment of the importance of folk-music venues is misleading. I propose that these places were significant because rural-urban migrants integrated them into broader networks. Thanks to these networks, the migrants faced and overcame the challenges of living in urban settings (controlled by upper and middle classes unfamiliar with or openly racist toward them). As a researcher and public official, Arguedas was genuinely interested in identifying these networks and helping to strengthen them. Furthermore, in his literary writing he followed a similar pattern, already evident in his first novel, *Yawar Fiesta* (1941), in the episode of the "Centro Unión Lucanas," where the 1920s rural-urban migrants in Lima gathered.

Similarly, *The Foxes* is a novel not primarily about the harbor or brothels in Chimbote (places where Braschi, or big capital, exerts his power) but about that broader network created by the rural-urban migrants to grapple with the uneven modernization process in Chimbote (and the whole country). In Lima these networks allow Maxwell to interact with Andean folklore for the first time; in Chimbote, these same networks accompany his further development: he moves to the slum La Esperanza, works as bricklayer with Cecilio Ramírez, establishes small businesses (a car wash and repair store), builds his own house, and plans to marry Fredesbinda, a neighbor of Cecilio Ramírez (*F*, 228–32). The transformation of Maxwell ends with the full revelation of his status as an Andean musician: he receives from the human-fox Diego a *charango* sent by the blind musician Antolín Crispín (235). If Maxwell learned *charango* songs from Huamanga in the Casa de la Cultura in Lima, he would learn musical styles from other regions of the Andes while living in Chimbote. In other words, Maxwell achieves his status as a folk performer and Indigenous-inspired authorial figure thanks to the networks of rural-urban migrants.

The Indigenous and mestizo characters who participate in these networks (notwithstanding the marginalization and poverty in the slums) have agency and develop survival or resistance strategies, which are successful to a certain degree. For instance, Moncada regularly denounces the exploitative system in Chimbote in his speeches, which take inspiration from his conversations with Esteban de la Cruz. Even the three female prostitutes, who are victims of persistent sexual abuse by the pimp Tinoco (one of Braschi's henchmen), do not express a pessimistic vision of the city—they report the violence in Chimbote by means of symbols and rituals of messianic sensibility (*F*, 48–52). Moreover, other lower-class characters experience significant improvements in their living conditions. Namely, Aurora,

Esteban de la Cruz's wife, obtains a stand in the municipal market Bolívar Alto after years of working as a street vendor. The list of successful cases goes on: Chaucato's brand-new house with furniture and electronic appliances (although the slums lack electricity), Hilario Caullama's economic success combined with ethnic pride, and Gregorio Bazalar's leadership in the slums.

While Braschi personifies the logic of capital (leading to a paranoid or conspiratorial representation of socioeconomic processes), no single character embodies the networks of rural-urban migrants similarly. Nevertheless, in the "Last Diary?" Arguedas summarizes his original plan to coalesce the stories of the above-mentioned characters, in which the mythical foxes play a crucial role:

> The Foxes run from one of their worlds to the other; they dance beneath the blue light, holding dry pieces of worm-eaten dung over their heads. They sense things; they have clearer, more intense presentiments than the half-demented people who have been overwhelmed and are aware of it, and therefore, not being mortal, they somehow stitch together and were going to continue to stitch together the materials and souls this narrative had begun to drag along. (*F*, 257–58)

In the fictional narration, the mythical foxes have decisive interactions with several characters: the manager Ángel, the stutterer Tarta, Esteban de la Cruz, Maxwell in Paratía, and all the people reunited in priest Cardozo's office. Moreover, the "Last Diary?" explains that, in the unwritten sections of the novel, the foxes were supposed to interact with the other characters, such as Loco Moncada and the three female prostitutes (256–57). In all these cases, the mythical foxes provoke a transfiguration in his interlocutors, who experience a sense of euphoria and perplexity combined with an urgent desire to speak, sing, and dance. In other words, these characters reveal their performative qualities and authorial dimensions.

In the final analysis, these characters' performances—triggered by the mythical foxes—challenge the rule of Braschi, who is ultimately responsible for the exploitation system in Chimbote. This is the reason for the attempted murder of Maxwell in the brothel. However, the novel also introduces the human-fox Diego as an agent of Lima's big capitalists. Ángel suspects that his visitor is not a mere employee of Braschi but a sort of disciple: "Is this frock-coated hippy somebody I can trust, some half de-jelled snob—could be one of Braschi's henchmen?" (*F*, 88).[35] What is the nature of the relationship between Diego (as igniter of rituals in the networks of rural-urban migrants) and Braschi (as a mythical figure who rules Chimbote's exploitation system)? The answer is of pivotal importance for the discussion about "Andean modernity" in *The Foxes*. Is one (Diego) subordinated to the other (Braschi)? Do they constitute discrete and opposite stances (capital against work)? I suggest that Arguedas's last novel attempts to negotiate between the relentless dynamics of modernization and the endangered Indigenous identities/communal values brought by rural-urban migrants. The networks created by these migrants respond to an immediate sense of loss in capitalist societies; nevertheless, these networks could not exist in the first place without the development of capitalism. In the end, rural-urban migrants find better living conditions in Chimbote than in the highlands, as well as unprecedented opportunities to improve their lives and transform their Indigenous identities. That is why the human-fox Diego appears as "hechura de Braschi"—in other words, as a product of the very capitalist process that Arguedas's last novel tries to understand. The uneven modernization is responsible for the challenges in Chimbote and is the source of their possible solutions. The networks of rural-urban migrants, which are an outcome of the modernization process, construct authorial figures with a strong and flexible Indigenous identity. Thanks to this attachment to Indigeneity, the characters beset by Braschi's exploitation system can negotiate their standing, call hierarchical structure into question, and foreclose commodification.

JAVIER ALONSO MUÑOZ-DIAZ is adjunct faculty of Spanish at the University of Denver. His research focuses on twentieth- and twenty-first-century Latin American literature and cultural history, with an emphasis on the Andean area.

Notes

1   Mariátegui, *7 ensayos de interpretación de la realidad peruana*, 240–42. For a comprehensive history of *Indigenismo* in Latin America, see Tarica, "Indigenismo."

2   *Primer encuentro de narradores peruanos*, 36–43.

3   Arguedas, *The Fox from Up Above and the Fox from Down Below*, 257 (hereafter cited as *F*).

4   Lienhard, *Cultura andina y forma novelesca*, 20; Portugal, *Las novelas de José María Arguedas*, 103. The *Huarochirí Manuscript* was composed in the first decade of the seventeenth century and had an important role in the extirpation campaigns of idolatry. Under the supervision of the secular priest Francisco de Ávila (1573–1647), an *indio ladino* (a bilingual assistant to the priest) interviewed the Indigenous population from the resettlement village of San Damian (thirty-eight miles from Lima) and had compiled the information in the preserved Quechua manuscript by 1608 (Salomon, "Introductory Essay," 26).

5   To depict the radical changes experienced by the mid-twentieth-century Peruvian society, *The Foxes* articulates three dimensions: autobiography, fiction, and myth. First, the autobiographical dimension is in the "Diaries," a text divided into four sections and intercalated with the fictional narrative. Arguedas begins to write the "Diaries" with a therapeutic goal: by uncovering his suicidal desire, he is supposed to reestablish his health and achieve the composition of his new novel. Second, the fictional dimension reconstructs the impact of the fishing boom and rural-urban migration on Chimbote—a process that Arguedas had started researching as an anthropologist by 1966. Lastly, the mythical dimension is rooted in Andean cultures and actively interacts with the other two. The leading role of this last dimension appears in the title of the novel, *The Fox from Up Above and the Fox from Down Below*, which refers to the *Huarochirí Manuscript*'s two mythical foxes who help the cultural hero Huatyacuri establish the cult of his father, the *huaca* Pariacaca. In Arguedas's novel, the mythical foxes first appear as two voices narrating and commenting on the events in both the "Diaries" and the fictional narrative; halfway through the novel these voices become the human-fox characters Diego and his brother.

6   In Peru liberal developmental policies found their most dynamic expression in fishing activities, which made this country the world-leading exporter of fish-meal in the 1960s. See Thorp and Bertram, *Peru, 1890–1977*, 180–82, 242–52.

7   Rama, "El boom en perspectiva," 271–73; Martin, "The 'Boom' of Spanish-American Fiction," 481.

8   Lienhard, *Cultura andina y forma novelesca*, 61–72. Regarding the definition of commodification, Georg Lukács explains that, in the capitalist mode of production, "the process of labour is progressively broken down into abstract, rational, specialised operations so that the worker loses contact with the finished product and his work is reduced to the

mechanical repetition of a specialised set of actions" (*History and Class Consciousness*, 88). As a consequence, exchange-value and commodities penetrate the whole life of society—including the subjectivity of the workers, who have a "reified mind" (93).

9   Jon Beasley-Murray rightfully observes that the fictional chapters of *The Foxes* include a roster of authorial figures who are projections of the diarist ("Arguedasmachine," 116). However, while Beasley-Murray highlights the relation of these fictional characters with the "machine" (a term that, based on Deleuze and Guattari's theory, the critic uses loosely), I analyze these characters as part of the novel's questioning of dominant models of authorship in 1960s Latin America.

10   Arguedas, "Del retablo mágico," 380 (my translation). In this article Arguedas explains that the *retablos* (portable boxes that depict religious, historical, or everyday events) experience displacement from sacred contexts (the so-called San Marcos, used during the branding of cattle) to secular and commercial ones. For an updated history of the *retablos* (in which the *Indigenista* painter Alicia Bustamante, sister-in-law of Arguedas during his first marriage, played a significant role), see Ulfe, *Cajones de la memoria*, 24–26, 32–37, 43–76.

11   According to Ulfe, López Antay modified his artistic production to fulfill Bustamante's expectation as a connoisseur who established a distinction between folklore and fine arts (*Cajones de la memoria*, 56). On the other hand, notwithstanding the social hierarchy among the *retablista* and the *Indigenista* painter, Ulfe points out their dialogical relationship and López Antay's agency (59).

12   Portugal, *Las novelas de José María Arguedas*, 194.

13   The model for Braschi in *The Foxes* is the Italian Peruvian entrepreneur Luis Banchero Rossi (1929–72), one of the most important "captains of industry" during the 1960s fish-meal boom. Regarding the participation of transnational capitalism, Thorp and Bertram argue that it did not play a significant role in an industry dominated by Peruvian and recent immigrant entrepreneurs of middle-class origin (*Peru, 1890–1977*, 248).

14   Salomon and Urioste's translation of the *Huarochirí Manuscript* presents Huatyacuri as "a poor friendless one" (*Huarochirí Manuscript*, 54). The manuscript also introduces the divinities Cuniraya Viracocha and Pariacaca following a similar pattern (9, 74).

15   For a discussion on *wakcha* motif in Arguedas's literature, see López-Baralt, "Wakcha, Pachakuti y Tinku," 303–20. López-Barat does not recognize Brachi as a *wakcha* because he is part of the exploiting class. However, following this critic's analysis of the relationship between *wakcha* and *pachacuti* (the inversion of the world), it could be argued that Braschi represents a degenerated Andean deity.

16   Lienhard, *Cultura andina y forma novelesca*, 32, 93, 166.

17   Rowe, "No hay mensajero de nada," 64 (my translation).

18   Beckman, "José María Arguedas' Epics."

19   Portugal, *Las novelas de José María Arguedas*, 440.

20   In *The Foxes* characters such Hilario Caullama or Gregorio Bazalar, rural-urban migrants whose first language is either Aymara or Quechua, speak in an idiosyncratic form of Spanish with an Indigenous accent. The English translation by Frances Barraclough attempts to reproduce it.

21   Regarding the commodification of Andean folklore, Arguedas mentions the persistence of the *incaísta* aesthetic, which reproduces prejudices toward contemporaneous indigenous populations. Basically, Peruvian ruling classes celebrate the mastery of Inca art, crafted hundreds of years ago, but dismiss living folk or popular production. As a consequence, folk groups have abandoned their traditional outfits and adopted stereotypical Cuzco costumes with Inca motifs ("Notas sobre el folklore peruano," 355–56). In other words, Andean folklore became *incaísta* to fit ruling classes' expectations and to succeed in cultural markets.

22   Following Lienhard, I intend not to discuss Fuentes's fictional narrative pieces in themselves but to analyze Arguedas's idea of a literary writer represented by the Mexican (*Cultura andina y forma novelesca*, 38–39).

23   Following Javier García Liendo, in these texts Arguedas attempted two complementary operations: first, to establish a historical continuity between voices and subjectivities founded in both colonial Quechua texts and contemporaneous folklore; and second, to recognize similarities between artistic works of folklore and those of prestigious literary writing. The result of these complementary operations is "to question the traditional concept of literature (given that he [Arguedas] included contemporary Quechua texts such as Huayno's lyrics) and the humanistic concept of culture (because of his work with anthropology

and folklore)" (*El intellectual y la cultura de masas*, 119; my translation).

24   Arguedas, "¿Qué es el folklore? (III)," 20 (my translation).

25   Arguedas, "¿Qué es el folklore? (III)," 20 (my translation).

26   This debate is a critique to European/ international modernism (represented by Cortázar) from a position attached to regional developments and infused with Indigenous identities (the position of Arguedas). See Moraña, "Territorialidad y forasterismo," 116–17.

27   Arguedas, "El arte popular religioso," 36 (my translation).

28   Arguedas, "El arte popular religioso," 49 (my translation).

29   Arguedas, "Del retablo mágico," 381 (my translation).

30   Arguedas, "Del retablo mágico," 382.

31   Arguedas, "Del retablo mágico," 381 (my translation).

32   Arguedas also linked Urbano Rojas's work with the sociocultural identity of *cholos*, acculturated Westernized individuals with Indigenous heritage ("Del retablo mágico," 382). With regard to *The Foxes*, this description of *cholo* mentality seems closer to the portrayal of certain characters, in particular Gregorio Bazalar. Although Maxwell and Cecilio Ramírez express their doubts about Bazalar's behavior and true intentions (*F*, 206), the following section presents another perspective about his complex identity: "Don Gregorio thought he was very close to the realization of this 'magnanimous' heroic deed, and he was feeling quite satisfied with the 'elegant impaction' with which he had told 'tactical' lies and truths in Cardozo's office. . . . 'Maybe I . . . ' he thought (no longer able to think in Quechua) 'It could be, maybe, in its lifetime of mine, that I won't be any longer a stranger in this country land where we've been born. First time and first person that ever finalizes that defficult [*sic*] deed in his lifetime existence'" (227–28). Despite Bazalar's questionable behavior, the diarist and author Arguedas would definitely subscribe to such a goal—the vindication of Andean subjects and communities.

33   Rama, *Writing across Cultures*, 18–35; Lienhard, "La 'andinización' del vanguardismo urbano," 326–32.

34   García Liendo, *El intelectual y la cultura de masas*, 163–65.

35   The original text says, "¿hechura de Braschi?," which literally means "handiwork of Braschi?" (*El zorro de arriba y el zorro de abajo*, 88).

Works Cited

Arguedas, José María. "Del retablo mágico al retablo mercantil." In vol. 10 of *Obras completas*, 378–83. Lima: Horizonte, 2012.

Arguedas, José María, trans. *Dioses y hombres de Huarochirí*. Universidad Antonio Ruiz de Montoya, Jesuitas, 2007.

Arguedas, José María. "El arte popular religioso y la cultura mestiza." In vol. 10 of *Obras completas*, 29–82. Lima: Horizonte, 2012.

Arguedas, José María. *El zorro de arriba y el zorro de abajo*, edited by Eve-Marie Fell. Nanterre: ALLCA XX, 1990.

Arguedas, José María. *The Fox from Up Above and the Fox from Down Below*, translated by Frances Barraclough. Pittsburgh, PA: University of Pittsburgh Press, 2000.

Arguedas, José María. "Notas sobre el folklore peruano." In vol. 10 of *Obras completas*, 351–54. Lima: Horizonte, 2012.

Arguedas, José María. "¿Qué es el folklore? (III)." In vol. 12 of *Obras completas*, 19–21. Lima: Horizonte, 2012.

Beasley-Murray, Jon. "Arguedasmachine: Modernity and Affect in the Andes." *Iberoamericana*, no. 30 (2014): 113–28.

Beckman, Ericka. "José María Arguedas' Epics of Expropriation." *Emiférica* 14, no. 1 (2018). hemisphericinstitute.org/en/emisferica-14-1 -expulsion/14-1-essays/jose-maria-arguedas -epics-of-expropriation.html.

García Liendo, Javier. *El intelectual y la cultura de masas: Argumentos latinoamericanos en torno a Ángel Rama y José María Arguedas*. West Lafayette, IN: Purdue University Press, 2017.

Lienhard, Martin. *Cultura andina y forma novelesca: Zorros y danzantes en la última novela de Arguedas*. Lima: Horizonte, 1990.

Lienhard, Martin. "La 'andinización' del vanguardismo urbano." In *El zorro de arriba y el zorro de abajo*, edited by Eve-Marie Fell, 321–32. Nanterre: ALLCA XX, 1990.

López-Baralt, Mercedes. "Wakcha, Pachakuti y Tinku: Tres llaves andinas para acceder a la escritura de Arguedas." In *Las cartas de Arguedas*, edited by John V. Murra and Mercedes López-Baralt, 299–330. Lima: Fondo Editorial, Pontificia Universidad Católica del Perú, 1996.

Lukács, Georg. *History and Class Consciousness: Studies in Marxist Dialectics*, translated by Rodney Livingstone. Cambridge, MA: MIT Press, 1971.

Mariátegui, José Carlos. *Siete ensayos de interpretación de la realidad peruana*. 17th ed. Lima: Biblioteca Amauta, 1969.

Martin, Gerald. "The 'Boom' of Spanish-American Fiction and the 1960s Revolutions (1958–

1975)." In *A Companion to Latin American Literature and Culture*, edited by Sara Castro-Klarén, 478–94. Malden, MA: Blackwell, 2008.

Moraña, Mabel. "Territorialidad y forasterismo: La polémica Arguedas/Cortázar revisitada." In *José María Arguedas: Hacia una poética migrante*, edited by Sergio R. Franco, 103–20. Pittsburgh: Instituto Internacional de Literatura Iberoamericana, 2006.

Portugal, José Alberto. *Las novelas de José María Arguedas: Una incursión en lo inarticulado*. Lima: Fondo Editorial, Pontificia Universidad Católica del Perú, 2007.

Primer encuentro de narradores peruanos. Lima: Casa de la Cultura del Perú, 1969.

Rama, Ángel. "El boom en perspectiva." In *La novela en América Latina: Panoramas (1920–1980)*, 235–93. Bogotá: Procultura, 1982.

Rama, Ángel. *Writing across Cultures: Narrative Transculturation in Latin America*, edited and translated by David L. Frye. Durham, NC: Duke University Press, 2012.

Rowe, William. "'No hay mensajero de nada': La modernidad andina según *Los Zorros* de Arguedas." *Revista de crítica literaria latinoamericana*, no. 72 (2010): 61–96.

Salomon, Frank. "Introductory Essay: The Huarochirí Manuscript." In *The Huarochirí Manuscript: A Testament of Ancient and Colonial Andean Religion*, translated by Frank Salomon and George Urioste, 1–38. Austin: University of Texas Press, 1991.

Salomon, Frank, and George Urioste, trans. *The Huarochirí Manuscript: A Testament of Ancient and Colonial Andean Religion*. Austin: University of Texas Press, 1991.

Tarica, Estelle. "Indigenismo." *Oxford Research Encyclopedia of Latin American History*. March 2016. oxfordre.com/latinamericanhistory/view/10.1093/acrefore/9780199366439.001.0001/acrefore-9780199366439-e-68.

Thorp, Rosemary, and Geoffrey Bertram. *Peru, 1890–1977: Growth and Policy in an Open Economy*. New York: Columbia University Press, 1978.

Ulfe, María Eugenia. *Cajones de la memoria: La historia reciente del Perú a través de los retablos andinos*. Lima: Fondo Editorial, Pontificia Universidad Católica del Perú, 2011.

The Past Embedded in Everyday Life

The Meseta del Collao as an Illustrative Case

ALEXANDRE BELMONTE

Abstract   The Andean experience of the everyday is affected markedly by respect and reverence for tradition, for teachings of the past, and for myths that explain and simplify reality. This article reflects on the uses of ancient rituals in Bolivia today, in the context that Xavier Albó named "the return of the Indian."

Keywords   Andean highlands, rituals, *yatiris*, Alasitas

In spite of the rupture represented by the European invasion and colonization, the antiquity of our continent continues to penetrate the present, composing the intrinsic way of being of our societies: the life of the majority of the original Andean, Mesoamerican, Amazonian, and Patagonian populations—just to cite a few examples still shows influences that date back millennia. This is visible in food, in construction (in the Andean case, superimposed stones without cement, adobe houses with roofs made out of *paja brava*, etc.), in ceramic patterns, in the geometric patterns of textiles, in musical instruments, in clothing, and in other items and practices. All these elements maintain a coherence and continuity that can be traced back over centuries. The brooms that are used nowadays in urban cleaning in Bolivia, for example, are handmade, produced from the *paja brava* (species *Stipa ichu*), an endemic highland plant used for centuries in the making of roofs and brooms and also in the treatment of various diseases.[1] In addition to these aspects of material cultures—Andean, Amazonian, Mesoamerican, and others—ancient myths and rites continue to be reelaborated and lived by a large part of the populations of these areas.

This peculiar antiquity, the American antiquity, appears in its complexity when history, anthropology, and archaeology are articulated with the cosmovision and the daily present of these societies. New parameters become necessary, therefore, when we study the past of our continent, and the permanence of manners and ways of acting publicly among many citizens is particularly discernible today.

ENGLISH LANGUAGE NOTES

58:1, April 2020 DOI 10.1215/00138282-8237432
© 2020 Regents of the University of Colorado

Like any other concept of antiquity, here too we are talking about a relative antiquity that needs to be understood in its own terms.[2]

One possible way of understanding this very different temporal record is through attention to the worldviews of those societies. In the Andes and its adjacent valleys, during the Inca era and even earlier, there are records that the world was thought of as a tripartite totality of kingdoms (*pachas*), which were distant from one another yet were (or should be) dynamically harmonized and interconnected. The intercommunication of the *pachas* depended on the action of priests in elaborate rituals. However, making *pachas* communicate was the function of the Inca himself, whose principal occupation as a ruler was to take care of the harmony between the people, the gods, and the *pachas*.

Hanan *pacha* was the celestial sphere, which encompassed gods such as the rainbow, the moon, the lightning, the thunder, and the sun and had as its chief divinity Wiracocha-Inti, represented in the Inca era by the sun (in Quechua, *inti*). Uku *pacha*, or Urin *pacha*, was the underworld, the world of the dead, spirits, and diseases; it was the domain of Pachamama, the lady of the earth and therefore of food and human survival. From the interaction and link between Wiracocha-Inti and Pachamama—between heaven and earth—arises Kay *pacha*, the world in which we live, which includes humans, plants, animals, mountains, lakes, and rivers.

The links between elements such as heaven and earth, night and day, the natural and the supernatural, typical of Andean thought, embody a conception of the world that explains not only the existence of the world and things but also the understanding of the visible, the invisible, time, the divine—in short, of all that really is. Andean material culture is impregnated with these symbolic and immaterial elements.

The Incas were responsible for appropriating the ancient Tiwanaku god Wiracocha and "transforming" it into Inti, a divinity subsequent to Tiwanaku's Wiracocha, or rather an avatar of him (fig. 1). The Tiwanaku civilization represented Wiracocha—the "god of the sticks" or "the creator god"—which, as Betty Meggers points out, was clearly inspired by the anthropomorphic figures of the culture of Chavín de Huántar (figs. 2–3).[3] This typical representation of Wiracocha, printed on so many textiles and often portrayed in Andean handicrafts from northern Chile and Argentina to Ecuador, makes us believe that the Tiwanaku themselves have appropriated the "god of the sticks" of the Chavín culture, adapting it for their religious purposes. On this subject, Thérèse Bouysse-Cassagne gives us various examples.[4] The Incas adored Wiracocha's avatars and somehow linked them to the cult of the sun, Inti (fig. 4). As elucidated by Bouysse-Cassagne, in many moments of Andean history prior to the Spanish invasion, Incas worshiped animals such as catfish, jaguars, and other feline species typical of Lake Titicaca and its surroundings.

Already during the Inca period, it was supposed that the Inca himself came from the earth and, since he was at the same time a son of the sun, it was he who guaranteed communication between the three worlds, having at his service an entire sacerdotal caste to corroborate his quasi divinity through complex ceremonies that vivified the myths. By its very nature and plasticity, myth is always modified and covered with new meanings with the passage of time. The Incas made

Figure 2. Central bas-relief of the monolith door of the sun gate at Tiwanaku, designed by Charles Wiener, as it appears in Puerta del Sol, located in the present-day Bolivian municipality of Tiwanaku. There are many controversies about the date of this work, but the general consensus is circa 200 BC. Image credit: es.wikipedia.org /wiki/Puerta_del_Sol_(Tiwanaku)#/media/Archivo:2Wiener -Tintin-Dieu_Soleil.jpg.

Figure 1. Graphic reproduction of the Raimondi Stele, representing a god with two rods, of the late phase that marks the decadence of Chavín de Huántar culture. Image credit: es.wikipedia.org/wiki/Estela_ de_Raimondi#/media/Archivo:Raimondi_ Stela_(Chavin_de_Huantar).svg.

many dominated peoples believe that the god they worshipped was indeed Inti, the solar disk that guaranteed and regulated all life cycles. This created Hanan *pacha*, the celestial plane, the mirror in which life in Kay *pacha*—the world here—was reflected.

The Native Americans did not perceive time in a linear way as the Europeans at the time of the "invasion" did: a time when the first ships were marvelously seen by amazed people in the Caribbean, along the coast of present-day Brazil and in many places in the sixteenth century. The Andean term *pachakuti*, so frequent in Andean history and mythology, is perfect to describe the new era that 1492 pro-

Figure 3. Puerta del Sol, Tiwanaku, Bolivia. In the center, above, high relief of Wiracocha. Personal archive.

voked. The idea of "time itself," as an abstract and universal concept, seemed simply not to exist for Native Americans. Despite enormous differences among American civilizations, in most of them, as between the Aztecs, many Amazonian nations, Chimus, Urus, Guaranis, Tiwanakots, and Incas, time was lived as a simultaneity of many dimensions of time and time living, acting as gears of a larger scheme. Each of these gears represented a dimension of time, which could encompass the cosmic time of planetary rotations and translations, the cycle of solstices and equinoxes, the time of sowing and harvesting, the time of rains and drought, the time of the lives of women and men, and, of course, an aspiration to recognize the absolute time of divinities. Natives were religious in what might be considered a purer way than their European antipodes, although both sides had no problem killing in the name of their gods: the empire of Christ was again shaken and dazed by this absolute otherness that included Native Americans' clothing (and the lack of it!) and adornments, gems, beautiful exotic plumes, and mother-of-pearl. Among many nations, as with the extinct Tupiniquim, anthropophagy was a current war practice. Also, the relationship that Native Atlantic and Caribbean peoples had with each other and their nudity defied all biblical principles and was regarded by Europeans as a temptation of Satan. It was not until the appearance of the detailed accounts of various writers—from Jean de Léry to Alexander von Humboldt, about how uncivilized and unconvertible to Christian faith those "primitive" Indians were—that they acquired the admiration and dignity of many voyagers, both religious and, in most cases, "scientific." Those first "uncivilized" populations did not even have to suffer idolatries extirpation or torture by the Inquisition. They perished as soon as Europeans arrived, in the first five decades of the sixteenth century.

Those people and civilizations living in highlands, as Aztecs and Incas did, had more time to wake up from forewarning nightmares and to prepare a great *pachakuti*, a great turn in the time wheel. For most Natives, 1492 originated a confusion in time. The multiple dimensions of time were (and still are) expressed in speech through verb tenses not found in Indo-European languages. They were

Figure 4. Pachacutec worshipping Inti inside Coricancha (representation of Martín de Murúa). Image credit: es.wikipedia.org/wiki/Inti#/media/Archivo:Pachacuteckoricancha.jpg.

Figure 5. Ekeko, always depicted loaded with various things, symbolizes abundance for many Andean peoples, from southern Peru to northern Argentina and Chile. This is a representation of Ekeko at the entrance of the Feria de las Alasitas, La Paz, Bolivia, 2016. Personal archive.

also expressed in the festivities and rituals that marked communal life and in the relationship of people with the harvest and perpetuation of the species—many of these rituals are still practiced in several communities and also in big cities like La Paz and El Alto. Here it is perhaps necessary to question the extent to which today's communities are aware of the meaning of the rituals they practice, or in any case to question what those rituals mean today. They were also manifested in their well-planned architecture, which was laid out in accordance with a cosmological order: pyramids that were also observatories; windows and portholes from which one could observe the first star that appeared in the sky in the afternoon; arches through which one could celebrate the entrance of a solstice.

The experience of a plural, dynamic time was not erased from the Natives' way of being. There is the experience of these cosmovisions in practical terms—what Simón Yampara calls *cosmovivencia*[5]—always subject to changes over time, in the more traditional communities of the highlands *ayllus*, especially in the most remote villages of the Andean puna, where up to this day Spanish is still not spoken. These cosmovisions are also resignified and lived, in various ways, in large cities such as La Paz and El Alto. The information provided by archaeological records must go hand in hand with historical information and an anthropological, ethnological approach to the study of these communities.

Bolivia: An Old Heart Beating like New

Simón Yampara prefers to use the term *cosmovivencia*, and not *cosmovision*, to refer to the relationship of the Aymara-speaking people with their present, past, tradition, and future. Their experience of everyday activities (such as work, the use of new technologies, the purchase of a car or a house) is markedly influenced by respect and reverence for tradition, for the teachings of the past, for the myths that explain reality and, in explaining it, make it simpler. This influence can be seen in many other ethnic/linguistic groups, such as Quichuan and Yampara. There are rituals for everything. To obtain success in the purchase of a house, many people search for a *yatiri*, either in the vicinity of Sagárnaga Street—the famous "street of the witches" in the center of La Paz—or in El Alto or in the diverse *ayllus* that extend along the Plateau of the Collao, the Bolivian highlands, *el altiplano*. They also look for *yatiris* in the great Alasitas fair, perhaps the largest miniature fair ever seen (fig. 5). *Yatiris*, considered heretics in the colonial period, were harshly repressed in the fight against idolatries, as demonstrated by the work of Iris Gareis, who cites an interesting document in a study on this subject:[6]

> Tenian muchos ydolos malquis que son cuerpos difuntos progenitores suyos a quienes dauan culto y beneraçion y otros muchos ydolos comunes y particulares . . . , y Domingo Mirca Capcha docmatiçador ministro de ydolos manifesto tres sepulcros de piedras como a manera de Bóbeda en que estauan tres ydolos malquis . . . que heran cuerpos gentiles y en dho sepulcro estauan nuebe ydolos conopa quatro de forma y manera de Carneritos de la tierra [llamas y alpacas] para aumentos de Carneros de la tierra y otro de hechura de vna maçorca de maiz. . . . Los qual ydolos Referidos mochavan el susso dho Domingo Mirca Capcha Con todos los yndios de su ayllu.

> [They had many malqui [mummy] idols, which are deceased bodies of their ancestors, whom they worshipped and venerated, and other common and particular idols . . . , and Domingo Mirca Capcha, dogmatizer minister of idols, manifested three sepulchers of stones as in the manner of an arch, in which there were three malqui idols . . . which were gentile bodies and in this tomb there were nine Conopa [miniature] idols, four in the form and manner of lambs of the earth [llamas and alpacas], for increases of lambs of the earth, and another in the form of a corn cob. . . . All the Indians of the Ayllu paid the aforementioned Domingo Mirca Capcha for those referred idols.][7]

Today, as in the past, people search for *yatiris* "for increases of lambs of the earth" (llamas)—that is, to obtain meals, material goods, and other items. Even detainees in Bolivian prisons request them.[8] In fact, in her ethnography on Miraflores women's prison in La Paz, Alison Spedding argues that the despair and helplessness felt by all prisoners leads sooner or later to their willingness to perform rituals in search of a positive outcome. The legal and governmental orders are tolerant with respect to the practice of magic, sorcery, and even various types of religions, such as those of *yatiris* and evangelicals, as well as some Catholics who hold masses inside Miraflores.[9]

In the Aymara language, *yatiri* means "the one who knows." Using methods of divination (which include the use of melted lead, the reading of the fall of coca leaves, chiromancy, etc.), the *yatiri* orients consultants in relation to their practical lives. The latter can acquire a miniature house, which will be *ch'allada* by the *yatiri*, between invocations to the *achachilas*—ancestral protective spirits—libations, and the use of incense from wood, seeds, and herbs. *Ch'alla* is a complex concept that goes beyond a Catholic-style blessing. The typical traditional Aymara or Quechua speakers, as well as other linguistic and ethnic communities, live in a world in which the natural and the supernatural coexist, and only the *ch'alla*—the reciprocity involved in the offering—can harmonize them. Through the use of typical herbs such as *k'oa* (*Clinopodium bolivianum*), *palo santo* (*Bursera graveolens*), and the omnipresent coca leaf (*Erythroxylum coca*) in rituals, the *yatiri* seeks to establish a rela-

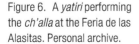

Figure 6. A *yatiri* performing the *ch'alla* at the Feria de las Alasitas. Personal archive.

Figure 7. Aymara *misa* (table), with a llama fetus in the center. Personal archive.

tionship of reciprocity between the client (located in the natural world) and his or her desires, future, and destiny, located in the supernatural world (fig. 6).

Miniatures symbolize the various things, material and immaterial, that the client longs to obtain, and for their effective concretion the *yatiri* arranges them on a table. The sacrifice of the llama, symbolized by the fetus, is ancestral in Andean cultures. The llama is the camelid that has accompanied the settlement of these peoples in the highlands for more than eight thousand years, and has had a fundamental importance in their systematic consumption of proteins. Sacrificing a llama (a source of meat, milk, wool, etc.), in the hardness of the *altiplano*, means to renounce a rich source of subsistence in the hope and faith that the earth, Pachamama, will compensate for it, rewarding the believer with abundance and health (fig. 7).

Through the ritual, the object represented by the miniature symbolizes the concrete object that one wants to obtain. Some proverbs say, in different highlands languages, that you can only see what is in front of you. Because it has already been lived, the past is exposed before our eyes. The future, on the contrary, cannot yet be seen; it is behind our back. It has not yet broken into the wheel of time. A Westerner might think that it is a world impregnated with magic, but an Aymara or Quechua speaker understands these rituals as common phenomena and devoid of any magical element: once the ritual is performed correctly and under the direction of a *yatiri*, it is only a matter of time before reciprocity occurs on the material plane. This is because for the one who realizes this "cosmoliving," the natural and the supernatural are not located in distant extremes; rather, they are part of the same reality, not only in the most solemn moments but also in the minutiae of everyday life. If reciprocity is not achieved, it is a sign that the *yatiri* did not perform well or perhaps that the "case" requires more elaborate rituals. Thus, in the daily life of these communities, the world of the *huacas*, the *achachilas*, and the souls of ancestors are dynamically connected to daily life.

Today in Bolivia we perceive not only a continuity of ancient practices but also a constant reelaboration of these practices. The miniatures referred to in the cited document (the llamas or "carneritos de la tierra") continue to be used, along with others that were used in colonial times (toads, condors, roosters, etc.). Likewise, next to these objects, whose usage and symbolism date back centuries, there are, for instance, miniatures of iPhones, computers, automobiles, modern houses, and bricks for the construction of houses and buildings. All these can be bought and made *ch'allar* by a *yatiri* inside the same Alasitas fair. There are other very interesting types of miniatures sold and *ch'alladas* in the Alasitas and other places destined for rituals: master's and doctoral diplomas in innumerable fields of study, certificates of "good health," family notebooks, marriage certificates, cancellation of debt notices, work contracts, and other documents. These miniatures on paper are often reproductions of the corresponding "official" documents, with university stamps and emblems, bank logos, drawings of couples in wedding gowns, and other depictions. One notices an ability and rapidity in the confection of new miniatures, which always represent material and symbolic longings that have to do with the present moment.

Other Chronos Experiences

In Native American history, from the South of today's United States to the southern Andes, the Amazon region and the Brazilian *sertão*, some periods are considered particularly nefarious because they closed a cycle and foreshadowed the beginning of a new time when nothing was predictable and cosmic harmony had to be recaptured through rituals, which sometimes included animal and/or collective human sacrifices. In April 2018 the remains of 140 children and 200 llamas were found on Huanchaquito beach, near the Peruvian city of Trujillo. The findings date back 550 years, in an area then inhabited by Chimus. There is evidence of dislocated ribs and cuts in the sternums of the children, suggesting that the chests of the victims were opened and separated to facilitate removal of the hearts.[10] The sacrificed llamas in this same ritual were brought from the highest lands; in fact, the footprints that have been found make us suppose that they were dragged by force to the place of sacrifice. It did not take long for the Incas to invade the Chimu kingdom, and perhaps this unusual ritual had been anticipated by the Chimus, as the Incas were known to be powerful and to have forced many peoples into submission.

The Spanish conquerors barely managed to erase the paths and footprints of powerful ancient civilizations. It is true that fertile valleys—where once corn, peanuts, and beans were planted and harvested—were transformed into deserts, as peasants were enslaved, transferred to haciendas, or held captive in the feared mines. Rarely would they return home from *mitayo* work or be reunited with their families. The Andean *mita* separated them in the deepest sense from family, destroying their blood relationships and also their familiarity with a language, a social code, and a way of being.

The Natives were defeated materially, because their roads, houses, and *huacas* were, for the most part, destroyed or looted. They were also defeated spiritually, because a new way of thinking was imposed on them, a "correct," "civilized," Christian way of thinking, while the way of life of their parents and grandparents was demonized throughout the centuries. From time to time, however, one can perceive the influence of older cultures. Although there have been areas such as the Mantaro Valley, where those who helped in the conquest were granted certain privileges as chiefs, such was not the case for most Natives. Here a comparison could be drawn with Mexico, and with Tlaxcala in particular.[11]

The antiquity of South America is perceived not only through material vestiges but also perhaps through the fundamental ways of being of the new American societies. In countries or regions in which Native traditions are still deeply rooted—as in the Andes, in some areas of North and Central America, and in some areas of the Amazon Basin—societies are true laboratories that allow us to investigate and conjecture about their remote past: languages such as Quechua, Aymara, Urú, Guaraní, and Nahuatl give us countless clues to how these peoples have organized their communal life, thinking, kinship blood relationships, and religiosity. The presence of numerous verb tenses to refer to the past, present, and future; the agglutinating languages that continually allow new words and ideas to be constructed through suffixes; the analysis of personal pronouns of so many types; the countless words to designate blood relationships—all these are keys to reading and rereading the past as well as the present of these populations, in the long duration of their existence. Alfredo Torero and his pioneering studies, especially on linguistic transformations, shed valuable light with respect to the forms of expansion/migration and the depth of colonial rule.[12]

The imposition of temporary regimes on the Natives has been inscribed in all the forms of sociability lived in the American colonies since the time of the invasions and colonization. In the new temporary regimes, they ultimately made Natives believe that they had no antiquity, only bones and fragments of a primitive epoch that, due to ethnocentric prejudice, was deemed to have no value. Today the antiquity of South America is studied in public schools. It is true that Brazil is, at present, the most backward country on the continent in this sense, especially since it removed the obligatory teaching of the history of Indigenous and African-descendant peoples from the public school curriculum.[13] It is necessary to resist this conservative wave of attempts to impose, semantically and hermeneutically, the values of the colonial era, with the Eurocentric discourse that Native Americans have no history, no religion, no laws, and no importance in a globalized liberal world. We need to recognize this unique and fascinating antiquity by teaching, studying, researching, and publicizing it from anthropological, religious, linguistic, technological, and cultural points of view—most important, because it is not merely the past but also the present: many cultures continue to rework, feel, and intensively live these ancient traditions.

In this sense, any work on South American history, anthropology, and archaeology that draws attention to the antiquity of this continent is also a manifesto that recovers the dignity of the descendants of Native American peoples. Far from being an ideological study or reconstruction, it is rather an exercise of alterity and respect for the other, a resignification and creative reconsideration of fundamental questions regarding the historical trajectory of Native American people. The time has come to be mature enough to tell the complete history, as we have the technical and intellectual tools to face this task.

ALEXANDRE BELMONTE is adjunct professor of history of ancient and colonial America at the Universidade do Estado do Rio de Janeiro (State University of Rio de Janeiro; UERJ). He is also professor in the Post-Graduation Program in History at UERJ and collaborating professor in the Post-Graduation Program in International Relations at UERJ and in the Post-Graduation in Ancient History at Núcleo de Estudos da Antiguidade, UERJ, where he teaches archaeology and ancient history of America. He is also collaborating professor in the Programa de Investigación y Docencia "Relaciones Internacionales, Globalización y Política Exterior" (lato sensu) at the Centro de Estudios Avanzados en Ciencias Sociales of the Universidad Nacional de Córdoba, Argentina. His research centers on the material culture of Indigenous peoples who participated in Andean uprisings in the late eighteenth century.

Notes

1   Villagrán, *Ciencia indígena de Los Andes del norte de Chile.*
2   Seda, "Sociedades sem história."
3   Meggers, *América pré-histórica*, 101–8.
4   Bouysse-Cassagne, "As minas de ouro dos incas."
5   Yampara Huarachi, "Cosmovivencia andina."
6   Cf. Gareis, "Extirpación de idolatrías e identidad cultural."
7   "Información y testimonio de la visita de idolatrías en Cajatambo," Los Reyes (Lima), November 22, 1664, cited in Gareis, "Extirpación de idolatrías e identidad cultural," n. 53.
8   Spedding, *La segunda vez como farsa.*
9   Spedding, *La segunda vez como farsa.*
10   "Nueva investigación arqueológica en sitio donde hallaron restos de 140 niños."
11   Manrique, *Vinieron los sarracenos.*
12   Torero Fernández de Córdova, "Los dialectos quechuas."
13   This was one of the measures of the education reform promoted by Michel Temer in Law 13.415 of February 16, 2017. In fact, it was one of his first acts as president of Brazil.

Works Cited

Bouysse-Cassagne, Thérèse. "As minas de ouro dos incas, o Sol e as culturas do Collasuyu." In *As minas e o cotidiano do mineral: Experiências humanas coloniais*, edited by Alexandre Belmonte and Christine Hunefeldt, 15–51. Rio de Janeiro: Estudos Americanos, 2018.

Gareis, Iris. "Extirpación de idolatrías e identidad cultural en las sociedades andinas del Perú virreinal (siglo XVII)." *Boletín de antropología* (Medellín, Colombia), no. 35 (2004): 262–82.

Manrique, Nelson. *Vinieron los sarracenos: El universo mental de la conquista de América.* Lima: Centro de Estudios y Promoción del Desarrollo, 1993.

Meggers, Betty. *América pré-histórica.* Rio de Janeiro: Paz e Terra, 1979.

"Nueva investigación arqueológica en sitio donde hallaron restos de 140 niños." www .arqueologiadelperu.com/nueva-investigacion -arqueologica-en-sitio-donde-hallaron-restos-de -140-ninos/?print=pdf (accessed August 15, 2019).

Seda, Paulo R. G. "Sociedades sem história: Por uma história antiga da América." In *América: Visões e versões—identidades em confronto*, edited by Maria Teresa Toribio Brittes Lemos and Alexis Toribio Dantas. Rio de Janeiro: 7Letras, 2010.

Spedding, Alison. *La segunda vez como farsa: Etnografía de una cárcel de mujeres en Bolivia.* La Paz: Editorial Mama Huaco, 2008.

Torero Fernández de Córdova, Alfredo A. "Los dialectos quechuas." *Anales científicos de la Universidad Agraria* (Lima) 2, no. 4 (1964): 446–78.

Villagrán, Carolina. *Ciencia indígena de los Andes del norte de Chile.* Santiago de Chile: Editorial Universitaria, 2004.

Yampara Huarachi, Simón. "Cosmovivencia andina: Vivir y convivir en armonía integral— *Suma Qamaña*." *Bolivian Studies Journal/ Revista de estudios bolivianos* 18 (2011). bsj.pitt .edu/ojs/index.php/bsj/article/download/42 /394.

Narrative of Origin and Utopia in Lucrecia Martel's *Nueva Argirópolis*

LEILA GÓMEZ

Abstract   This article offers a reading of Lucrecia Martel's film short *Nueva Argirópolis* (2010) in light of Domingo F. Sarmiento's treatise *Argirópolis* (1850). Both Sarmiento's text and Martel's film address the question of landownership, river navigation, and the inequal distribution of territorial and national wealth. *Nueva Argirópolis* is one part of a cinematographic project that brought together twenty-five directors for the occasion of the bicentennial of the Argentine revolution. Martel's eight-minute story takes as its point of departure the ideas of Sarmiento, one of the founders of the nation: through her fiction, she tells how original Argentine peoples adopted Sarmiento's proposal. In speaking of her inspiration for the film, Martel refers to both her work and Sarmiento's as bold texts that fall within the genre of science fiction. The present essay considers the reasons for the audacity of the proposals in both texts and, at the same time, why both were unsuccessful.

Keywords   Lucrecia Martel, Qom, Argirópolis, Sarmiento

In 2010 the Qom community of Formosa, Argentina, claiming ownership of the fifteen hundred acres where they lived as well as their right to potable water, carried out a roadblock of Interstate 86, which in turn was violently removed by the state police and federal army. Qom houses were burned, and their leader, Roberto López, was killed.[1]

The short film *Nueva Argirópolis* (2010), by Lucrecia Martel, shows in eight minutes a series of scenes in which a few members of the Qom or Tobas community in the Argentine region of Chaco embark on a raft trip on the Bermejo River with the aim of reaching certain uninhabited, unclaimed islands in the Paraná's delta. Their attempt fails when they are apprehended by federal authorities. Some scenes show the detention process and the intention of the police to determine the reason for this unusual trip. Other scenes reveal that the voyagers belong to a group of people that has been summoned by an Indigenous leader who transmits a message of liberation on YouTube. This message is partly translated by two girls who

ENGLISH LANGUAGE NOTES

58:1, April 2020   DOI 10.1215/00138282-8237443
© 2020 Regents of the University of Colorado

understand it but decide not to reveal it completely to the police. It bears noting here that the raft is made of plastic bottles tied together and that the travelers go under the raft to hide. In another scene, the geological formation of these islands and the role the river plays in their formation are explained in a school lesson. The Qom peoples inhabit mainly the northernmost region of Argentina, and therefore the short movie was filmed in the provinces of Corrientes, Chaco, and Salta.[2]

For the bicentennial of the revolution against the Spanish empire, the Argentine government summoned twenty-five film directors to shoot eight-minute short films that ended up forming a two-hundred-minute mosaic of styles and voices.[3] These short films were screened in more than 125 theaters across the country. With respect to the inspiration and idea for the film, Martel refers to her story, which is fictional, as a conspiracy:

The Confederation of Rivers

A conspiracy. News clips about something that would be happening upstream of Buenos Aires. It is a fictional story, partly inspired by Sarmiento's *Argirópolis*. In 1850 Sarmiento proposed creating a capital on Martín García Island for the Confederation composed of Uruguay, Paraguay and Argentina. And in that same text he writes about the importance of the navigability of rivers. I was always struck by the audacity of that political text. *Nueva Argirópolis* is inspired by that audacity. We liked the pretense of founding a space that is a new social order. Science fiction would be the genre, I think. The distant islands, the unknown languages. Fragments of a foundational movement.[4]

At first glance, one might situate *Nueva Argirópolis* within two popular genres of contemporary cinema: ethnographic cinema created by directors who do not belong to Native communities,[5] and environmentalist cinema, specifically the subgenre that focuses on the topic of water, its pollution, and its privatization.[6] Nonetheless, my reading aims to highlight other aspects of the short that are also relevant to its interpretation and that to some extent question its potential classification in the aforementioned genres. My reading is based on two key clues Martel herself gives in the interview excerpt cited above, in which she describes and explains the history of *Nueva Argirópolis*. First, merely from the film's title we can see a strong reference to Domingo Faustino Sarmiento's treatise *Argirópolis* (1850) and suppose that through the name *Nueva Argirópolis* Martel is proposing a reconsideration, a reinterpretation, and even a parody of the text written by Sarmiento, the intellectual who coined the binomial "civilization and barbarism" to refer to the opposition between European and non-European cultures and values.[7] However, this would be an incomplete reading, in my opinion, given the complexity of Martel's cinema, its keen cultural reflection, and also Sarmiento's text itself. Contrary to what critics have pointed out, *Argirópolis* is not just a text about civilization and barbarism but in addition an analysis and a solution to a historical, economic, and political drama at the very foundation of the Argentine state.[8]

The second of Martel's clues is precisely her choice not to mention the protagonists of her story even once in her description of the movie. She only mentions

Sarmiento. In so doing, she distinguishes herself from the other directors of the twenty-five shorts, such as Pablo Trapero, who, in describing his short film *Nómade*, speaks precisely of the debt of the Argentine state and society to their original peoples, many of whom are now impoverished and "confused," living in the cities:[9] "For the indigenous peoples, what did the independence mean, what does Argentina mean today, what has it given them and how much has the revolution, carried out by criollos and former colonizers, taken away from them?"[10] By contrast, Martel talks about the audacity of a book and science fiction.

Why is Sarmiento's *Argirópolis* an audacious text? Why is Martel's story of *Nueva Argirópolis* also audacious? What is it that leads these texts to be classified as science fiction? Let's start by analyzing the audacity of *Argirópolis*. In 1850, prior to the formation of Argentina, the Confederation of Rio de la Plata states had neither a congress nor a constitution nor laws to rule the navigation of its rivers. The only customs house was that of the port of Buenos Aires, which enriched itself through foreign trade, importing and exporting goods and regulating market prices, and thus impoverishing the provinces of the interior, particularly those distant to Buenos Aires. The transportation of goods was done mainly overland, which increased both their cost and their losses. This manner of commerce proved a great source of conflict between Buenos Aires and the provinces, especially those with rivers that flow into the River Plate, which naturally disputed the customs centralism of Buenos Aires. In *Argirópolis* Sarmiento writes of the necessity to undo the customs monopoly of Buenos Aires and to create a congress as well as laws that would promote the free navigation of other rivers, such as the Paraná and the Bermejo, in the transfer of goods. To do so, he argued, it was also necessary to establish a new customs office, one that would not benefit only one province but would be strategically located at the junction of several rivers with access to the River Plate and thus take advantage of trade. In Sarmiento's estimation in 1850, this strategic location was on Martín García Island.[11] Sarmiento himself called this island Argirópolis. He proposed that this island belong not to one country but instead to the three interested in navigating the rivers that led to it: Argentina, Paraguay, and Uruguay. In his view, the creation of *Argirópolis* would also put an end to the internal wars of the confederation and to conflicts with bordering countries, which would then become unified against a common enemy, Brazil.

Argirópolis is thus a text about the modernization of river navigation, the demonopolization of customs revenues, and the breakdown of regional hierarchies. It is a text about the equal distribution of wealth throughout the Argentine national territory. In addition, it is a text that proposes a way of resolving international conflicts. Sarmiento's essay is visionary, audacious, and therefore, unsuccessful.

The story of *Nueva Argirópolis* is also audacious in that it tells of an Indigenous conspiracy to reclaim land that the Qom own yet that has been displaced by the currents of the rivers. The members of this conspiracy seek to promote the Argirópolis utopia and occupy the islands formed by silt that comes from the Bermejo to where it meets the Paraná, upriver from Martín García Island. These are lands that do not belong to anyone, as the girl says in the school lesson in the film, yet her use of the word *anyone* could be perceived as a reference to the invisibility of the original peoples.[12] The choice of location is no accident. The land displaced from the Bermejo to the Paraná is the land inhabited by the Qom and other Indigenous peoples, who, like the silt displaced by the river, are forced to migrate to other cities. These islands are also located in a strategic position that antagonizes the domain of Buenos Aires, the Argentine capital, in economic and geopolitical terms and therefore the entire national structure. This antagonism is not explicit in the short film. However, this is clear if the film is read on the palimpsest of Sarmiento's *Argirópolis*. Remarking on this geographic place, from where this trip and conspiracy are conceived, Martel explains:

> I spent about five years studying the mechanics of the river, the delta, the Paraná; I am very envious of this river that you have here. . . . It happens that this color that your river has is thanks to us, the people from Salta: Why? Because the river that reddens the Paraná is the Bermejo—which is, I do not know if it is the second or third in the world in terms of sedimentary load— and all that land that brings the Bermejo River (it is called Bermejo because it carries red soil; it is a red, red, red river)—all that land of the Bermejo River comes out of the Iruya River basin, in the region of the Collas communities. . . . With the summer rains this Bermejo River is loaded with sediment, and if you, who doubt it is so, think this is Salta chauvinism, then travel past Corrientes, go farther, and when you reach the confluence of the Bermejo and the Paraná rivers and then go to the Paraguay River, you will clearly notice the differences in color. Then, with this idea of science fiction, that all the sediments that the Paraná River brings (if you see the movie you will say [that is] completely incomprehensible; eight minutes is hardly enough to explain all this). Then, the sediments that come from the Paraná River settle in the delta, where the current slows down because the depth changes . . . and because of the kind of plug that the sea applies to the water of the Paraná, carrying the soil that we send you down from Salta. Then . . . —this was the theory—deltas are the only places in the world, with the exception of a few volcanic islands, where new lands appear, lands that belong to no one. Well, they are from the countries that contain the deltas, but whose exactly is the new land that appears? Almost 90 meters of new land appears every year; the delta is growing. . . . And the idea was that this new land was the only land without a conflict—that's why they [the Indigenous people] went there. What naiveté! But of course, it was a naive time.[13]

Sarmiento wanted Martín García, an island that "belonged to no one," to be the center of government for the new republic. The Indigenous people of northern Argentina want to move to these new islands to inhabit lands that "belong to no one" but are formed from the land they currently inhabit. What also is addressed in the film, therefore, is the entwined relationship of land and water: the two are inseparable because it is impossible in Indigenous communities to fight for one and not the other.

Thus the film shows a new story of origin, of both the land's inhabitation and its possession. It is a story that also speaks of a new beginning, a new life cycle, and a new opportunity for survival, in a kind of promised and mythical land. It is, in this way, a story that focuses on the heart of the problem of land for the Indigenous in relation to the nation and addresses their subordination and submission, their dislocations and migrations. The characters who are part of the conspiracy reflect on this condition in Spanish and in Qom: "All those who speak in Wichí, Mocobí, Ilarrá, Toba, Guaraní. All poor. What, will we all be fools?" In appropriating Sarmiento's *Argirópolis*, the film foregrounds a historical conflict that has much relevance today and, like Sarmiento's essay, proposes a solution that is bold yet destined to fail.

The leader of the conspiracy transmits her message on YouTube. It is she who gives the name Nueva Argirópolis to the islands, citing not only Sarmiento but also the Argentine national anthem. Her message is in the native language and thus impossible to decipher for the police who apprehend the navigators of the plastic bottle raft. They task two girls with translating the message: "Let us go to the rafts. Let us uphold noble equality. Let us distinguish 'indigenous' from 'indigent.' Let us not be afraid to move. We are invisible." What's curious is not only that the youngest are the sole ones capable of translating the message—since we know that the language is no longer learned by the new generations—but also that the message itself is directed toward a diverse linguistic community. The other characters' mention of the Wichí, Mocobí, Illará, Toba, and Guaraní languages suggests conformation to a panlinguistic community, as opposed to subjugation to the monolingualism of the nation-state.

According to Darko Suvin and Patrick Parrinder, science fiction's main characteristic is the novum, validated by "cognitive estrangement." Scientific findings that diverge from what is known have inspired science fiction writers to propose worlds that, based on these new findings, expand beyond scientific proof. This is the novum.[14] In Martel's short film, the science that explains the forming of new land through the sedimentation at the rivers' confluence inspires the fictional narrative of new possible landownership by the Qom people. It also inspires the conspirative movement of Indigenous communities that project their utopian ideals onto the new (is)lands.

In combining scientific facts pertaining to nature with both fiction and utopia, the story adopts key characteristics of science fiction. "Utopia has always been a political issue," posits Fredric Jameson in *Archaeologies of the Future*.[15] These new islands, like Martín García, would be what Ernst Bloch, in *The Principle of Hope*, would call "utopian enclaves"—that is, new spatial and social totalities.[16] In the film the appellation *Argirópolis* and the national anthem are also references to the (national) past, to a way of imagining the historical underpinnings of the present. Jameson's proposal offers a valuable perspective on this history; in his view, the fundamental dynamic of a political utopia rests on a dialectic of identity and difference. The reality imagined in the film is inspired by the one imagined by Sarmiento. Jameson says: "On the social level, it means that our imaginations are hostages to our own mode of production. . . . It suggests that at best utopia can serve the negative purpose of making us more aware of our mental and ideological imprisonment—and that therefore the best utopias are those that fail the most comprehensively."[17] In this way, the new Argirópolis is trapped in its own "ideological imprisonment" and fails, making us more conscious of the historical drama of land dispossession. This failure imparts a sense of tragedy to the arrest of the conspirators as well as to the last scene of the short film, where we see a movement of people who, apparently, intend to continue the conspiracy. We see schoolchildren perhaps returning home and the conspirators also walking along the same riverbank, perhaps toward the raft that will take them to the new islands. The nonlinearity of the film and its temporal fragmentations are proof that the conspiratorial attempt is no isolated event but a repetitive or cyclical one in a dialectic of hope and failure.

Toward the end of his text Sarmiento stresses that the creation of a new customs and administrative center would help bring about the end of the nation's domestic strife as well as the end of wars with Paraguay and Uruguay. In this way the national army would have more resources to wage war against Indigenous peoples. The principal objective of these frontier wars was expansion of the national territory toward the lands of the Indigenous communities:

> Between the river to the south, the Paraná to the east, and the Bermejo to the
> north lies an extension of land of more than four thousand six hundred square
> leagues that has not yet been occupied, and although this country is flooded
> in many places and dry in others, the State needs to occupy it to drive the
> barbarians back to the north bank of the Bermejo, and clear the lines of
> communication between Jujuy, Salta, Tucumán and Santiago del Estero with
> Corrientes, Paraguay and Entre Ríos. The fact that it has been inhabited by
> the Indians shows that the Christian population can thrive there.[18]

Nonetheless, Martín García Island did not become an administrative center, nor did the navigation of the Bermejo to the Paraná modernize or enrich that region of the country. Nor did the situation of the Indigenous peoples improve. In 1870, when Sarmiento became president, Martín García Island functioned as a detention center for the Indigenous kidnapped in the military campaigns against them. Mariano Nagy and Alexis Papazian have discovered records of five hundred Native Americans in the general archive of the army, including women and children, who between 1871 and 1886 were held in what Nagy and Papazian have called the concentration camp of the island. These Indigenous people were detained and kept there before, during, and after the military campaigns in La Pampa, Patagonia, and Chaco. Today Martín García Island is a nature reserve.[19]

In placing her film inside the sphere of science fiction and foundational fiction, Martel explains, she is opting not to delineate the struggle of the original inhabitants involved, because doing so is unnecessary. Sarmiento's text *Argirópolis*, Martín García Island, the unclaimed islands, the silt of the Bermejo, the multilingualism of her characters, the conspiracy, and the short dialogues all make reference to both the political history of the Qom and the Argentine nation itself. The land she depicts acquires both mythic connotations and multiple layers of meaning in the context of the nation's founding. It is the utopian geography of an unsuccessful conspiracy, of an unfulfilled hope. In this failure one can nevertheless appreciate what Jameson observes in the best utopias: those that make us aware that our ways of imagining the future cannot be extricated from either our past or our present. Martel's story is the story of the land question itself, precisely what Mariátegui in 1928 asserted to be the "Indian's problem." In eight minutes Martel recovers the history of more than five centuries of colonization that continued with the Argentine nation and still persists today.

LEILA GÓMEZ is associate professor of Spanish and director of the Latin American Studies Center at the University of Colorado Boulder. Among her books are *Iluminados y tránsfugas: Relatos de viajeros y ficciones fundacionales en Argentina, Paraguay y Perú* (2009) and the edited collection *Darwin in Argentina (Major Texts, 1845–1909)* (2011). She is also coeditor of *Entre Borges y Conrad: Estética y territorio en W. H. Hudson* (2012) and *Teaching Gender through Latin American, Spanish, and Latino Literature and Culture* (2015). Gómez is writing a book about the mythical image of Mexico in travel writing of the nineteenth to the twenty-first centuries. For this book project she was awarded the Alexander von Humboldt Fellowship for Advanced Researchers in Germany.

Notes

1   The same year, the Qom community carried out a protest in Buenos Aires, the Argentine capital, to garner national attention. They demanded the restoration of their land and the liberation of many of their imprisoned leaders. Despite months of camping outside the national government house, they were never granted a meeting with the government. In 2015 this protest continued, with the same result (*Política*, "La 'mala memoria' de Cristina").

2   The Qom (alternatively referred to as the Toba) comprise one of the largest indigenous groups in Argentina, with more than 120,000 Qom living in the country today. (In all South America close to 130,000 people currently identify as Toba or Qom.) Prior to and during the colonial period, the Qom resided in the Central Chaco region. Today they live in northern Argentina, in the Salta, Chaco, Santiago del Estero, and Formosa provinces. Due to persecution, many have migrated to the suburbs of Buenos Aires and other major cities. Like other indigenous groups in South America, the Qom have persisted, since the Spanish settlers' arrival, through a long history of discrimination, conflict, and land struggles.

3   This project, titled *25 miradas, 200 minutos* (2010), includes films of several major Argentine directors, such as Carlos Sorín, Pablo Trapero, Albertina Carri, and Lucrecia Martel.

4   Martel, "Los cortos sobre la historia argentina por sus directores."

5   In contemporary Latin American cinema one can find several notable examples of ethnographic movies, such as Ciro Guerra's *Embrace of the Serpent* (Colombia, 2015), Jayro Bustamante's *Ixcanul* (Guatemala, 2015), Sebastián Sepúlveda's *Quispe Girls* (Chile, 2014), and Claudia Llosa's *Madeinusa* (Peru, 2015). These films are focused on Indigenous characters and situations and are partly or completely shot in Indigenous languages but directed and produced by non-Indigenous people.

6   Some films, such as Ernesto Cabellos's documentary *The Daughter of the Lake* (Peru, 2015) and Icíar Bollaín's *Even the Rain* (Spain and Bolivia, 2010), focus on environmental issues, in particular the pollution and privatization of water on the lands of Indigenous families and communities.

7   In "Lucrecia Martel's *Nueva Argirópolis*" Deborah Martin quotes the critics Lorena Amaro Castro and Ruth Hill, who propose a reading of Sarmiento's text through the lens of civilization and barbarism. My reading differs from theirs and focuses on Sarmiento's proposal as revolutionary—or "audacious," as Martel puts it.

8   Domingo F. Sarmiento (1811–88) was a writer, teacher, and politician and the founder of the Argentine nation.

9   "La cámara, en un movimiento continuo, acompaña el viaje del personaje más afectado por esta confusión: Tonolec, el descendiente de indígenas tobas que participa de la filmación, y que pasa del set cruzando la autopista—esa realidad que tiene tan poco que ver con sus raíces—a su realidad actual, al barrio humilde

en el que vive, para luego llevar las sobras del catering de la filmación a un comedor comunitario. Nómade se presenta al espectador también como una experiencia sensorial. El hipnótico movimiento sigue a Tonolec y deja adivinar cómo él y sus ancestros han quedado perdidos, enredados en la historia" (The camera, in a continuous movement, tracks the journey of the character most affected by this confusion, Tonolec, the descendant of Indigenous Tobas, who took part in the filming, and what happens on the set as he crosses the highway—this reality that has so little to do with his roots—to his present reality, to the poor neighborhood where he lives, in order to bring the catering leftovers from the filming to a community dining hall. Nómade also engages the viewer with a sensory experience. The hypnotic movement follows Tonolec and leaves the audience wondering how he and his ancestors have been forgotten, entangled in history) (Trapero, "Los cortos sobre la historia argentina por sus directores").

10   "Para los pueblos originarios, ¿qué significó la Independencia, qué significa hoy día la Argentina, qué les ha dado y cuánto les ha quitado la Revolución protagonizada por criollos y antiguos colonizadores?" (Trapero, "Los cortos sobre la historia argentina por sus directores").

11   See, for example, the map at mapsof.net /argentina/riodelaplata.

12   "Cuando llueve el agua baja. Lleva toda esa tierra al río Iruya. De ahí va al Bermejo, al Paraná y llega al Río de la Plata. Como ahí merma la velocidad, se asienta la tierra y se van formando . . . ¡islas!" (When it rains, the water descends. It carries an enormous quantity of dirt to the Iruya River. From the Iruya it goes to the Bermejo, then to the Paraná and finally to the River Plate. Since at that point its velocity decreases, all of this dirt sinks and becomes sediment, slowly forming . . . islands!) (*Nueva Argirópolis*, 4:01–4:16).

13   Martel and Llosa, "Pensar con imágenes."

14   Parrinder, *Learning from Other Worlds*.

15   Jameson, *Archaeologies of the Future*, xi.

16   Bloch, *Principle of Hope*, 763.

17   Jameson, *Archaeologies of the Future*, xii–xiii.

18   Sarmiento, *Argirópolis*, 178–79.

19   Nagy and Papazian, "El campo de concentración de Martín García."

Works Cited

Amaro Castro, Lorena. "La América reinventada: Notas sobre la utopía de la 'civilización' en *Argirópolis*, de Domingo Faustino Sarmiento." *Revista de estudios literarios* 25 (2003). pendientedemigracion.ucm.es/info/especulo /numero25/argiropo.html.

Bloch, Ernst. *The Principle of Hope*. Vol. 2. Cambridge, MA: MIT Press, 1995.

Hill, Ruth. "Ariana Crosses the Atlantic: An Archaeology of Aryanism in the Nineteenth-Century River Plate." In "Troubled Waters: Rivers in Latin American Imagination," edited by Elizabeth M. Pettinaroli and Ana María Mutis. Special issue, *Hispanic Issues On Line* (2013): 92–110. hispanicissues.umn.edu/assets /doc/05_HILL.pdf.

Jameson, Fredric. *Archaeologies of the Future: The Desire Called Utopia and Other Science Fictions*. London: Verso, 2005.

Mariátegui, José Carlos. *Siete ensayos de interpretación de la realidad peruana*. Lima: Biblioteca Amauta, 1928.

Martel, Lucrecia. "Los cortos sobre la historia argentina por sus directores." *Página/12*, October 3, 2010. www.pagina12.com.ar/diario /suplementos/radar/9-6511-2010-10-03.html.

Martel, Lucrecia, and Claudia Llosa. "Pensar con imágenes." Santa Fe Debate Ideas. Uploaded December 17, 2018. www.youtube.com/watch ?v=odi9ZvvxL9I.

Martin, Deborah. "Lucrecia Martel's *Nueva Argirópolis*: Rivers, Rumours, and Resistance." *Journal of Latin American Cultural Studies* 25, no. 3 (2016): 449–65.

Nagy, Mariano, and Alexis Papazian. "El campo de concentración de Martín García: Entre el control estatal dentro de la isla y las prácticas de distribución de indígenas (1871–1886)." *Corpus: Archivos virtuales de la alternidad americana* 1, no. 2 (2011). journals.openedition .org/corpusarchivos/1176.

Parrinder, Patrick. *Learning from Other Worlds: Estrangement, Cognition, and the Politics of Science Fiction and Utopia*. Liverpool: Liverpool University Press, 2010.

Política. "La 'mala memoria' de Cristina: 'Nunca hubo persecución y judicialización a los qom.'" September 21, 2017. www .laizquierdadiario.com/La-mala-memoria-de -Cristina-Nunca-hubo-persecucion-y -judicializacion-a-los-qom.

Sarmiento, Domingo Faustino. *Argirópolis*. Buenos Aires: La Cultura Argentina, 1916.

Trapero, Pablo. "Los cortos sobre la historia argentina por sus directores." *Página/12*, October 3, 2010. www.pagina12.com.ar/diario /suplementos/radar/9-6511-2010-10-03.html.

Yotsi'tsishon and the Language of the Seed in the Haudenosaunee Story of Earth's Creation

AMBER MEADOW ADAMS

Abstract   Kanyen'keha and Onoñda'gega' versions of the Haudenosaunee story of Earth's creation transcribed in the late 1880s by J. N. B. Hewitt contain ethnobotanical detail not present in many other recorded versions of the story. They also, especially the version told by Skanyatarí:yo John Arthur Gibson, build nuanced actors and articulate the negotiations of relationship through dialogue, imagery, and arcs of naming. Using close readings of these versions, I argue that the narrative arc of biome, as described through ethnobotanical detail, and of the story's dynamic actors, as described through the poetic devices present in fuller versions, inform one another. The intersection of these arcs encodes a matrix of human responses to catastrophic climate change specific to the narrative's home biome.

Keywords   Haudenosaunee, Indigenous languages, ecology, ethnobotany

In the summer of 1888, a young man from Tuscarora, fresh on the job at the newly formed Bureau of American Ethnology (BAE),[1] sat down in a small, smoky house at Six Nations, land deeded to His Majesty's allies the Haudenosaunee on the Grand River in present-day Ontario.[2] Over the course of two years, when the young man, John Napoleon Brinton Hewitt, could get away from the BAE in Washington, DC, for what he learned to call "fieldwork" and his host would almost certainly have called "visits,"[3] he was told a story about the beginnings of life on Earth. The storyteller, Skanyatarí:yo John Arthur Gibson, was blind, his sightlessness trained into memory by women and men of his grandparents' generation who had brought their knowledge and their history from the Haudenosaunee heartland of New York State, at the end of the War of American Independence, up to the Grand River lands in Canada.[4]

The story Skanyatarí:yo[5] told Hewitt remains the longest known written version of the Haudenosaunee story of Earth's creation. At 164 manuscript pages, its length exceeds that of the next three longest versions combined, those Hewitt published as *Iroquoian Cosmology* in 1903. The Kanyen'keha (Mohawk-language)

ENGLISH LANGUAGE NOTES

58:1, April 2020   DOI 10.1215/00138282-8237454
© 2020 Regents of the University of Colorado

version retold by Dayodekane Seth Newhouse, at half as many pages, represents the next longest. Of the approximately forty published versions of this story, Skanyatarí:yo's presents not only exceptional richness of detail but a store of ethnobotanical data. Twenty-eight distinct plant species appear in roughly 130 distinct narrative moments, averaging just over 1.2 mentions per page. Other ethnographic work from this era catalogs Haudenosaunee ethnobotany, notably that of Frederick Wilkerson Waugh, whose field notes taken for the Canadian Geological Survey were published, in heavily edited form, as *Iroquois Foods and Food Preparation* in 1916.[6] However, despite the bonanza for collection characterizing the ethnography of the late nineteenth and early twentieth centuries, no other published source in the field of Haudenosaunee studies integrates the ethnobotanical and the narrative as comprehensively as Skanyatarí:yo's version of the Haudenosaunee story of Creation.

Despite the richness of the source, scholarship treating it has been limited.[7] Hewitt's own was the earliest and, perhaps, the most exhaustive work. Though he transcribed Skanyatarí:yo's version first among the four he published, a full thirty-nine years of editing and translation lay between the end of his work on this story with Skanyatarí:yo in 1889 and his publication of it as *Iroquoian Cosmology, Second Part* in 1928.[8] William N. Fenton, Hewitt's successor in his post at the BAE, offers a brief comparison of these versions' plot points in "This Island, the World on Turtle's Back" (1962). Joseph Campbell retells the story with an accompanying meta-analysis of its place in the mythology of other "primitive planters" in *Mythologies of the Primitive Planters: The Northern Americas* (1989).[9] In 2005 Sotsisowah John C. Mohawk, Onöndowa:'ga:' (Seneca) scholar, published *John Arthur Gibson's "Myth of the Earth Grasper,"* an edited version of Hewitt's English free translation of Skanyatarí:yo's Onoñda'gega' (Onondaga) retelling.[10] Sotsisowah's introduction examines some of the historiography of the version, including a reading of Hewitt's own narrative motives in crafting *Myth of the Earth Grasper*. Ahkwesashne scholar Kevin J. White's 2007 doctoral thesis "Haudenosaunee Worldviews through Iroquoian Cosmologies" and 2013 article "Rousing a Curiosity in Hewitt's Iroquois Cosmologies" compare Hewitt's and earlier versions, with emphasis on distinctly Onöndowa:'ga:' narrative differences.[11] Although valuable in building a historiography of the story's variations and addressing the complexities of a culture of orality that remains wary of the canonical (even when its stories are reduced to text), most scholarship to date has addressed Skanyatarí:yo's (and his peers') work in translation.[12] Thus it has mostly avoided language-based interpretations of narrative meaning and their implications, especially where verb morphology encodes relational matrices.

Here I offer a reading of Skanyatarí:yo's and Dayodekane's versions of the Haudenosaunee story of creation that addresses those matrices, specifically in relation to local ecology. Building on the theoretical work I present in my doctoral thesis "Teyotsi'tsiahsonhátye," I argue that the sequential appearance of plant species indigenous to the Haudenosaunee home biome represents an arc of ecological succession that defines the story as not one of a first emergence of life, but as one of the reemergence of life following catastrophic ecological loss.[13] Against this arc, I read the Onoñda'gega' and Kanyen'keha poetics of the protagonist's naming as it—again, sequentially—changes through the narrative's arc. These concentric arcs of personal and biomic loss and (re)creation present a model for ecological recovery after catastrophic loss within a specific biome. Further, they present a model for intra- and interpersonal recovery from such loss as an adaptational strategy to ecological catastrophe.

Within the narrative, the indigenous plant species that appear in the Skanyatarí:yo and Dayodekane versions work, before all else, to locate the audience. Anchoring creation narratives in a specific geographic location is a common feature of what are often, in the context of criticism, called cosmologies not only among Indigenous nations but, more broadly, within what might be called the religions of text.[14] Although in other Haudenosaunee narratives fixed geographic locations or features do appear, the story of creation distinguishes itself, even within its own internarrative context, by emphasizing biome over place. This ecotype, in Canada, is called the Carolinian biome; in the United States, the Laurentian Mixed Forest ecoregion, with some areas of Adirondack–New England Mixed Forest. This temperate deciduous forest grows in deep, fine-loamy soils and is defined by the presence of hardwood species, particularly American chestnut (*Castanea dentata*), hickory (*Carya spp.*), black walnut (*Juglans nigra*), a range of oaks (*Quercus spp.*), and sugar maple (*Acer saccharum*), with dependent varieties of grasses, forbs, and fungi. In North America, the Carolinian biome stretches from the St. Lawrence riparian system in the north to the Carolinas in the south, and from the Atlantic to the Ohio Valley, east to west. New York State, southern Ontario, southern Québec, northern Pennsylvania, and eastern Ohio, the core of the Haudenosaunee homeland, exemplify this ecotype.[15]

That generations of a story's narrators would establish place, build imagery and mimetic detail, and construct metaphor from the biome in which they live is hardly surprising. Indeed, the same biome-based poetics appear in other major Haudenosaunee narratives, such as Kayanerenhtsherakó:wa, or the Great Law of Peace. However, the deliberate refusal to tie the narrative to particular geographic spots within this biome allows the narrative mobility within the biome. That is, nations with breathing borders may comfortably carry the story to different physical locations within a broad geographic range. It also makes the story lendable to neighboring nations, whose home biome may, at various historical points, have overlapped with that of the Haudenosaunee, or whose political institutions borrowed from the Haudenosaunee via treaty alliance.[16] This locational flexibility defines "Creation" as *tsi niyonhwentsyò:ten*, not "one's" place or jurisdictional claims about place but the kind or type of earth in which one lives (i.e., one's nation).[17] Further, this type is defined primarily by what grows within it.

The story begins with a detailed description of a stable climax community characteristic of a Carolinian biome. This community is stable to the point of stasis, such that "ratinakere ne èneken, nène yah tehatiyenteri nène tayonhshentho', ne oni nène taya'iheye" (they were living in a place above, and they did not know what it was to weep. And they did not know what it was to die).[18] Ignorance of death extends to all beings in this place. Its single light source, a great tree growing at the spatial and narrative center of the place *ne èneken*, above this one, sheds constant light from its flowers.[19] There are no seasons, and so no seasonal death. There is no division between night and day, and so no daily death of light. This deathlessness is so total and so constant that it extends from the static light source up the food chain, comprehending all plant species within a Carolinian-like biome and all animal species, including humans, that depend on them. This biomic stability forms the setting of the first third of the narrative.[20]

The first narrative crisis arrives when a man becomes ill and announces to his mother that he will die:

Ne' ka'tī ne' nĕñ' oⁿ'hwă''djok iă'tĕⁿhatoñr'seratkoñ'tĕⁿ' nĕñ' wă'shakawĕⁿ'hă'se' ne' ro'nīstĕⁿ''hă', wă'hĕñ'roⁿ': "Nĕñ' oⁿ'hwă''djok ĕⁿki''heyă'." Ne' o'ni' ro'nīstĕⁿ''hă' wă'i'roⁿ': "O'' ne' nă'ho'tĕⁿ' ne' dji' nă'ho'tĕⁿ' sā'toⁿ'? O'' ne' nĕⁿiă' wĕñne'?" Ne' o'ni' ne' toñtă'hata'tī' wă'hĕñ'roⁿ': "Ĕⁿwă''tkă'we' ne' dji' katoñrie'' se', tă'hnoⁿ'' ĕⁿkawis'to'te' ne' kieroñ'ke',['] nĕñ' tă'hnoⁿ'' ĕⁿio'hnir''hă'ne ne' dji' tewăksthoñteroñ'nioⁿ'. Ne' o'ni' ne' neñ' ĕⁿwă''tkă'we' ne' dji' katoñ'rie'se' tĕⁿskeroñ'weke.

[So, then, when his breathing had nearly ended, he then told his mother, saying to her: "Now, very soon shall I die." To that, also, his mother replied, saying: "What thing is that, the thing that thou sayest? What is about to happen?" When he answered, he said: "My breathing will cease; besides that, my flesh will become cold, and then, also, the joints of my bones will become stiff. And when I cease breathing, thou must close my eyes."] (translation by J. N. B. Hewitt)[21]

As death is a biological unknown, this man must describe the physical parameters of death explicitly: he will not move, he will not breathe, and, in the absence of breath, he will not talk. As it is also a social unknown, he must explain to his mother how the *kahwatsire*, the immediate family, should deal with his inanimate body: "'Gaeⁿ'hageⁿ'hiada' heⁿga'hä'k ne' agieeⁿ'da'.' T'ho'ge' oneⁿ ne' goksteñ'a' oneⁿ wa'a-goio'deⁿ'ha', wa'e'señnia' tsa' noñwe' enhoñwaia'doñdāk. Nāie' ne' ga'soⁿ'da' nāie' wa'e'hoⁿseñnia'da" ("When I am gone, take my body and place it at the top of the highest tree" . . . [She] fashioned a bark coffin, and the young man took the body and the coffin and carried it aloft to the top of the highest pine tree where he laid the body to rest) (translation by J. N. B. Hewitt).[22] These instructions also begin to define the parameters of death as an ecological crisis, even if here confined to one organism, a man. The absence of movement, respiration, speech, and its attendant consciousness defines and foreshadows the biological parameters and, in the aggregate, ecological consequences of other deaths. More immediately consequent to this crisis, however, is a renegotiation of the first quality of the place ne èneken, above, as the narrator describes it in the story's first lines: this man's young daughter weeps.[23] Grief, for a moment in this narrative episode, turns narrative focus onto the *eksa'a*, the female child whose response to death becomes as distressing a matter to her kahwatsire as the intrusion of death itself.[24] Eventually, her family lifts her up into the rafters, where her father's body lies, and she no longer cries, and appears to communicate with the man.[25] This crisis and its local consequence—the death of an organism and the manifestation of the eksa'a's grief—are resolved through the kahwatsire's adaptations and, though an unprecedented rupture in the biostasis of the place ne èneken, is seemingly contained.

A second crisis arrives when Hoda'he, the man who guards and cares for the tree whose blossoms shed all light, falls ill.[26] Death and grief, seemingly confined to the kahwatsire of the man and his daughter, appears in another place. The threat of death this illness presents Hoda'he threatens all creation, as his bond with the tree, called Ono'dja, "Tooth," in Skanyatarí:yo's version, causes one to sicken with the other: "'Agadä'he' ne' awe^{n}hāi'" (Look! My Standing Tree now bears a mass of dead flowers!).[27] Hoda'he's awareness of an impending catastrophe—personal and ecological—leads him to draw on the advice of all beings of that world. Unaware of the first death ne èneken, he seeks counsel of the man who has died. The man's daughter, an eksa'a at the moment of his death, is now grown into *yeya'taseha*, a new, fresh, or beautiful body, and sent on behalf of the kahwatsire in his place. "E^{n}si'heñ', 'I' hiia' ne' Awe^{n}hai'," the dead man, still communicating with his daughter, tells her before she leaves to ultimately marry Hoda'he: "You will say that you are called Awe(n)ha'i', Mature Blossoms."[28] Awenha'i', an Onoñda'gega' term often rendered as "Yotsi'tsishon" in Kanyen'keha, travels from her family's house to Hoda'he's. The trip takes several days, moving her through a landscape filled with Carolinian climax community species, the *o'heia'da'* (*Castanea dentata*) and other mature trees[29] of a fully developed and, apparently, still healthy biome. Even after the yeya'taseha's arrival at Hoda'he's house, all advice fails him until he uproots the light-bearing tree and causes her to fall through the hole this rupture creates.[30]

Up to this point, no single figure's perspective dominates the narrative. Third-person omniscience allows the audience an unmediated view of the actions and dialogue of several actors, with no single figure's perspective privileged. When the girl who is now called Awenha'i' or Yotsi'tsishon falls, narrative focus stays with her almost exclusively for the next third of the story. This abrupt change in point of view collapses the consciousness of existence ne èneken, above, into a single actor. She carries not only the entire social and relational matrix of kahwatsire and *kentyohkwa*, the larger human population of the place, but also the biological requirements, sense memory, expectations, and survival strategies of an ecology lost in the violence of a single moment. This also represents the ecology's physical collapse into a single representative organism. In some versions, she tries to prevent her fall by clutching roots and seeds, or soil from their footing, from plants—especially *niyohonhtehsha* (*Fragraria virginiana*) and *oyen'kwa'on:we* (*Nicotiana rustica*)—that become embedded under her fingernails, between her fingers, and even in the folds of her clothing.[31] Through different iterations of the story, these materials become the medium of the growth of a biome like—though not exactly like—the one she leaves. More fundamentally, however, this woman herself falls as organic material capable of seeding another biome like its parent. She herself, as a physical organ of a specific ecology's food chain with *o'nikòn:ra*—the will, desire, habits, memories, and preferences—housed and supported by that physicality, is a product and a piece of the ecology of the place above. Whatever she carries, she falls as a seed from one biome into the potential growing medium of another.

Further reinforcing the metaphor, she is pregnant when she falls: a seed within a seed. Tuscarora scholar Richard W. Hill Sr. has interpreted the moment Yotsi'tsishon falls from the world above as an act of birth.[32] An apt comparison: the unchanging, unconditionally life-sustaining womb ne èneken contrasts with the cold, darkness, and survival pressures of existence beyond it, the sudden and (in most versions) involuntary expulsion from it, and the vulnerability of the newly expelled being. However, if we read Yotsi'tsishon's development linguistically, the next phase in her development as a literal "Mature Blossom" is to fruit and drop as a seed. *Yotsi'tsishon*[33] consists of the pronominal prefix *yo-*, the bound noun root *-tsi'tsa-*, translating as "flower," and the verb root *-ishon-*, describing something completed, finished, matured. The translation Hewitt favors is "it is a Sear (Ripe) Flower";[34] in Sotsisowah's edited version, it is "Mature Blossom." These somewhat stilted phrases point to the specific moment in the reproductive cycle of flowering plants at which the female pistil of the fully developed flower becomes capable of receiving pollen from the male anther. The biological moment the name describes, however, does not specify whether or not that fertilization has taken place. Yotsi'tsishon's deceased father gives her this name when she leaves her home to travel to Hoda'he and the failing light tree. She carries that name through the negotiation of her marriage to him, her conceiving a child, and the moment of her fall through the hole Hoda'he makes by uprooting the tree. That she carries this name on both sides of her own fertilization—before her pregnancy is recognized, and after—subtly emphasizes ako'nikòn:ra, her will, desires, perception, and mind, rather than *ako'shatstenhsera*, her strength, ability, and capacity, specifically here her capacity to conceive and carry a child. Ako'shatstenhsera makes her Yotsi'tsishon, creating a passive capacity for her carrying, and carrying herself as, a seed. Ako'nikòn:ra, the exercise of her will, choice, fear, and ingenuity, consciously brings this capacity into the fruition that is Earth.

The act of emergence that can be read as one of both birth and insemination becomes the linguistic birth of another self for the woman called Yotsi'tsishon. From the moment the ordeal of her fall begins, the story's narrators call her "yakon:kwe,"[35] *yako-* the feminine pronominal prefix bound to *-onkwe-* the root meaning "human," or "person."[36] In other words, she is called a fully realized human being for the first time at the moment she faces catastrophe, and faces it alone. By this point in the narrative she remains the only actor whose outward sign of grief— weeping—the audience has been shown. Her grief appears to isolate her within her kahwatsire and, implicitly, within the larger kentyohkwa that populates the place ne èneken, above what will become Earth. However they do, or do not, respond, other actors in the narrative up to this point have confronted at least the concept of death; likewise, those old enough to hear and internalize the story on Earth have been introduced, however obliquely, to the idea of their own mortality. In this moment, this yakon:kwe that is the metonym and physical vessel of her entire biome confronts a loss unprecedented in the world of the narrative. The audience is invited to empathize with that loss, for which they have no direct experiential reference. They grasp the concept but must imagine the scope.

Nor need the specificity of her gender or her pregnancy limit the exercise of that empathy. The morphology of *yakon:kwe* reinforces this universalizing turn. Although this actor is, indeed, a woman, feminine pronominal prefixes, including *yako-*, are routinely used in Kanyen'keha to refer to groups of multiple genders, unknown persons, the "they" of fluidity, the hypothetical, and the imagined. In this universe, where everything, in the moment of her fall, is yet to be, the whole potentiality of event and perception can be expressed only in the unmarked feminine. Yakon:kwe is not only specifically female but the they/she/all[37] of an audience invited to adopt the only remaining perspective in the narrative world—hers—in this moment. This fall, through the gaze of the person falling, is the death of that biome, not only its biological structures and boundaries but all the social, emotional, and psychological structures that biome supports. Even her name, the word she is called—eksa'a, yeya'taseha, Yotsi'tsishon—requires calling by another. She loses the physical presence of other human beings, their recognition of her within a matrix of familial relationships, and consequently her own consciousness of their recognition. In this extraordinary narrative moment, the protagonist both loses a personhood that is socially—which is, ultimately, biomically—constructed and gains a personhood that depends on her choice of whether and how to act in (re)construction of another biome that will sustain it.

This yakon:kwe falls toward a limitless expanse of water. Her fall is broken; Ranyahtenhkowa, the great snapping turtle, agrees to support her on his[38] back, and any light from the hole where the tree was uprooted is gone. This, in the parlance of disaster response, is ground zero. Although she finds water birds, shore-dwelling mammals, and other living beings—fellow climate refugees from the place above—snapping turtle's carapace is nearly bare rock. Neither she nor the other beings can sustain themselves in the long term under these conditions. In both Skanyatarí:yo's and Dayodekane's versions, the animals already in the water below and the yakon:kwe discuss their course of action. There is dialogue between these animals before the yakon:kwe's arrival in most of the versions Hewitt transcribed.[39] However, her arrival, and the council that follows, catalyzes the formation of Earth.[40] This scene demonstrates yoti'nikòn:ra, the will and thought and decision of all, unified to address the needs of one's survival. Dialogue does the work of externalizing the interiority not only of ka'nikòn:ra but of how multiple iterations of ka'nikòn:ra are negotiated, within actors and between actors, through narrative time. The yakon:kwe's decision to spread the soil that muskrat collects from the bottom of the water represents a deliberate, and deliberated, response to an ecological crisis. Here she councils with all other parties concerned, arrives at a decision with them, and then acts to hold the life she carries and grow it further by working to (re)create a biome. This choice enables her to give birth to and care for a daughter. She becomes "ako'nihstenha," she who is mother to a daughter.

The verb root -'*nihstenh*- is glossed as "to mother someone."[41] However, this verb root appears to incorporate another morpheme, -*stenh*-,[42] meaning "strength" or "capacity," the same root incorporated in the term introduced above, ka'shat-stenhsera, describing capacity, ability, and potentiality. As each of the protagonist's names is given her not only to describe each developmental stage she has reached but to define that developmental stage socially through her actions in the narrative, "ako'nihstenha," like "yakon:kwe," works as a psychosocial narrative pivot. The narrators call her "ako'nihstenha" when the physiological event of childbirth takes place. In the same narrative moment, however, she must begin constructing her motherhood by (re)constructing the biome that she and now her daughter require to survive. Insofar as the verb root -'*nihstenh*- incorporates the verb root -*stenh*-, this episode of the narrative asks its audience to again imagine, as it does when the protagonist is called Yotsi'tsishon, how the intersection of *ako'shatstenhsera*, her capacity and strength, and *ako'nikòn:ra*, the ways in which she deploys it, creates. How does she use the tension at the intersection of these two terms creatively?

It is at precisely this moment of potential insight that the versions of the narrative left to us now, transcribed and archived, become most blurred. Ako'nihstenha and her daughter grow Earth and begin to form geographic features, shrubs, trees, and other parts of what will become a recognizable biome. However, not until Taharonhiawakon and Tawiskaron, the unnamed daughter's twin sons, are born and grow do specific species reappear in the narrative. The narrative's historiography partly explains this gap. The earliest known written account dates from 1632, with Gabriel Sagard's *Le grand voyage au pays des Hurons*.[43] The Jesuit missionary Paul Le Jeune's version, appearing as told by Montagnais and Wendat narrators two years later in the *Rélations jésuits de la Nouvelle-France*, is little less truncated and, per his interpretation, appears to be "some tradition of the great universal deluge which happened in the time of Noë [Noah], but they have burdened this truth with a great many irrelevant fables."[44] The remainder of the story, in these and many other versions (including those produced by some Haudenosaunee narrators) to follow in the nineteenth and early twentieth centuries, is largely devoted to the twin boys born to ako'nihstenha's daughter. The episodes of their creatorship shift close third-person perspective onto these twins, mostly marginalizing other actors. Taharonhiawakon becomes de facto protagonist, with Tawiskaron the antagonist, sometimes abetted by rohsotha, their grandmother. The twins' conflict, beginning in utero and building to near-apocalyptic violence at the episode's climax, has historically been used as a vehicle for Christian evangelism; the twins, as Le Jeune's contemporary Jean de Brébeuf writes, "hav[e] some quarrel with each other," and Brébeuf invites his audience to "judge if this does not relate in some way to the murder of Abel."[45] Neither a feminine Creator nor the conceptualizing of multiple creators serves a Christianizing (or, later, syncretizing) agenda; narrative investment in the creative methodology of Yotsi'tsishon–yakon:kwe–ako'nihstenha becomes proportionately minimized. Even in the versions Skanyatarí:yo and, to a lesser degree, Dayodekane narrate, in which Taharonhiawkon's and Tawiskaron's creative methodologies, negotiations, and conflicts are richly, even minutely, detailed, little narrative space is given to the ako'nihstenha's and her daughter's (re)creation of a functional biome. The historiographical record is suggestive, but not explicit.

When the ako'nihstenha assists her daughter in childbirth and the girl dies, she becomes "rohsotha," his or their grandmother. The motif of narrative renaming following sudden loss remains consistent. The emotional devastation of losing a child hardly needs explication. Yet this loss carries additional layers in the context of traditionally matrilineal and matrilocal Haudenosaunee society. A daughter represents the continuity of one's kahwatsire. As an adult, a daughter would customarily continue to live in her mother's house; would typically raise her children in an environment of co-mothering (and co-grandmothering); would contribute to the kahwatsire's economic capacity by gardening, gleaning, harvesting, and processing plant species and other resources, and would, perhaps, assume leadership by taking the role of yakoyaner.[46] Within the narrative, loss of this daughter also empties two other roles. As the child of Yotsi'tsishon and Hoda'he, she represents the only other physical piece of the ecology lost and, as both representative of that biome and co–re-creator with her mother, halves with her death their combined ka'sha'stenhsera, their capacity and potentiality, and so the survival odds of the fragile new earth. Absent her daughter, the rohsotha must choose to continue to create alone, or to discontinue creation.

At this point in Skanyatarí:yo's and Dayodekane's narratives, perspective shifts and the close third person follows the brothers Taharonhiawakon and Tawiskaron. Building from and upon the earth/Earth that their grandmother and their mother have already made, they begin to create the plant species found in the Carolinian-like biome of the place ne èneken, above Earth. First to appear is *niyohonhtehsha*, wild strawberries (*Fragraria virginiana*) in English but "plants that are short" in Kanyen'keha, those growing nearest the ground. Propagating by suckers and quick to establish themselves and spread, *Fragraria* are typical of a seral community in what successional ecology is called primary succession. Successional phases, or seres, represent a series of developmental phases characterized by communities of plant species (and their dependents) that build toward a climax community, that of greatest biodiversity possible given the limitations of climate.[47] Capable of establishing themselves quickly in disturbed soils under relatively poor growing conditions, they are early to appear and serve to stabilize and enrich the soil. They are also, in traditional Haudenosaunee herbology, what might be called emergency medicine—high in ascorbic acid (both fruit and leaves), bearing vital fructose for replenishing fat after winter scarcity. Regarded by many Haudenosaunee herbalists as useful in treating depression, grief, and malaise, they are often simultaneously applied for what Western medicine usually distinguishes as emotional versus physical distress.[48]

The next wave of new species on Earth includes shrubs and small fruit-bearing trees. Representing a secondary successional stage, *skanekwenhtará:nenh* (*Rubus occidentalis*), *shá:yehse'* (*Rubus canadensis*), *sewahyó:waneh* (*Malus coronaria*), and *tsyotsyò:renh* (*Prunus serotina*) thrive in open sites, requiring deeper soil with higher humus content than the species of a primary succession seral community. *Rubus* species characterize secondary succession and are typically found within three to four years of the initial disturbance of a site in the Carolinian biome. *Prunus* and *Malus*, both medium-size fruit-bearing trees, exemplify tertiary succession, usually appearing within five to seven years of the initial site disturbance.[49]

Up to this point, all creation has taken place in darkness. Taharonhiawakon creates *otsi'tsakó:wah* (*Helianthus annuus*), a "great, large flower" whose single blossom, like the tree in the place above, sheds light. The next species to appear in the story is *ò:nenhste* (*Zea mays indurata*), although its emergence is not the work of one actor, and there are several reemergences in successive episodes. Here the Earth begins to bear *kayenthoshera* for the first time, the root *-yentho-* meaning "to plant," the prefix *ka-* referring to something altered or initiated by human agency.[50] In the Carolinian biome, imported species like *Zea mays*, *Helianthus annuus*, and later (both historically in the Carolinian biome and within the narrative) *Phaseolus vulgaris* and *Cucurbita* have traditionally thrived in cleared areas of hardwood forest—that is, in soil that represents the biodiversity, on the macro and micro levels, of a climax community already rich in decomposing organic matter. Even so, and despite traditional patterns of Haudenosaunee intercropping, land use patterns and village site occupation depended on allowing soil to rest after a decade or two of gardening.[51] Kayenthosera make heavy nutritional demands even in carefully managed horticultural sites. When Taharonhiawakon begins to grow otsi't-sakó:wa and ò:nenhste, the Earth has reached a point in its development at which the soil can support a Carolinian climax community but has not yet realized one.

The seral curve that the appearance of plant species forms up to this point in the narrative also repeats the annual cycle of ceremonies many Haudenosaunee observe.[52] If one begins with Midwinter,[53] now usually held in January,[54] the time of year in which there is least daylight and during which nothing grows, one (re)starts the cycle at the point of least ecological activity—Yotsi'tsishon's nadir, the catastrophe point in the narrative. From there, the tapping of sap from *wáhta'* (*Acer saccharum*), the emergence of niyohonhtehsha' (*Fragraria virginiana*), the ripening of skanekwenhtará:nenh (*Rubus occidentalis*) and shá:yehse' (*Rubus canadensis*), the growth of green corn, and finally the harvest of maize and other staple crops are each marked with ceremonial acknowledgments of the (re)emergence of *tyonn-hehkwen*, literally "they (feminine) that sustain life."[55] The cyclical, successional reappearance of these species repeats, on a smaller annual scale, the greater circle of the catastrophic loss, seral recovery, and maturity of the biome narrated in the story of Earth's creation. That these seasonally reemerging species within the Haudenosaunee home biome are also major elements of the core story about the creation of life on Earth—within a Haudenosaunee context and for most of Haudenosaunee history—firmly embeds the concept of the death and rebirth of a biome in a daily, lived reality. It does so not only in terms of routine gathering, preparation, and sharing of meals but also in terms of the routine ceremonial acknowledgment of their return after a period of absence. In other words, narrative impact relies on intertextuality (for lack of a better term in English), but the most significant referents are not other texts but the communal gathering, growing, preparing, eating, and digesting of food. Ceremonies that feature the sharing of the newly available foods as they reappear annually perform and reinforce these daily acts.[56] Historically, a Haudenosaunee audience brings sense-memory awareness to the seasonal order—the successional curve—of the appearance of plant species in this episode of the story. To evoke the imagining of greater successional scale—biomic, global, universal—the narrator need only evoke greater time scale.

At this point of biomic near realization, rohsotha reemerges. Perspective remains a close third person on Taharonhiawakon, now in the act of completing his engineering of ò:nenhste. His grandmother interrupts him with her hunger: "The two visitors entered the lodge and there they saw him roasting something. Fatness flowed from the ears and into the fire in streamlets. . . . Then he brought corn and roasted it and the aroma of corn was exceedingly pleasant and the juices flowed from the ears. 'Would it be all right,' the grandmother asked, 'if I take a single grain and eat it?'"[57] The significance of this particular species in the story is hard to overstate. Of the twenty-eight distinct plant species appearing in Skanyatarí:yo's version, 60 percent of these appearances include ò:nenhste. As a sign of biomic stability and largesse, Hoda'he causes ò:nenhste to rain down on Yotsi'tsishon's home ne èneken in some versions, as a gift to her family on her marriage to him.[58] A major source of calories, storable almost indefinitely, portable, and relatively easy to prepare, ò:nenhste represents both a high level of biomic capacity and the security, nutritional and social, this capacity ensures. Its reappearance promises relief from multiple stressors that her grandson frustrates. His argument that "it is not our custom. . . . We will eat it together. . . . We will be together when we eat, and each will have an equal right to the food" does not convince her.[59] Although the Sewatohkwatshera't[60] ethos that Skanyatarí:yo's version of Taharonhiawakon explains remains a core principle of Haudenosaunee law, the conflict he identifies—between feeding a few now or everyone later—is not the only one in play in this narrative moment: "'I can't believe how stingy you are,' the old woman said. Then she went to stand near the fire and she picked up a handful of ashes and she threw them on his roasting corn. As soon as she did this, the appealing aroma ceased and she said, 'Is it only human beings who should be pleased?'"[61] The hypothetical "we" Taharonhiawakon imagines (a projected and, implicitly, unlimited population) represents a pace of growth strikingly at odds with the biomic resources available to the here-and-now "we" of the kahwatsire inhabiting an Earth that still barely feeds it. The rohsotha reacts in frustration, throwing ash on the roasting cobs, thereby drying up the kenye, the liquid fat,[62] that the ò:nenhste had contained and making it less nutritionally dense than Taharonhiawakon intended it be. Ako'shatstenhsera, her creative capacity, comes into direct conflict with ro'shatstenhsera, his creative capacity; her action does not negate his creation, but it does alter it. On its face, her action represents a misuse of ako'nikòn:ra: her frustration has interfered with her reason, to everyone's detriment. However, she remains the only actor in the narrative who has experienced the sudden and total collapse of a complex ecosystem, and the only surviving actor carrying the sense memory of hunger that defines its recovery. Her irrational act, which places limits on what she, as a creator of and on Earth, will permit, or at least participate in, serves as a rational warning to a fellow creator that, even in the midst of exponential growth, growth is not, and should not be imagined as, limitless.

The principle of creative equity this scene illustrates becomes more explicit in the building conflict and final violence between Tawiskaron and Taharonhiawkon. At first they negotiate creative methodology, their conversations suggesting an equity of creative ka'shatstenhsera even while still in the womb:

> She was surprised to hear two male voices conversing from within her body. The first voice said to the other, "What will you do after you leave this womb and we are born?" The second answered, "I will create human beings and they will live together as groups. . . . And what will you do?" "I will make the attempt to do as you say. It must come to pass that I will have an impact on the earth."[63]

They work in common purpose here and throughout the story. They differ only in approach. Much of the length of Skanyatarí:yo's narrative comes from their dialogue. They negotiate in full awareness of one another's ka'shatstenhsera. Their failure to resolve conflict by negotiation erupts into a physical fight so violent that they threaten to destroy the painstakingly grown Earth. At the end of their fighting, the brothers reiterate not only their inability but their refusal to delegitimize one another's creation: "'That is enough!' [Tawiskaron] cried. 'You have demonstrated your powers. I surrender. . . . All I will retain is my mind.'"[64] This creative equity means that, throughout the episodes detailing the building conflict between Taharonhiawakon and Tawiskaron, one's ro'nikòn:ra, his will, desire, intent, and character, can affect the work of another's, but no actor's ka'shatstenhsera, capacity and potentiality, has legitimate primacy over another's. Earth was made, and continues to be made, as a place of multiple creators.

Yet this principle is subjected to one last narrative proof, a dramatization of how equity works under extreme pressure. Rohsotha, not a party to Taharonhiawakon's agreement with Tawiskaron, emerges one last time, with precisely the agenda from which the brothers have retreated: to put an end to life on Earth. The audience must assume she has the ka'shatstenhsera to make good on her threat, which means that the creative equity the brothers have established is something she can, despite her only partial interference with the development of ò:nenhste, supersede if she chooses to. Instead of a physical contest, she proposes a game of chance, what is now referred to as the Peach-Stone or Bowl Game, to Taharonhiawakon. If he wins, life on Earth continues. If she wins, life on Earth ends. Taharonhiawakon solicits the help of all living beings, asking them to direct their *oren:na*[65]—a physical manifestation of both their ka'shatstenhsera and their o'nikòn:ra—toward his throw. He wins, and life continues, but it requires all the capacity and will of all living things to neutralize the capacity and will of the rohsotha, whose motherhood—ako'nihstenhsera, which is ako'shatstenhsera—makes her capacity the senior of all of theirs.

Earth's life continues. In the last episodes of Skanyatarí:yo's and Dayodekane's versions, the tree species indicate, as do the kayenthoshera, a biome nearing the Carolinian-like climax community of the place ne èneken, above Earth. *Platanus occidentalis*, a mature sycamore, features in a late scene in which Taharonhiawakon steals the head of his mother to place in the sky as "yethihsotha asonnthanekha karahkwa,"[66] literally "grandmother to all of us, the nighttime sphere," the moon. Sycamores, while not the defining nut-bearing hardwood of a Carolinian climax community, are found in Carolinian ecoregions[67] and point to a nearly mature, almost fully realized ecology. Although Skanyatarí:yo's version of the story includes several more episodes, it closes without any further explicit references to the kinds of trees—chestnuts, maples, and hickories—we see ne èneken. In Dayodekane's version, Taharonhiawakon hangs not his mother's but his grandmother's head in the sky, grandmother and mother merging in the fulfillment of this ecological role. The form of address "yethihsotha," common in Haudenosaunee ceremony,[68] incorporates the prefix *yethi-* (also, in nonceremonial usage, *yonkhi-*), meaning "she to all of us." If human beings are finished by Taharonhiawakon, then, to humanity "grandmother" would be the mother of Taharonhiawakon, the (usually) unnamed daughter of the rohsotha. It is also the case, however, that speakers of Haudenosaunee languages can comfortably address their great-grandmothers with the same term as their grandmothers: rohsotha or, less formally, sota or tota.[69] This terminological collapse, if it allows us to think of yethihsotha as both, or either, grandmother or great-grandmother, puts the woman who came from the place above in a halfway state in terms of where she ends the story. If we imagine her head hanging in the sky, assuming responsibility as timekeeper and guider of Earth's fertility, then she too comes near to fulfilling her return journey to a mature, stable, even timeless, biome. Yet she does not fully return.

The narrative curve of the woman called Yotsi'tsishon nests within the narrative curve of the seral succession of a Carolinian biome in the Haudenosaunee story of creation. Neither make full circles; both end in a place near where they began, but not to full restoration of their beginning states. The double protagonist these narrative arcs form—the woman whose name changes throughout the story, and the biome she regrows—represents the story's only three-dimensional character, in the discourse of literary criticism. We might call her/it/them a character of four dimensions, as the temporality these dual curves build together distinguishes the yakon:kwe biome even further from the story's other characters, and certainly from the Bahktinian adventure time of other narrative traditions. In this version of how Earth came to be, death initiates a temporality that makes restoration impossible but leaves room for adaptation and experiment through multiple yoti'nikonhrashon'a: wills, desires, hungers, and minds.

Movement in the narrative—spatial, temporal, and developmental—is driven by the tension at the axis of ka'shatstenhsera, capacity, and ka'nikònra, choice. This is true between actors, as the narrative space given to dialogue, especially in Skanyatarí:yo's version, demonstrates. It is also true within actors, as we see in the changing names, roles, reactions, and motives of the woman whose entire human life cycle the narrative describes. Absent her ako'nikòn:ra, the conceit of her, the female character as personification of a landscape, might become no more than the kind of feminized-earth trope abundant in Western discourse,[70] in which the earth's femaleness, and the female's earthness, are both metaphors for and reinscriptions of passivity, even to the point of unconsciousness. This story's Earth begins with one woman's ako'nikòn:ra, which becomes the carrier of her whole home biome, and develops into a place of multiple creators. The narrative trajectory from Hoda'he, the exclusive holder of that world's only light source, to the negotiated resolutions of conflicts on Earth—over access to food, over sharing of light sources, over the continuance of all life—traces a move from a monopolist[71] to a redistributive relationship with the biome's resources. The driver of this redistributive ethic is creative equity. The principle of creative equity is illustrated through conflicts of ka'nikòn:ra that cannot be resolved by the application of ka'shatstenhsera and so are renegotiated through a matured ka'nikòn:ra refined by discussion and redirected toward consensus.

Finally, the role of ka'nikòn:ra in this story offers a model of creation—life on Earth and beyond it—vulnerable not only to sudden, catastrophic ecological loss, but to loss precipitated by human action. While human ka'shatstenhsera alone does not drive ecological loss ne èneken, in the place of no death, the pace of that loss is affected by human response to ecological threat. On what will become Earth, ecological recovery comes from yoti'shatstenhsera, all beings' capacities together, but informed by ka'nikòn:ra, the direction of those capacities by human beings dependent on the growing biome for their (narrow) survival. Grief, as the prime dimension of this response, is also presented as the defining parameter for a range of human responses to loss of an ecology. The definition of life, and life on Earth, begins with the loss of life in the place above: here there is time, which means death, which means grief. This story about response to ecological catastrophe must, first, be a story about response to loss. Our response to that loss at the levels of ka'nikòn:ra, the single will, kahwatsire, close family, and kentyohkwa, the human collective, alters and redirects the intersection between ka'shatstenhsera and ka'nikòn:ra. If this is truly a universe of creators, then each of our creative choices acts on all other elements of creation, and those elements of creation react on them in turn, in a constant and exponentially complex matrix of creative ka'shatstenhsera.

Western science has yet no narrative vernacular for this dynamic. Ecology, a relatively young discipline, deals effectively in the data of the particular, increasingly well in the construction of system models, and poorly in the integration of the former two with the graspable, the reactive, the imaginative, and the experiential of human response in all its ka'nikonhrashon'a variety. Until policy becomes story, and story told and understood tsi niyonhwentsyò:ten—in the context and at the level of one's lived earth—the global human commitment to comprehend and grieve catastrophic ecological loss and then to act to recover a functional ecology remains uncertain. The Haudenosaunee story of Earth's creation stands as one extraordinarily durable example of what the bundling of specific biomic data, narrative orientation to complex systemic collapse, and reproduction of an ethic informing practical response can teach a world in the midst of ecological emergency. Let the world observe.

AMBER MEADOW ADAMS is a writer living in Six Nations of the Grand River Territory.

Notes

1   Merriam, "Preservation of Iroquois Thought," 78–79. For an overview of Hewitt's professional history and working methods, see Merriam's dissertation. I present further information on Hewitt's working relationships with sources living at Six Nations in my unpublished "Report on the 'Hewitt Collection.'"

2   Frederick Haldimand, governor of Québec and commander of the Forces, set apart six miles on each side of the Grand River, from source to mouth, for "the Mohawk Nation and such other of the Six nations as wish to settle in that quarter," in 1748. Haldimand Deed, October 25, 1784. One version generated at the time of the deed is now housed in Library and Archives Canada, Ottawa. Another, contemporaneous version is reputed to be held by a group of Kanyen'kehaka at Six Nations.

3   See, e.g., J. N. B. Hewitt to Laura M. Cornelius, March 1, 1902, MS Box 2, "Hewitt Collection," National Anthropological Archives, Smithsonian Institution; also Adams, "Report on the 'Hewitt Collection,'" 12n54. The relationship between Skanyatarí:yo and Hewitt was a long one, complex and, at times, vexed. Hewitt's surviving correspondence, including with relatives and friends in the Haudenosaunee community of Tuscarora, paints the self-portrait of an earnest, uncompromising scholar. This portrait is at odds with some of his scholarship and with his attempts to acquire wampum belts, hadu'is (medicine masks), and other cultural property from sources at Six Nations on behalf of the BAE.

4   In the "John Arthur Gibson" entry of the *Dictionary of Canadian Biography*, Geoffrey E. Buerger includes the following quote: "While a young man, Gibson became the pupil of one of the oldest [*sic*] of the Onondaga, whose memory went back to the years before the dispersion of the Six Nations, in the aftermath of the American Revolution." The "likely" attribution, he writes, is "The Death of Chief John A. Gibson," *American Anthropologist* (Lancaster, PA), new ser. 14 (1912): 692–94. Although Buerger offers a history of Skanyatarí:yo's education in keeping with the contemporary political history of the Haudenosaunee at Grand River, and with contemporary methods of reproducing oral tradition, I cannot confirm the information referred to in this citation via another written source.

5   I introduce those with Haudenosaunee names—including a political title, as in Skanyatarí:yo—with their Haudenosaunee and English names and refer to them by their Haudenosaunee names thereafter. Here I use the Kanyen'keha form of Skanyatarí:yo's title (which is an Onöndowa:'ga:' Genyadeh [Turtle Clan] title and is rendered as *Ganyodai:yo* in modern Onöndowa:'ga:' gawe:no orthography), partly out of greater personal familiarity with Kanyen'keha and partly in recognition of the historical usage of Kanyen'keha as the language of Council.

6   Waugh, *Iroquois Foods and Food Preparation*.

7   These limits reflect scholarly disinterest less than the offices of William N. Fenton, self-styled "dean of Iroquoianism," who assumed Hewitt's post at the BAE in 1939, two years after Hewitt's death. He also borrowed the field notes of both Waugh and Alexander Goldenweiser, both of whom conducted interviews in several Haudenosaunee communities, from what is now the Canadian Museum of History, for a term of six decades (Benoit Thériault, Collections Information Specialist—Archives, Canadian Museum of History, conversation with author, December 12, 2014). Thus these crucial primary source materials have been available to scholars and community researchers for no more than the past fifteen years.

8   I base this comparative chronology on what appears to be Hewitt's annotation of his own notes and drafts. See NAA 482, which is Hewitt's manuscript of Skanawati John Buck Sr.'s version dated 1889, versus NAA 2336, which is labeled as Hewitt's "final translation" of Skanyatarí:yo's version, tentatively dated 1899, "Hewitt Collection," National Anthropological Archives, Smithsonian Institution. However, I am no expert in the comparative analysis of handwriting and, as stated in the previous note, this collection passed through other hands after Hewitt's death.

9   Fenton, "This Island, the World on Turtle's Back"; Campbell, *Mythologies of the Primitive Planters*.

10   Sotsisowah, *Iroquois Creation Story*. Sotsisowah worked from Hewitt's free translation of

Skanyataríːyo's words. A close comparative reading of these two sources—Sotsisowah's and Skanyataríːyo's via Hewitt, *Iroquoian Cosmology, Second Part*—reveals emendations and additions that, it might be argued, fall beyond the scope of what is usually understood by the term *edit*. In the exegetical sense, Sotsisowah's version could be read as a secondary source. However, the Western construction of single authorship ill fits Haudenosaunee orality; several published versions of the Haudenosaunee story of creation begin with the teller's acknowledgment of his or her own primary source, often a grandparent. As the event of each telling represents the synthesis of shared narrative material and the teller's own interpretation—the acts of transcription and translation add yet more elements to resulting narrative—every version of the story, including Sotsisowah's, can be read as a primary text that reflects both narrative historiography and the historical moment in which it was produced.

11   White, "Haudenosaunee Worldviews through Iroquoian Cosmologies"; White, "Rousing a Curiosity in Hewitt's Iroquois Cosmologies."

12   I use the term *scholarship* narrowly here, referring to work done in adherence to the conventions of academe. This is in no way to marginalize the living orality of the story or its representations in visual arts, material culture, dance, poetry, prose, symbolism, and shared referents that create the cultural matrix in which most of the work of interpretation—and, I would argue, the work most vital to cultural health—is done.

13   Adams, "Teyotsiʼtsiahsonhátye." The *Oxford English Dictionary*, 2nd ed. (1989), defines *biome* as "the plant and animal community of a major climatic region or type of habitat" (n.1). While this relatively new term in English remains subject to negotiation, I argue elsewhere in this essay that the principle of defining space by what grows in it has been part of tsi niyonkwarihòːten, traditional Haudenosaunee culture, for centuries and has much to contribute to current discussion of the term and its implications.

14   *Cosmology* is a word I avoid when discussing this narrative. Both the denotation of the Greek root κόσμος and connotations of the modern English *cosmos* suggest a universality to which the narrators of Haudenosaunee stories of Creation make no claim. The Jesuit missionary Jean de Brébeuf complained that "when we preach to them of one God, Creator of Heaven and earth, and of all things, and even when we talk to them of Hell and Paradise and of our other mysteries, the headstrong savages reply

that this is good for our Country and not for theirs; that every Country has its own fashions" (Thwaites and Kenton, *Jesuit Relations*, 169). A diplomatic put-off, perhaps, but one that reveals an approach to narrative deeply embedded tsi niyonhwentsyòːten, in the kind of earth one narrates.

15   For an overview of temperate forest ecoregions see Yale School of Forestry and Environmental Studies, *Global Forest Atlas*. For regularly updated guides to species of the Carolinian biome, see Ontario Ministry of the Environment, Conservation and Parks.

16   For example, elements of the creation story told by the four nations of the Wabanaki Confederacy (the westernmost of which touch Kanyen'kehaka lands to the east), along with those of their Condolence ceremony, include identifiably Haudenosaunee details within a distinctly Wabanaki narrative context. Frank Speck, writing in the early the twentieth century, argues that "we can readily see what a profound effect this steady contact with the superior culture of the Iroquois must have had upon the simpler nomadic hunting tribes of the Wabanaki group. The effect appears clearly in the wampum procedures, the condolence, and the election of chiefs, the sending of delegates, and functions in general which characterized the internal operations of the Wabanaki confederacy, the whole fabric of which was manifestly modelled after the pattern of the Iroquois League" ("Eastern Algonkian Wabanaki Confederacy," 493–94). Sakom Hugh Akagi of the Peskatomuhkati at Skutik offers a similarly (though less aggressively) comparative account of his own Condolence, put through in 1998 (interview with author, Peskatomuhkati Nation at Skutik, April 25, 2016). The English phrase *put through* is commonly used in Haudenosaunee communities when referring to ceremony. It not only accurately conveys the meaning of relevant Haudenosaunee language verb phrases but also eschews the white gaze connotations of such substitutions as *performing*, *conducting*, or *undertaking*.

17   In Kanyen'keha one identifies one's nation by saying "Kanyen'kehaka niwakonhwentsyòːten," literally "where the flint or chert is located is my kind of earth." Describing such broad and (often) ephemeral concepts as nationhood requires reference to the details of what grows or occurs in that part of Earth, rather than, for example, a line marked with a fence. Throughout this essay I introduce Kanyen'keha terms in italics; thereafter they appear in regular typeface. While I am aware of the

scholarly convention of presenting "foreign" words in italics, I am unaware of what qualifies the words of the languages of peoples Indigenous to North America—where this publication is being produced—as "foreign."

18   Tehahenteh and Kanatawakhon, *Ratinakere Ne È:neken*, 1. Translations are my own unless otherwise noted.

19   Throughout this essay I refer to the place beyond Earth from which its creators come with the phrase ne èneken, which translates as "above" or "up(ward)" (Kanatawakhon, *Karoron Ne Owennashonha*, 100). This is the verb phrase that Skanyatarí:yo and Dayodekane choose to describe this place throughout their versions of the story, and its directionality—up—implies a place with the same spatial rules and descriptors as those used for, and on, Earth as these narrators know it. The more popular English rendition, "Skyworld," not only bears no linguistic relationship to the verb phrase presented in the texts but implies a "world" with different spatial and physical rules from those on Earth. While temporal rules differ greatly between these places, if, as I argue, the narrative addresses parallel crises of space—that is, of biome—then the dissimilarity of place suggested by the English translation "Skyworld," versus the verb phrase "ne èneken," obscures a significant theme of the narrative.

20   This episode, which makes a full third of the narrative in Skanyatarí:yo's version, is often truncated or discarded entirely in later versions of the story. Popularly, those who are familiar with the story today often begin it at the moment Yotsi'tsishon, the woman who falls from the sky, begins her fall. The reasons for this particular abridgment may make a fruitful inquiry into what parts of narrative cultural production become discarded, and when and why. This discarding begins in the early seventeenth century, when Jesuit missionaries like Paul Le Jeune and Jean de Brébeuf quite consciously refashioned Wendat versions of the story into a version of the Cain and Abel episode of the book of Genesis. The "Woman Who Falls from the Sky" then becomes merely a vehicle for the brothers to act out binary concepts of good and evil, and whatever brought the woman to her fall becomes irrelevant for the purpose of Christian evangelizing.

21   Dayodekane transcribed and translated by Hewitt, *Iroquoian Cosmology (First Part)*, 258–59. The same scene narrated by Skanyatarí:yo appears in Hewitt, *Iroquoian Cosmology: Second Part*, 614, and in Sotsisowah, *Iroquois Creation*

Story, 2, with some additions. Neither Skanyatarí:yo's nor Sotsisowah's version offers explicit descriptions of what death is, however.

22   Skanyatarí:yo via Hewitt, *Iroquoian Cosmology: Second Part*, 614; Sotsisowah, *Iroquois Creation Story*, 2.

23   Skanyatarí:yo via Hewitt, *Iroquoian Cosmology: Second Part*, 614–15. See also Sotsisowah, *Iroquois Creation Story*, 2 and Dayodekane via Tehahenteh and Kanatawakhon, *Ratinakere Ne È:neken*, 4–5.

24   Skanyatarí:yo via Hewitt, *Iroquoian Cosmology: Second Part*, 616.

25   Skanyatarí:yo via Hewitt, *Iroquoian Cosmology: Second Part*, 616, 619–20, et al.

26   Hewitt glosses the name he renders as Hodä'he' as "he has a Standing Tree" (*Iroquoian Cosmology: Second Part*, 615). However, he identifies the man who marries "Awenhāi" as "Ha'oñ-hweñ-tcyá-wa'koⁿ" (MS p. 5) and "Haoñhweñtcyawa'ki'" or "Thaeñhyawaki" (MS pp. 32–36) in NAA 3853, National Anthropological Archives, Smithsonian Institution. "Ha'oñ-hweñ-tcyá-wa'koⁿ" and "Haoñhweñtcyawa'ki'" contain the root -onhwentsy-, referring to Earth. "Thaeñhyawaki" may be a variation of the name Thaharonhiawakon, the elder of the twin boys to whom Awenha'i's daughter gives birth. However, a proficient speaker of Onoñda'gega' is required for proper linguistic analysis.

27   Skanyatarí:yo via Hewitt, *Iroquoian Cosmology: Second Part*, 621; Sotsisowah, *Iroquois Creation Story*, 6.

28   Skanyatarí:yo via Hewitt, *Iroquoian Cosmology: Second Part*, 620; Sotsisowah, *Iroquois Creation Story*, 5.

29   Skanyatarí:yo via Hewitt, *Iroquoian Cosmology: Second Part*, 620, 619. See also Dayodekane via Tehahenteh and Kanatawakhon, *Ratinakere Ne È:neken*, 9, 19.

30   A deliberately unagented phrasing, as there are several versions of what precipitates her fall. In most, Hoda'he decisively pushes her. In some, she stumbles or is tricked. Skanyatarí:yo description is among the most humane: Hoda'he tells her what must happen, explains some of what comes next, and lowers her until she is out of the world and through the hole. Whatever the method, she leaves one world and enters the darkness that will become another.

31   It should be noted that these plant materials, on and embedded in her body, do not appear in the Skanyatarí:yo, Dayodekane, or other Hewitt-collected materials, or in the *Jesuit Relations* or other contemporary versions. However, this moment is so deeply embedded in current

representations of the story—both verbal and visual—that to overlook them would misrepresent the narrative continuum as it exists today.

32   Hill, "Traditional Ecological Knowledge"; Hill, "Haudenosaunee Art."

33   This represents one version of her name in Kanyen'keha. Another is *Yotsi'tsakayon*, the suffix *-kayon* meaning "aged" or "worn" (Kanatawakhon, *Akwekon Tetewakhanyon*, 48). I prefer Yotsi'tsishon because the completion and fulfillment the verb root *-ihsa-* (44) connotes better expresses a developmental, rather than a temporal, understanding of her name and of the developmental moment her name represents.

34   Hewitt glosses the verb root *-kayon* (see n. 33) as "Sear" (also "Sere"), which the *Oxford English Dictionary*, 2nd ed. (1989), defines as "dry" or "withered" (adj. 1a.). Given her youth, as she has not yet left the state of being a yeya'taseha, a "fresh body," and her fertility in the preceding scenes, Hewitt's editorial choice of "sere" seems more poetic than strictly accurate.

35   Skanyatarí:yo via Hewitt, *Iroquoian Cosmology: Second Part*, 633. See also Sotsisowah, *Iroquois Creation Story*, 20; and Dayodekane via Tehahenteh and Kanatawakhon, *Ratinakere Ne È:neken*, 21.

36   Kanatawakhon, *Akwekon Tetewakhanyon*, 65.

37   For a fuller discussion of the usage of feminine pronominal prefixes in Kanyen'keha morphology, see Kanatawakhon, *Karoron Ne Owennashonha*; and Kanatawakhon, *Akwekon Tetewakhanyon*.

38   The pronominal prefix *ra-* refers to a male actor specifically. Thus this particular turtle is he.

39   Skanyatarí:yo via Hewitt, *Iroquoian Cosmology: Second Part*, 632–33; Dayodekane via Tehahenteh and Kanatawakhon, *Ratinakere Ne È:neken*, 21–24.

40   Kayanesenh Paul Williams points out the parallels, down to elements of protocol, between this first, proto-terran council and what happens in Haudenosaunee Council, historically and in the present day, in *Kayanerenhkó:wa*, 29n7. Skanyatarí:yo's familiarity with Council procedure is hardly surprising, given the *royaner* (Chief's) title he held on the Onöndowa:'ga:' bench, and that his father held, of Thadodaho, on the Onoñda'gega' bench.

41   Kanatawakhon, *Akwekon Tetewakhanyon*, 2. This is distinct from the verb root *-yen(h)-*, "to parent," which is related to the verb root *-yen(a)-*, "to hold or receive something" (111). It is also distinct from *rakeniha*, the word for "father," which incorporates the root *-nihon*,

meaning to lend someone (59; men, upon marriage, would typically move to their wife's mother's home; a father is a man lent one woman's family by another woman's family). That is, Kanyen'keha grammar treats mothering as a verb and categorizes one who mothers as distinct from one who parents, gives care, or assists. What, then, is "mothering" in the Haudenosaunee intellectiverse? The story of Creation forms a significant part of the answer.

42   This linguistic interpretation is offered by Ahkwesashne Bear Clan yakoyaner Wa'kerahkats:teh Louise MacDonald as a panelist for the "Practicing Peace for Climate Justice: Haudenosaunee Knowledge in Global Context" event at Cornell University, March 14, 2019. Etymology and deep meaning remain areas of healthy debate among proficient speakers of Kanyen'keha and other Haudenosaunee languages. I offer Wa'kerahkats:teh's interpretation here with the caveat that some speakers may parse the verb root *-'nihstenh-* in other ways.

43   Sagard, *Le grand voyage au pays des Hurons*.

44   Thwaites and Kenton, *Jesuit Relations*, 52.

45   Thwaites and Kenton, *Jesuit Relations*, 129.

46   Often translated as "Clan Mother," the word *yakoyaner* incorporates the verb root *-yaner-*. This is usually translated as "good," but, as Kanyen'keha teacher Tehahenhteh Frank Miller points out, its core phoneme *-yan-* refers to the trace of a stride, a "track, pace, [or] path" (Kanatawakhon, *Akwekon Tetewakhanyon*, 107). In other words, the word describes a woman who shows the way, the path, the pace of life within the society. Although the linguistic counterpart to royaner, a Haudenosaunee Chief, a yakoyaner is charged with (among other things) representing the interests of her o'tara (Clan) in choosing a royaner and installing him into office. She, at her family's behest, has the authority to remove him from that office should his performance prove unsatisfactory. For a discussion of women's roles in Haudenosaunee society that is contemporaneous with the primary sources used here, see Hewitt, "Status of Women in Iroquois Polity before 1784," 476; and Hale, *Iroquois Book of Rites*, 64–66.

47   Sally Morgan provides a basic introduction to the Western model of successional ecology in *Ecology and Environment*. Alfred W. Crosby discusses the implications of ecological disturbance by colonialism, specifically within Carolinian and adjacent ecoregions, in *Ecological Imperialism*. Charles C. Mann

updates and elaborates on Crosby's work in *1491: New Revelations*.

48 Adams, "Teyotsi'tsiahsonhátye," 86; Teharonhiakarenrons Edmund Gray, Kanonhkwatsheriio, interview with author, Kana:ton (St. Regis Village), Akwesasne Mohawk Territory, April 16, 2010. A full discussion of Haudenosaunee herbology, its history, and its role within Haudenosaunee communities today falls beyond the scope of this essay. For a discussion of some of the medicinal and nutritional properties of plants appearing in the Creation story, as well as for perceptions of how they are perceived and used, see my dissertation "Teyotsi'tsiahsonhátye." For a catalog of plants used in traditional Haudenosaunee herbology, see Herrick, *Iroquois Medical Botany*. Herrick's work, though a useful compendium, fails to recognize the relationship between usage as food and usage as medicine that is a major part of Haudenosaunee medical philosophy. As many of Herrick's sources come from the Frederick Wilkerson Waugh field notes housed in the Canadian Museum of History, along with methodologies, preparations, and some insight into how they were used by practitioners with whom Hewitt was working roughly contemporarily, Waugh's and Hewitt's notes make altogether better resources on the subject.

49 Morgan, *Ecology and Environment*; Mann, *1491: New Revelations*.

50 Adams, "Teyotsi'tsiahsonhátye," 57, 58n3, 59.

51 For descriptions of historical Haudenosaunee horticultural land use patterns, see Mt. Pleasant, "Science behind the Three Sisters Mound System"; and Hart, *Current Northeast Paleoethnobotany*.

52 After four centuries of Christian evangelism, nearly two hundred years of church-run Indian residential schools, and wave upon wave of New Ageist co-optation, discussion of present-day Haudenosaunee spirituality and practice is complicated. There is enormous variety between and within individuals, communities, and historical moments, and I do not wish to use the term *Haudenosaunee* to suggest an undifferentiated bolus of beliefs and practices. However, a degree of cosmopolitanism has always been a part of tsi niyonkwarihò:ten (our culture, the way we do things). Historical records from the early seventeenth century onward show Haudenosaunee voluntarily and comfortably practicing many forms of religious syncretism, integrating not just Christianity but practices from Anishinaabeg, Plains, and other peoples into Haudenosaunee spirituality. (This, of course, constitutes a discussion

entirely separate from that of the involuntary religious conditioning administered—violently—by residential school staff, invader state policy, and the pressures and distortions of racism.)

53 One need not. Various anthropologists have erroneously called Midwinter "the Iroquois New Year" in reflection of their own cultural frame. I would argue that these ceremonies of season are cyclical precisely because they have no fixed beginning point and so are not linear. An interpretation of the Creation story that aligns Midwinter with the point in the story of least (observable) biodiversity must also take into account the point preceding it, ne èneken, in the place above, where there is greatest biodiversity in the narrative.

54 At some longhouses, Midwinter ceremony is held as late as mid-February. This may have more to do with historical periods, especially during the mid-twentieth century, when state-sponsored linguicide and suppression of Indigenous ceremony of all kinds reduced the number of speakers capable of putting through ceremonies. Because of their limited availability, speakers might travel from longhouse to longhouse, or community to community, thus putting the ceremony off until later in the year.

55 The term *tyonnhehkwen* is often used in reference to the ò:nenhste (*Zea mays indurata*), ohsahè:ta (*Phaseolus vulgaris*), and ono'onhsera (*Cucurbita*) that form the "Three Sisters" of Haudenosaunee horticulture. While these three species have certainly sustained life among the Haudenosaunee since the introduction of ò:nenhste into the biome some eleven hundred years ago, tyonnhehkwen remains a descriptor equally applicable to many other plant and animal species in the biome that sustain human life directly, and to those that sustain the life of the biome in toto.

56 Sharing of food, especially newly available food based on the season, forms a core part of much of Haudenosaunee ceremonial life. This aspect of ceremony functions as a form of economic redistribution: everyone eats what is served, down to the last bite. This ensures equity of access to resources, especially (relatively) ephemeral ones like soft fruit that dries poorly (as compared to, for example, ò:nenhste or ohsahè:ta) and must, in the absence of refrigeration, be gathered and consumed quickly. It also reminds all present and eating to maintain a relationship with these resources most conducive to their returning again and

again—gratitude and responsibility, rather than indifference and overconsumption.

57   Sotsisowah, *Iroquois Creation Story*, 24, 40.

58   Dayodekane via Tehahenteh and Kanatawakhon, *Ratinakere Ne È:neken*, 16.

59   Sotsisowah, *Iroquois Creation Story*, 40.

60   Sewatohkwatshera't, usually translated as "the Dish with One Spoon," represents a law formalized after Kayanerenhtsherakó:wa, the Great Law or Great Peace, was established. Its principle of equitable access to resources—encoded in the metaphor of eating communally, that is, of using a shared spoon—is anticipated by Skanyatarí:yo's retelling, as the Haudenosaunee story of creation antedates both Kayanerenhtsherakó:wa and (at least, a more formalized iteration of) Sewatohkwatshera't. However, as Kayanesenh argues in *Kayanerenhkó:wa*, later institutions were built on older narratives and the legal principles they encoded. In *The Common Pot* Lisa Brooks also offers a discussion of some of the ways in which Sewatohkwatshera't was applied during periods of colonial upheaval throughout northeastern North America.

61   Sotsisowah, *Iroquois Creation Story*, 40.

62   Dayodekane via Tehahenteh and Kanatawakhon, *Ratinakere Ne È:neken*, 41.

63   Sotsisowah, *Iroquois Creation Story*, 15.

64   Sotsisowah, *Iroquois Creation Story*, 68.

65   The root *-renn-*, meaning a song, poem, chant (Kanatawakhon, *Akwekon Tetewakhanyon*, 68), is the root from which Hewitt coined the term *orenda* in his 1902 paper "Orenda and a Definition of Religion." In that paper he claims to have used Wendat morphology (this is less than convincing, as his surviving field notes reflect much greater familiarity with Haudenosaunee languages than with Wendat, and little or no work done at Wendake or in any other Wendat community) to explain a broad set of spiritual beliefs that do not necessarily reflect any contemporaneous Haudenosaunee practices or tenets (at least not insofar as his notes over years attending many, and many forms of, ceremonies in Haudenosaunee communities would suggest). However, Hewitt's semi-neologism *orenda* has since been popularized to discouraging effect.

66   Dayodekane via Tehahenteh and Kanatawakhon, *Ratinakere Ne È:neken*, 46.

67   Sullivan, "Platanus occidentalis."

68   Kanatawakhon, *Karoron Ne Owennashonha*, 321n1.

69   Kanatawakhon, *Karoron Ne Owennashonha*, 332.

70   To choose one from myriad examples, see Jane Austen's *Mansfield Park*. Throughout, Fanny Price and the grounds at the parsonage, Sotherton Court, and the Antigua plantation are projects for Sir Thomas's "improvements" (and those of his positional heirs, Mr. Rushworth and Mr. Crawford). Though acutely aware of the pain and danger inherent in these ill-conceived plans, Fanny remains unable to consent, or to withhold consent, still and mute under the weight of patriarchal whim.

71   That is, in relative terms. I do not suggest that the physical configuration of the place *ne èneken* represents some kind of protocapitalist foil to a latter redistributive economy, or that Hoda'he's position should be read as the patriarchal starting point of a profeminist evolution. I argue only that Ono'dja, the tree Hoda'he lives with and through, represents a climax community stable to the point of staticity.

Works Cited

Adams, Amber Meadow. "Report on the Deyohahá:ge: Indigenous Knowledge Centre's Holdings of the National Anthropological Archives Hewitt Collection." Unpublished report. Deyohahá:ge Indigenous Knowledge Centre, Ohsweken, ON, 2014.

Adams, Amber Meadow. "Teyotsi'tsiahsonhátye: Meaning and Medicine in the Haudenosaunee (Iroquois) Story of Life's Renewal." PhD diss., State University of New York at Buffalo, 2013.

Brooks, Lisa. *The Common Pot: The Recovery of Native Space in the Northeast*. Minneapolis: University of Minnesota Press, 2008.

Buerger, Geoffrey E. "Gibson, John Arthur." In vol. 14 of *Dictionary of Canadian Biography*. www.biographi.ca/en/bio/gibson_john_arthur_14E.html (accessed December 2, 2019).

Campbell, Joseph. "The Iroquois." In *Mythologies of the Primitive Planters: The Northern Americas*. Part 2 of *The Way of the Seeded Earth*. Vol. 2 of *Historical Atlas of World Mythology*, 131–63. New York: Harper and Row, 1989.

Campbell, Joseph. *Mythologies of the Primitive Planters: The Northern Americas*. Part 2 of *The Way of the Seeded Earth*. Vol. 2 of *Historical Atlas of World Mythology*. New York: Harper and Row, 1989.

Crosby, Alfred W. *Ecological Imperialism: The Biological Expansion of Europe, 900–1900*. New York: Cambridge University Press, 1996.

Fenton, William N. "This Island, the World on Turtle's Back." *Journal of American Folklore*, no. 298 (1962): 283–300.

Hale, Horatio. *The Iroquois Book of Rites*. Philadelphia, 1883.

Hart, John P., ed. *Current Northeast Paleoethnobotany*. New York State Museum

Bulletin 494. Albany: New York State Department of Education, 1999.

Herrick, James W. *Iroquois Medical Botany*. Syracuse, NY: Syracuse University Press, 1995.

Hewitt, J. N. B. *Iroquoian Cosmology (First Part)*. Washington, DC: Bureau of American Ethnology, 1903.

Hewitt, J. N. B. *Iroquoian Cosmology: Second Part, with Introduction and Notes*. Washington, DC: Bureau of American Ethnology, 1928.

Hewitt, J. N. B. "Orenda and a Definition of Religion." *American Anthropologist* 4, no. 1 (1902): 33–46. www.jstor.org/stable/658926.

Hewitt, J. N. B. "Status of Women in Iroquois Polity before 1784." *Annual Report of the Board of Regents of the Smithsonian Institution for the Year Ending June 30, 1932*. Washington, DC: Smithsonian Institution, 1933.

Hill, Richard W., Sr. "Haudenosaunee Art." Unpublished manuscript, 2013.

Hill, Richard W., Sr. "Traditional Ecological Knowledge." Lecture at Deyohahá:ge: Indigenous Knowledge Centre, Six Nations Polytechnic, May 12–26, 2010.

Kanatawakhon David R. Maracle. *Akwekon Tetewakhanyon: Let's Put It All Together*. London: Centre for Research and Teaching of Canadian Native Languages, University of Western Ontario, 2003.

Kanatawakhon David R. Maracle. *Karoron Ne Owennashonha: Mohawk Language Thematic Dictionary*. London: Centre for Research and Teaching of Canadian Native Languages, University of Western Ontario, 2001.

Kayanesenh Paul Williams. *Kayanerenhkó:wa: The Great Law of Peace*. Winnipeg: University of Manitoba Press, 2018.

Mann, Charles C. *1491: New Revelations of the Americas before Columbus*. New York: Knopf, 2005.

Merriam, Kathryn Lavely. "The Preservation of Iroquois Thought: J. N. B. Hewitt's Legacy of Scholarship for His People." PhD diss., University of Massachusetts Amherst, 2010.

Morgan, Sally. *Ecology and Environment: The Cycles of Life*. New York: Oxford University Press, 1995.

Mt. Pleasant, Jane. "The Science behind the Three Sisters Mound System: An Agronomic Assessment of an Indigenous Agricultural System in the Northeast." In *Histories of Maize: Multidisciplinary Approaches to the Prehistory, Biogeography, Domestication, and Evolution of Maize*, edited by John E. Staller, Robert H. Tykot, and Bruce F. Benz, 529–38. Burlington, MA: Academic, 2006.

Ontario Ministry of the Environment, Conservation and Parks. *Species at Risk*. March 30, 2019. www.ontario.ca/page/species-risk.

Sagard, Gabriel. *Le grand voyage au pays des Hurons*. 1632. Project Gutenberg. October 24, 2012. www.gutenberg.org/files/23828/23828-h /23828-h.htm.

Sotsisowah John C. Mohawk. *Iroquois Creation Story: John Arthur Gibson's "Myth of the Earth Grasper."* Buffalo, NY: Mohawk, 2005.

Speck, Frank. "The Eastern Algonkian Wabanaki Confederacy." *American Anthropologist* 17 (1915): 492–511.

Sullivan, Janet. "Platanus occidentalis." *Fire Effects Information System (FEIS)*. US Department of Agriculture, Forest Service, Rocky Mountain Research Station, Fire Sciences Laboratory, 1994. www.feis-crs.org/feis.

Tehahenteh Franklin Miller and Kanatawakhon David R. Maracle. *Ratinakere Ne É:neken*. Ohsweken, ON: n.d.

Thwaites, Reuben Gold, and Edna Kenton, trans. *The Jesuit Relations and Allied Documents: Travels and Explorations of the Jesuit Missionaries in North America, 1610–1791*. LaVergne, TN: Kessinger, 2010.

Wa'kerahkats:teh Louise MacDonald. "Practicing Peace for Climate Justice: Haudenosaunee Knowledge in Global Context." Panel presentation at Cornell University, Ithaca, NY, March 14, 2019.

Waugh, Frederick W. *Iroquois Foods and Food Preparation*. Ohsweken, ON: Iroqrafts, 1991.

White, Kevin J. "Haudenosaunee Worldviews through Iroquoian Cosmologies: The Published Narratives in Historical Context." PhD diss., State University of New York at Buffalo, 2007.

White, Kevin J. "Rousing a Curiosity in Hewitt's Iroquois Cosmologies." *Wicazo Sa Review* 28, no. 2 (2013): 87–111.

Yale School of Forestry and Environmental Studies. *Global Forest Atlas*. New Haven, CT: Yale University, 2019. globalforestatlas.yale.edu.

A Central Sierra Miwok Origins Story
The Theft of the Sun

ANDREW COWELL

Abstract   This article examines an Indigenous origins narrative from central California. The text is an oral narrative about the theft of the sun by Coyote, recorded in the Central Sierra Miwok language. The article presents a formal analysis of the structure, language, and poetics of the text from the perspective of ethnopoetics, focusing on structural and lexical metaphors developed for describing the pathway of the sun. It then offers reflections on the ethnogeography and worldview presented in the text, linking it to Penutian migrations from the western Great Basin into central California's Sierra Nevada several thousand years ago. The article also provides a general contextualization of the themes of the text in relation to California and western North American coyote stories and origins stories more generally.

Keywords   origin myths, ethnopoetics, coyote stories, Native American oral narrative, Miwok people

A number of Sierra Miwok narratives have been published, in both English and Sierra Miwok, but little attention has been paid to the texts in the original language, especially from the perspective of verbal arts. Indeed, speaking of the oral literature of California generally, William Bright wrote in 1994 that "studies of Native narratives from the viewpoint of literary aesthetics are almost nonexistent."[1] The situation is only marginally improved since that time. In this article I analyze a Sierra Miwok origins story. It describes the theft of the sun, resulting in the arrival of daylight in the Miwok world and the beginning of day/night cycles. I offer a close structural and semantic analysis of the narrative, based on the original language, from a verbal artistry perspective. I argue that although similar stories are widespread in central California, the particular structural and lexical details and oral artistry of the story make it understandable specifically in relation to the ecological surroundings, landscape, and deep history of the Central Sierra Miwok people.

The Sierra Miwok languages are divided into the Northern, Central, and Southern languages, with Central Sierra Miwok further divided into eastern (the

ENGLISH LANGUAGE NOTES

58:1, April 2020   DOI 10.1215/00138282-8237465
© 2020 Regents of the University of Colorado

dialect of this text) and western varieties. The territory of the languages roughly covers modern Amador and Calaveras Counties (Northern), Tuolumne County (Central), and Mariposa County (Southern) in California. There are reportedly no fully fluent native speakers of Central Sierra Miwok alive today. A grammar has been published, along with a dictionary and collection of texts, and a second collection of texts.[2] The work here is based on my knowledge of Sierra Miwok acquired through the published literature. I have not done fieldwork on the languages myself, and I am not of Miwok (or Native American) descent. My interest in Sierra Miwok developed during my time as a graduate student at the University of California, Berkeley, and during hiking trips to the Sierra Nevada.

The text analyzed here was told by Lena Cox to the linguist Lucy Freeland sometime during the 1930s. Cox, who spoke the east-central dialect of Central Sierra Miwok, was from Groveland, California.[3] A very similar version of this narrative ("Coyote Steals the Sun") can be found, in English only, in a collection of Southern Sierra Miwok narratives done by S. A. Barrett in 1919.[4] A somewhat different version has been published in the Southern Sierra Miwok language.[5]

More generally, the theft of the sun is a widespread feature of western North American myths.[6] It is especially characteristic of central California, but such narratives are widespread in the northern as well as central regions of the state.[7] Many figures other than Coyote are responsible for the theft in the various narratives, however, and the plots are often quite different from the one found here. Even within the Miwok tradition there is a considerable range of fire/sun stealers, as can be seen in Merriam's 1910 collection.[8]

Coyote himself is a key figure in many Native American oral traditions. That prominence perhaps reaches its apex in the myth traditions of central California.[9] As a figure specifically in creation narratives, however, Coyote is most prominent in the Miwok and Yokuts traditions of the south-central region of California.[10] In summary, general theft of fire/sun narratives are widespread, as are Coyote narratives, and both types are very common in California in particular. Narratives that link Coyote and the theft of the sun, however, are more restricted, and most characteristic of the south-central California cultural region.

The version of the narrative presented here remained in manuscript form until Howard Berman made a hand copy of Freeland's manuscript in the 1970s and then published this and other texts from Freeland in 1982.[11] Berman provides a free translation of the text, done by Freeland's husband at the time, Jaime de Angulo.[12] I have altered the original sentence divisions and translation to conform more closely to the original language. Underlining is explained following the text. The apostrophe represents a glottal stop, as in English *uh-oh* (said when one makes a mistake); /š/ represents *sh* in English *ship*; /ŋ/ represents *ng* in English *sing*; /ṭ/ represents a retroflex *t* sound, made with the tongue touching the roof of the mouth farther back than with English *t*; /y/ represents a high middle vowel, between /i/ and /u/, similar to French *peu*, "a little"; /j/ represents *y* in English *year*; and /č/ represents *ch* in English *child*. Both vowels and consonants can be short or long. A short vowel at the end of a word prior to a pause or period lengthens in Central Sierra Miwok.

Most Miwok communities have adopted a newer orthography that does not match the one used below, which is taken directly from Berman. There are some important practical and pedagogical reasons for this. However, I assume that readers of this article are mostly not learning Miwok but may, on the other hand, want to consult existing published sources on the language for comparative scholarly purposes. Those sources are all either in the orthography used here or in an earlier version of it in Freeland's work, so I retain the older orthography in this case. The differences between the orthography used here and the newer one are: /c/ here is replaced by /ch/; /j/ is replaced by /y/; /ŋ/ is replaced by /ng/; /y/ is replaced by /ï/; /š/ is replaced by /sh/; /ṭ/ is replaced by /th/; and /'/ is replaced by /^/.

Coyote Steals the Sun

Line	Miwok	English
1	waty' lakkyšewaššy' 'oloowin, kome'joo.	The sun used not to come over to the west, or the moon either.
2	pušiiṭašy nunaašaj.	It was always dark.
3	luṭiisašy' 'itaanon'ok.	It was different at that time.
4	'ašeeli' wynnytiššy',	Coyote used to hunt,
5	'ynny'iššy' hiišyym.	He used to go to the east.
6	laamaametij hajje'paak, hiišym 'eṭṭuj šyjeŋŋeššy'.	When he got [down] near the timberline, he saw sunlight to the east.
7	'itan'ok hyyjakkeššy' liilemmy' lemeet,	Then he reached the top of the mountain,
8	šyjeŋŋeššy' 'itan 'eṭṭuuj,	and there he saw sunlight,
9	šyjeŋŋeššy' luuṭiikoj miwwyykooj.	and he saw strange people.
10	'etaltuuŋ, kojowmunit hajaapooš.	When he returned home, he told his chief about it.
11	tinnyjši mič'yjnyys? kačyššeššy' hajaapoš 'ašeeliiŋ.	"What do you want to do about it?" Coyote's chief asked him.
12	'ašeeliŋ: wyksynni'kaan, kaččyy,	"I would go," Coyote said,
13	wylaaŋyjjiŋkynni'kan 'ij'ok watyj,	"I would go to steal that sun,"
14	wylaatynniš 'ajtuj tolleej.	"It would light up the whole world."
15	'ašeelij je"apewaŋkyt kojownaš miwwyykooŋ.	The people did not believe Coyote when he told them this.
16	'issakyŋ wyyšit tyntynny'pak keŋŋettiŋ.	He set out, pondering over it.
17	wyyšiit,	He set out,
18	wyyneet;	he traveled along;
19	'eṭṭuj šyjŋejjiikaat.	he went to see the sunlight.
20	woṭiilet laamaŋ 'allammyytooš, luṭiisypoksu'paak.	He lay down at the bottom of a tree, transforming himself [into a stick of wood].
21	hajaapoŋ wo'ultuŋ mukkukčij 'unuutuŋ 'yššaa.	After a while the chief of that land came along a little trail on his way home.

22	pejjymaj šyššyj paṭyytet 'uučutoš šyššyyjiiš.
	He took home the broken stick for his firewood.
23	wyyket 'ij'ok kawyylyyj.
	He made a fire that night.
24	šyššyŋšyy 'iišyŋ'ok septupoot.
	That stick jumped out of the fire.
25	hojiiket šyššykčiij.
	He put the little stick in again.
26	'iišyŋ'ok 'owlet wykej hawimmaṭyyj.
	It circled itself around the fire.
27	wiiket wekeelet šyššyyj.
	He put the stick in again crosswise.
28	'išyŋ'ok hačiitet, lilettyyt.
	But it stood upright.
29	ṭiwwyyšiit.
	It stood on end.
30	ṭyj'eṭit hajaapoŋ 'yṭṭys,
	The chief was very sleepy,
31	ṭyjjekotjoo.
	and he dropped off to sleep.
32	ṭyjeemuŋkaš 'ašeeliŋ šyjŋe'paak, luṭiisypoot.
	When Coyote saw that the chief was asleep, he turned himself into Coyote again.
33	'ašeeliŋ šyyjakkat watyj,
	Coyote saw the sun,
34	'itan hywatkunit 'ečam.
	and he ran outside with it.
35	hajaapoŋ talliit,
	The chief awoke;
36	wykasaš šyyjakkaat.
	He saw [Coyote] as he was going.
37	'ašeeliŋ hywwaŋ manik miwwyykoj.
	But Coyote was a better runner than the people.
38	hywaaty'pak 'elleet.
	He outdistanced them as he ran.
39	hyyjakot puušiṭat tolleet.
	He came to the dark land.
40	miwwyykoŋjoo šekyyjakkat puušiṭaaj.
	And the people were afraid of the dark.
41	'etaltuŋ lakšet 'uučutoš 'issakyŋ hajnaak.
	He arrived back again slowly [approaching] his home.
42	wiiket hojkimmyytoš hajaapoŋ 'uučuŋšuu watuuj.
	He laid the sun down in front of the chief's house.
43	haṭṭeesyš čikkakoot.
	The chief pointed at it with his foot.
44	tinnyjši kuči' 'i"okʔ kaččeet.
	"What is it good for?" he had asked.
45	'ašeeliŋ kaččeet, welattim watuuj,
	Coyote said, "We will have the sun for light."
46	kaččeet, wellatyyji'.
	He said, "It will be a light."
47	'ašeeliŋ 'ojšeet.
	Coyote fixed it.
48	waty' wynnik liileṭṭiij, kaččeet.
	"The sun will travel along with us," he said.
49	hiišym lakyššik;
	"It will appear in the east;"
50	'oloowin wy"iik, kaččeet.
	"and it will travel to the west," he said.
51	'yny"ik 'aalaṭṭiij;
	"Then it will go below us;"
52	'etallik hiišyym, kaččeet.
	"and return to the east," he said.
53	'ojšeet.
	He fixed it that way.
54	'yny"ik 'aalaṭṭiij, kaččeet;
	"It will go below us," he said;
55	'etallikjoo,
	"[then] return,"
56	hiišym 'etalliik.
	"return to the east."

Each sentence of the text is structured as in the table below. The Sierra Miwok languages have a case system similar to Latin, and free word order. They also have inflectional markers on the verb, so the subject/actor need not appear as an overt noun or pronoun in a sentence. When a subject *is* overtly mentioned, it is most commonly preverbal, so postverbal (linguistically marked) occurrences are underlined. Conversely, adverbial elements and grammatical objects are most commonly postverbal (especially in this text), so marked, preverbal occurrences are also underlined. When lines of the story are told by a character in the story (always Coyote), the verb is in quotation marks. The citational verb *says/said* is not treated as part of the structure.

Line	Subject/actor	Overt preverbal elements	Verb	Postverbal elements
St. 1				
1	sun	sun	not appear	in the west
2	world		dark	always
3	world		different	then
St. 2				
4	Coyote	Coyote	hunt	
5	Coyote		go	to the east
6	Coyote	<u>in the east, sunlight</u>	see	
St. 3				
7	Coyote		arrive	top of the mountain
8	Coyote		see	sunlight
9	Coyote		see	strange people
St. 4				
10	Coyote	(sub. cl.)[a]	tell[b]	his chief
11	chief #1	"what do about it?"	ask	chief, coyote
St. 5				
12	Coyote		"I would go"	
13	Coyote		"I would steal"	the sun
14	sun		"would light"	the world
15	people	<u>Coyote</u>	not believe	<u>the people</u>, when he tells this
St. 6				
16	Coyote	he	set out	pondering
17	Coyote		set out	
18	Coyote		traveled along	
19	Coyote	<u>sunlight</u>	go see	
St. 7				
20	Coyote		lay down	at base of tree, transforming
21	chief #2		return along	path
22	chief #2	<u>broken stick</u>	take	home, for firewood

St. 8

23	chief #2		make fire	that night
24	stick	stick	jump out	of fire
25	chief #2		put in again	
26	stick	it	circle	around the fire
27	chief #2		put in	stick, crosswise
28	stick	it	stand	upright
29	stick		stand on end	
30	chief #2		sleepy	
31	chief #2		fall asleep	

St. 9

32	Coyote	(sub. cl.)	transform self (back)	
33	Coyote	Coyote	see	sun
34	Coyote		run	outside

St. 10

35	chief #2	chief	wake up	
36	chief #2	<u>coyote's departure</u>	see	

St. 11

37	Coyote	Coyote	run	better, than people
38	Coyote	(sub. cl.)	outdistance	
39	Coyote		arrive	dark land
40	people	people	fear	dark

St. 12

41	Coyote	(sub. cl.)	arrive	at his home
42	Coyote		lie down	at chief's house, sun

St. 13

43	chief #1	<u>with his foot</u>	point	
44	chief #1	"what is it good for?"	say	

St. 14

45	Coyote/ chief #1		"we have for light"	sun
46	sun		"light"	
47	Coyote		fix things	

St. 15

48	sun	sun	"walk"	above us
49	sun	<u>in east</u>	"appear"	
50	sun	<u>westward</u>	"go"	
51	sun		"go"	below us
52	sun		"return"	to the east
53	Coyote		fix things	

St. 16

54	sun	"go"	below us
55	sun	"return"	
56	sun	"return"	to the east

[a]"Sub. cl." means subordinate clause.

[b]The narrator switches tense usage here, beginning use of narrative past tense, other than in dialogue. Notice the disappearance of the regular past tense suffix /-ššy-/ on verbs after line 11.

The story can be broken down largely into three- or four-line stanzas. Little California oral narrative has been examined from this type of ethnopoetic perspective, though Bright provides one analysis of a Karok text.[13] The ends of stanzas, as I analyze the story, are indicated by shifts to another main character as actor/subject, shifts into or out of dialogue, and/or the use of marked sentence structures with preverbal elements.

Once we appreciate this overall structure, we can then note two stanzas that stand out. The first is stanza 15, where Coyote summarizes the result of the story. The long six-line stanza (perhaps divisible after line 50 into two stanzas, based on the marked preverbal elements in lines 49 and 50) is not unexpected at the culmination of the story.

On the other hand, stanza 8, at the middle of the story (it is grouped around line 28, at the exact midpoint of the story), is less expected. Also of note in this stanza, unlike any of the others in the story, is the rapid shifting of actor/subject roles from one line to the next. The chief puts the stick in the fire three times (lines 23, 25, 27), but it gets out again three times (lines 24, 26, 28/29), before the chief falls asleep (30/31).

Symbolically, this series of actions seems to predict the cycles of night and day, darkness/"out of the fire" and daylight/"into the fire," that will be the eventual result of this sequence of action. The three series of "in-and-out-of-the-fire" could be understood as three twenty-four-hour cycles, after which the chief can no longer stay awake to guard the fire (and thus the sun). But most notable is that the actual structure of this stanza carefully replicates, on a purely formal level, the back-and-forth sequence of events. The stick appears overtly as a noun or pronoun each time it acts (though the chief never does), further reinforcing the back-and-forth cyclic rhythm that presages day and night. In other words, the poetic structure of the lines in the story are themselves an abstract representation of the subject and theme of the story—a kind of structural and rhythmic wampum, to echo another example of abstract representation found in Indigenous art.[14] Moreover, the stick seeks to "encircle" the fire, just as the sun will circle around the world. In line 26 the word used for "(all) around" is *hawimmaṭyj* (with the final vowel lengthened in the story due to sentence-final position, as occurs with all Central Sierra Miwok words), a rare form related to *hawittyt* "all around, in all directions, in both directions." This word clearly echoes the east-west, back-and-forth focus of the sun's path as well as the cyclicity that Coyote emphasizes in his concluding remarks.

The stick also seeks to stand upright, just as the sun will rise above the Miwok world eventually. In line 28 the word for "upright" is *lilettyt*, which is derived from *lille-* "above."

Once we recognize how carefully structured the story is, and how various lexical items echo across multiple parts of the story, we are invited to think further about the world and paths on it. We can note, for example, that the preverbal marked elements in the story are almost entirely restricted to the key foci: the east; sunlight; Coyote; the stick into which Coyote transforms himself; and his return journey, westward.

Coyote's own journey in the story, from west to east and then back west (twice), again metaphorically presages the path the sun will take, though Coyote goes over the mountains rather than under them. The verbs in the story at first seem restricted, even dull—there is no effort at colorful description. This is not the point, however. The teller carefully restricts word choice to a few key verbs, which are then repeated for both Coyote and the path of the sun in close parallel. Coyote's two journeys are described using forms of the verbs *'ynny-* "come" (line 5; the sun does the same in lines 51, 54), *'etaal-* "return" (lines 10, 41; sun lines 52, 55, 56), *lakšy-* "appear/approach/arrive" (41; sun line 49), *wyyn-* "walk" (line 18; sun line 48), *wy-* "go" (lines 16, 17; sun line 50). These are all very common verbs in Sierra Miwok discourse. Yet none of them are used to describe the motion of the chiefs and the peoples, and none of the verbs used in that regard are used for Coyote or the sun. There is a very strict segregation of verbs in the narrative. Poetic effect is achieved through parsimony and a kind of sacred/profane opposition created internal to this particular story rather than through "flowery" elaboration. This is a style of verbal art noted elsewhere in Native America.[15] The lexical style described here echoes the structural style of the narrative discussed earlier: the full power of the back-and-forth nature of stanza 8 and the associated metaphorical suggestions— the symbolic structure, we might say—function effectively only if the other stanzas in the story are carefully controlled and structured in clear *opposition* to this unique structure.

In summary, we have found in this relatively short narrative two carefully developed metaphors for the cycle of day and night and the pathway of the sun in relation to the land. One (in and out of the fire) is elaborated and enhanced through strictly controlled structural means, while the other (the journey of Coyote as parallel to that of the sun) evolves out of strictly controlled lexical usage. In reality, however, these domains reinforce each other. As we noticed, structurally marked preverbal adverbs and grammatical objects are closely connected to the central themes of the story. There are also many uses of lexical and grammatical parallelism, especially in verb usage, which contribute to the unity of individual stanzas. See stanza 4, for example, where the first three lines all have a volitional verb (indicated by the /-ni-/ prefinal suffix). In the last three stanzas, all the verbs are in the future tense (indicated by prefinal /-i-/ plus doubling of the consonant preceding the /i/). The first three stanzas all use distant past tense, but then in line 10 the narrator switches into narrative past tense for the rest of the story, thus clearly separating the background framework and events from the central narrative. Many more details of this sort could be pointed out, but the examples given so far illustrate the extremely detailed and elaborate interdependencies in this story.

It is intriguing that the theft of the sun seems closely connected to forests and fire. When Coyote first sees the sun, the text says specifically in line 6:

> laamaametij hajje'paak,   hiišym   'eṭṭuj   šyjeŋŋeššy'.
> trees   reaching/approaching in the east sunlight he saw
> "When he got [down] near [the western] timberline, he saw sunlight
>   to the east."

At this point, he does not yet see the sun itself, only the distant glow. The next two lines say, "Then he reached the top of the mountain, and there he saw sunlight."

The same concept is echoed in the second voyage, in line 20:

> woṭiilet   laamaŋ 'allammyytooš, luṭiisypoksu'paak.
> he laid down of a tree at its base/bottom transforming himself
> "He lay down at the bottom of a tree, transforming himself
>   [into a stick of wood]."

The sun is not to be found at the top of the mountain, or even just over on the other side, but far toward the eastern base, below the eastern timberline. This makes sense, as the sun would appear to rise from the eastern lowlands, if one were looking from the highlands in the west. This means, however, that the Miwok storyteller is conceiving of the Miwok world not just as going from the western foothills and lower mountains (where the villages all were) to the upper mountains and perhaps the summit (the territory as indicated in ethnographic sources).[16] If so, the sun would appear to rise from the summit of the mountains. Rather, the Miwok world is conceived as extending from the western base of the mountains to the eastern base. The full Sierra Nevada are "the World," conceptually speaking, even if Washo, Mono, Paiute, and Shoshone peoples may have actually occupied the eastern Sierra slopes in the post-contact period. And the "privileged" or originary visual perspective, at least in this story, is on the summit of the Sierra and, more specifically, sees the origin as being on the *eastern* slope of the Sierra.

Historical linguists and archaeologists have suggested that pre-Miwok speakers (particularly groups that spoke a pre-Utian language, which eventually developed into the Miwok and Costanoan languages) did most likely originally arrive in California from the Great Basin in western Nevada around forty-five hundred years ago.[17] It so happens that another narrative tradition, focused on Coyote and the theft of fire, is shared specifically among California Penutian groups such as the Miwok and Plateau/Great Basin Penutian groups of northwestern Nevada and northern California.[18] If we assume that early Miwok storytellers preserved the idea of Great Basin origins themselves (if only in indirect and mythic ways in shared narratives), then this story implicitly aligns the original sunrise and original source of the sun with the original—or at least earlier—homeland of the pre-Miwok peoples, as if the sun were "left behind" in the past and Coyote had to go and fetch it. Both sides of the mountains seem to have roughly similar people and chiefs—in other words, the eastern side is not notably "alien." The word *miwwyyko-* "people" (the source of the name Miwok) is used in lines 15 and 37 to describe the people on both sides of the Sierra. Although the narrator characterizes the people on the other side as *luuṭi-* "different" (line 9), the land of the Miwok itself is initially described using the same word (line 3), since there is as yet no sun. This root is also the source of the verb "transform oneself" (*luṭiisypoksu-*) used to describe Coyote's actions (lines 20, 32). In transforming himself, Coyote also transforms the formerly dark Miwok world and the Miwok people themselves. Thus the narrative seems to be in part about ethnogenesis and transformation into a "different" people but one with roots in a previous homeland and connected to those left behind.

The source of the sun here is clearly the eastern woodlands of the Sierra, however, not the Great Basin sagebrush. This suggests a more specific view of "the World" as seen by Lena Cox and those from whom she received this narrative: the World is wooded. This makes sense for recent historical times, as the territories of the Sierra Miwok all ran along the wooded base of the western Sierra foothills, while the plains farther west were occupied primarily by the Yokuts peoples (along with the Plains Miwok to the northwest). Whatever ecological adaptations existed in the western Great Basin (likely a wetland/marsh focus),[19] the historical Miwok relied most fundamentally on acorns and oaks for food, and thus show a fundamentally woodland adaptation.[20] This transformed adaptation, to a new environment, would certainly have been a key aspect of ethnogenesis and the process of becoming a "new" people in a new land.

As noted earlier, there is much more that could be said about this narrative, and possibly more to be learned from fieldwork as well. Why, for example, does the chief's using his foot to point at the newfound sun merit a marked, preverbal placement in line 43? This same detail occurs in the other versions of the story mentioned above, so it clearly has some significance—which, however, is unknown to me. Most generally, much of my analysis here has been formalistic, treating the text as a self-contained entity. This kind of treatment has been criticized by Greg Sarris, a noted scholar of central California culture and narrative, as inadequate to a rich understanding of oral narratives.[21] As my own primary field research is heavily focused on contextual and emergent meanings of oral narrative,[22] I am sympathetic to this perspective, but in the case of Central Sierra Miwok little such contextual information has been preserved for us, and the narrative tradition and language are no longer fluently practiced. As Sarris also points out, texts such as this one, which were produced as "linguistic units" for language researchers, are especially likely to be presented by the tellers themselves as "isolated pieces of information devoid of meaningful contexts" and "close[d to] the oral context."[23] Nevertheless, these are the only texts we have from Central Sierra Miwok, and while they may be devoid of context, they are not devoid of meaning. Moreover, we must first understand the individual, unique text before seeking broader context, and give the text its due as a single, specific performance. I offer this study as a first step in that regard. The concluding paragraphs of my analysis are of course partly speculative, but I hope that they illustrate how this narrative potentially links fire, woodlands, the Sierra Nevada massif, the pathways of the sun, and the journeys of Coyote.

As noted earlier, narratives of the theft of the sun are quite common in central California, shared by various groups, not all of whom may share the same histories. Many decades ago Gifford and Block noted that California myths often seem to belong to regions, not specific groups; in particular, groups that had clearly migrated into areas more recently, such as Pacific Coast Athabaskan groups, shared key myths with surrounding groups of long residence.[24] From this perspective, groups would have adopted the myths of a region as part of a regional identity, and therefore it would be difficult to read a widely shared narrative plot as specific to an individual group. One response to this fact would be that all the groups of central California—Miwok, Costanoan, Maiduan, Wintuan, Yokuts—are part of the broader California Penutian grouping that did in fact arrive from the east or northeast, interceding into an area likely earlier occupied by Hokan groups,[25] and thus regional narrative themes in this case could be allied to a general shared regional history. But my analysis of the specific text in this article is also intended to show how this particular version of the general story potentially links all the themes in question to the deep historical journeys and transformations of the Miwok peoples, through the carefully developed poetics of Lena Cox, of the Central Sierra Miwok language, and of the oral tradition emergent in this narrative. Rather than just look for common regional themes, plots, and motifs in English translations of myths, we must give the stories and their tellers their utmost due through a careful engagement with the original languages of the land.

ANDREW COWELL is professor of linguistic anthropology at the University of Colorado Boulder. He has done extensive field documentation of the Arapaho and Aaniiih/Gros Ventre languages, including recording traditional oral narratives. He has published a grammar of Arapaho and three bilingual anthologies of Arapaho and Aaniiih/Gros Ventre oral literature, as well as a linguistic ethnography of the Northern Arapaho. His current work includes transcription and analysis of Coast Miwok narratives and a study of the syntax of that language, and compilation and analysis of Central and Southern Sierra Miwok narratives, based on archival materials.

Notes

1   Bright, "Oral Literature of California," 48.
2   Freeland, *Language of the Sierra Miwok*; Freeland and Broadbent, *Central Sierra Miwok Dictionary, with Texts*; Berman, *Freeland's Central Sierra Miwok Myths*.
3   Freeland, *Language of the Sierra Miwok*, ii.
4   Barrett, "Myths of the Southern Sierra Miwok," 19–20.
5   Broadbent, *The Southern Sierra Miwok Language*, 168–71.
6   Carlson, *Northwest Coast Texts*.
7   Wallace, "Comparative Literature," 659; Gifford and Block, *Californian Indian Nights*, 63–65, 129–41, 153–61.
8   Merriam, *The Dawn of the World*, 33, 35, 45, 49, 62, 89, 135, 153, 201.
9   Golla and Silver, introduction, 1; Bright, introduction, 1; Heizer, "Mythology," 655;

Bright, "Oral Literature of California," 49–50; Luthin, *Surviving through the Days*, 520–22. See Golla and Silver, *Northern California Texts*, and Bright, *Coyote Stories*, for many general Coyote narratives.

10 Bright, introduction, 1; Bright, "Oral Literature of California," 50; Heizer, "Mythology," 656; Luthin, *Surviving through the Days*, 517.

11 See Berman, *Freeland's Central Sierra Miwok Myths*.

12 See Schelling, *Tracks along the Left Coast*, for details on Freeland, de Angulo, and their work with the Miwok and others.

13 Bright, "A Karok Myth in Measured Verse."

14 Kelsey, *Reading the Wampum*.

15 Cowell, C'Hair, and Moss, *Arapaho Stories, Songs, and Prayers*, 25–28. See also Kroeber, "An Introduction."

16 Kroeber, *Handbook of the Indians of California*, plate 37.

17 Callaghan, *Proto-Utian Grammar and Dictionary*, 24–27.

18 Golla and Silver, introduction, 1.

19 Callaghan, *Proto-Utian Grammar and Dictionary*, 24–27.

20 See Ortiz and Parker, *It Will Live Forever: Traditional Yosemite Indian Acorn Preparation*.

21 See esp. Sarris, *Keeping Slug Woman Alive*, 20–33.

22 Cowell, *Naming the World*.

23 Sarris, *Keeping Slug Woman Alive*, 21, 23, 47.

24 Gifford and Block, *Californian Indian Nights*, 16–17.

25 See Nevin, introduction, 128.

Works Cited

Barrett, S. A. "Myths of the Southern Sierra Miwok." *University of California Publications in American Archaeology and Ethnology* 16, no. 1 (1919): 1–28.

Berman, Howard, ed. *Freeland's Central Sierra Miwok Myths*. Survey of California and Other Indian Languages, Report 3. Berkeley, CA: Department of Linguistics, 1982.

Bright, William, ed. *Coyote Stories*. Chicago: University of Chicago Press, 1978.

Bright, William. Introduction to *Coyote Stories*, edited by William Bright, 1–2. Chicago: University of Chicago Press, 1978.

Bright, William. "A Karok Myth in Measured Verse: The Translation of Performance." *Journal of California and Great Basin Anthropology* 1, no. 1 (1979): 117–23.

Bright, William. "Oral Literature of California and the Intermountain Region." In *Dictionary of Native American Literature*, edited by Andrew Wiget, 47–52. New York: Garland, 1994.

Broadbent, Sylvia. *The Southern Sierra Miwok Language*. Berkeley: University of California Press, 1964.

Callaghan, Catherine. *Proto-Utian Grammar and Dictionary*. Berlin: de Gruyter, 2013.

Carlson, Barry F., ed. *Northwest Coast Texts*. Chicago: University of Chicago Press, 1977.

Cowell, Andrew. *Naming the World: Language and Power among the Northern Arapaho*. Tucson: University of Arizona Press, 2018.

Cowell, Andrew, William C'Hair, and Alonzo Moss Sr. *Arapaho Stories, Songs, and Prayers: A Bilingual Anthology*. Norman: University of Oklahoma Press, 2014.

Freeland, L. S. *Language of the Sierra Miwok*. Baltimore: Waverly, 1951.

Freeland, L. S., and Sylvia M. Broadbent. *Central Sierra Miwok Dictionary, with Texts*. Berkeley: University of California Press, 1960.

Gifford, Edward Winslow, and Gwendoline Harris Block, comps. *Californian Indian Nights*. Lincoln: University of Nebraska Press, 1990.

Golla, Victor, and Shirley Silver. Introduction to *Northern California Texts*, edited by Victor Golla and Shirley Silver, 1–3. Chicago: University of Chicago Press, 1977.

Golla, Victor, and Shirley Silver, eds. *Northern California Texts*. Chicago: University of Chicago Press, 1977.

Heizer, Robert F. "Mythology: Regional Patterns and History of Research." In vol. 8 of *Smithsonian Handbook of North American Indians*, edited by Robert F. Heizer, 654–57. Washington, DC: Smithsonian Institution, 1978.

Kelsey, Penelope Myrtle. *Reading the Wampum: Essays on Hodinöhsö:ni' Visual Code and Epistemological Recovery*. Syracuse, NY: Syracuse University Press, 2014.

Kroeber, Alfred L. *Handbook of the Indians of California*. Washington, DC: Smithsonian Institution, 1925.

Kroeber, Karl. "An Introduction to the Art of Traditional American Indian Storytelling." In *Traditional Literatures of the American Indian: Texts and Interpretations*, edited by Karl Kroeber, 1–24. 2nd ed. Lincoln: University of Nebraska Press, 1997.

Luthin, Herbert W., ed. *Surviving through the Days: Translations of Native California Stories and Songs; A California Indian Reader*. Berkeley: University of California Press, 2002.

Merriam, C. Hart. *The Dawn of the World: Myths and Tales of the Miwok Indians of California*. Lincoln: University of Nebraska Press, 1993.

Nevin, Bruce. 2002. Introduction to "How My Father Found a Deer." In *Surviving through the*

_Days: Translations of Native California Stories
and Songs; A California Indian Reader_, edited
by Herbert W. Luthin, 127–32. Berkeley:
University of California Press, 2002.

Ortiz, Beverly J., and Julia F. Parker. _It Will Live
Forever: Traditional Yosemite Indian Acorn
Preparation_. Berkeley, CA: Heyday, 1991.

Sarris, Greg. _Keeping Slug Woman Alive: A Holistic
Approach to American Indian Texts_. Berkeley:
University of California Press, 1993.

Schelling, Andrew. _Tracks along the Left Coast: Jaime
de Angulo and Pacific Coast Culture_. Berkeley,
CA: Counterpoint, 2017.

Wallace, William J. "Comparative Literature." In vol.
8 of _Smithsonian Handbook of North American
Indians_, edited by Robert F. Heizer, 658–61.
Washington, DC: Smithsonian Institution,
1978.

American Indians Encounter the Bible

Reception, Resistance, and Reinterpretation

CHRISTOPHER VECSEY

Abstract   This article explores how Native Americans have received the Bible. Over the centuries some Indians have been inspired by the Bible, and some have been repelled by its long-standing place in colonization. The Christian invaders in the New World carried the Bible in their minds. It served as their inspiration, their justification, and their frame of reference as they encountered Indigenous peoples. In effect, the Bible was the template for exploration, conquest, identification of selves and others. The Christian invaders brought along or produced physical Bibles, which served their catechetical purposes, and in time they began to translate the Bible—in whole and in part—into American Indian languages. Therefore this article illustrates that to the present day Native Americans continue to receive the Bible actively and variously, attempting to fit it to their unfolding cultural stories. Ultimately, it has not lost its potency, nor have they lost their power to consider it on their own terms.

Keywords   Bible, American Indian reception, Christianity, resistance, reinterpretation

The Christian invaders in the New World carried the Bible in their minds. It served as their inspiration, their justification, and their frame of reference, as they encountered Indigenous peoples. The Bible was the template for exploration, conquest, and identification of selves and others. It was the basis of the colonists' "genuine spiritual aspirations."[1] Throughout the world, as R. S. Sugirtharajah writes in *The Bible and the Third World*, "the Christian Bible became a defining symbol of European expansion."[2]

The Christian invaders brought along or produced physical Bibles, which served their catechetical purposes, and in time they began to translate the Bible— in whole and in part—into American Indian languages. In this light, "the conquest of the Americas was as much a linguistic as a political or military venture."[3] The invaders' hope was that Indians would learn to read these Bibles, perhaps in their own languages, or perhaps in English and other colonizers' tongues.

ENGLISH LANGUAGE NOTES

58:1, April 2020 DOI 10.1215/00138282-8237476
© 2020 Regents of the University of Colorado

Protestant biblical translations began in the mid-1600s in New England. John Eliot's signal contribution was his 1663 Indian Bible, *Mamusse Wunneetupanatemwe Up-Biblum God* (*The Whole Holy His-Bible God*), translated completely, sixty-six books of the Old and New Testament, into the Massachusett language with the help of James Printer, a Nipmuck convert. For Eliot and those who have followed him (there are about fifty translations of the Bible—in whole or in part—in American Indian languages north of Mexico), the translation was an "agent of conversion" and "social reform."[4]

Into the nineteenth century and beyond, across the continent, missionizing was understood as a process that introduced Indians to the "Book," the gospel's announcement of sinfulness, forgiveness, and moral revolution. With the "Book" came a "very intense" literate culture, including the Bible's "complex of literary forms and literary interpretations"[5] as part of a worldwide process of "scriptural imperialism," or "mass circulation of the Bible."[6] From Eliot's time to the present, the Bible has been utilized as the "'sword of God[']s word,'"[7] as Thomas Shepard called it in the 1600s, a weapon of spiritual conquest. However, Kristina Bross has remarked, "Once forged, the 'sword' could be wielded by the people who were supposed to be pierced by it. . . . [Indians] made creative use of the Bible and perhaps not always as . . . missionaries imagined they would."[8]

Christian missionaries have imagined the Bible to possess radically innovative power over Native peoples. Therefore, the question is, How has "the urtext of European culture . . . been transmitted, received, appropriated and even subverted by Third World people?" Of course, colonized peoples were not passive in their reception of the Bible; they engaged in "reading back: resistance as a discursive practi[c]e."[9]

How have Native Americans received the Bible? They have sometimes apprehended Bibles as powerful objects and the ability to read them as an expression of spiritual prowess.[10] Thus literacy enhanced the appeal of Christianity and was embedded in Indigenous experiences of the Bible.[11] Yet from the outset Native Americans have questioned the content of the Bible. They questioned the mores of biblical lessons: Why should men rule over women? Why is allegiance to Christ more valued than the ties of kinship? What causes faith healings? They found inconsistencies in scriptural texts (e.g., regarding theodicy [why God permits evil]). They wondered why there was sectarian bickering among Christian parties. They puzzled over the identity of God: Was He equivalent to their own deities? The most foreign Christian concept explicated from the Bible was the notion of original sin, which the Indians struggled to understand and accept.[12] Yet, armed with Bibles, Christian missions produced "converts and native preachers" who exhorted each other to follow the teachings of Holy Writ.[13] The Bible was affective among these independent Indian Christians; however, "the Bible was only one source of revelation and inspiration for Indian Separates," amid "dreams, visions, and trances," which Indians viewed as superior sources of spiritual truth.[14]

Bibles helped produce forms of Indian Christians. At the same time, they produced a "traditionalist movement . . . sharply critical of missionary teachings."[15] In fomenting Nativist reactions to Christian colonialism, sometimes even forming new religious movements such as the Delaware Prophet's nativism, or Handsome Lake's new Longhouse Religion among the Iroquois, which took the eschatological biblical insistence on imminent last days and applied it to their present condition, emphasizing "apocalyptic themes."[16]

Inspired by the Bible under missionary influence, Indians have produced their own forms of "liberation theology," which have included biblical critiques of their white Christian oppressors.[17] William Apess, a Pequot Methodist, writing in the early 1800s, used numerous biblical passages (Matthew 22:37–40; John 13:35; John 1:3–4; 1 Peter 1:22; 1 John 1:20; Romans 8:9) describing true disciples to critique Americans who have stolen "almost . . . their whole continent" yet "profess to have pure principles and who tell us to follow Jesus Christ." Do they love God and their neighbor as themselves? Apess asked. If so, he asked, "Did you ever hear or read of Christ teaching his disciples that they ought to despise one because his skin was different from theirs?"[18] Apess employed the Bible to claim for Indians an "equal status before God, . . . a single parentage," along with whites and other peoples.[19]

In face-to-face relations with Indians, missionaries often espoused an "unreal gospel" aimed only at censuring Indian ways of life.[20] Evangelists have often been intent on replacing Indigenous culture with American culture, and thus focused the critical edge of the Bible only at Indians. This type of messaging has often been debilitating to Indian esteem; however, the Christian Bible had a strong impact on Indian converts as well, for it "recounted tales of a tribal people, of encounters with a greater power, and of a God who freed captives. The Christian scriptures resonated with the stories of people who were tied together by kinship relationships, who revered the transcendent world and its temporal manifestations, and could identify with the oppressed."[21]

Over time thousands of American Indians have immersed themselves in biblical worldview, employing the Good Book for inspiration and guidance. In the latter half of the eighteenth century, Joseph Johnson, a Mohegan and a founder of the Brotherton community of Christian Indians, was an active, devout, biblical Christian, not only in his God-fearing but also in his emulation of Old Testament models, especially in Jewish nationhood, which reminded him of his own people. Johnson wanted his congregation to be like the Christian community of Corinthians, set apart from nonbelievers. As a pastor, he modeled himself on biblical models: Joseph in the Old Testament, Jesus in the New. He exhorted his Indian community to trust in God and live in a Christlike manner. In 1771 he described himself, thinking about Christ's "'Second Coming,'" and thinking of his own "'salvation with fear and trembling'" while reading scripture.[22] He was obsessed with his own sinfulness and every day he wrote and sought after Christ through biblical Christianity.

Johnson's more famous Mohegan compatriot, Samson Occom—listed on the Episcopal Calendar of Saints (July 14), although a professed Presbyterian—shared Johnson's reliance on the Bible to exhort the Brotherton Christian community to seek a destination for themselves free of white domination. Both Occom and Johnson rejected the notion of their "Red Brethren" as a cursed race of sinners. For example, Johnson preached from Ezekiel 36:24—"I will take you from among the heathen, and gather you out of all countries, and will bring you into your own land"—and Occom drew explicitly on Joshua 24:22 to compare his Brothertons to the Israelites who would escape their "captivity" and enter their own promised land. Thus, "rather than be cursed by an angry God for their racial status as Christian Indians, Occom and Johnson spoke of exodus, redemption, hope, and this-worldly salvation for the Native children of God."[23]

Occom preached a gospel of pan-Indian love from Luke 10:26–27, depicting the Good Samaritan as a model, "regardless of race or station in life. In a sermon called 'Thou Shalt Love Thy Neighbor as Thy Self,' he decried slaveholding as anathema to Christian brotherhood." He also drew on Galatians 5:1, "Stand Fast Therefore in Liberty," proclaiming that "reborn Christians would exercise republican virtue and democratic self-government: 'that is the great Duty of Christian People both to God and to themselves, to Stand fast in the LIBERTY where Christ has made them Free.'"[24]

Because of his prolific literacy, Occom's ministry evidenced his immersion in the Bible. He delivered homilies grounded in Romans 6:23, Matthew 22:42, Ephesians 5:14, Ezekiel 33:11, Timothy 6:12, 2 Corinthians 5:17, Daniel 5:25, Revelation 22:12, Psalms 139:7, Canticles 2:3, Isaiah 58:1, Habakkuk 2:15, and others,[25] focusing his listeners' attention on the Christian gospel of human sin, the need for repentance, Christ's merciful promise of redemption, the power of prayer in spiritual warfare, God's sovereignty, and the crucial importance of "giving thanks always for all things unto God" (Ephesians 5:20).[26]

A century later David Pendleton Oakerhater, a Cheyenne Episcopal deacon in Indian Territory—also included on the Episcopal Calendar of Saints (September 1)—relied on the Bible in his ministry as a counterweight to "all images" and as a means to "repent." He wrote in 1885:

> I visit the sick almost every day, with prayers to our Lord Jesus Christ, and read the Bible to Indian, and tell about history that he is the Son of God. I am glad to tell poor heathen people of that Blessed Lord who hast caused Holy Scriptures to be written for our learning great that we may in such wise hear them read . . . and inwardly digest them, that by patience and comfort of the Holy words we may embrace and ever Hold fast the blessed hope of everlasting life which thou hast given us in our Saviour [sic] Jesus Christ.[27]

Not all Indians have adopted the Bible at the expense of their Native traditions. Some, like the Yaqui Catholics of southern Arizona, have fitted scripture into their own legendary locale in northern Mexico. Peter Nabokov writes that the Yaquis "did not consider the Old Testament heroes and prophets to be Middle Eastern characters. They were Indians. The Garden of Eden, Noah's Ark, all the rest of it happened here. Nor did the Passion unfold in Galilee. Christ first walked the Americas. His miracles took place along the Yaqui River. This was not any Holy Land; here lay *the* Holy Land."[28]

For many Indians, biblical stories constituted mythemes to be adapted to their own storytelling corpus. Jarold Ramsey writes: "[It] is clear that the Indians did accept stories from the Christian Bible into their oral repertories, with or without accepting the doctrines that the stories embody for Christians. . . . Assimilated Bible stories, . . . Bible-derived texts," underwent alterations in the telling and retelling; it was "in the minds of the Indians that the stories underwent their most striking changes," for "the redemptive value of the Crucifixion did not easily 'take' among people lacking any traditional yearning for redemption." Many Indians harked to the narrative medium of the Bible but not necessarily to the spiritual message of original sin and the need for redemption. They learned legends of the Creation, Adam and Eve, the Flood, the Tower of Babel, Jonah and the Whale, the Red Sea Crossing, and main episodes of Jesus's birth, life, death, and resurrection, but they adapted and incorporated them into their own Native mode. For example, "Coyote the Transformer and Jesus the Redeemer" became storied foils for each other, and so forth, in a "fusion of Indian and Christian ideas" within the process of "unstable mythopoetic playing with parallel elements of two cultures." One can even see in some cases how the adaptation of Bible stories "becomes the vehicle of a direct attack on Anglo culture."[29]

In their stories various American Indian peoples have sometimes syncretized, sometimes compartmentalized Christian and Native aspects in an overall culture of belief. Some American Indians have taken the Bible into their hearts, even if that has meant putting aside traditional fundaments. Other Indians have rejected the Bible, along with Christianity, as a product of white identity. In recent decades, disdain for the Bible has become a commonplace, particularly among Indian academics. In *Custer Died for Your Sins* Vine Deloria Jr. famously wrote: "It has been said of missionaries that when they arrived they had only the Book and we had the land; now we have the Book and they have the land."[30] Thus began the critique by erstwhile Indian Christians. Deloria, the offspring of pioneering Sioux clergy, and his imitators have come to cast off the Bible as a colonialist tool. Deloria exhorted his fellow Natives to put down the Bible and embrace nature-filled, land-based neopaganism as an act of decolonization. Deloria wrote that the Bible cannot be the touchstone of Indians' contemporary experiences and that Christianity is not a universal panacea, despite its conceits. In his view, Indians will have to look to their own experiences, in their own homelands, to seek their own solutions to the existential and immanent, and to transcend questions of life. Indians' own solutions must come from their own myths and visions in their own sacred times and places. Thus, by turning back to the ways of the ancestors and their own sense of relatedness, Deloria and other Indians of the late 1900s became post-Christians. Indeed, Deloria wrote, "I have in my lifetime concluded that Christianity is the chief evil ever to have been loosed on the planet."[31]

One of the central biblical themes repudiated by some contemporary Indians is that of the book of Exodus. Whereas some earlier Indians, like Joseph Johnson and Samson Occom (and even Deloria!), found in Exodus a model for liberation from injustice, today's Native critics identify their people with the Canaanites, whose lands were usurped by the Israelites under the conquering direction of Yahweh. In short, the biblical narrative—epitomized in Exodus 23:31–33 and Deuteronomy 7:1–2—justifies the dispossession of Indigenous peoples, and it has been adopted by invading Christians claiming to be God's new Chosen People. "Do Native Americans and other indigenous people dare trust the same god in their struggle for justice?" asked the Osage scholar Robert Warrior in 1989. "Maybe, for once, we just have to listen to ourselves."[32]

On the Web one can find Indians repeating Warrior's argument about the Canaanites and censuring violent passages from Deuteronomy, for instance, in an item called "Native American Christians—Surviving Christianity,"[33] or in a condemnatory blog, "Christian Devils: How the Bible Was Used to Mobilize Oppression of Native Americans," in which it is stated, with citations from Deuteronomy 17:2–5, Psalms 2:8, and Romans 13:2: "The European colonizers and conquerors did not misinterpret the bible. They did not twist the bible's words. No, their actions were *truly* supported by biblical commandments, because the bible *is* a violent text. . . . The bible calls for, and Jehovah-God advocates for *righteous violence*— precisely what the conquerors and colonizers used as justification to attack the First People."[34] In print one can follow the ongoing denunciation by Steven T. Newcomb, Shawnee-Lenape, and others, of the so-called Doctrine of Discovery— the justification for Indigenous dispossession used by papal fiat, settler colonists, and even the United States Supreme Court—grounded in Bible-based Christian nationalism.[35]

One can also observe attempts at "decolonizing" the Bible by American Indian writers and academics.[36] For Native people, "biblical reading has produced traumatic disruptions within Native societies and facilitated what we now call culturecide," according to Laura E. Donaldson (Cherokee). But, she says, Native peoples have "resisted deracinating processes by reading the Bible on their own terms."[37] The Ojibwe poet Kimberly M. Blaeser writes: "Subverting the pagan epithet" imposed on Indians since the arrival of Columbus, "much contemporary Native writing enacts a literary resistance . . . to the narrow strictures of orthodox religion," especially Christianity. Indeed, "Native American writers have made the Christian/Native American religious conflict a central motif in tribal fiction," including subversion of the Bible and its putative authority.[38] "Postcolonialism"[39] has included a rereading and rewriting of scripture according to the rubrics of "intertextuality,"[40] in which Native novelists such as Linda Hogan, Louise Erdrich, Leslie Silko, and Thomas King, among many others, have shaped their own works in allusion to and parody of biblical texts. As a result, these works become "an absurd replication of norms that actually undermines them."[41]

In asking how should "contemporary Native people respond to scripture," Indian academics suggest that Indigenous people should interpret the Bible with Indian sensitivities based on their experiences of oppression at the hands of Christians. This form of "hermeneutics" rejects the claim of biblical inerrancy along with the concept of Jesus as "the Lord," as a conqueror and ruler of a "Kingdom," by emphasizing Indigenous concerns.[42]

The postcolonial project can be seen as parallel to the prophetic, related to the biblical call to "proclaim the need for justice at all levels of society." It is a "critical focus on imperialism, neo-colonialism, and Eurocentrism." As such, Native postcolonialism looks with a jaundiced gaze at the Great Commission of Matthew 28:19–

20: "Go, therefore, and make disciples of all nations, baptizing them in the name of the Father and the Son and of the Holy Spirit, and teaching them to obey everything that I have commanded you." Donaldson writes that this missionary-motivating passage "has too often unleashed the lethal weapons of the Word and the European world against aboriginal peoples," creating what she has called "the most brutal system of conquest and exploitation the world has ever known."[43]

Donaldson shows how Christian invaders have used chapters 19 and 20 of the book of Judges to vindicate the annihilation of Indian peoples, most specifically in 1637, when Puritans massacred the Pequots in Connecticut—a parallel to the Israelites' war with the Benjaminites of Gibeah: "Just as God delivered the Benjaminites into the hands of the Israelites, so He delivered the Pequot [sic] to the Massachusetts Bay Colony." Thus, when Native people encounter the Bible and its justification for Israelite colonization and conquest, she encourages Native people to read the Bible "like Canaanites."[44]

George E. Tinker, Osage-Cherokee Lutheran professor of cross-cultural ministries at Iliff School of Theology, has championed rethinking of biblical values of hierarchy and control in favor of a worldview he finds more holistic, mutually dependent, nurturing, healing, and ultimately liberating. The starting point for American Indian liberation theology, he attests, is not in the scriptural history of the Hebrew people; it is not in the Jesus of the gospels; indeed, it is not in the Bible or Christian theology. Rather, he avows, Indians should look to themselves as the sources of their own liberation: "We American Indians are just arrogant enough in the midst of our oppression and poverty to think that our perception of the world is at least as adequate, more satisfying, and certainly more egalitarian than anything the West has produced." He concludes that "an American Indian theology coupled with an American Indian reading of the gospel might provide the theological imagination to generate a more immediate and attainable vision of a just and peaceful world."[45]

Rethinking the Bible in Indigenous terms has led some contemporary Native women to reconsider female characters in scripture. For example, Donaldson looks in the book of Ruth at the character of Orpah, who stays among her people, the Moabites, rather than join the Israelites. Jewish and Christian Bible readers usually perceive her choice as a failure, but "to Cherokee women . . . , Orpah connotes hope rather than perversity, because she is the one who does not reject her traditions or her sacred ancestors."[46] Native feminists, Donaldson writes, have a particular perspective, carrying the "double cross" of approbation under male Christian hegemony, and therefore have worked to transform the theological category of Christology.[47] Some Native evangelicals echo a "complementarian philosophy" that puts women in their submissive roles,[48] but others think that the Bible is misused to justify male headship. They see biblical women (Mary, Martha, Mary Magdalene) as strong faith keepers, and they call for gender equality in ways that are based on biblical models.

For many contemporary Indian Christians, decolonizing the Bible means indigenizing scripture, learning, as Sister Marie Therese Archambault (Hunkpapa Lakota) once said, to "subtract the chauvinism and the cultural superiority with which this Gospel was often presented to our people" and then make it their own.[49] The Catholic Ojibwe medicine priest John Hascall, O.F.M.Cap., indigenizes the Bible by employing it along with nature symbols of the Indian world. He says that "God speaks to us through the Bible, but also through leaves and grass and other aspects of His creation, as well as in the special revelations of vision guests."[50] The Protestant Odawa minister Mike Peters takes part in the same type of ceremonial melding of Native and Christian spirituality in his 4 Fires Ministry: burning incense, dancing, and drumming in liturgy. Disparagers tell him "'how we do things is pagan and evil' and yet," he affirms, "when I read my Bible, my culture is in the Bible. . . . The spiritual ways of my ancestors reflect what's in the Bible."[51]

If there is any group of contemporary American Indians who are immersed in the Bible—reading it with Native eyes, indigenizing its messages, and attempting to live according to its principles—it is Native evangelicals. As Andrea Smith and Jason E. Purvis have depicted in depth, and as the late Lakota Richard Twiss and the Cherokee Randy Woodley, among others, have represented vividly, Native evangelicals have sought to demonstrate that they can be authentic, sovereignty-affirming Indians—not "dupes for white supremacy"—and still be members of "Native Bible-believing communities" such as Wiconi International (Twiss), Eagle's Wings Ministry (Woodley), and the North American Institute for Indigenous Theological Studies (NAIITS).[52] Ultimately, they recognize how missionizing has oppressed their people; however, they belong to a long-standing tradition of "Native Christians who hold the Bible as authoritative."[53]

A few emphasize "traditionalism over Christianity" or wish to combine Indigenous and Christian spirituality, yet most wish to avoid any syncretism, viewing the two religious traditions as "completely separate" even though they "may desire to hear the Bible in their language." When faced with two roads—one aboriginal, one Christian—Twiss and others have opted for, as he has called it, "'a journey of internal reconciliation.'"[54]

For these Native evangelicals of many persuasions, the question is, "What is acceptable within the bounds of Bible-based Christianity?" Is scripture "the framework by which cultural practices are interpreted" and judged (perhaps as demonic, perhaps as godly)? Does the Bible not condemn white behaviors (oppressing Indians, breaking treaties, etc.) as thoroughly as Native ones, and are there not Indigenous practices (sharing the earth's goods in common) that find praise in scripture? Does the Bible encourage political activity on behalf of Native people, against colonization, or is Jesus "concerned more with personal transformation than with political transformation"? Decolonization is a positive goal, according to Native evangelicals; however, the Bible also speaks clearly on the need for peoples to reconcile with enemies "rather than to simply separate from their oppressors."[55]

Native evangelicals take seriously the argument that the Bible is "the inerrant word of God," but they treat that inerrancy variously. Some, like the Potawatomi Casey Church, regard the Bible as thoroughly truthful "'as a whole,'" guided by the Holy Spirit but not necessarily so in every utterance. Others emphasize "biblical infallibility" in contradistinction to church "teaching or theology." As Twiss contends, "the Bible may be error-free [but] it is never interpreted error-free."[56] He finds the gospel redemptive, but not as the "Cowboys" have interpreted and lived it.[57]

To instruct Indian Christians in biblical literacy, Pentecostals like the Assemblies of God ministry established an all-Indian Bible College, hoping to train Indians to be effective, knowledgeable preachers to their own people. The All-Tribes Bible School opened in Phoenix in 1957 and became a four-year Bible college in the 1980s.[58] It is known today as American Indian College, in partnership with Southwestern Assemblies of God University (SAGU). Its mission is "equipping Native Americans for Christian Service," according to the principle that "the Bible is the inspired Word of God."[59] Today there are several organizations for Native Christian leadership and pastoral training, such as the American Indian Bible Institute in Los Angeles; Cook Native American Ministries Foundation in Tempe, Arizona; Indian Bible College in Flagstaff, Arizona; the Center for Indian Ministries in Bemidji, Minnesota; and Native Ministries International, online. These institutions are conducted primarily under non-Indian leadership. Their instruction is in English, and their attitude toward Native culture hardly stresses traditional revival. Indeed, in addressing the "questions concerning Native spirituality and Biblical truth," it is said:

> We must renounce and avoid any form of idolatry and syncretism, because
> they are forbidden in Scripture. . . . As believers, we should not, therefore, use
> or attach any spiritual value to items regarded as sacred such as tobacco, cedar
> smoke, sweet grass, peyote, prayer feathers, fetishes, masks, drums, dances,
> etc.; to places regarded as sacred such as mother earth, kivas, mountains, sweat
> lodge, longhouse, or other traditional religious places of worship, etc.; or
> to spirit beings such as kachinas, skin walkers, animal and nature spirits,
> etc. . . . Christ should not be used as a license to introduce anything from
> the native traditional ways that would hinder our lives in Christ. . . . We
> believe that Christ reigns supreme above all cultures.[60]

Native Ministries International provides numerous biblical references for its theological principles against syncretism.

At the same time, the "Pauline example" of the Indigenous principle has been cited by the founders of the All-Tribes Bible School to argue that "native peoples, with the help of the Holy Spirit, were completely capable of running their own churches." Some Indian communities have "read their Bibles in their Native languages," receiving "not simply a replication of the texts of the dominant culture [but rather] an oppositional text to the English Bible."[61] Whether reading the Bible in English or in Indigenous languages, some contemporary Native evangelicals have formulated "a theology of Biblical indigeneity."[62] Twiss and other founders of NAIITS in 2001 understood syncretism as "normative. Yes normal!"[63] Even more, Twiss viewed syncretism as biblically sanctioned and the means by which the gospel can be embedded in Native cultures. He and his coauthors, Adrian Jacobs (Cayuga) and Terry LeBlanc (Mi'kmaq), have not advocated "syncretism without boundaries";[64] they have reaffirmed the biblical position of God's sovereignty. Yet they and their NAIITS colleagues say that Native implements like drums and rattles can be redeemed by Christian worship, creating an indigenized Christianity with an indigenized understanding of the Bible.

Woodley has gone even farther by "contextualizing the Gospel [and] adapting the message to the culture of the people." He states that there are "redemptive analogies," for instance, between the biblical Christ and *the risen bear* of Cherokee myth, who saves a lost hunter, nurtures him over the winter, and then offers his body to hunters in the spring, only to rise from the dead and return to his cave.[65] Through this kind of intertextual Bible analysis, Woodley hopes to learn about and proclaim "the real Jesus, . . . not the one who was used to take our land and rob us of our cultures," but the Jesus who can have meaning for Indigenous peoples.[66]

Twiss heralded indigenized Christianity in biblical terms: "At this time in history, almighty God has raised up the First Nations people of North America as a new wave of ambassadors for the gospel of Jesus Christ."[67] To proclaim the gospel, however, Indians have to rise above criticizing oppressive whites. According to Twiss, Native Christians must invite whites to share in Christian renewal, according to the essential spirit of the gospel: forgiveness, hospitality, welcome, and inclusion—which are, after all, Native virtues, too.[68]

Embracing the Bible, embodying the Gospel, has meant forgiving (although certainly not forgetting) colonial oppression. John McPherson, Cherokee Pentecostal, has told how he had to overcome hatred of whites who forced the Trail of Tears on his people: "By becoming a Christian, he could move forward and leave behind his anger at those who inflicted so much pain. In essence, Pentecostal Christianity healed him from the wrongs of the past and allowed him to overcome his hate"; hence he "reshaped the Gospel" and overcame the debilitation of victimhood.[69]

In like manner, the Choctaw Episcopalian bishop Steven Charleston tells how he "came to read and interpret the Bible through the eyes of traditional Native American religion." To do so, he had to overcome the disillusion he felt when he read Vine Deloria Jr.'s excoriation of Christian colonialism. Was there nothing of worth in Christianity? In seminary Charleston came to interpret Matthew 4:1–11, where Jesus goes into the Wilderness, as a story akin to a Native American vision quest. He discovered other visions of Jesus: in the Transfiguration (Matthew 17:1–8), Gethsemane (Matthew 26:36–46), and Golgotha (Matthew 27:32–55). In all four of these episodes Jesus broke barriers between the human and the godly, like a Native American spiritual seeker. Coming to this biblical understanding helped revive Charleston's Christian faith. As he avows, "I believe Jesus is the fulfillment of both the Hebrew Covenant and the Native Covenant."[70]

Now in the sixth century since first contact with Christianity, Native Americans are still encountering the Bible afresh. Some are moved, even transformed, by its words. One can read on the Web about Nicholas Ross-Dick, a Yakama student, who "was challenged to read the New Testament" and, while studying Jesus's ministry in Matthew 9 (in which He heals the sick and forgives their sins), was moved to tears: "I needed to know I was forgiven. I finally gave my heart to the Lord. I was given a better heart and a clearer conscience and a new life."[71] Some contemporary

Indians are inspired by the Bible, and some are repelled by its long-standing place in colonization. They continue to receive it actively and variously, attempting to fit it to their unfolding cultural stories. It has not lost its potency, nor have they lost their power to consider it on their own terms.

CHRISTOPHER VECSEY is Colgate University's Harry Emerson Fosdick Professor of the Humanities, Native American Studies, and Religion and chair of the Department of Religion. He is a founding member of Colgate's Native American Studies Program. He is author of five books and editor of eight about American Indian subjects. Since 2001 he has served as editor of the series The Iroquois and Their Neighbors at Syracuse University Press.

Notes

1   Gregerson and Juster, *Empires of God*, 2.
2   Sugirtharajah, *The Bible and the Third World*, 1.
3   Gregerson and Juster, *Empires of God*, 6.
4   Round, *Removable Type*, 74; Ronda, "The Bible and Early American Indian Missions," 9.
5   Furtwangler, *Bringing Indians to the Book*, 116, 123.
6   Sugirtharajah, *The Bible and the Third World*, 60.
7   Bross, *Dry Bones and Indian Sermons*, 52.
8   Bross, *Dry Bones and Indian Sermons*, 73.
9   Sugirtharajah, *The Bible and the Third World*, 1, 74.
10 Murray, "Spreading the Word."
11 Hackel and Wyss, "Print Culture and the Power of Native Literacy."
12 Silverman, *Faith and Boundaries*, 56–62.
13 Ronda, "The Bible and Early American Indian Missions," 23.
14 Fisher, *The Indian Great Awakening*, 130.
15 Ronda, "The Bible and Early American Indian Missions," 23.
16 Wallace, *The Death and Rebirth of the Seneca*, 239.
17 McLoughlin, *Champions of the Cherokees*, 484.
18 Apess, *A Son of the Forest*, 97–98.
19 Sugirtharajah, *The Bible and the Third World*, 90.
20 Cox, *The Impact of Christian Missions on Indigenous Cultures*, 211–34.
21 Lewis, *Creating Christian Indians*, 46.
22 Johnson, *To Do Good to My Indian Brethren*, 104.
23 Rubin, *Tears of Repentance*, 241, 243, 141.
24 Rubin, *Tears of Repentance*, 242, 240.
25 Occom, *Collected Writings*, 166–225.
26 Occom, *Collected Writings*, 220.
27 David Pendleton Oakerhater to Mrs. Deaconess Mary Burnham, June 6, 1885, Burnham Collection, Oklahoma State University Library. dc.library.okstate.edu/digital/collection/oaker/id/164/rec/43.
28 Nabokov, *Where the Lightning Strikes*, 112.
29 Ramsey, "The Bible in Western Indian Mythology," 442–43, 444, 446, 449, 453, 454, 450.
30 Deloria, *Custer Died for Your Sins*, 101.
31 Deloria, *For This Land*, 146.
32 Warrior, "Canaanites, Cowboys, and Indians," 289, 290.
33 Schenk, "Native American Christians—Surviving Christianity."
34 Pardue, "Christian Devils."
35 Newcomb, *Pagans in the Promised Land*.
36 Tinker, *American Indian Liberation*, 91.
37 Donaldson, "The Sign of Orpah," 21.
38 Blaeser, "Pagans Rewriting the Bible," 13, 16.
39 Donaldson, "Postcolonialism and Biblical Reading."
40 Donaldson, "Noah Meets Old Coyote."
41 Donaldson, "Response," 281.
42 Kidwell, Noley, Tinker [and Weaver], *A Native American Theology*, 25, 21, 62.
43 Donaldson, "Postcolonialism and Biblical Reading," 1, 6, 7.
44 Donaldson, "Postcolonialism and Biblical Reading," 9, 11.
45 Tinker, *Spirit and Resistance*, 107, 111.
46 Donaldson, "The Sign of Orpah," 34.
47 Donaldson, "Native Women's Double Cross."
48 Smith, "Native Evangelicals and Scriptural Ethnologies," 67.
49 Archambault, "Native Americans and Evangelization," 135.
50 Vecsey, *Where the Two Roads Meet*, 211.
51 Kopenkoskey, "Religion."
52 Smith, "Native Evangelicals and Scriptural Ethnologies"; Purvis, "A 'Circle in a Rectangle'"; Twiss, *One Church, Many Tribes*;

Twiss, *Rescuing the Gospel from the Cowboys*; Woodley, *Living in Color*; Woodley, *Mixed Blood. Not Mixed Up*; Woodley, *When Going to Church Is Sin*.

53   Smith, "Native Evangelicals and Scriptural Ethnologies," 27, 29, 33.

54   Smith, "Native Evangelicals and Scriptural Ethnologies," 35, 37, 39, 38.

55   Smith, "Native Evangelicals and Scriptural Ethnologies," 42, 50, 55.

56   Smith, "Native Evangelicals and Scriptural Ethnologies," 60, 61, 62.

57   Twiss, *Rescuing the Gospel from the Cowboys*.

58   See Tarango, *Choosing the Jesus Way*.

59   SAGU American Indian College, "Mission and Core Values."

60   Native Ministries International, "Statement on Native Spirituality."

61   Tarango, *Choosing the Jesus Way*, 31, 39, 64, 65.

62   Purvis, "A 'Circle in a Rectangle,'" 137.

63   Twiss, *Rescuing the Gospel from the Cowboys*, 31.

64   Purvis, "A 'Circle in a Rectangle,'" 141.

65   Woodley, *Mixed Blood. Not Mixed Up*, 47, 90.

66   Woodley, *When Going to Church Is Sin*, xiii.

67   Twiss, *One Church, Many Tribes*, 20.

68   See Twiss, *Rescuing the Gospel from the Cowboys*.

69   Tarango, *Choosing the Jesus Way*, 99.

70   Charleston, *The Four Vision Quests of Jesus*, 2, 57.

71   Ross-Dick, "My Story."

Works Cited

Apess, William. *A Son of the Forest and Other Writings by William Apess, a Pequot*, edited by Barry O'Connell. Amherst: University of Massachusetts Press, 1997.

Archambault, Marie Therese. "Native Americans and Evangelization." In *Native and Christian: Indigenous Voices on Religious Identity in the United States and Canada*, edited by James Treat, 132–53. New York: Routledge, 1996.

Blaeser, Kimberly M. "Pagans Rewriting the Bible: Heterodoxy and the Representation of Spirituality in Native American Literature." *ARIEL: A Review of International English Literature* 25, no. 1 (1994): 12–31.

Bross, Kristina. *Dry Bones and Indian Sermons: Praying Indians in Colonial America*. Ithaca, NY: Cornell University Press, 2004.

Charleston, Steven. *The Four Vision Quests of Jesus*. New York: Morehouse, 2015.

Cox, James L. *The Impact of Christian Missions on Indigenous Cultures: The "Real People" and the Unreal Gospel*. Lewiston, NY: Mellen, 1991.

Deloria, Vine, Jr. *Custer Died for Your Sins: An Indian Manifesto*. New York: Macmillan, 1969.

Deloria, Vine, Jr. *For This Land: Writings on Religion in America*, edited by James Treat. New York: Routledge, 1999.

Donaldson, Laura E. "Native Women's Double Cross: Christology from the Contact Zone." *Feminist Theology* 10, no. 29 (2002): 96–117.

Donaldson, Laura E. "Noah Meets Old Coyote, or Singing in the Rain: Intertextuality in Thomas King's *Green Grass, Running Water*." *Studies in American Indian Literatures*, ser. 2, 7, no. 2 (1995): 27–43.

Donaldson, Laura E. "Postcolonialism and Biblical Reading: An Introduction." *Semeia*, no. 75 (1996): 1–14.

Donaldson, Laura E. "Response: 'When Jesus Rewrote the Corn Mothers: Intertextuality as Transnational Critical Practice.'" *Semeia*, nos. 69–70 (1995): 281–92.

Donaldson, Laura E. "The Sign of Orpah: Reading Ruth through Native Eyes." In *Vernacular Hermeneutics*, edited by R. S. Sugirtharajah, 20–36. Sheffield: Sheffield Academic Press, 1999.

Fisher, Linford D. *The Indian Great Awakening: Religion and the Shaping of Native Cultures in Early America*. New York: Oxford University Press, 2012.

Furtwangler, Albert. *Bringing Indians to the Book*. Seattle: University of Washington Press, 2005.

Gregerson, Linda, and Susan Juster, eds. *Empires of God: Religious Encounters in the Early Modern Atlantic*. Philadelphia: University of Pennsylvania Press, 2011.

Hackel, Steven W., and Hilary E. Wyss. "Print Culture and the Power of Native Literacy in California and New England Missions." In *Native Americans, Christianity, and the Reshaping of the American Religious Landscape*, edited by Joel W. Martin and Mark A. Nicholas, 201–22. Chapel Hill: University of North Carolina Press, 2010.

Johnson, Joseph. *To Do Good to My Indian Brethren: The Writings of Joseph Johnson, 1751–1776*, edited by Laura J. Murray. Amherst: University of Massachusetts Press, 1998.

Kidwell, Clara Sue, Homer Noley, George E. "Tink" Tinker [and Jace Weaver]. *A Native American Theology*. Maryknoll, NY: Orbis, 2006.

Kopenkoskey, Paul R. "Religion: American Indian and Christian Beliefs Blend at Michigan Church." *Huffington Post*, May 25, 2011. www.huffingtonpost.com/2010/10/29/american-indian-and-christian_n_775645.html.

Lewis, Bonnie Sue. *Creating Christian Indians: Native Clergy in the Presbyterian Church*. Norman: University of Oklahoma Press, 2003.

McLoughlin, William G. *Champions of the Cherokees: Evan and John B. Jones*. Princeton, NJ: Princeton University Press, 1990.

Murray, David. "Spreading the Word: Missionaries, Conversion, and Circulation in the Northeast." In *Spiritual Encounters: Interactions between Christianity and Native Religions in Colonial America*, edited by Nicholas Griffiths and Fernando Cervantes, 43–64. Birmingham: University of Birmingham Press, 1999.

Nabokov, Peter. *Where the Lightning Strikes: The Lives of American Indian Sacred Places*. New York: Viking, 2006.

Native Ministries International. "Statement on Native Spirituality." nativemi.org/statement-on -native-spirituality (accessed November 23, 2019).

Newcomb, Steven T. *Pagans in the Promised Land: Decoding the Doctrine of Christian Discovery*. Golden, CO: Fulcrum, 2008.

Occom, Samson. *The Collected Writings of Samson Occom: Mohegan Leadership and Literature in Eighteenth-Century Native America*, edited by Joanna Brooks. New York: Oxford University Press, 2006.

Pardue, Crystal. "Christian Devils: How the Bible Was Used to Mobilize Oppression of Native Americans." *Last Real Indians*, March 6, 2018. lastrealindians.com/news/2018/3/6/mar-6 -2018-christian-devils-how-the-bible-was-used -to-mobilize-oppression-of-native-americans-by -crystal-pardue.

Purvis, Jason E. "A 'Circle in a Rectangle': Native Evangelicals, Trans-Indigenous Networks, and the Negotiation between Legitimation and Evasion." PhD diss., University of Florida, 2017.

Ramsey, Jarold. "The Bible in Western Indian Mythology." *Journal of American Folklore*, no. 358 (1977): 442–54.

Ronda, James P. "The Bible and Early American Indian Missions." In *The Bible and Social Reform*, edited by Ernest R. Sandeen, 9–30. Philadelphia: Fortress, 1982.

Ross-Dick, Nicholas. "My Story: How My Life Changed; Can I Be Native American and Christian?," with Rich Atkinson. *Cru*, 1994– 2018. www.cru.org/us/en/how-to-know-god /my-story-a-life-changed/nick-ross.html.

Round, Phillip H. *Removable Type: Histories of the Book in Indian Country, 1663–1880*. Chapel Hill: University of North Carolina Press, 2010.

Rubin, Julius H. *Tears of Repentance: Christian Indian Identity and Community in Colonial Southern New England*. Lincoln: University of Nebraska Press, 2013.

SAGU American Indian College. "Mission and Core Values." www.aicag.edu/about/mission-and -values (accessed November 23, 2019).

Schenk, Edwin. "Native American Christians— Surviving Christianity." *The Salt Collective*. thesaltcollective.org/native-american -christians-surviving-christianity (accessed October 2, 2019).

Silverman, David J. *Faith and Boundaries: Colonists, Christianity, and Community among the Wampanoag Indians of Martha's Vineyard, 1600–1871*. Cambridge: Cambridge University Press, 2005.

Smith, Andrea. "Native Evangelicals and Scriptural Ethnologies." In *MisReading America: Scriptures and Differences*, edited by Vincent L. Wimbush, 23–85. Oxford: Oxford University Press, 2013.

Sugirtharajah, R. S. *The Bible and the Third World: Precolonial, Colonial, and Postcolonial Encounters*. Cambridge: Cambridge University Press, 2001.

Tarango, Angela. *Choosing the Jesus Way: American Indian Pentecostals and the Fight for the Indigenous Principle*. Chapel Hill: University of North Carolina Press, 2014.

Tinker, George E. *American Indian Liberation: A Theology of Sovereignty*. Maryknoll, NY: Orbis, 2008.

Tinker, George E. *Spirit and Resistance: Political Theology and American Indian Liberation*. Minneapolis: Fortress, 2004.

Twiss, Richard. *One Church, Many Tribes*. Ventura, CA: Regal, 2000.

Twiss, Richard. *Rescuing the Gospel from the Cowboys: A Native American Expression of the Jesus Way*. Downers Grove, IL: InterVarsity, 2015.

Vecsey, Christopher. *Where the Two Roads Meet*. Notre Dame, IN: University of Notre Dame Press, 1999.

Wallace, Anthony F. C. *The Death and Rebirth of the Seneca*. New York: Vintage, 1972.

Warrior, Robert Allen. "Canaanites, Cowboys, and Indians." In *Voices from the Margin: Interpreting the Bible in the Third World*, edited by R. S. Sugirtharajah, 283–90. Rev. ed. Maryknoll, NY: Orbis, 2006.

Woodley, Randy. *Living in Color: Embracing God's Passion for Ethnic Diversity*. Downers Grove, IL: InterVarsity, 2001.

Woodley, Randy. *Mixed Blood. Not Mixed Up: Finding God-Given Identity in a Multi-cultural World*. Hayden, AL: Randy Woodley, 2004.

Woodley, Randy. *When Going to Church Is Sin, and Other Essays on Native American Christian Missions*. Scotland, PA: Healing the Land, 2007.

Fallen Star

ELLA DELORIA

> I have been steeped in Dakota lore and seen and felt it around me ever since
> childhood, it is in fact the very texture of my being.
> —Ella Cara Deloria

Born on January 31, 1889, to Mary and Reverend Philip J. Deloria on the Yank-
ton Reservation, Ella Cara Deloria spent much of her life deeply immersed in
the Dakota and Lakota oral storytelling traditions.[1] As a member of the Dakota
nation, Deloria was familiar with both storytelling traditions because shortly after
she was born, her family moved to the Standing Rock Reservation, where she was
exposed to the Lakota dialect and also began attending boarding school. In 1910
Deloria graduated from All Saints Boarding School and continued her education
at the University of Chicago, Oberlin College, and Columbia College. At Columbia
College, Deloria met the famed anthropologist Franz Boas, who hired her in 1927 to
correct and retranslate Dakota and Lakota texts collected by early nineteenth-
century missionaries and ethnologists who desperately wanted to preserve traditional oral stories as a record of a primitive people rapidly nearing extinction.

In 1938 Deloria began interviewing tribal storytellers and historians on the
Flandreau Reservation to learn more about these traditional oral stories. Deloria's
letters to Boas hint at several discrepancies between oral and print versions of
"Fallen Star."[2] For example, Deloria observes that the tribal storytellers and historians she interviewed were troubled that these early translations often seemed to con-
flate the Dakota oral storytelling tradition with Christian and Greek mythology.
Although Deloria expressed these concerns to Boas, he largely dismissed them,
eventually republishing Stephen Riggs's translation with just a few minor grammatical corrections. Deloria, on the other hand, seemed to take these concerns to
heart and completely rewrote "Fallen Star" as well as several other *ohų'kaką* tales
to reflect a tribal worldview that honored and celebrated the Dakota way of life.

These nineteen stories are part of Deloria's unpublished manuscript "Dakota
Legends," housed in the Ella Deloria Archive at the Dakota Indian Foundation (DIF)
in Chamberlain, South Dakota.[3] I would like to thank the DIF for preserving Deloria's incredible body of work and for giving *English Language Notes* permission to
publish "Fallen Star" for the first time. *Wopila!*

ENGLISH LANGUAGE NOTES

58:1, April 2020 DOI 10.1215/00138282-8237487
© 2020 Regents of the University of Colorado

Fallen Star

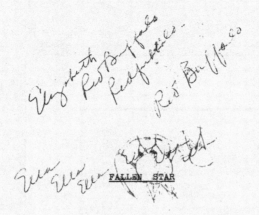

FALLEN STAR

In a certain Dakota village, long ago, there
lived two girl-cousins who were also constant companions.
They were now of that age when girls' thought turn naturally towards men and marriage.

One summer evening, when their mothers finished
a fine new tipi and set it up to inspect its proportions,
they begged to be allowed to sleep in it the first night,
while it was so new and fresh. Of course their mothers
said yes.

So they spread their beds on the clean grass in
the very centre and lay down to sleep; but first they must
exchange confidences, as young girls will. So they lay
talking and watching the stars that shone brightly through
the smoke-opening where the flaps had been left spread
out for the night, for ventilation. They were especially

--2--

near tonight, almost human, those stars.

After a while, one girl said idly, "Cousin, do you
see that biggest, most brilliant star? I am sure he must be
the chief. I wish he were my husband!"

And the other answered, "Yes. And do you see the
one near it? Not so big, nor so bright, but sparkling continuously? I wish he were my husband!"

Soon afterward they both fell asleep. And, lo and
behold, they woke in the heaven-world where all the stars were
people, and each girl was the wife of the star of her own
choosing.

This upper world was both beautiful and strange. And
the tipsila, usually something of a task to find on earth, grew
everywhere, with their flowers much larger up there, dotting the entire landscape. The handsome male plants stood out conspicu-
ously far above the grasses; and invariably their shy wives,
in plainer dress, were close by, just as they are on earth.

Since Dakota women can never resist digging tipsila,
the two cousins prepared speedily to do so now, by borrowing digging sticks from their neighbors. But their husbands returned just then.

"No, do not dig them. Nobody does so, up here. Why
not pick instead the beautiful twin-flowers that are so plentiful?" they advised. And indeed the purple furry-stemmed and
·petalled spring flowers were thick everywhere, though it was
long past their season down below. So they picked twin-flowers instead.

One day when the Star Nation moved camp to a

--3--

new site, the Dakota women arranged to place their tipis
side by side. And when the wife of the Great Star, now
with child, entered her tipi to lay the mats and robes for
the beds, she saw a magnificent tipsila, growing in the very
centre. The temptation was too great.

"I will dig it. Inside my own lodge here, who will
ever know of it?" she thought.

So she brought in a digging stick and worked it
into the ground far enough to uproot the plant by overturning
the sod all around it. But lo! directly she did this, she
made a hole that proved to be an opening in the sky through
which she fell headlong down, down, down to earth!

And there she lay dead, her young body broken by
the fall. And, near by, her infant son lay kicking and crying,
still linked to his lifeless mother. Thus So little Fallen Star
was born.

away was the tipi of
Not far from here there lived an aged couple and
every morning the husband went forth to walk about in the
woods for whatever he might find. So once again he was going
along when he heard a feeble infant-voice crying. He followed
till he
the sound and found the child and its dead mother. So He placed
the tiny child in his bosom inside his robe, and took it home.

"Wife, something I have seen this day which makes me
sad," he began. "Why! What is it, old man?" she said, impati-
annoying
ently, for it was his way to be slow of speech.

"I saw today a beautiful young woman. She lay
dead upon the ground. Her body was broken; and a babe lay

--4--

near by, kicking and crying. It was a man child," he finished.

"You stupid old man, why must you take so long? Why didn't you take him up and bring him home?" she almost scream-ed, and now began to whimper to hold back the tears, at the thought of the pity of it all. But, just then the old man took the red squirming infant out of his blanket. "This is he," he said.

Then she laughed to see. "O, old man, what if, at our age, we should manage to bring him up?" she exclaimed.

"We can; and we will," he answered. "I shall roll him down the tipi-side."

"O yes, do! Do!" She was all eagerness. So he stood up inside the tipi, and tossed the babe upward through the smoke opening at the top, and he rolled down the outside, to the ground. In a moment or so, a child in the creeping stage came in through the doorway.

But Mercilessly he picked him up and threw him upward again. And lo, presently a small boy ran nimbly in. A third time, and they heard him bounce and bump down the side, and strike the ground outside with a thud; and a very talkative boy ran in with some twigs in his hand.

"Grandfather, make me some toy arrows at once!" he begged. But for the fourth and last time, the old man picked him up. It was not easy now, but with great effort he heaved him up out of the opening. Then the two sat and waiting. For a long time they sat waiting. But finally a handsome youth entered the tipi, carrying some saplings suitable for arrows. "Make these for me, grandfather. I want to go hunting," he said.

--5--

How happy the old pair were now, for they had a grandson, grown up from helpless infancy to his full stature, all in a day! They hastened to take him into their home and into their lives. The youth proved himself an excellent hunter, and brought in an abundance of game daily, so that very soon the little household was well provisioned, with many skins for new garments and a tent, and with much food stored away.

In the honor-place the grandmother built the youth a bed banked high with the softest robes. And many friends and strangers came to visit, and nobody was turned away without food. And the old man said,

"Wife, so full of joy am I, let me stand on some high hill, and proclaim my good luck to the world, by inviting all to a feast," and she replied, "Then do so!"

Accordingly he did so; and invited all who heard him to a feast. And they shared in the great supply of food which Fallen Star had provided, and all went away happy.

Soon after, Fallen Star grew restless, as young men will. "Grandfather, I want to go traveling," he told him. And the old man was wise. "That is as it should be, grandson. When one is young, one should do his journeying; and when he is old, let him sit at home. Yes, you shall go."

So Fallen Star set out to see the world. After some days, he came to a people in a tribal camp nestled close in the bend of a river. In the open space within the circle of tipis, community games were going on. He entered and reached a group of men who were watching a hoop-and-stick contest, and stood next to a young man of perhaps his own age.

--6--

"Well, I may as well stop here, next to my friend, and look on with him," he said to himself, but loud enough to be heard. And the young man moved quietly over to give him room, as he hoped he would. So the two stood, exchanging opinions about the game.

After it was over, the friend asked Fallen Star where he came from. And upon learning that he was a traveler from another tribe, he took him home to his grandmother's tipi, for he was an orphan, raised by his grandmother, *whose lodge was his only home.*

As they approached it, he called out, "Grandmother, I am bringing my friend Fallen Star. Hurry and set food before him, for he has journeyed far today." But the old woman replied in distress, "Alas, grandson, what can I do? You know the curse we are under!"

Fallen Star asked what it was. It seemed that the entire tribe was slowly dying for lack of water. For whenever anyone went for water, after he had dipped it out and turned about to come home, he was no longer seen.

Here ~~This~~ was a challenge *for Fallen Star —* "Get a water container. You and I are going for water!" he said to his friend.

Whereupon the old woman started to wail. "Alas, grandson! What will become of you, after all the trouble it cost me to bring you up!" And she bent low where she stood, and wept, letting her tears fall of themselves to the ground.

But the youth said lightly, "Come now, grandmother, do not be always worrying over trifling things!" and he departed with Fallen Star.

--7-- *long since*

Near the stream there stood wooden troughs filled with *very clear* water, for the sand had settled in the bottom. It sparkled in the sun. Fallen Star dipped his container into it, calling out defiantly as he did so,

"Whither have you gone? You who are said to punish all ~~that~~ come for water? For I Fallen Star have come for water!"

Forthwith the two young men vanished, and for a time even they themselves did not know where they were. But afterwards they found themselves in a great room. It was very long, extending far into the distance, and seemed made of logs ~~and~~ parallel. And along the wall ~~sat~~ countless youtns and maidens imprisoned there for having tried to get water.

Doubtless there was a time when these were beautiful and vigorous; but now they were in a piteous state. Some were already dead ~~and~~ the rest were about to die. They had had no water or food since they came in.

Fallen Star questioned those who were still strong enough to talk. "Now, how is it that you are all here?" And they said, "You ought to know, ~~for~~ you have been swallowed by the monster, just as we were, for getting water." So the two latest arrivals sat down at the end, and Fallen Star leaned back on the wall to rest his head. As he did so, he felt and heard something ticking regularly.

"Why, what's this?" he asked, jumping up. "Hush!" they whispered, "that is the *heart* of It!"

Immediately he took ~~out~~ his knife *out* of its sheath, and boldly slashed and sliced it to pieces, to the horror of all who sat within. It stopped ticking then; and the whole

Page 8 is
missing
from the
Original

--9--

seen to it that all things had been accomplished correctly,
as if for him; and ˄he traveled on for many days, coming at length
to another tribe in a great circular ˄summer camp on the open prairie.

In the centre was great commotion and much cheering and
laughter. From time to time, the entire multitude of onlookers
moved in droves from one point to another. When he went to see
the cause of it all, he found ˄that a shinney game ˄was being played by
Dakota women. Handsome, lithe-bodied women ran, swiftly, as
one might draw a line, here and there over the field, intent only on the ball. It was truly a sight to see.

Fallen Star took his place amid the spectators, and saw
that the one near him was an especially agreeable looking young
man. So he remarked, as though to himself, "Here will I stop
a while, and look on with my friend."

At once the young man courteously moved to give him room.
When the game was over, he said, "Friend, where do you come
from?" And when he realized that Fallen Star was a visitor,
not ˄even from the next tribe, but ~~beyond it~~ from, farther off, he invited
him to his home ~~at once~~. with no delay.

"Grandmother, hasten some food. My friend here is a traveler from far off," he called, as he entered. But the old woman
shook her head sadly, as she greeted Fallen Star -

"Alas, grandson, it is good you have come to visit. But
in our tribe, the people are dying for want of ~~food~~ Whoever
goes for ~~fuel~~ wood fails to return so that by now we are not able to
cook our ~~food.~~ meat. And when winter comes, we shall probably freeze
to death. How can I ~~cook to give~~ prepare you food?"

--10--

But Fallen Star was undaunted by this news. "Take up a
pack strap," he told his friend, "we are going after wood!"

The old woman began to raise objections, but ended by
weeping helplessly, being old and easily ~~given to~~ *moved to tears*.

"Alas, *my* grandson, with what difficulty I brought him up!
Now he will surely die!" she wailed.

But the youth laughed away her fears, "Stop worrying,
grandmother, you only *beckon to* ~~borrow~~ trouble, *by* fearing trifling things.
I shall be all right, with my friend here," and he left with *it.*

As the two walked through camp, Fallen Star cried out,
"I am going after firewood. If there be any who wish to join
me, come on!" And the word passed rapidly from tipi to tipi,

"A young man...... Oh, very fearless! .... he has
come from somewhere away...... he says this......." and soon
from here and there other young braves came running out to
join him with pack straps thrown over their shoulder.

They arrived in the wood. All about lay great bundles of
fuel which had been gathered and strapped ready for carrying
home--and then abandoned. Some apparently had lain there a
long time, while others had been gathered only recently. Those
who came with Fallen Star took up these bundles and started
home, being told by Fallen Star to go. But he remained behind
and when the rest were well out of the wood, he cried *out in a voice* aloud ~~so~~
that ~~it~~ rang and echoed down the river,

"Whither are you gone, you who are said to kill those
who come for firewood? For I, Fallen Star, have come for firewood!"

Straightway he vanished from view, and himself did

--11--

not know where he was. After a time, however, he found himself
in a great round room. And it was filled with youths and maidens.
Some were dead and others were dying from long imprisonment.

As Fallen Star was about to take a seat, he ~~saw~~ *noticed* overhead a spot which appeared to be drawn very tightly together in
a pucker. *While he ~~took~~ was taking careful aim at it,*
~~He aimed his arrow at it, but then~~ the ones who saw
him laid hands on him to restrain him. "Take care," they ad-
monished, "for that is It." But even so he let fly the arrow
which struck the pursed spot and stood impaled in the folds.
And at once the tipi-like room opened out and the prisoners
stepped out into daylight again. For it was none other than
the Owl ~~Monster,~~ who had thus caught the youth of the tribe and
thrown them into his enormous ear and kept them trapped there.

They ~~ran in~~ *hastened home* to the village; and there
was great joy everywhere, And again these people gave ~~him~~ *Fallen Star* their
two finest maidens, revered for their chastity, that he might
take them for his wives.

But he refused them. "Ah, ~~but~~ they are lovely! Not
every man gets *the* ~~a~~ tribe's two ~~loveliest~~ *best maidens* for his wives. But,
alas, for me they can not be, for I am a roving man. There-
fore my friend here shall take them to wife." So all the rites
and formalities for a young chieftain's taking a wife were
carried out for the humbly-reared youth who had befriended
Fallen Star.

As for him, he went on far~~ther~~ *he*, and in due time
arrived at another encampment. ~~This was the fourth tribe
he was to know.~~ Here a moccasin game was being played. Men

--12--

participants

crowded around the seated ~~players~~, intent on watching every
movement of the skillful players whose sleight-of-hand in
hiding the "moccasin" was unbelievable. Fallen Star pushed
his way in as politely as that could be done, and stopped,
saying as if to himself,.

"I'll just stand here and watch, over my friend's
shoulder,"and at once the young man moved to give him room.
When the game was over, he invited him home.

"Hurry, grandmother, here is my friend, Fallen Star,
who has come from a far-off tribe. He is my guest, so get him
some food!" he called. But the old woman came limping around
from the back of the tipi, looking greatly troubled. "Alas,
how can I provide food for your guest?" she asked.

Fallen Star asked why not, and he learned that the
tribe was being dominated by the cruel cold-god.

"Waziya lives near us," the old woman told him," and
abuses this tribe beyond endurance. Whenever there is a chase
and the people are butchering the animals they have killed,
he goes along claiming all the meat. Thus it is that he alone
has food in abundance stored about his home, while all the
people are perishing slowly."

Fallen Star was indignant. "Grandmother, go to the
lodge of Waziya and tell him this: Fallen Star, my grandson,
has come on a journey but I have no food for him, so he has
sent me to tell you about it.'"

In fear and trembling she went forth, and stopped
~~well~~ *safe* at a distance from the cold-god's home, too timid to

--13--

go nearer, and called out weakly, "Waziya, my grandson Fallen
Star has come on a journey but I have no food for him, so he
has sent me to tell you about it."

Waziya was furious that she should dare to annoy him.
"You worthless old thing, get you gone, and do not come here
again, making a nuisance of yourself!" he shouted, causing
her to hobble back, shaking *all the way*

She came home crying, "I think he intends to kill me
outright--the way he yelled at me who am a ~~cautious~~ *timid* woman by
nature!" she sobbed,"I can not stand to be shouted at!"

Fallen Star instructed his friend to get a pack-strap
and go with him. Together they arrived at Waziya's tipi. All
around outside the giant lodge great bales of dried jerked meat
lay in high piles. Fallen Star took several of them and strapped them on his friend's back, and sent him home to the grandmother. "Tell her to cook some and have it ready," he said.

Then he entered the lodge where Waziya sat scowling,
cross-legged, in his bed-space. What is this, Waziya?" he
asked curiously, pointing to a huge bow of ice which hung
from a tipi-pole.

"Let that be!" Waziya warned, "for whoever touches
it gets a broken arm!"

I will touch it, and see if I do get a broken arm,
thought Fallen Star. So he took it down, but it was *too* cold
and ~~burnt~~ *numb* his hands, and heavy withal, so that it slipped
from his hands. And ~~because it was also brittle,~~ it crashed
to the ground, shattered to countless bits; but Fallen Star's
arm remained whole.

--14--

Next day there was a communal hunt and many buffaloes
were killed. But as the men were busy cutting up the meat, Waziya walked about in and out among the groups at work and selected the best of all the meat and took it, placing it inside his
emmense robe which he wore ǿpǿ held about his body by a strong
belt.

When he came to the fat cow which Fallen Star ahd
killed and was now skinning, he asked, "And whose is this one?"
Fallen Star, without looking up, replied, "I am dressing this
one. You may tell by that that it is mine!"

And Waziya was put out by his insolence. "Where do
you hail from, Fallen Star, that you dare to be so haughty and
impudent even to Waziya?" he asked.

But Fallen Star came back at him with, "And you, Waziya, what makes you think yourself so important?"

The cold-god went on, "Fallen Star, let me tell you
this: Whoever defies me by pointing a finger at me, dies on
the spot!"

Fallen Star said in turn, "Waziya, know this: Whoever points a finger at Fallen Star become paralyzed to the
elbow!"

"Why!" and Waziya in fury pointed his finger and his
arm was useless instantly. Frantically he tried with the other
hand, and that arm also became utterly limp and without life.

This emboldened Fallen Star to go further. He took
his knife and slashed the helpless Waziya's blanket into strips,
causing all the meat he had taken from the people and packed

--15--

away in it to fall to earth with a thud, all about him, The people who had watched in amazement ran and took up their meat and hurried home to their starving families. It is said that there was great feasting and much happiness in every tipi that night.

On the morrow, the herald went along proclaiming that Waziya's wife had pieced together her man's blanket which Fallen Star had almost ruined; and that presently she would stand outside and shake it out to rid it of lint, grasses and other bits.

All the people watched, apprehensive, as she stepped outside and stood facing the north, and began shaking the robe with a mighty effort, for it was very big.

And straightway, like an answer, a strong northwind began to blow, and with it appeared particles of snow. Both wind and snow gradually increased, and and soon a supernatural snow-storm was in full force. The snow piled steadily higher and higher until at last only the tops of the tallest tipis were visible; a cluster of lodge-pole tips alone indicating where the smaller ones stood.

Then the people became frightened, and began to complain, as people will, of the one who but lately they had acclaimed as their saviour.

"Alas! We did live, after a fashion at least, formerly....... but now we are undone!" they wailed.

Still Fallen Star was undaunted. "Grandmother, go out and find me a fan," he ordered. Now, with rare foresight a network of passages had been maintained from tipi to tipi under the snow, so she was able to walk along those tunnels,

--16--

looking for a fan.

"My grandson Fallen Star needs a fan!" she planned to
say at each tipi. But at the very first place she found a
group of older men gathered for the evening. To them she
put her quest.

One said, "Well, give him this!" and he threw her an
eagle's wing such as men on the decline of life carried habit-
ually, as essential to their dress as a pipe and kinnikinick
pouch.

Others commented, drily, "Whatever he wants with a fan,
this kind of weather! He is a queer lad....... well, he can
hardly harm us much more!"

When the old woman returned with the fan, Fallen Star
removed all his clothing and climbed naked to the top of the
tipi, ~~There he sat down at the place~~ where all the poles are
tied together, he seated himself, ~~there,~~ facing the south;
and began to fan himself, in all that snow.

Soon he brought forth a hint of warmth, and a south
breeze which quietly struggled with the boisterous northwind
for supremacy; and by its very stealth, overcame it.

A tremendous heat-wave, a supernatural thing, swept
over the land now, turning the snow into water at a magic
speed, equalled only when ~~one throws~~ is poured boiling water over a
pile of snow. In no time at all, what was so shortly before
a sold white now became a flowing sea.

And only Fallen Star, nude and fanning himself, was
comfortable in all that heat.

--17--

All the people suffered somewhat in the heat and the flood;
but those who fared hardest were Waziya himself and his wife and
their many mischievous children. Running amuck in an effort to
escape the unaccustomed heat, they died by the way. Only the
smooth-bellied little last-born of Waziya, the cold-god, managed
to escape with his life.

Neglected by his elders who were too frenzied to think
of him, he ran about by himself, trying to find safety. At last
he fell into a deep hole at the base of a tipi-pole, and there
he found it comfortable; for the heat did not reach the frost down
there.

And so he alone survived, And if you think it gets cold
in winter now, you are sampling only such cold as a weak little
last-born can bring. Just think what winter used to be long ago,
when Waziya, the king of the north, and his wife and stal-
wart sons, were alive to bring it on!

Notes

1   The epigraph is found in Ella Deloria to
    Virginia Dorsey Lightfoot, August 8, 1949,
    Dakota Indian Foundation, Chamberlain,
    South Dakota.

2   Ella Deloria to Franz Boas, June 28, 1938, Franz
    Boas Archive, American Philosophical Society,
    Philadelphia.

3   The DIF and Indiana University have made this
    work available at zia.aisri.indiana.edu/deloria
    _archive/index.php.

Translating and Retranslating "Fallen Star"

An *Oḣu'kaka* Tale

SARAH HERNANDEZ

Abstract   This article provides a comparative close reading of Ella Deloria's and Stephen Riggs's translations of the ancient and sacred Dakota creation story "Fallen Star." Although Deloria, a fluent Dakota/Lakota speaker, published several books on the Dakota oral storytelling tradition, Riggs is often viewed as the expert on Dakota culture, language, and literature. The impulse to privilege Riggs is problematic, because it is a new iteration of settler colonialism and patriarchy that further oppresses the Dakota nation and delegitimizes its rich and complex literary traditions. As an ethnologist and linguist, Riggs transformed the rich and complex Dakota oral storytelling tradition into a static cultural artifact. This article examines how Deloria corrected Riggs's work to incorporate tribally specific beliefs, values, and worldviews into a new interpretation of "Fallen Star."

Keywords   Dakota, indigenous, literature, translation, Ella Deloria, Stephen Riggs

In 1927 the famed anthropologist Franz Boas hired Ella Deloria to correct and translate Dakota and Lakota texts collected by several missionaries and ethnologists. This collaboration culminated in the publication of two books—*Dakota Texts* (1932) and *Dakota Grammar* (1941)—that were intended to standardize Dakota language and literature.[1] According to Lakota anthropologist Bea Medicine, these books were not well received by Dakota scholars and students, who dismissed them as "too technical." Medicine observes that many scholars and students, specifically at the tribal college level, were "disenchant[ed] with ethnological work" that often reduced Dakota language to a scientific form.[2] Ironically, Ella Deloria's nephew, Vine Deloria Jr., points out that his aunt also felt that these texts, especially *Dakota Grammar*, were problematic because they helped reduce the rich Dakota language to a series of abstract rules: "Ella did not like [that] kind of translation, which suggested that words and ideas could be easily matched across complex linguistic traditions."[3] Deloria was likely dissatisfied with this approach, because Dakota and Lakota languages "cannot be compared to single terms, or words, in English" but must be translated as "word-units" with "important knowledge . . . and cultural

ENGLISH LANGUAGE NOTES

58:1, April 2020 DOI 10.1215/00138282-8237498
© 2020 Regents of the University of Colorado

implications . . . encoded in [them]."[4] In other words, Deloria and Boas's translations not only were "too technical" but also failed to account for the cultural and linguistic nuances inherent in the Dakota oral storytelling tradition.

As an emerging anthropologist and linguist, Deloria often worked with problematic methods of analysis that altered the cultural context of Dakota language and literature. However, as a creative writer, she developed new and innovative methods that allowed her to reclaim the Dakota oral storytelling tradition and reimagine it in a more modern form as print literature. This article explores how Deloria translated and reinterpreted "Fallen Star," an *ohu'kaką* tale, an ancient and sacred Dakota oral story passed down from generation to generation to preserve and perpetuate traditional Dakota beliefs and values.[5] Although several missionaries, ethnologists, and other scholars have tried to translate "Fallen Star" in the past, I argue that Deloria is one of the few translators to incorporate tribally specific beliefs, values, and worldviews into her interpretation. While early translators trivialized and simplified "Fallen Star," thus delegitimizing the Dakota oral storytelling tradition, Deloria consciously and deliberately used her interpretations to honor and celebrate Dakota culture, language, literature, and lifeways.

"Fallen Star": A Brief Literary/Translation History

"Fallen Star" is often one of the earliest oral stories shared among the Oceti Šakowiŋ or "the Seven Council Fires." In Dakota culture it is known as an *ohu'kaką* tale or traditional story that conveys a specific cultural lesson or value.[6] Because of its rich cultural significance, "Fallen Star" was also one of the first oral stories that early Dakota storytellers shared with missionaries, ethnologists, and other translators.[7] In 1881 the Reverend Stephen Return Riggs transformed "Fallen Star" from an oral story expressed in Dakota to written forms published in both Dakota and English. Riggs's Dakota transcription was a literal translation that did not make sense in the English language. Subsequently, he composed a free translation of "Fallen Star" that captured the general meaning of the *ohu'kaką* tale. Unfortunately, however, Riggs's English translation lacked many important cultural details that inevitably altered the scope and meaning of this traditional oral story.

More than half a century later Boas recruited Ella Deloria to correct Riggs's Dakota translations. He hired Deloria, a fluent Dakota-speaker, to proofread Riggs's literal translation of "Fallen Star" for superficial errors such as grammar and spelling. However, Deloria quickly realized that Riggs's translations, both literal and free, actually required deeper revisions, as his use of "Christian idioms" had transformed "Fallen Star" from an *ohu'kaką* tale about a young Dakota hero who saves several tribal communities in peril to a Christian parable resembling Adam and Eve's fall from grace.[8] Riggs's translation focuses heavily on the theme of good and evil, denigrates women, and simplifies many important cultural and linguistic references. Although Deloria emphasized these discrepancies to Boas, he largely dismissed her concerns and republished Riggs's translation in 1941 with a few minor grammatical corrections.[9]

Dissatisfied with Boas's updated translation, Deloria took it upon herself to compose a new interpretation of "Fallen Star"—an English translation that honors and celebrates Dakota culture. Deloria's Dakota-centered interpretation of "Fallen Star" is the first story in her unpublished manuscript "Dakota Legends."[10] Unfortunately, Deloria's interpretation of "Fallen Star" has never seen the light of day, as it is buried in an archive at the Dakota Indian Foundation in Chamberlain, South Dakota. Meanwhile, Riggs's deeply flawed translations have been published and republished numerous times, with some contemporary scholars even praising them as "the only truly authentic voice to document the American Indian past."[11] The impulse to privilege Riggs as an authority of the Dakota oral storytelling tradition is problematic, because his translation of "Fallen Star" tends to diminish and devalue Dakota culture, language, literature, and lifeways. Furthermore, it displaces Deloria from the traditional role that Dakota women have always played in Dakota society as "keeper[s] of the stories."[12]

In Dakota society, "women were traditionally seen as carriers of the culture and were the primary figures responsible for imparting Dakota values."[13] Therefore many scholars theorize that Deloria consciously or unconsciously used her extensive writing and research to fulfill this traditional role in a modern tribal context. Although Deloria was firmly committed to fulfilling this cultural role, Cheryl Suzack et al. point out that it was not uncommon for male colonizers to forcibly remove Indigenous women "from their positions of power, [by] replacing their traditional gender roles with Western patriarchal practices."[14] The next section of this article demonstrates the consequences of displacing Deloria and other Dakota women as culture keepers in their tribal communities.

"Fallen Star": A Close Reading of Riggs and Deloria's Translations

Although Riggs and Deloria provided different interpretations of "Fallen Star," the basic plot of this myth remains the same. In both versions, a young woman marries a star, becomes pregnant, falls through a hole in the sky, and plummets to the earth, where she gives birth to a baby boy, who ages quickly into a young man. This young hero, known as Fallen Star, embarks on a series of adventures that allow him to assist several tribal camps in peril. Often the members of these camps are terrorized by supernatural forces that threaten their physical and emotional well-being. In their translations both Riggs and Deloria add small, subtle details that tend to alter the context and meaning of the story. For instance, Riggs filters his translation through a Western, largely Christian lens that recasts Fallen Star's parents in the roles of Adam and Eve. Meanwhile, Deloria retranslates this myth to reflect a more tribal worldview that emphasizes the importance of the Dakota kinship system and that acknowledges Dakota women's traditional role as culture keepers.

The difference between Riggs and Deloria's translation of "Fallen Star" is evident in the very first line of the text. Riggs opens his translation by simply saying, "A people had this camp."[15] This statement is generic: it fails to specify the tribe. Meanwhile, Deloria's translation refers to "a certain Dakota village" that represents one of seven unique nations among the Oceti Šakowiŋ.[16] In the first paragraph Riggs vaguely refers to the people's homes as "tents," while Deloria uses the cultural reference *tipi*, a Lakota word that "means 'they live there.'"[17] While Riggs mentions the "tents" only in passing, Deloria devotes an entire paragraph to describing how

Dakota women carefully "set up" and "inspected" their tipis.[18] This is not only a cultural reference but also a gender-specific one, as tipis "were the exclusive responsibility of the women."[19] According to Lakota linguist Albert White Hat, women are "the keeper of all our traditions and . . . the foundation of the home."[20] These different word choices emphasize that Deloria, unlike Riggs, is well aware of the cultural and linguistic nuances that exist among tribes and tribal women and men. This opening scene sets the tone for the rest of these two translations. Riggs's descriptions are often vague, lacking in detail, and inclined to ignore the significant role that women play in Dakota/Lakota culture. His translations contain the basic elements of the story but otherwise are cold and largely detached. As a result, Riggs's English translation of "Fallen Star" is less than five typed pages, while Deloria's translation is nearly twenty pages long and includes more descriptive words and modifiers. In addition to being more detailed, Deloria's literary translation is warmer and much more empathetic, especially toward Dakota women, suggesting that she is intimately connected to the people and community that she describes.

The main difference between Riggs's and Deloria's translations is, perhaps, most evident in their portrayals of Fallen Star's mother. Fallen Star is the son of a human mother and a not-so-human father. Both translations introduce Fallen Star's mother as one of two females lying under the night sky gazing at the stars. Riggs suggests the two females are grown women; meanwhile, Deloria describes them as "two girl-cousins," adding that they "exchange confidences as young girls will."[21] The women in Riggs's story are older and more mature, while Deloria suggests that the two females are younger and more innocent. The older, more mature women in Riggs's translation are sinful and willfully disobedient, bearing a striking resemblance to Eve and thus reflecting Riggs's strong Christian worldview. While Riggs condemns the actions of Fallen Star's mother as a sin, Deloria suggests that the two "girl-cousins" are merely naive, inexperienced, and prone to human error. White Hat emphasizes that "to the Lakota, a mistake is simply a mistake, and it's one of the ways we learn."[22] These different perspectives on a "sin" as opposed to a "mistake" further underscore Riggs's and Deloria's two worldviews: Christian and Dakota.

Deloria's literary translation embodies her firm belief in the Dakota kinship system. According to Deloria, "The ultimate aim of Dakota life . . . is quite simple: One must obey kinship rules; one must be a good relative."[23] Adamant about the importance of the Dakota kinship system, Deloria discusses it both directly and indirectly in much of her life's work. She discusses the Dakota kinship system explicitly in her book *Speaking of Indians* as well as in her ethnographic book *The Dakota Way of Life*. Several literary scholars also point out that it is a major theme in her posthumously published novel *Waterlily*.[24] The Dakota kinship system is also undeniably present in her retranslation of "Fallen Star," which emphasizes how the two females in this story are related (i.e., they are "girl-cousins") and how they are expected to behave toward each other (i.e., as "close friends and confidantes"). Deloria even discusses their mothers and how they care for the two "girl-cousins" and the rest of the community. In contrast, Riggs, who approaches "Fallen Star" from a Western perspective, is unconcerned with these women or their kinship relationships.

Such cultural and linguistic nuances seem small, subtle, and largely insignificant, but when ignored or dismissed, they can alter the context and meaning of the story. In Riggs's translation, Fallen Star's father explicitly "forbids" his wife to pick turnips.[25] Instead of listening to her husband, she secretly picks the forbidden turnip, slyly reasoning that "I will pick this—no one will see it."[26] Like Eve, Fallen Star's mother succumbs to temptation, picks a forbidden fruit (or vegetable), falls from paradise (literally), and is punished with the pains of childbirth. In effect, Riggs transforms this *ohu'kaka* tale from an oral story about a simple mistake to a Christian parable about the fall of humanity and the entrance of sin into the world. White Hat observes that the "Christian bias[es]" embedded in these early missionary translations still impact Dakota/Lakota language and literature today.[27]

In his translation Riggs reinterprets the death of Fallen Star's mother as punishment for deliberately disobeying her husband. After she picks the forbidden turnip, Riggs writes, "immediately the country opened," and she plummets to the earth.[28] He describes her death bluntly: "Her belly burst open. And so the woman died, but the child did not die, but lay there stretched out."[29] This description is gratuitous and violent, especially given that Riggs's translation, up until this point, lacks detail or emotion, suggesting that he means to condemn Fallen Star's mother for her supposed transgression. The decision to characterize pregnancy as punishment is biblical in nature, as God punishes Eve for eating the forbidden apple by "greatly multiply[ing]" woman's "sorrow" and "conception" (Gen. 35:16–18). Likewise, Riggs multiplies the "sorrow" of Fallen Star's mother for picking the forbidden turnip by punishing her with a pregnancy that ends in death. Riggs's condemnation of Fallen Star's mother is unsurprising, as the Christian Bible often "emphasize[s] women's sin and inferiority."[30] According to Alice Ogden Bellis, out of "all the stories in the Hebrew bible, the story of Eve has been used more than any other as the theological base for sexism."[31]

In contrast, the Lakota creation story suggests that "Winyan, woman, was created before Wicasa, man, and she was created to be like the earth and give life and nourishment."[32] In Riggs's translation, Fallen Star's mother does not give life or nourishment but rather is just as destructive as Eve, who causes the fall of humanity. Deloria provides a tribal, more feminist interpretation of the life and death of Fallen Star's mother. In Deloria's translation, Fallen Star's mother picks the turnip because "Dakota women can never resist *tipsila*," a traditional food staple with strong cultural connotations.[33] Deloria's protagonist picks the forbidden turnip because it reminds her of her culture and community. Her intentions are not sinful or evil. Nor does anybody ever explicitly "forbid" her to pick the turnip; rather, her husband cautions her that "nobody does so up here" and "advises" her to pick "the beautiful twin flowers [that] are so plentiful."[34] He does not explain why she cannot pick *tipsila* in the star world; however, she quickly learns the reason when she picks the turnip and inadvertently "make[s] a hole . . . in the sky," which she falls through, "headlong down, down, down to the earth."[35] This description suggests that Deloria imagines Fallen Star's mother as impulsive and immature, thus characterizing her death as an unfortunate tragedy.

According to White Hat, early missionaries such as Riggs often mistranslated and misinterpreted the Dakota oral storytelling tradition. He observes that Christians "tell you that if you . . . do something wrong, then something bad will happen to you. . . . What the church calls sin is simply a mistake."[36] The tone of Riggs's and Deloria's translations again underscores these two different worldviews. In his translation Riggs condemns Fallen Star's mother for her sins of succumbing to temptation and causing the fall of humanity. Deloria, on the other hand, is much more sympathetic and compassionate toward Fallen Star's mother than Riggs. She describes her death not as a form of punishment but as a tragic mistake that costs the young woman her life. Deloria writes: "There she lay dead, her young body broken by the fall. And, nearby, her infant son lay kicking and crying, still linked to his lifeless mother."[37] Deloria's description of the lifeless body of Fallen Star's mother is tragic because she is young and her death is violent and untimely. Even more heartbreaking is the image of a newborn baby without his mother. Moreover, this powerful image reinforces the power of the kinship system, because even in death the child is linked to his mother, both literally by an unsevered umbilical cord and symbolically by the unbreakable emotional bond between mother and child. Riggs's description fails to capture this bond. He does not mention any link between mother and child—physical or otherwise—emphasizing his disinterest in the Dakota kinship system, which is so important to Deloria both personally and professionally.

Clearly, Deloria and Riggs approached "Fallen Star" from very different perspectives, each of which altered the context and meaning of the story. Riggs relays the story of "Fallen Star" through a Christian lens that nearly erases the Dakota perspective and introduces the concept of sin to Dakota people. The context of his translation is not surprising, given that he was an Episcopalian minister determined to "put the word of God in their [i.e., the Dakota's] speech."[38] In many ways he succeeded. His biblical reinterpretation of "Fallen Star" has been published numerous times: in 1881, 1883, 1941, 1977, 2004, and 2015.[39] The privileging of Riggs as an authority of the Dakota oral storytelling tradition is troubling, as it is a new iteration of settler colonialism and patriarchy that further oppresses the Dakota nation and delegitimizes their rich and complex literary traditions.

Historically, Dakota women were responsible for preserving and perpetuating the Dakota oral storytelling tradition. "Women are the keeper of our way of life. They are the teachers of our way of life," says White Hat. "[But] we've lost that understanding. In the boarding schools we were taught that the man was the head of the household, the head of the family, that the man was in control."[40] Riggs, who helped establish some of the first boarding schools in Dakota Territory, used his many translations of the Dakota oral storytelling tradition to perpetuate the misogyny that White Hat references.[41] Despite Riggs's hindrance of the Dakota oral storytelling tradition, White Hat argues that "our traditional respect for women . . . [is not] gone forever. . . . It's like most of our traditional beliefs: they're still here and can still be practiced if we are willing to do so."[42] Deloria's ability to adapt and modify these traditional oral stories as print literature is further evidence that the

Dakota oral storytelling tradition (like many of our other traditions) is still alive and well in the twenty-first century.

Concluding Remarks

In "Tribalography" Leanne Howe reminds us that "the story you get depends on the writer."[43] From Riggs's point of view, "Fallen Star" (and the Dakota oral story-telling tradition in general) is a quaint story from a primitive people rapidly nearing extinction. Riggs's goal was to document and record "the Dakota race" before "they passed away, as their own buffalo of the prairie." He and his colleagues wanted to "retain an adequate memorial of them" before he (and other missionaries) forced Dakota/Lakota people to convert to Christianity and assimilate to Western society.[44] Deloria, on the other hand, used her interpretation of "Fallen Star" to challenge the damaging and pervasive myth that Dakota people were an inferior, dying race. As was often the case, Deloria used her writing and research to protect and defend the Oceti Šakowiŋ and their traditional knowledge systems by composing a representation that helps honor and celebrate Dakota literature and the important role that women play (and continue to play) in preserving Dakota culture. In effect, Deloria used her translation of "Fallen Star" and other Dakota oral stories to embrace the traditional role that Dakota women have long played in their communities as "keeper[s] of the stories." She reimagined this role in a modern tribal context that allowed her to preserve and perpetuate Dakota culture, language, literature, and lifeways for countless generations.

SARAH HERNANDEZ (Sicangu Lakota) is assistant professor of Native American literature at the University of New Mexico. Her research focuses on Oceti Šakowiŋ (Dakota, Lakota, and Nakota) literatures. She is also executive director of the Oak Lake Writers Society, a tribal group established in 1993 for Dakota, Lakota, and Nakota writers.

Notes

1   Deloria, *Dakota Texts*; Boas and Deloria, *Dakota Grammar*.
2   Medicine, "Ella Cara Deloria," 260.
3   Deloria, introduction, xiv.
4   Red Shirt Shaw, "George Sword's Warrior Narratives," 8, 161.
5   Deloria, introduction, ix.
6   Deloria, introduction, ix.
7   Goodman, *Lakota Star Knowledge*, 142.
8   Jahner, *Lakota Myth*, 22.
9   Prater, "Ella Deloria," 41–42.
10   Ella Cara Deloria, "Dakota Legends." MS, n.d., Ella C. Deloria Archive, Dakota Indian Foundation, Chamberlain, South Dakota.
11   Parks and DeMallie, "Plains Indian Native Literatures," 106.
12   Cook-Lynn, *Aurelia*, 254.
13   Kelsey, *Tribal Theory in Native American Literature*, 26.
14   Suzack et al., *Indigenous Women and Feminism*, 1.
15   Riggs, "The Fallen Star," 90.
16   Ella Cara Deloria, "Fallen Star," 1. MS, Box 2, Ella C. Deloria Archive, Dakota Indian Foundation, Chamberlain, South Dakota.
17   Marshall, *Lakota Way*, 44.
18   Riggs, "The Fallen Star," 90; Deloria, "Fallen Star," 1.
19   Marshall, *Lakota Way*, 45.
20   White Hat and Cunningham, *Life's Journey*, 57.
21   Riggs, "The Fallen Star," 90; Deloria, "Fallen Star," 1.
22   White Hat and Cunningham, *Life's Journey*, 76.
23   Deloria, *Speaking of Indians*, 25.
24   For more information on *Waterlily* and the kinship system, see Gardner, "'Though It Broke

My Heart to Cut Some Bits I Fancied'"; Cotera, "'All My Relatives Are Noble'"; Prater, "Ella Deloria"; and Medicine, "Ella Cara Deloria."

25 Riggs, "The Fallen Star," 90.

26 Riggs, "The Fallen Star," 90.

27 White Hat, *Reading and Writing the Lakota Language*, 8–9.

28 Riggs, "The Fallen Star," 90.

29 Riggs, "The Fallen Star," 90.

30 Bellis, *Helpmates, Harlots, and Heroes*, 47.

31 Bellis, *Helpmates, Harlots, and Heroes*, 47.

32 White Hat and Cunningham, *Life's Journey*, 50.

33 Deloria, "Fallen Star," 2.

34 Deloria, "Fallen Star," 2.

35 Deloria, "Fallen Star," 3.

36 White Hat and Cunningham, *Life's Journey*, 108.

37 Deloria, "Fallen Star," 3.

38 Riggs, *Mary and I*, 31.

39 Murray, "Dakota Resources," 340.

40 White Hat and Cunningham, *Life's Journey*, 76.

41 Fear-Segal, *White Man's Club*, 78.

42 White Hat and Cunningham, *Life's Journey*, 62.

43 Howe, "Tribalography," 123.

44 Riggs, "Dakota Language," 89.

Works Cited

Bellis, Alice Ogden. *Helpmates, Harlots, and Heroes: Women's Stories in the Hebrew Bible*. Louisville, KY: Westminster/John Knox Press, 1994.

Boas, Franz, and Ella Cara Deloria. *Dakota Grammar*. Washington DC: Memoirs of the National Academy of Sciencesy, 1941.

Cook-Lynn, Elizabeth. *Aurelia: A Crow Creek Trilogy*. Boulder: University Press of Colorado, 1999.

Cotera, Maria Eugenia. "'All My Relatives Are Noble': Recovering the Feminine in Ella Cara Deloria's *Waterlily*." *American Indian Quarterly* 28, no. 1 (2004): 52–72.

Deloria, Ella Cara. *The Dakota Way of Life*. Sioux Falls, SD: Mariah, 2007.

Deloria, Ella Cara. Introduction to *Dakota Texts*, ix–xi. Vermillion, SD: Dakota, 1978.

Deloria, Ella Cara. *Speaking of Indians*. Lincoln: University of Nebraska Press, 1998.

Deloria, Vine, Jr. Introduction to *Speaking of Indians*, by Ella Cara Deloria, xiv. Lincoln: University of Nebraska Press, 1998.

Fear-Segal, Jacqueline. *White Man's Club: Schools, Race, and the Struggle of Indian Acculturation*. Lincoln: University of Nebraska Press, 2007.

Gardner, Susan. "'Though It Broke My Heart to Cut Some Bits I Fancied': Ella Deloria's Original Design for *Waterlily*." *American Indian Quarterly* 27, nos. 3–4 (2003): 667–96.

Goodman, Ronald. *Lakota Star Knowledge: Studies in Lakota Stellar Theology*. Mission, SD: SGU, 1992.

Howe, Leanne A. "Tribalography: The Power of Native Stories." *Journal of Dramatic Theory and Criticism* 14, no. 1 (1999): 117–25.

Jahner, Elaine. *Lakota Myth*. Lincoln: University of Nebraska Press, 2006.

Kelsey, Penelope Myrtle. *Tribal Theory in Native American Literature: Dakota and Haudenosaunee Writing and Indigenous Worldviews*. Lincoln: University of Nebraska Press, 2008.

Marshall, Joseph. *The Lakota Way: Stories and Lessons for Living*. New York: Penguin Compass, 2002.

Medicine, Beatrice. "Ella Cara Deloria: Early Lakota Ethnologist (Newly Discovered Novelist)." In *Theorizing the Americanist Tradition*, edited by Lisa Philips Valentine and Regna Darnell, 259–67. Toronto: University of Toronto Press, 1999.

Murray, Janette. "Dakota Resources: Historical Sketch and Selected Bibliography of Early Linguistic Research in Dakota/Lakota Language." *South Dakota History* 9, no. 10 (1979): 337–48.

Parks, Douglas R., and Raymond J. DeMallie. "Plains Indian Native Literatures." *boundary 2* 19, no. 3 (1992): 105–47.

Prater, John. "Ella Deloria: Varied Intercourse; Ella Deloria's Life and Work." *Wicazo Sa Review* 11, no. 2 (1995): 40–46.

Red Shirt Shaw, Delphine R. "George Sword's Warrior Narratives: A Study in the Processes of Composition of Lakota Oral Narrative." PhD diss., Arizona State University, 2013.

Riggs, Stephen Return. "The Dakota Language." In vol. 1 of *Collections of the Minnesota Historical Society*, 89–107. St. Paul, MN, 1872.

Riggs, Stephen Return. "Fallen Star." In *Dakota Grammar: With Texts and Ethnography*, edited by John Nichols, 83–94. St. Paul: Minnesota Historical Society Press, 2004.

Riggs, Stephen Return. *Mary and I: Forty Years with the Sioux*. Boston, 1880.

Suzack, Cheryl, Shari M. Huhndorf, Jeanne Perreault, and Jean Barman. *Indigenous Women and Feminism: Politics, Activism, Culture*. Vancouver: University of British Columbia Press, 2010.

White Hat, Albert, Sr., and John Cunningham. *Life's Journey—Zuya: Oral Teachings from Rosebud*. Salt Lake City: University of Utah Press, 2012.

White Hat, Albert, Sr. *Reading and Writing the Lakota Language: Lakota Iyapi Un Wowapi Nahan Yawapi*, edited by Jael Kampfe. Salt Lake City: University of Utah Press, 2006.

Tales of (De)colonization in the Peruvian Amazon

The Case of the Iskonawa

JOSÉ ANTONIO MAZZOTTI

Abstract   This article presents some results of a long-term research project on the Iskonawa, a Peruvian Amazon community that until recently many specialists considered
gone. The few living speakers hold a world of knowledge and oral tradition that a team
of Peruvian researchers has been collecting since 2010. Some Iskonawa myths of origin
and survival tell us about their relationship with nature, their use of animals and plants,
and a bleak future of deforestation, contamination, drug trafficking, and other crimes. In
some of these narratives, it is possible to find alternative views of nature and the world
in general that challenge the Western and neoliberal approach to the Amazonian basin.
Keywords   Iskonawa, Peruvian Amazon, decolonization, myth, origin

The Iskonawa oral tradition is full of knowledge about nature and survival strategies that speak volumes about the environment and the possibility of coexistence among humans and between humans and nature. Let us start with a few basic
concepts. The Amazon rain forest covers an area of over 2 million square miles, and
it is estimated to host over three hundred indigenous languages and their corresponding ethnic groups.[1] In Brazil there are around two hundred of these communities, sixty of them still in voluntary isolation. In Peru there are seventeen linguistic families and around fifty originary languages, at least ten of them in imminent
danger of disappearance in the next few years due to rapid deforestation, contamination, cultural contact, and forced migration.

Iskonawa is one of those languages. My work with the small community that
still speaks it in the Peruvian jungle could not have been done without a serious
and comprehensive documentation of its culture. As opposed to traditional linguistics and anthropology, language and cultural documentation implies, first, a large
amount of audiovisual data that serves as a bank of information for future researchers. No documentation team can presume to record all cultural manifestations in a
given community, however small it is, much less presume to produce a total and
detailed description and analysis of that culture. Documentation does not mean

ENGLISH LANGUAGE NOTES

58:1, April 2020 DOI 10.1215/00138282-8237509
© 2020 Regents of the University of Colorado

an extensive lexicon or a detailed grammar, either. That will be the task of other specialists, who will ultimately impose their own criteria in their selection and organization of the material. It is not that linguistic description does not occur in a documentation and revitalization project but that it does so to a lesser degree than in a traditional linguistic endeavor. A documentation project of endangered cultures will be interdisciplinary in nature and also more ambitious, especially when it includes a revitalization component that has a direct impact on the life of the community.

I started to work on this project in 2010. At that time I was looking for a research interest beyond literary and historical analysis, which is what I have been doing most of my professional life. Going back to my juvenile years as a linguist, and in talking to old professors and colleagues in Lima, I decided to find out about a language that some thought had completely disappeared.

The Iskonawa language is an almost extinct variety of the Pano family in the Amazonian basin (in the Pucallpa area and the "Sierra del Divisor," near the border with Brazil). The area is privileged because of its unique volcanic origin, with mountains reaching up to three thousand feet and numerous thermal waterfalls, a condition favoring what biologists call a rapid process of "speciation."

The Iskonawa language has been poorly documented and increasingly displaced by the Shipibo-Konibo language (also from the Pano family) and, obviously, by Spanish. Because of its extreme vulnerability and the real risk that it will disappear in the next generation, the Iskonawa case is a sad example of the ongoing process of colonization in the Amazon. It constitutes modern evidence of the failure of modern states in countries with large originary populations, like Peru, whose approximately 7 million "indigenous" inhabitants constitute 24 percent of the entire population.

I began doing research on this community with a multidisciplinary team of researchers, including Roberto Zariquiey and Rodolfo Cerrón-Palomino (two linguists from Peru) as co–principal investigators. We also secured a few research assistants to aid in the collection and formatting of data. One of them, Carolina Rodríguez Alzza, has become a specialist on Iskonawa culture.

In July 2010 I planned a visit to the community of Chachi Bai, located about eight hours by boat from Yarinacocha, the lakeside port of the city of Pucallpa. Chachi Bai is the name of an ancient Iskonawa chief who was also an important *curandero*, or medicine man. While both Iskonawas and Shipibos inhabited this town, the place-name indicates that Chachi Bai had been home to a number of Iskonawa families.

The history of the Iskonawa people is tragic. According to the anthropologists Louis Whiton, H. Bruce Greene, Richard P. Momsen, and André Marcel D'Ans, the Iskonawa are the last remnants of a larger group called the Remo, who were gradually expelled from western Brazil and killed by neighboring tribes and modern *caucheros* (rubber privateers) in the early twentieth century.[2]

The Iskonawa call themselves the Iskubakebu but used their current name more frequently after 1959. That year Protestant missionaries from the South American Mission tracked the noncontacted Iskonawa and convinced twenty-four of them to leave the jungle. The missionaries relocated those twenty-four Iskonawas from the upper Utiquinía river to the current Shipibo community of Callería.

The original name Iskubakebu is a compound word formed by the roots *isko/ isku*, a type of bird (the oriole), and *bake*, "child," to which the collective/plural suffix *ûbo/-bu* has been added. It is probable that those Iskubakebu or Iskonawa who were not relocated—and their descendants—today constitute a community in voluntary isolation of around a hundred members.

In terms of field research, this was a privileged situation: we got to work on the language of an isolated community but without having direct contact with them, just with members of the group who were assimilated and their children and grandchildren. The Iskonawa who worked with us are basically trilingual: they speak Iskonawa (especially the elders), Shipibo, and Spanish.

Iskonawa is not yet extinct, but it will be soon. André D'Ans registered only twenty speakers in 1973. Other linguists and anthropologists have identified a few Iskonawa speakers dispersed among the Shipibo communities on the borders of the Callería River, one of the Ucayali's tributaries.[3] Despite the existence of few Iskonawa speakers, the handful of modern scholars who have approached them provided only some cultural and historical—not linguistic—description. We were left only with short vocabularies totaling merely a hundred words combined.

Our project filled this gap in the knowledge and, because most Iskonawas have to speak Shipibo to survive in their host communities, we also measured the degree of linguistic interference. We identified at least fourteen native speakers, five of them completely fluent. They are the last survivors of the group of twenty-four who split from the main community in 1959.

The other identified speakers of Iskonawa have an intermediate to minimal command of the language. They live within larger Shipibo communities; in scattered *caseríos*, or small farms, along the Callería River; in the communities of Callería, San Miguel, and Guacamayo; and in the cities of Pucallpa and Tingo María.

I met doña Nelita Rodríguez Campos (or Nawá Niká), a seventy-year-old Iskonawa woman with whom I conversed in Spanish. Doña Nelita was born in an old Iskonawa village near the head of the Utiquinía River, some seventy miles east of the Callería community, where she was living in 2010. My initial contact with her allowed me to map the situation of the surviving Iskonawa.

A year later, in August 2011, Roberto Zariquiey (one of my co–principal investigators and a specialist in Pano languages) and I traveled again to the area. We met with doña Nelita, her son Felipe, and four of her grandchildren, now in their early twenties. This second trip allowed both of us to confirm that Iskonawa still existed as an independent language, although it already presented some traces of language attrition. Doña Nelita and her family completed several lists of vocabulary. She also produced complete sentences, narrated some passages of her personal life, and told a popular tale about a local bird in Iskonawa. All this material was immediately translated into Spanish and compared to Shipibo with the help of our Iskonawa collaborators. After collecting over two hundred lexical entries, many simple and compound sentences, and samples of oral narrative, we verified that Iskonawa still has its own grammatical and phonological features.

We also learned that the surviving Iskonawa of the area continually move to Chachi Bai, where they still have *chacras*, or orchards. They congregate in Chachi Bai, moreover, to keep their language and ethnic identity alive. They fear that Shipibo families living in Chachi Bai may overpower them and expel them from their traditional town. They understand that at least some sporadic presence in Chachi Bai is the best way to keep the members of the Iskonawa community together and to defend their rights against the log privateers who abound in the area.

The initial fieldwork demonstrated the feasibility of the project, so we presented it to the National Science Foundation and received a grant in 2012.[4] Our original idea was to complete the project in three and a half years, from July 2012 to December 2015, but circumstances delayed the conclusion of the project until 2018.

During 2012 we traveled to the area to help set up basic infrastructure and work closely with the community in the initial compilation of recordings and raw material, as well as in training young members of the community in basic techniques of data compilation.

During 2013–14 the team returned to Chachi Bai to complete data recording and continue the training of the young native speakers. The training included travel to Lima for ten Iskonawa members to attend a seminar on data compilation and processing at Pontifical Catholic University (PUCP), our partner institution. The team worked on the completion of the database, including an archive with lexical specificities and oral history materials that serve as future references for native speakers and researchers.

We had four specific goals: (1) produce a database, a website, and publications with linguistic, ethnohistorical, and environmental information; (2) train PUCP and Tufts University students in language documentation; (3) train native speakers in the preservation and revitalization of the Iskonawa language; and (4) empower the Iskonawa community.

These materials are being disseminated through various dedicated web pages and printed publications available to both specialists and the general public. Our research project is a first step in preserving the language and culture of the Iskonawa people. Our long-term goal is to develop local resources to participate in much-needed language revitalization, thus preserving the linguistic diversity of the region and providing scholars with additional insight into the intersections of language and culture.

Background and Rationale

Going back to the big picture: Peru is the territory of at least nineteen originary linguistic families: the Quechua family, the Aimara family, and seventeen Amazonian families, where there is a largely understudied linguistic variety. The Quechua and Aimara families each include a set of linguistic variables that are languages in their own right. The Amazonian families include the Pano, Jíbaro, Bora, Tucano, Huitoto, Arahuaca, and others, all with different degrees of complexity, numbers of languages, and distinctive grammatical features. In the Pano family, for example, at least seventeen of thirty registered languages are still spoken in the central-east area of Peru and the central-west area of Brazil. Iskonawa is one of them. As I mention above, there are still five elders who speak Iskonawa fluently and nine others who have some speaking ability. These individuals form part of the contacted Iskonawa group, the few who remain so long after the forced relocations and assimilation.

However, a 1995 report by the Inter-Ethnic Development Association of the Peruvian Rainforest (Asociación Interétnica de Desarrollo de la Selva Peruana—Ucayali Chapter) indicates that, in addition to the known Iskonawa people who live in Chachi Bai and on the banks of the Callería River, there are still about a hundred members in complete isolation, distributed in twenty-one families.[5] In 1998 the Peruvian government created the Iskonawa Territorial Reservation on 275,665 hectares at the heads of the Abujao, Utiquinía, and Callería Rivers, next to the border with Brazil. There may be other Iskonawa families living in isolation on the Brazilian side as well. For obvious legal, sanitary, and ethical reasons, nobody can contact those voluntarily isolated members of the Iskonawa group. The journal *Ethnologue* mentions eighty-two speakers in 2000 (www.ethnologue.com/language/isc), but it is not clear if those are the noncontacted members of the Iskonawa community. Our direct experience in the area points to the lower number of fourteen, at least in terms of known speakers with different degrees of competency. While this small group of speakers is sufficient for documenting the phonology, syntax, lexicon, and oral tradition of the Iskonawa language, it implies that immediate preservation of these data is crucial.

Iskonawa Language and Its Social and Historical Contexts

Very little was known about the Iskonawa language. Some of the Shipibo speakers we consulted claimed that they could barely understand the Iskonawas when they spoke "in their dialect." However, from the few lexical examples that linguists have compiled, there do seem to be an important number of cognates between Iskonawa and Shipibo, in part owing to genetic reasons and the prolonged contact between the two languages. Our conclusion is that there is an overlap of about 60 percent between the two languages.

In regard to Iskonawa oral tradition, Bernd Brabec de Mori and Jefferson Pérez Casapía refer to a type of song or chant called *yoamai*, which healing *curanderos* or shamans use to ward off the evils plaguing their patients.[6] Also important to an understanding of Iskonawa oral culture is the list that Whiton, Greene, and Momsen compiled of the names of various Iskonawa divinities and their associations with particular beings, plants, animals, or forces of nature.[7] During our conversation in 2010, doña Nelita acknowledged her familiarity with a number of these divinities and offered her own interpretation of their characteristics. For example, she identified names like *yoshi* (spirit or demon), *waca* (a good spirit of water), *rumu* (spirit of tobacco), *hawa* (a good spirit of the sky), and *aboco* (an evil water spirit) and described the principal features of these spirits. In one of our visits to Chachi Bai in 2013, she offered a moving testimony of her hard life and a short popular tale about a bird, the *isko*, or oriole, in fluent Iskonawa. We have collected more than fifty tales about animals, the origin of natural phenomena, how humans started to use plants, and so on. Here I will concentrate on the telling of the oriole tale and the tale of the moon and then relate this kind of narrative to the revitalization aspect of the project. I will also relate the "Tale of the *Isko* Bird" to a branch of Peruvian literature that looks to native forms of knowledge as the source of its aesthetic and ideological agenda. Here is the tale:[8]

El cuento del pájaro *isko*

En la noche, el curioso había pensado: "Esta noche vamos a ir a sacar su nido del páucar." Había tomado purga con tabaco el curioso Hanebo [hombre médico, brujo, *yoshinya*]. El curioso ha tomado purga para ver el páucar. Su hijo le dice: "Vamos papá a sacar el nido del páucar." Al amanecer su hijo le dice: "El páucar tiene toda clase de maní." El papá respondió: "Hay que pedirle al páucar." El papá advierte: "El páucar es bien bravo." Le había visto en su tomadera. El hijo le dice que vayan. Dos días han caminado. Eran seis iskonawas. El curioso y sus cinco hijos. El único malcriado era el que le contestaba. Llevaban su fariña (de maíz). Los hijos se adelantaron y el curioso iba atrás. Los cinco muchachos han llegado primero al nido del páucar. El papá les dice a sus hijos: "Espérenme hasta que yo llegue para ver cómo está el páucar." El páucar estaba escuchando.

El muchacho malcriado desobedece y dice: "Yo voy a ver." Los hermanos le dicen "no te vayas, que llegue papá." El malcriado no les hacía caso a sus hermanos. Se fue solo.

El maní es un arbusto largo y grande. Cuando el pájaro páucar vio al malcriado desde el arbusto le cantaba *tsitsa keterés, ashpa keterés* (voy a soltar pluma amarilla, voy a lanzar hacia abajo). Lo mató con un lanzazo en la cabeza.

El curioso ha visto al hijo muerto. Los hermanos han llorado. Estaban de pena. Ahí el curioso se ha hecho amigo con el páucar. Ha tomado tabaco. Ha soplado. "No me hagas nada, somos familia, no me mates." De ahí el páucar sacudía sus plumas. Después conversaban. "Hemos venido a pedir tu maní," dice el curioso. "Yo voy a coger tu maní." El páucar le aceptó. Ahí canta: *keska keterés, choish keterés, betsis keterés*. El curioso jala la rama del nido con un palo y la rama se rompe (*keska keterés*). Le pone candela al nido (*chuis keterés*). El páucar dice "yo le voy a apagar." Llama a la lluvia y el fuego se apaga (*betsis keterés*).

El páucar explica los tipos de maní: "Este es *manko tama*, este es *heoh tama*, este es *boshta tama*." Le dice: "Siembra el maní." "Después de sembrar, cosechas el maní y haces tu chicha de maní." Los hombres sembrarían el maní y las mujeres harían chicha. Pero al sembrar no crecía nada. Entonces hamaquearon todo el día, un mes, dos meses. Después creció el maní. Estaba grandecito y lo cosechan para la chicha y después le comen.

El páucar le explica: "Cuando cosechas, corta un palo grande, rodando." De ahí le sale el maní. Le dijo al curioso: "Vete a sembrar *tashi kari* (camote amarillo), *nawan kari* (camote blanco)." Y le da dos clases de camote para que siembre.

El curioso ha sembrado. El páucar le dice: "Cuando crezca invita a toda tu familia, no les mezquines." Cuando el camote creció, las mujeres fueron a la chacra y encontraron unos camotazos grandes. Han traído a la casa y le han cocido para que coman entre la familia y los muchachos.[9]

[Tale of the *Isko* Bird

One night a curious man thought: "We should go and sack the nest of the oriole." He then took his tobacco to clean his body with the help of Jánebu, a medicine man, a sorcerer or *yuushiña*. The curious man cleaned his body to be able to see the oriole. His son told him: "Let's go and sack the nest of the oriole. He has all kinds of peanuts." The father responded: "We should ask the oriole." He added: "The oriole is wild." He had seen him in his cleansing process. The son insisted that they go. So they walked for two days. They were six Iskonawa in total: the curious guy and his five sons. The naughty one insisted the most that they go and talked back to his father. They took corn flour with them. The five children went ahead and the father stayed behind. The sons arrived first at the nest of the oriole. The father had told them: "Wait for me to see how the oriole is doing." But the oriole was listening to the conversation. The naughty son disobeyed and said: "I am going to see by myself." His brothers tried to dissuade him: "Don't go. Wait for father." But he didn't listen and went by himself.

The peanut plant is a tall and big bush. When the oriole saw the mischievous son, it started to sing: "Tsitsa kuturú, ashpa kuturú" [I will release my yellow feather, I will throw it down below]. Then the bird killed the man with the feather-spear in his head.

The curious man saw his dead son. The brothers cried. They were sad. Then the curious man became friends with the oriole. He brought tobacco and appeased it. "Don't do anything to me, we are family, don't kill me." The oriole shook its feathers. They started to talk. "We came to ask for your peanuts," the curious man said. The oriole assented. Then it sang: "Kuska kuturús, chuis kuturús, buytsis kuturús" [I will bring the rain to put off any fire].

The oriole explained the different types of peanut: "This is *manku tama*, this is *jeus tama*, this is *buyshta tama*." He told the man: "Plant the peanut. After you do that, you harvest the peanut and make peanut *chicha* [beer]." Men planted the peanut and women made the *chicha*. But when they planted, nothing grew. So they rested in their hammocks all day for one, two months. Then the peanuts grew. They were big and the people made *chicha* and also ate them.

The oriole explains to the curious man: "When you harvest, cut the peanuts with a big stick, rolling it over the plant. The peanuts come from there." Then he told the man: "Go and plant *tashi kari* [yellow sweet potato] and *nawan kari* [white sweet potato]." And then he showed him the two types of sweet potato to plant.

So the curious man planted the sweet potatoes. The oriole told him: "When the plants grow, invite your entire family; don't be cheap with them." When the sweet potatoes grew, the women went to the orchard and found huge sweet potatoes. They took them to the house and cooked them, and all the family and the children ate.]

This myth of origin presents some of the most common elements found in the oral traditions of many Amazonian cultures.[10] For example, communication between humans and sacred or primordial animals requires some sort of spiritual alteration, which begins with the cleansing of the body before consuming tobacco, usually through the nose. As contradictory as this may sound, the process implies a fast of several days before consuming tobacco or any other substance, such as the more usual *ayahuasca* or *yagé*, a hallucinogenic compost of tree skins and herbs. The myth of the oriole creates a timeless context wherein communication between humans and animals seems normal. Given this premise, the curious man can embark on the kind of search for knowledge traditionally attributed to animals. Similarly, the primordial time referenced in the narration can recur in the present time during specific activities, for instance, hunting. When a member of the community goes out to hunt, he traditionally recites a designated prayer asking for the animal's forgiveness. In the myth of the oriole, there are two models of conduct: on the one hand, there is the disobedient son acting with no respect for his father or the oriole; on the other, there is the understanding father correcting his son's mistake and easily making peace with the oriole by showing respect. The respectful approach is effective because it does not alter the well-being of the bird or its surroundings. What is more, the oriole—in addition to giving the humans peanut seeds and the knowledge of how to process them—provides them with sweet potatoes and even advises them about social norms of conduct, suggesting that they ensure the communal enjoyment of the harvest. Rather than seek revenge for his son's death, the father understands the danger of provoking a powerful force of nature and protects the rest of his family and his community by negotiating the terms of his communication with the oriole. The myth shows that there is a form of knowledge that, if shared among living beings, may lead to peaceful coexistence. It does not question the authority of the oriole; rather, it acknowledges that the bird can teach humans much and will give more than what is asked if humans respect its well-being.

There is no way of knowing how old this myth is. Doña Nelita and her aunt doña Juana Rodríguez Meza (Pibi Awin) both recalled this tale as they were remembering their childhood in the rain forest. It may date back hundreds of years to the original Iskonawa community that inhabited its territory before Hispanic times, like most Amazonian communities in voluntary isolation today.

There are many other aspects of this origin myth to explore, but at this point I would like to focus on a second one:

El cuento de la luna

Un hombre mayor vivía con su hermana y tenía relaciones con ella, sin que ella se diera cuenta. No lo reconocía de noche. Después ella ha traído *huito* (pintura negra) y le pintó su cara para saber quién era.

En la mañana venían varios hombres y pasaban y pasaban. Ella contaba. "No es éste," decía. Otro y otro más. Al último viene su hermano. Se dio cuenta de que él era el que se acostaba con ella. "Ah, mi hermano, él ha sido." Ella lloró.

Después estaba cantando el mono coto, que era comestible. "Vamos a matar el coto. Sube allá a ese palo," le dice. Han subido cuatro hombres, donde estaba el coto. El hermano destripó al coto. Primero le cortó el brazo. Poco a poco iban cayendo las partes del mono. También su costilla. Todito botaba. "Hay otro mono," dice la joven. Voy a mirar, dice el hermano. Y un joven descuartizó al hermano también.

Luego ese joven fue a su casa y la cerraron porque la cabeza del hermano estaba viniendo.

De ahí la cabeza subió a la casa. Dijo, "yo voy a ser comegente." "Voy a ser lupuna." "Pero mejor voy a ser luna para que nadie me fastidie." Y así apareció la luna con sus manchas.

[Tale of the Moon

An older man lived with his sister and had sexual relations with her without her realizing it. She did not recognize him at night. Then she brought *huito* [black paint] and painted his face to know who he was.

In the morning several men came and went. She counted. "It's not this one," she said. Another one, and another one. The last one who came was her brother. She realized that he was the one who was sleeping with her. "Ah, my brother, he has been the one." She cried.

Then the monkey *coto* was singing, it was edible. "We are going to kill the *coto*. Go up there to that branch," she said. Four men climbed where the monkey was. The brother disemboweled the *coto*. First he cut his arm. Little by little the monkey parts were falling. Also his rib. He threw out everything. "There's another monkey," said the young woman. "I'm going to look," said the brother. And a young man dismembered the brother, too.

Then that young man went to his house and they closed it because the brother's head was coming.

From there the head went up to the house. He said, "I'm going to be a people eater. I'm going to be *lupuna*. But it would be better if I were the moon so no one bothers me." And so the moon appeared with its spots.]

This short narrative traces the spots on the moon to a brother's incestuous violation of his sister. She, realizing the abuse, plans to kill her brother, yet he, through the powers he has, does not die at all; his head decides to become the moon and go up to heaven "so no one bothers me."

The story is in some ways similar to that of other Amazonian peoples concerning the origin of the lunar spots. In the case of the Iskonawa myth, however, a strongly sexual theme explains the prohibition of incest, strengthens community bonds, and grants male gender to the nocturnal celestial body. At the same time, the Iskonawa tale gives this male moon negative features that explain and warn us about the dangers of the night in the jungle, when the animals go out to hunt. It is a narration about primordial times that allows us to understand the origin and conformation of many elements of nature, always with a strong animistic content.

The existence of the moon, moreover, is the result of a mechanism of protection by which the Iskonawa people avoid the presence of the *lupuna* and his cannibalistic practice. The moon thus acquires a regulating function of coexistence among humans. It also symbolizes the relationship with animals and limits hunting to the need to eat, as opposed to modern Western society, in which hunting is basically a sport.

The Decolonization of Literature

Such tales have nurtured modern Andean literature with a cultural framework that contemporary decolonial studies refer to as "indigenous episteme." Let me refer briefly to the cases of two Peruvian writers, José María Arguedas and César Calvo.[11]

In terms of the epistemological and ontological categories present in the oriole myth (and also pivotal in Quechua oral tradition), José María Arguedas's now-celebrated poem titled "Huk Doktorkunaman Qayan" (published in 1966), also known as "Llamado a algunos doctores" ("An Appeal to Some Learned Doctors"), is instructive. Here Arguedas carries out a brilliant defense of indigenous cultural identity and of the relationship between humans and nature in the indigenous world. He writes:

> Quinientas flores de papa crecen en los balcones de los abismos que tus ojos
> no alcanzan, sobre la tierra en que la noche y el oro, la plata y el día, se mezclan.
> Esas quinientas flores son mis sesos, mi carne. . . .
>> Las plumas de los cóndores, de los pequeños pájaros se han convertido
> en arcoiris y alumbran. . . .
>> Las cien flores de la quinua que sembré en las cumbres hierven al sol en
> colores, en flor se ha convertido la negra ala del cóndor. . . .
>> En esta fría tierra siembro quinua de cien colores, de cien clases, de semilla
> poderosa. Los cien colores son también mi alma, mis infatigables ojos.[12]

> [Five hundred potato flowers grow on the balconies of the abysses that your
> eyes cannot reach, on the land where night and gold, silver and day, intertwine.
> Those five hundred flowers are my brain, my flesh. . . .
>> The feathers of the condors, of the small birds, have turned into rainbows
> and shine. . . .
>> The hundred flowers of the quinoa that I sowed on the summits boil in
> colors under the sun; the black wing of the condor has turned into a
> flower. . . .
>> In this cold land I plant quinoa of one hundred colors, of a hundred types,
> of powerful seed. The one hundred colors are also my soul, my relentless eyes.]

The speaker (who in other parts of the poem identifies himself as a plural subject, interchangeably using "I" and "we") here transforms himself into multiple elements, some minimal, some grandiose, all interconnected by their belonging to the natural world. In that universe, the subject of the poem finds a knowledge that identifies him as part of that world: he learns from that knowledge and gets nurtured by it; from the perspective of that knowledge he can challenge the supposedly modernizing and "scientific" knowledge of the "doctors" to whom he addresses the poem; scholars who come from distant lands assume that they know everything about Andean culture but fail to recognize the importance of the environment as part of local identity. Roxana Molinié, in her essay "For a Poetics of Recognition," argues that Arguedas's poem challenges the traditional recognition of the other.[13] That is, Arguedas is not claiming that indigenous thought be recognized because of its resemblance to a Western episteme; rather, he insists that this knowledge be recognized for its power to transform Western preconceptions about human beings and nature inhabiting separate universes in a hierarchical order where the human realm reigns supreme.

César Calvo, in his *Las tres mitades de Ino Moxo y otro brujos de la Amazonía* (*Three Halves of Ino Moxo: Teachings of the Wizard of the Upper Amazon*), makes another important attempt to express an indigenous worldview, in this case that of the Ashaninka community of the Peruvian jungle. This is a heterogeneous book in which the personal story of the protagonist, the poet César Calvo himself, intermingles with the story of Ino Moxo, a shaman whose name means "Black Panther." Ino Moxo was the son of a rubber privateer, kidnapped at an early age by the Ashaninka so he could be raised in their culture. Because he was white, the Ashaninkas believed that Ino Moxo could better defend their rights and their culture. The plot consists of Calvo's search for Ino Moxo, a paternal figure who will teach the poet the most profound secrets of the Amazon and how to achieve personal happiness. This book, originally published in 1981 yet still ignored by most conventional literary criticism, has many redeeming qualities that I could discuss at length; let me just quote two short paragraphs that suggest the importance of Calvo's book to my own project of cultural documentation:

> No solamente suenan tantos y tantos animales que has visto, que no has visto, que nadie verá jamás, bichos que aprenden a pensar y conversar como personas. . . . Suenan también las plantas, los vegetales.
>
> Y más que nada suenan los pasos de los animales que uno ha sido antes de humano, los pasos de las piedras y los vegetales y las cosas que cada humano ha sido.[14]

> [Not only do the many, many animals resound that you have seen, that you have not seen, that will never be seen by anyone, bugs that learn to think and converse like people. . . . The plants and vegetables resound as well.
>
> And above all, the footsteps resound of the animals that one was before being human; the footsteps of the stones and plants and things that each human being has been.]

This passage presents an animistic and humanizing concept of nature in which animals and plants, as potential human beings, learn how to communicate with people in a nonhierarchical way. Ino Moxo has achieved a form of wisdom that breaks apart the more traditional notions of "real maravilloso" and "magical real-ism," two styles of narrative that tend to incorporate "irrational" elements in a more general framework of "normality." In contrast, the literature that attempts to reproduce mythical thought dismantles the Western notion of rationality, along with its presupposed opposition between culture and nature. Both Arguedas and Calvo represent a particular approach to originary forms of knowledge that is primarily accessible through field research alone.

Returning, then, to the oriole and the moon tales, I believe that recollection and documentation of such stories offer an example of how to revitalize a language and culture, since it is the elders who recount the myths of origin that the younger generations then learn. Members of endangered cultures are usually very interested in their own oral tradition, and through the remembrance of these stories the elders can pass on the knowledge about traditional ways to maintain a good relationship with the environment.

The involvement of native speakers in the process of data collection proves even more valuable when they act as agents and not just as objects of study. The training of native speakers in data recording and transcription enables the project participants to engage more personally and professionally with the native speakers, thus gaining more access to their daily lives. At the end of this project, they are qualified to help with some recordings and to learn the basic phonetic literacy of their own language, enhancing their knowledge of their own tradition. Through this achievement they will help slow the rapid process of disappearance of their language by transcribing more material in the future for educational purposes within their community.

Conclusion

The knowledge gained through documentation and study of Iskonawa contributes to the field of linguistics as a whole and to the preservation of endangered languages in particular. It also helps preserve a vast legacy of cultural production in the form of songs, rituals, dances, and, especially, oral narratives, thus contributing to the fields of literary studies and cultural studies. The grammar outline (*Bosquejo gramatical de la lengua iskonawa*, by Roberto Zariquiey) follows all international standards of phonetic notation, phonological classification, and morphologic and syntactic analysis. The lexicon (*Vocabulario de la lengua iskonawa*, by Roberto Zariquiey) has about sixteen hundred entries, covering most aspects of the culture and social life of the studied community. In compiling a selection of oral narratives (*Tradición oral iskonawa*, by José Antonio Mazzotti, Roberto Zariquiey, and Carolina Rodríguez Alzza) and video recordings, we take into consideration their accessibility to a broad sector of the general public—an accessibility that will help ensure the preservation of the rich cultural legacy of this indigenous community.[15]

However, the imminent threat of deforestation and contamination of the Amazon Basin will mean the disappearance of entire ethnic nations and their millenary knowledge of how to preserve the environment and use it in a sustainable way. In this sense, one cannot approach this reality with the assumption that the processes of colonization ended two hundred years ago with the birth of the Spanish American "sovereign" nations. On the contrary, these processes have accelerated over the past thirty years with the implementation of neoliberal economic policies that facilitate the exploitation of natural resources, spurred on by a hierarchical mentality that privileges "progress" over nature and Westerners over natives. In short, internal colonialism has been invigorated by the international world economic order.

Whatever claims are made by postcolonial or decolonial theories, activists and academics can do little without true knowledge of the culture of endangered communities. In the field of literature, authors such as Arguedas and Calvo will be increasingly exceptional unless literary criticism explores other disciplines and embarks on true and meticulous field research.

JOSÉ ANTONIO MAZZOTTI is King Felipe VI of Spain Professor of Spanish Culture and Civilization and professor of Latin American literature at Tufts University. He is also president of the International Association of Peruvianists and director and chief editor of the *Revista de crítica literaria latinoamericana*. He is author, most recently, of *The Creole Invention of Peru: Nation and Epic Poetry in Colonial Lima* (2019). He received the International Poetry Prize "José Lezama Lima" from Casa de las Américas, Cuba, in 2018 for his book *El zorro y la luna: Poemas reunidos 1981–2016*.

Notes

1   From *ethnos* (in Greek) or *natio* (Latin), that is, a group with a common language, culture, and ancestry that can claim a collective identity. I prefer to talk about "ethnic groups" in the sense of "ethnic nations," as was the original sense of the word *ethnos*. The term *indigenous*, unfortunately, refers to a category ("Indian") imposed by the European invaders from 1492 on in the so-called New World. Modern "indigenous" studies tend to overlook this colonizing aspect of the word.

2   Whiton, Greene, and Momsen, *The Isconahua of the Remo*; D'Ans, "Reclasificación de las lenguas pano."

3   E.g., Matorela, *Estudio de actualización*; Brabec de Mori and Pérez Casapía, "Los Iskobakebo," 12).

4   Details about the grant can be found in Mazzotti, Cerrón-Palomino, and Zariquiey, abstract.

5   See Rodríguez, "Establecimiento y delimitación territorial," 90–91.

6   Brabec de Mori and Pérez Casapía, "Los Iskobakebo," 3.

7   Whiton, Greene, and Momsen, *The Isconahua of the Remo*.

8   These and other tales can be found in their original Iskonawa form at sites such as the "Archivo de Lenguas Peruanas" of the PUCP

(repositorio.pucp.edu.pe/index/handle /123456789/124187) and the Archive of Indigenous Languages of Latin America of the University of Texas at Austin (ailla.utexas .org/islandora/object/ailla%3A256718).

9   Mazzotti, Zariquiey, and Rodríguez Alzza, *Tradición oral iskonawa*, 169–70.

10   I use the term *myth* in its original meaning of "tale of origin" or "foundational narrative." It is not used in the sense of "fable" or "fiction," mainly because for many originary peoples those stories constitute the best explanation of the beginnings of their culture and identity.

11   For a critique of decolonial studies, see Browitt, "La teoría decolonial." José María Arguedas (1911–69) is probably the most important Peruvian novelist of the twentieth century. Some of his books (such as *Los ríos profundos* [*Deep Rivers*, 1958] and *El zorro de arriba y el zorro de abajo* [*The Fox from Up Above and the Fox from Down Below*, 1971]) form part of the most exigent Peruvian literary canon. He also has a posthumous book of poems, *Katatay* (*To Tremble*, 1972). César Calvo (1940–2000) is fundamentally a poet, with numerous books and literary awards. However, he is better known for his experimental novel *Las tres mitades de Ino Moxo y otros brujos de la Amazonía* (*Three Halves of Ino Moxo: Teachings of the Wizard of the Upper Amazon*, 1981),

in which he tells the story of a shaman, Ino Moxo, who holds the secrets of plants and animals and teaches the way to preserve nature and the well-being of people in the Amazon Basin.

12   Arguedas, *Katatay y otros poemas*, 25–26.
13   Molinié, "'Llamado a algunos doctores.'"
14   Calvo, *Las tres mitades de Ino Moxo*, 27, 30.
15   Zariquiey, *Bosquejo gramatical de la lengua iskonawa*; Zariquiey, *Vocabulario de la lengua iskonawa*; Mazzotti, Zariquiey, and Rodríguez Alzza, *Tradición oral iskonawa*. The three books are downloadable at sites.tufts.edu/iskonawa.

Works Cited

Arguedas, José María. *Katatay y otros poemas: Huc Jayllucunapas*. Lima: Instituto Nacional de Cultura, 1972.

Brabec de Mori, Bernd, and Jefferson Pérez Casapía. "Los Iskobakebo: La historia del contacto de los misioneros con un pueblo de habla pano en Ucayali." Centro de Recursos Interculturales, 2006. centroderecursos.cultura.pe/es/registrobibliografico/los-iskobakebo-la-historia-del-contacto-de-los-misioneros-con-un-pueblo-de.

Browitt, Jeff. "La teoría decolonial: Buscando la identidad en el mercado académico." *Cuadernos de literatura*, no. 36 (2014): 25–46.

Calvo, César. *Las tres mitades de Ino Moxo y otro brujos de la Amazonía*. Havana: Casa de las Américas, 2009.

D'Ans, André Marcel. "Reclasificación de las lenguas pano y datos glotocronológicos para la etnohistoria de la Amazonía peruana." *Revista del Museo Nacional* (Lima), no. 39 (1973): 349–69.

Matorela, Miriam. *Estudio de actualización del grupo indígena en aislamiento voluntario Isconahua, en el área propuesta para el establecimiento de la zona reservada Sierra del Divisor*. Lima: Pronaturaleza, 2004.

Mazzotti, José Antonio, Rodolfo Cerrón-Palomino, and Roberto Zariquiey. Abstract of "Documenting Isconahua (isc) in Peru: An Interdisciplinary Project." Research project conducted from July 1, 2012, to August 31, 2018 (estimate). Division of Behavioral and Cognitive Sciences, National Science Foundation. www.nsf.gov/awardsearch/showAward?AWD_ID=1160679.

Mazzotti, José Antonio, Roberto Zariquiey, and Carolina Rodríguez Alzza. *Tradición oral iskonawa*. Boston: Revista de Crítica Literaria Latinoamericana, 2018.

Molinié, Roxana. "'Llamado a algunos doctores': Para una poética del reconocimiento." *Tinkuy* 5 (2007): 95–104.

Rodríguez, Genaro. "Establecimiento y delimitación territorial para el grupo indígena no contactado Isconahua." Report. Ucayali: Asociación Interétnica de Desarrollo de la Selva Peruana, 1995.

Whiton, Louis C., H. Bruce Greene, and Richard P. Momsen Jr. *The Isconahua of the Remo*. Winter Park, FL: Rollins College, 1961.

Zariquiey, Roberto. *Bosquejo gramatical de la lengua iskonawa*. Boston: CELACP, Latinoamericana Editores y Revista de Crítica Literaria Latinoamericana, 2015.

Zariquiey, Roberto. *Vocabulario iskonawa-castellano*. Boston: Revista de Crítica Literaria Latinoamericana, 2017.

Indigenous Narratives of Creation and Origin in *Embrace of the Serpent*, by Ciro Guerra

ENRIQUE BERNALES ALBITES

Abstract   In Ciro Guerra's film *Embrace of the Serpent* (2015), cultural exchanges between the central characters reveal the origin narratives and the curative power of plants valued by Indigenous cultures of the Amazon. This article analyzes how *Embrace of the Serpent* expresses Indigenous rationality in the origin narratives as the shaman Karamakate confronts Western travelers and scientists. For these Indigenous cultures, knowledge and its reproduction are equivalent to ancestral songs and rituals such as the ceremony of the Ayahuasca. This article supports these ideas not in a filmic analysis but by exploring central aspects and scenes in the film associated with intercultural exchanges and the ritual of Ayahuasca. Finally, *Embrace of the Serpent* highlights the difficulty of distinguishing between the rationality of orality and writing with which Native cultures of the Americas understand the world that surrounds them.

Keywords   song, travel, origin narrative, Amazon, Ayahuasca

mbrace of the Serpent (2015) centers on Karamakate, an Amazonian shaman, and two scientists, Theo and Evan,[1] who are in search of a mythical plant, yakruna, the secrets of which are held by the last survivor of Karamakate's people. The film is based on the journals of the German ethnologist Theodor Koch-Grünberg and the American biologist Richard Evans Schultes, who sought to unveil the secrets of the Amazon for the advancement of Western hegemony.[2] Karamakate is a fictional character, and, as the narrative liaison between the two expeditions, he embraces all the virtues of an Amazonian shaman.

Karamakate grew up in the margins, on the frontier of the Amazon civilization. This gave him insight into his culture and the Western world. In *La semiósfera* Yuri Lotman points out that the characters of the semiotic frontier, like Karamakate, "belong to two worlds and are translators, establishing themselves in the frontier of the cultural and mythological space."[3] The frontier translator is a key element in the Semiosphere. This pathfinder of signs, the trickster of the universal mythology, an ambiguous being who is unbalanced, feared, and loved, is the ultimate guar-

ENGLISH LANGUAGE NOTES

58:1, April 2020 DOI 10.1215/00138282-8237520
© 2020 Regents of the University of Colorado

antor for the survival of the semiotic universe. Karamakate belongs to this category of archetypal characters. Finally, Karamakate, as a trickster, kills Theo, but decades later he decides to transfer the knowledge and wisdom of his dying culture to Evan.

Embrace of the Serpent is not an Indigenous-made film. But it is a Latin American motion picture that portrays Native languages and their people, as do other Latin American movies like *Madeinusa* (2006) and *The Milk of Sorrow* (2009), by the Peruvian Claudia Llosa; *The Quispe Girls* (2013), by the Chilean Sebastián Sepúlveda; *Ixcanul* (2015), by the Guatemalan Jayro Bustamante; *Wiñaypacha* (2017), by the Indigenous Peruvian Óscar Catacora (aimara); and *Roma* (2018), by the Mexican Alfonso Cuarón. Besides Catacora, there are other Indigenous filmmakers doing extraordinary work, like Jeannette Paillan (Mapuche), David Hernandez Palmar (Wayuu), and Divino Tserewahú (Xavánte). One can read Ciro Guerra's films as an idealization of the rural life in contrast to the urban world, using Michel Foucault's concept of heterotopia as developed by María Luna and Eylin Rojas Hernández: "These dreamy landscapes become idyllic because of the quietness that they communicate, a quality highly appreciated by a citizen of a big city."[4] However, despite the idealization, death and violence are in full swing in this landscape.

Foucault states that the place-other, or heterotopia, is a locus that exists historically differently from utopias. It works as a mirror of reality. The mirror for the Amazon rain forest portrayed in Guerra's film is the world of the modern Western cities. Additionally, these spaces are not split from the economic reality to which they belong; on the contrary, they constitute a fundamental part of the capitalist system. In this sense, Foucault stresses that the heterotopia par excellence of the Western world is the ship. This synonym for adventure and imagination since the sixteenth century has strengthened the economic progress of the capitalist system.[5] Likewise, in *Embrace of the Serpent* the heterotopia of the Amazon rain forest is not isolated from colonial forces. These forces have threatened the survival of the forest and the Indigenous people who have inhabited those lands for thousands of years.

In addition to heterotopia, another tool useful in analyzing the film is the concept of the glocal:

> The strategy of the glocal in the cinema works as a claim by the audience that is questioned with a discourse identified with the authenticity that is matched with the figure of the traveler in opposition to the tourist. The problem is that all the cinema of non-English-speaking countries is introduced to the cosmopolitan audiences as "a different cinema," a cinema that connects us (to whom, one can ask) to the discovery of "other worlds." So, in addition to the good intentions of the films, in the catalogs of international distribution one can see a uniformity of the diversity that represents a cinema as exotic from the same presentation.[6]

As Luna suggests, this strategy generates heterotopic spaces in films like *Wind Journeys* (2009), *Embrace of the Serpent* (2015), *Ixcanul* (2015), and *Madeinusa* (2006) and allows a cosmopolitan, international spectator to approach a reality identified as more authentic than the life in the urban environments of the global market. These representations of an alternative life in a rural or Indigenous space make the consumers of global products feel better about themselves by supporting glocal productions.

Embrace of the Serpent thus reproduces a *more authentic* way of life, far from cosmopolitan values,[7] and then visualizes a space that Foucault called heterotopia— the place-other that is nonetheless not separated from the economic conditions of capitalist expansion. Indeed, the expansion can be of the imagination, but it remains capital all the same, a playful investment in the sustainability of the bourgeois structures of global capitalism.

Finally, *Embrace of the Serpent* is not an Indigenous film of Abiayala,[8] but it has been created with care to protect the images and representations of Indigenous people of the rain forest and their way of life, including their origin narratives recorded in writing (petroglyphs), Icaros (Amazon songs), and the use of medicinal plants.

Coloniality

Karamakate is the medium for the sacred plant called yakruna. Because of the relations of power that are established in the film, one can visualize the effects of coloniality in the relations between Western rationality ("criollo") and the Indigenous one. In her study *Aurality* Ana María Ochoa Gautier writes:

> The history of the rise of the modern since the sixteenth century has been associated with the emergence of vision as the privileged sense for perception and for ideas about the subject and its relation to knowledge and the world in the West.
>
>   For [the Colombian philosopher Santiago] Castro-Gómez such an emphasis on the gaze is crucial to the relation between colonialism as power and coloniality as knowledge because it gives an external observer the power to universalize its categories of knowledge and posit its own point of view as a despatialized omniscience. For Castro-Gómez, the "ocularcentrism" of Western epistemologies is a critical element in the constitution of the colonial modern itself.[9]

For Ochoa Gautier, following Castro-Gómez, the privilege of the gaze (rational and scientific) in the Western logocentrism sprang from the creation of the scientific method and the development of the sciences in the sixteenth century. This was especially notable in the American territories where power relations and coloniality created their own complexity. A written and scientific discourse of a criollo rational gaze developed. This criollo discourse distanced itself from the non-criollos (the Afro-Latin and Indigenous groups). About this, Castro-Gómez writes:

> I will defend the hypothesis that *la limpieza de sangre*, I mean, the belief of the racial superiority of the criollos over the other ethnic groups of Nueva Granada. This worked as a habitus from where the European Enlightenment was translated and enunciated in Colombia. For the enlightened criollos, whiteness was their most valuable cultural capital. Because of it, they were granted access

to the scientific and literary knowledge of the time, and it secured them the social distance from "el otro colonial" that was the subject of their research. In the study of the "Neogradina" population, the enlightened criollos projected their own habitus of ethnic displacement in the scientific discourse. This habitus was conveniently hidden under the pretense of truth, objectivity and neutrality.[10]

The characters of the film, Theo, Evan, and Karamakate, meet in disputed territories, in a very active frontier. Colombia, Brazil, and Perú were fighting in these territories during the first half of the twentieth century over exploitation of rubber. These events brought the Amazon people slavery, genocide, and an ecological disaster that changed their lives forever. The history of the exploitation of rubber in South America has left a rich literature that includes novels like *La Vorágine* (1924), by José Eustacio Rivera; *Canaima* (1935), by Rómulo Gallegos; *Las tres mitades de Ino Moxo y otros brujos de la Amazonía* (1981), by César Calvo; and *La casa verde* (1966) and *El sueño del celta* (2010), by Mario Vargas Llosa. About this human tragedy, Ana Pizarro stresses:

> The rubber laborers, the indigenous that did and do still the extraction in the area of the Andean piedmont, were the ethnic groups of the area connected by the River Negro, the Solimoes, el Putumayo, el Caquetá, el Madre de Dios, the Juruá, the Muru, among other tributaries of the Amazon River. The worst stories about the slave work of the indigenous come from that geographical area. They cover the end of the nineteenth and the beginning of the twentieth century, the period of the "rubber barons": Julio César Arana, Carlos Fermín Fiscarraldo, Nicolás Suárez, in the Hispanic part, and some other "coronéis do barranco" in the Luso-American part. This left a sad memory, branding the indigenous memories of the region. These historical memories sometimes create a trauma for the mythical memory, in order to impose the beginning of the narration of their stories.[11]

On the pretext of Westernizing the Indigenous nations, the governments of Peru, Colombia, and Brazil enslaved and exterminated thousands of Indigenous people in the Amazon. The people from this region did not identify with the national imagined communities of South America. They already had their own identity. In this frontier Karamakate has grown up alone, separated from the Cohiuanos, his Indigenous group.[12] He thinks that his group has been exterminated or, worse, evangelized by the missionaries who saved children from rubber slavery but who punished them for speaking their own languages or practicing their rituals, both of which are considered barbaric and primitive by the Catholic Church. The objective of the priests was to force the children to succumb to acculturation.

Icaros

The singing of the Icaros for the Amazon people is a basic way to understand their origin narratives. To cure people, you must sing. Singing is also a heritage (gift) of the ancestors. However, singing is not the only way to record a mythical origin. Amazonian people recognize that to ensure the transmission and recording of knowledge, they need to use different platforms. These platforms are, first, the Icaros, which come from the visions triggered by the medicinal plants. Other platforms are the medicinal plants themselves that trigger oral stories. Still others are petroglyphs and the knitting of artisanal fabrics that record their origin. Finally, when the Natives migrate to Western-influenced cities, they record their myths through paintings.

The Icaros sung in the film are from Colombia, but the Icaro is a tradition shared with other Indigenous people across the Amazon of Peru, Ecuador, and Brazil. My description of the Icaro comes from the bibliography of the Peruvian Amazon rain forest:

> Icaro is the generic name given to the songs utilized by the urban mestizo curanderos—or mixed race healer—of the Peruvian Amazon Basin and by some indigenous healers in this region during their ritual works. . . . With no direct translation from native languages, Luna speculates that the word *icaro* would be a Castilianism from the verb *ikaray*. In Quichua—a dialect of Quechua, the main stem tongue of several ethnic groups of the Amazon Basin—the word means "to blow smoke" in order to heal. . . . Interestingly, the Shipibo-Conibo people of Peru refer to their magic melodies as *taquina*, *masha*, and *cusho*, which mean "to work by blowing." In both cases, the use of the ritual song is linked to blowing or infusing breath or smoke.[13]

The lyrics of the Icaros normally address the plants, the spirits, to make them act on the person's body. The shaman invites the spirit of the plant to dance around the ceremonial place. The spirit works together with the shaman to heal the person's body.[14] Also, as Rosa Giore writes, every shaman owns his own Icaro, received from his mentor or from manifestations of Amazon nature—plants or animals—in dreams.[15] The shamans in the Amazon assert that everything they know they have learned from dreams or visions. This aspect of the Amazon cultures is portrayed correctly in the film. The shamans receive the melody and the lyrics from the Icaros without using will or reason. This is also stressed by Karamakate to Evan, the American traveler. At the moment of using the Icaro in the Ayahuasca ceremony, the Icaro comes spontaneously from the mouth of the shaman.[16]

The film portrays these rituals of origin at the beginning of the twentieth century and during World War II (1940). During this last period American capitalism was looking for resources to win the war. Many things have changed in the Amazon rain forest since then. Nowadays there is a Western demand for Indigenous rituals like the ones represented in the film. There is an ongoing trend of Western appropriation of Indigenous knowledge for commercial and capitalist purposes. As Ricardo Badini claims: "The system of Amazon indigenous thought and its intimate relation with the environment are at the crossroads of a conflict with Western interests. This includes the economic sphere but also the imaginary and its symbolic correspondences."[17]

Figure 1. "Karamakate writing on the rock." Reprinted from *Embrace of the Serpent*, by Ciro Guerra.

Yet there is an intellectual tradition in Andean studies to think of South American Native cultures as excluded from written rationality. When Karamakate meets Evan, the American scientist, he is drawing petroglyphs. In Karamakate's design there is crucial information about the Amazon cultures. An internal voice communicates to the shaman which designs he will record on the stone. Hence there is no radical division between the orality logos and writing in these cultures:

EVAN: What do they mean?

KARAMAKATE: I don't know. I can't remember. These rocks used to talk to me. They answered my questions. The line is broken. My memories are gone. Rocks, trees, animals, they all went silent. Now they are just pictures on rocks. Now, I am empty. I'm a chullachaqui.

EVAN: This is similar to a drawing I saw of yakruna. These are mountains. A group of mountains. It is the "Workshop of the Gods." That is where yakruna grows.

Evan, familiar with the signs recorded on the stone, reminds Karamakate of their meaning. As a scientist, Evan proves with his notes that Karamakate's design refers to an actual location in the Amazon. The shaman confesses to him that he does not remember the meaning of the petroglyphs, these designs that describe a geographic location in Colombia. The Workshop of the Gods is in reality the Mavecure Hills, located in the Amazonian region of Guainía. This is a real sacred place of origin for the Native people of the Colombian Amazon Basin. The shaman Karamakate, as a trickster archetype, hides information about his culture from the Western travelers and scientists. In doing so, he even brings about death if necessary, as happened with Theo, the German explorer. But the shaman has other intentions with the second visitor, Evan. He wants him to understand the songs and rites of the Cohiuano culture. Thus Evan needs to surrender completely to the domain of the logic and wisdom of the Cohiuano world. If Evan listens, he will understand.

The first traveler, Theo, did not respect the domain of the wisdom of the Amazon cultures in part because of his racism. He could not accept the idea that a Native shaman was in control with his cure through the rite of the yakruna (*ayahuasca* or *togé*). At the end, Theo dies; Evan, however, survives. The latter understood the need to abandon all his measurement instruments, his maps, his samples—all his Western rationality—to become a Cohiuano warrior.

On studying the cultures of the Amazon, one must take into account the platforms (devices) that enable the production and reading (singing) of images and inscriptions. In Peru, Antonio Cornejo Polar, in his famous study *Escribir en el aire*, developed the crucial opposition between the oral Andean cultures and the Western and Creole writing culture:

> Now, I am interested in examining what might be named the "grado cero" of that interaction; in other words, the moment when orality and writing encounter the biggest differences, their own alienation and their reciprocal and aggressive repulsion. That moment of total friction has a date, circumstances and concrete protagonists. I am talking about the "dialogue" between the Inca Atahuallpa and the priest Vicente Valverde that took place in Cajamarca on the afternoon of Saturday, November 16, 1532.[18]

Evidently the Andean cultures did not use a writing platform contained in books or documents but developed a type of writing or reading device in the form of landscapes, petroglyphs, quipus, knitting, and so on:[19]

> This broader non-Western definition of "writing" is echoed in Andean terminology. Qillqa, in the sense of an engraved painted image, was transposed to writing from the early colonial period. Today, modern weavers readily adapt their terminology of weaving techniques to the writing skills of modern young women, so that the Aymara word *p'itaña* can be used just as well for "picking out threads" with a bone weaving pick as for "picking out writing" with a pencil.[20]

In the film there is evidence of recording of narratives of origin in the form of petroglyphs. Also, when the Ayahuasca ritual is performed on Evan, the audience can see a series of colorful drawings or images that represent the worldview of the Amazon people:

> KARAMAKATE: This is the Medora caapi. The most powerful of all. It existed before creation, before the snake descended. It will take you to see her. She is enormous, fearsome. But you must not fear it. You must let her embrace you. Her embrace will take you to ancient places, where life doesn't exist, not even its embryo. Drink. . . . Give them more than what they asked for. Give them a song. Tell them everything you see. Everything you feel. Come back a whole man. You are Cohiuano. [*Icaro singing*]

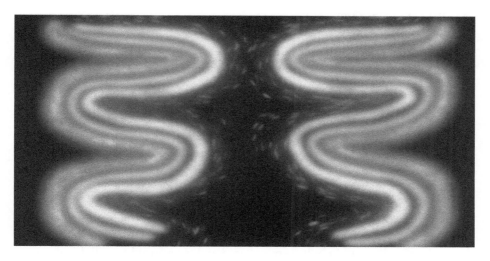

Figure 2. "Ayahuasca dream." Reprinted from *Embrace of the Serpent*, by Ciro Guerra.

There is a long tradition of recording on canvas all the information received by the Peruvian shamans from the plants and animals that they encounter in their hallucinatory dreams and visions. The canvases of the Huitoto painter Santiago Yahuarcani are similar to the one reproduced in the film.[21] One can see represented a shaman with half his body in the shape of a jaguar. The hand of the shaman and the feet of the feline merge in the figure of the serpent that untangles the rings, the symbol of the Ayahuasca.[22] The jaguar, the serpent, and the rings are crucial symbols and forces that bring balance to life in Amazon cultures.

Ritual of the Ayahuasca

Plants in the film, such as the chiricaspi, the caapi, and the yakruna, are essential for the origin narratives of the Amazon cultures.[23] Plants trigger folktales, legends, and myths of the Amazon cultures. This wisdom is preserved through oral transmission. In the film Karamakate, the only survivor of his culture, transmits his knowledge orally to Evan.[24] However, the church and its representatives in this environment, the missionaries, regard this knowledge differently. For them, these Native languages are a product of the devil, synonyms of cannibalism and barbarism. To save the souls of the recently converted, the church must eradicate Amazon culture.

In a scene in the film, a young Karamakate meets Cohiuano children at the Misión of Vaupes, run by the Capuchin order. He tells them in their language the origin of the plant chiricaspi, a gift from their ancestors:

> KARAMAKATE: Look. This is chiricaspi. A gift that our Karipulakena ancestors received from the gods. We received the sun's semen when Yeba, the sun's daughter, scratched his penis and ground the semen to dust. We must do the same with this plant before boiling it. Help me. This is the strongest defense we have against any disease. It will help you endure.

This story shows the different layers of knowledge that are present in the origin narratives of the Amazon people. First, the acceptance of gifts is key in the Amazon worldview. There are different moments where gifts are central in the film, for example, when Theo loses his compass to his hosts. From the German perspective, the Natives stole the compass; for the Amazon people, it was a gift that they want to exchange for other goods. The compass as a gift will help them know more about their stars, the origin of this people. Karamakate is aware of this, because he stresses to the German: "You can't forbid them to learn." Later Evan and Karamakate go back to the now-dystopian Misión of Vaupes. In this failed mission the now-adult Indigenous people are led by a mad priest who believes that he is God. In the scene, the Indigenous collect artifacts from Evan's pockets and call them gifts ("mi regalo"). Second, myth is a way to remember a more practical benefit that the chiricaspi plant contains. This plant has attributes that protect the health of Amazon people and enables them to endure this rough environment. Without the myth, the story, this gift would not be remembered and transferred to individuals of the group. Therefore the myth is a vehicle for the scientific transmission of knowledge. In Western science, the transmission of knowledge first requires scrutiny using the scientific method. In the Amazon, in contrast, the myth is the quintessential mechanism for the spread of wisdom.

Plants, together with the Icaro (the singing), are essential to the Ayahuasca ritual. Ayahuasca is the name for a liana, *Banisteriopsis caapi*, and the different infusions prepared with this main ingredient. Infusions vary according to the additives that are included, generally plants that have dimethyltryptamine in their composition. The term *Ayahuasca*, originally from Quechua, means "vine of souls." There are other synonyms depending on the specific geography and language spoken. Ayahuasca has other names, like *yajé o yage, mihi, dapa*, and *pinde*.[25] Evan wants to learn from Karamakate, "who moves the world" through the Ayahuasca ritual. He also wants to share with Karamakate his culture, all his Western heritage. This is a peculiar aspect that differentiates Evan from the racist German traveler, Theo. But how did this occur? Evan gets rid of all his research but retains one artifact, his phonograph, that lacks any usefulness for scientific exploration. He keeps it to tell Karamakate his story, the song of his culture and his ancestors from Boston:

> EVAN: This sound calms me. It takes me back to my father's house in Boston, to my ancestors.
> KARAMAKATE: To become a warrior, every Cohiuano man must leave everything behind and go into the jungle, guided only by his dreams. In that journey, he has to discover, in solitude and silence, who he really is. He has to become a vagabond of dreams. Some get lost and never come back, but those that do are ready to face whatever may come. . . .
> KARAMAKATE: What story is it telling?
> EVAN: How God created the world.
> KARAMAKATE: This is the way you seek. Listen to it.
> EVAN: It is beautiful, but it is only a story.
> KARAMAKATE: It's not a story. It's is a dream. You must follow it.

Therefore the film not only represents the origin narratives of the Amazon cultures but, through an exercise of cultural exchange, adds the narrative of origin of a Western explorer. This does not occur with Theo. Even though he dances some Bavarian folk songs with his translator, Manduka, before an Indigenous tribe, he does not show a deep level of understanding of the Amazon world. He does not disengage from his Western rationality. In this world of the Amazon cultures, it is essential to dream. As Guerra's film depicts, dreaming in the Ayahuasca ritual enables contact with the secret powers that share messages, their songs, the love for their world. Karamakate admitted to Evan in his language: "The world speaks. I can only listen. Listen to the song of your ancestors, not only with your ears." In an interview Guerra stresses:

> They [beings descended from the Milky Way] also left behind a few presents, including *coca*, the sacred plant; tobacco, which is also another kind of sacred plant; and *yagé*, the equivalent of *ayahuasca*, which is what you use to communicate with them in case you have a question or a doubt about how to exist in the world. When you use *yagé*, the serpent descends again from the Milky Way and embraces you. That embrace takes you to faraway places; to the beginning where life doesn't even exist; to a place where you can see the world in a different way. I hope that's what the film means to the audience.[26]

Guerra is telling the Western audience a narrative of origin from the Amazon people. It has characteristics in common with the story of Chiricaspi, such as the concept of the gift and the importance of transmitting knowledge through oral stories. Finally, the myth is the vehicle that leads to more practical benefits.

At its conclusion the film authentically reproduces a Ayahuasca ceremony. The shaman Karamakate prepares the subject Evan at the sacred place, the Workshop of the Gods. There they find what are thought the last flowers of yakruna. This flower is the main ingredient of the Ayahuasca drink. But what is a ceremony of Ayahuasca about? The Ayahuasca ceremony has different purposes. Evan and Karamakate want, respectively, to be cured and to transmit the knowledge of the Cohiaunos. Generally, the Ayahuasca is taken to communicate with the spirits, diagnose and/or treat diseases, do or undo sorcery, gain knowledge through divination, travel to distant places, and, finally, enhance interpersonal and community bonds, social identity, and cohesion.[27] During the ceremony shown in the film, some of these goals are accomplished. There is communication with the spirits, which is necessary for one to be cured. The ceremony heals Evan. Viewers can also see the Indigenous drawings of origin, the visions that the drinking of the Ayahuasca produces in the people. They can listen to the Icaros. In addition, the ceremony portrays consciousness traveling to distant places in the Amazon rain forest. Finally, this ceremony enhances interpersonal bonds between Karamakate and Evan. When Evan wakes the next day, Karamakate is not there. He has disappeared. His goal has been accomplished with the ceremony. Evan is cured, and through the dreams he experimented with, he has received the wisdom of the Cohiaunos. He is ready to be back in his country.

Against Idealization of Indigenous Cultures

The film, far from introducing the viewer to a stereotypical idea that the Indigenous people in the Amazon reproduce an idealized peaceful coexistence between people and their environment, makes us think about the concept of violence that permeates this world. As Greg Garrard acknowledges:

> The image of the Ecological Indian is certainly potent, but it does not accurately represent the environmental record of historical Native Americans. There seems little reason to question the destructiveness and, at times, genocidal racism of the Euro-American culture that opposed it. Yet the idealization that would make Indians and other indigenous people models of ecological dwelling arguably derives primarily from the latter, not the former, culture.[28]

There is no idealization of the Amazon people in *Embrace of the Serpent*, because this is a projection of the guilt complex of the Western cultures. The portrayal of the shaman Karamakate is one of the film's successes. In addition, the Indigenous people who defend their "regalo" of the compass, with violence if necessary, show that the Amazon people also are open to learning and not only to repeating the rituals of millenary traditions. There are scenes in the film where there is not peaceful coexistence. In one, Karamakate destroys all the flowers of the yakruna because his people are corrupt and do not use yakruna in a therapeutic and respectful manner. He also kills the German traveler Theo and admits it with no remorse. In another scene, before the ceremony of Ayahuasca at the Workshop of the Gods, a jaguar eats a snake; this is not peaceful coexistence but evidence that the balance of life in the Amazon is far from some Western-imagined ecological peace. The little kids whom the young Karamakate meets need to take chiricaspi to survive in the Amazon. Finally, before the ceremony of Ayahuasca, Evan and Karamakate fight. The shaman wants the American to kill him with his pocketknife, but the latter decides not to do it. Then the space of interpersonal connection opens for both of them during the ritual. Although violence and destruction are not the focus of this article, they must be considered for us to understand the balance that the cultures of the Amazon rain forest create with their surroundings.

Conclusion

In this article I have analyzed how *Embrace of the Serpent* reproduces recent trends, like the glocal and heterotopic, in world cinema. However, the film is also a coherent portrayal of Amazon cultures. For the Amazon people, music and singing are associated with narratives around the origin of their medicinal plants. The tradition of the Icaro is crucial to highlighting the importance of music and singing for Amazon people as a healing mechanism and as a repository for ancient knowledge. Amazon shamans like Karamakate own their own Icaro, received from their mentor or from manifestations of the Amazon nature—plants or animals—in dreams. The Icaro possesses curative powers. Finally, in *Embrace of the Serpent*, Indigenous logos expressed in the narratives of origin by Karamakate confront the Western travelers and scientists: Theo, the German, and Evan, the American. For Amazon Indigenous cultures, knowledge and its reproduction are equivalent to singing the songs of the ancestors and enacting rituals like the ceremony of the Ayahuasca.

ENRIQUE BERNALES ALBITES is assistant professor of Spanish at the University of Northern Colorado. He specializes in contemporary Latin American literature and cultural production, ecocriticism and psychoanalysis, Chicano literature, homoerotic cultural production in Peru, and Andean cinema. His most recent publications are an article on the Peruvian film *The Milk of Sorrow*, published in *Revista iberoamericana* (2017), and an article on the poetry of Eduardo Atilio Romano, an author of the Argentine Northwest, published in the *Hispanic Studies Review* (2018).

Notes

1   The film starts when the young Karamakate meets Theo Von Martius and his translator, Manduka. The German is looking for a cure for his disease. He needs the help of the Cohiauno shaman, who knows the secrets of the yakruna plant. Theo must take Karamakate to a town where the yakruna grows. From that moment Theo will take part in an initiation ceremony (Ayahuasca) with Karamakate. They travel to different towns. In one, Theo gives away his compass. Later they arrive at the Misión of Vaupes, run by the Capuchin order. There Karamakate tells the Indigenous children the legend of the chiricaspi plant in their language. Afterward a priest physically punishes the kids, and the characters need to run. Finally, they arrive in the town where yakruna grows. Karamakate, however, has other intentions. He burns out all the yakruna plants after realizing that they are cultivated by the Indigenous people and are not found growing wild. Moreover, they are used by the Natives as a hallucinogenic drug for entertainment and not for curative purposes. This seals Theo's fate. In 1940, now an old man, Karamakate meets the American biologist Evan. He too is looking for the yakruna plant to take it to the United States and find his own cure. They set out for the Workshop of the Gods, a hill where the last yakruna plant is believed to exist. Before they reach the sacred hill, they come to the Misión of Vaupes, which the Capuchins have abandoned. There they are imprisoned by the onetime Native kids of the original Misión," who as adults live in a dystopian community run by a former Brazilian priest who believes himself the Messiah. They escape after Karamakate poisons a drink used during a group ceremony with a hallucinogenic plant. Finally,

Karamakate wants to remedy the mistake he made with Theo. He decides to bequeath Evan all his Cohiauno knowledge. For this to happen, they need to organize an Ayahuasca ceremony at the Workshop of the Gods. There Evan symbolically becomes a Cohiauno warrior. After he wakes from the ceremony the next day, Evan starts looking for Karamakate but does not find him.

2   Koch-Grünberg, *Indianertypen*; Schultes, *Where the Gods Reign*. Schultes's expedition took place in 1942–43, but the book was published in 1988.

3   Lotman, *La semiósfera I*, 14. All translations from the Spanish are my own.

4   Rojas Hernández, "Cine de arte y ensayo en Colombia," 17. See also Luna, "Los viajes transnacionales del cine colombiano."

5   Foucault, "Of Other Spaces," 24–27.

6   Luna, "Los viajes transnacionales del cine colombiano," 71.

7   In the context of global capitalism, there is a trend to find more authentic life experiences to make them part of an expanding market. These experiences are inserted into the circulation of global goods under the tag of primitive authentic events. I can mention different examples, such as the pet food that makes dogs become wolves; the Paleo diet, which helps you lose weight but is inspired by the diet of the people of the Paleolithic; the ceremony of Ayahuasca that takes place in the United States or in Europe and is conducted by real Indigenous shamans from South America; or the visualization of films that reproduce the lives of aboriginals in different corners of the world and include the use of Native languages instead of Spanish, English, or other Western languages.

8 Abiayala is the Indigenous name for the American continents. In the Indigenous Guna language from Panama, it means "land in its full maturity." It is a name intended to replace the Western names of "America," the "Americas," or the more partial "Latin America" (Cárcamo-Huechante, "Lenguas, lenguajes y literaturas de Abiayala," 6).

9 Ochoa Gautier, *Aurality*, 13.

10 Castro-Gómez, *La hybris del punto cero*, 15.

11 Pizarro, "El trabajador del caucho y la representación narrativa," 316.

12 *Cohiuano* is a fictional Indigenous name.

13 Bustos, "The Healing Power of the Icaros," 10. Bustos refers to Luna, *Vegetalismo*, who in turn cites Arévalo, "El ayahuasca," for the meanings of *taquina*, *masha*, and *cusho*.

14 Bustos, "The Healing Power of the Icaros," 10.

15 Giore, "Acerca del Icaro o canto shamánico." Riccardo Badini observes in this genealogy of the Icaro that the shaman first receives the music and then the lyrics from the spirit of the plant or the animal in dreams or visions ("Reapropiación simbólica de la Ayahuasca," 179).

16 Giore, "Acerca del Icaro o canto shamánico," 7.

17 Badini, "Reapropiación simbólica de la Ayahuasca," 175.

18 Cornejo Polar, *Escribir en el aire*, 20.

19 Petroglyphs, as we have seen, play a role in *Embrace of the Serpent*. About landscapes, Rebecca Carte writes: "Landscapes were read by humans long before their inventions of signs and symbols. Landscapes had to be translated into signs and symbols" ("Translating Landscape and the Huarochirí Manuscript").

20 Arnold and Yapita, "The Nature of Indigenous Literatures in the Andes," 386.

21 His works are inspired by the ritual of the Ayahuasca. He is the father of another famous Huitoto artist, Rember Yahuarcani.

22 Badini, "Reapropiación simbólica de la Ayahuasca," 182.

23 In the film the names of different Amazon plants are stated, but only two are real names: that of chiricaspi (*Brunfelsia chiricaspi*) and caapi (*Banisteriopsis caapi*). As mentioned above, the name of yakruna is invented.

24 Most of this Amazon wisdom is transmitted through the Icaros, a musical dimension of knowledge. In addition, to transmit their knowledge, the Amazon people use petroglyphs, oral stories, and paintings.

25 Avendaño, "Estudio de los ícaros," 110.

26 Guillén, "Embrace of the Serpent."

27 See Bustos, "The Healing Power of the Icaros," 21.

28 Garrard, *Ecocriticism*, 124.

Works Cited

Arévalo, Guillermo. "El ayahuasca y el curandero Shipibo-Conibo del Ucayali (Perú)." *América indígena* 46, no. 1 (1986): 147–61.

Arnold, D. Y., and J. de D. Yapita. "The Nature of Indigenous Literatures in the Andes." In *Literary Cultures of Latin America: A Comparative History*, edited by M. Valdés and D. Kadir, 385–415. Oxford: Oxford University Press, 2004.

Avendaño, Diego. "Estudio de los ícaros: Dentro de los chamanes ayahuasqueros de la Amazonía." *Cáñamo: La revista de la cultura del cannabis*, no. 198 (2014): 108–12.

Badini, Riccardo. "Reapropiación simbólica de la Ayahuasca: Entre prácticas de representación y participación política." In *Pensamiento social italiano sobre América Latina*, edited by Stefano Tedeschi and Alessio Surian, 175–89. Buenos Aires: CLACSO, 2017.

Bustos, Susana. "The Healing Power of the Icaros: A Phenomenological Study of Ayahuasca Experiences." PhD diss., California Institute of Integral Studies, 2008.

Cárcamo-Huechante, Luis E. "Lenguas, lenguajes y literaturas de Abiayala: ¿Descolonizando o re-colonizando en la era del capital extractivista?" *LASA Forum* 50, no. 1 (2019): 6–10.

Carte, Rebecca. "Translating Landscape and the Huarochirí Manuscript." In *Hawansuyo: Poéticas indígenas y originarias*, 2012. hawansuyo.com/2012/09/10/translating-landscape-and-the-huarochiri-manuscript-rebecca-carte.

Castro-Gómez, Santiago. *La hybris del punto cero: Ciencia, raza e ilustración en la Nueva Granada (1750–1816)*. Bogotá: Editorial Pontificia Universidad Javeriana, 2005.

Cornejo Polar, Antonio. *Escribir en el aire: Ensayo sobre la heterogeneidad socio- cultural en las literaturas andinas*. Lima: CELACP, 2003.

Foucault, Michel. "Of Other Spaces." *Diacritics* 16, no. 1 (1986): 22–27.

Garrard, Greg. *Ecocriticism*. London: Routledge, 2011.

Giore, Rosa. "Acerca del Icaro o canto shamánico." *Revista Takiwasi* 1, no. 2 (1993): 7–27.

Guillén, Michael. "Embrace of the Serpent: An Interview with Ciro Guerra." *Cineaste*, 41, no. 2 (2016). www.cineaste.com/spring2016/embrace-of-the-serpent-ciro-guerra.

Koch-Grünberg, Theodor. *Indianertypen aus dem Amazonasgebiet nach eigenen Aufnahmen während seiner Reise in Brasilien*. Berlin: Wasmuth, 1906.

Lotman, Yuri. *La semiósfera I: Semiótica de la cultura y del texto*, translated by Desiderio Navarro. Madrid: Ediciones Cátedra, 1996.

Luna, L. E. *Vegetalismo: Shamanism among the mestizo population of the Peruvian Amazon.* Stockholm: Almqvist och Wiksell, 1986.

Luna, María. "Los viajes transnacionales del cine colombiano." *Archivos de la Filmoteca*, no. 71 (2013): 69–82.

Ochoa Gautier, Ana María. *Aurality: Listening and Knowledge in Nineteenth-Century Colombia.* Durham, NC: Duke University Press, 2014.

Pizarro, Ana. "El trabajador del caucho y la representación narrativa." *Cuadernos de literatura*, no. 37 (2015): 313–27.

Rojas Hernández, Eylin. "Cine de arte y ensayo en Colombia: *Los viajes del viento* (2009), *El vuelco del cangrejo* (2010), *La sirga* (2012), *Porfirio* (2012) y *La Playa D.C.* (2012)." *Revista Luciérnaga*, no. 14 (2015): 1–21.

Schultes, Richard Evans. *Where the Gods Reign: Plants and Peoples of the Colombian Amazon.* Oracle, AZ: Synergetic, 1988.

World(build)ing in Mohawk-
and Seneca-Language Films

PENELOPE KELSEY

Abstract   This essay brings Zayin Cabot's concept of "ecologies of participation" into conversation with contemporary Mohawk- and Seneca-language films and language revitalization movements. For Indigenous peoples, these participatory events are often interactive storying of worlds, whether told in film, social media, or oral tradition. As a particularly salient example, the essay considers Mohawk director Karahkwenhawi Zoe Hopkins's adaptation of *Star Wars: A New Hope* in *Star Wars Tsyorì:wat IV—Yonhská:neks* (2013) in a comparative analysis with both the Navajo-language *Star Wars: Episode IV* and the Seneca-language films *Kohgeh and Tših* to highlight critical choices Karahkwenhawi makes in translation, both linguistic and visual, vis-à-vis settler colonial consumer culture. The essay concludes that her adaptation foregrounds supposed "advances" of Western technocratic capitalism; highlights the constructed, fallible, and ephemeral nature of these technologies; and potentiates other technologies and ecologies based in Mohawk ontologies.

Keywords   ecology, Mohawk, Seneca, language, technology, Haudenosaunee

Recent trends in Iroquois use of social media have shown a movement toward inclusion of individuals formerly understood as outsiders (i.e., those with patrilineal descent) and thus non-Hodínöhšö:ni:h; these actions evince a desire to invite supposedly liminal figures to participate in worldmaking with other Iroquois with nations and clans, *and* point to Indigenous understandings of identity and ontology that disallow notions of "purity." From the Seneca Nation of Indians' use of Facebook and YouTube as platforms to promote and undertake Seneca-language study to the formation of social media groups hinging on "traditional teachings" that promote a transpatrilineal/matrilineal sociality, bonding, and equivalence, these examples ask us to consider more diverse theories of Iro-social engagement, including the framing of "ecologies of participation," a term coined by the linguist Zayin Cabot. In the case of this essay, I specifically consider participation across a range of Hodínöhšö:ni:h identities, experiences, and situations of living, and I contend that these digital deployments invite us to examine their revitalization of Hodínöhšö:ni:h conceptions of the natural world and their focus on Iroquois

ENGLISH LANGUAGE NOTES

58:1, April 2020   DOI 10.1215/00138282-8237531
© 2020 Regents of the University of Colorado

languages through the medium of film as expressive of a collective agency, one that reflects and moves beyond Cabot's theorization of Indigenous ontologies in ways that I outline in the following pages.[1]

In *Ecologies of Participation* Cabot studies both settler and Indigenous frameworks, seeking to find where their associated ontologies might "move [us] forward" out of our current "planetary predicament." Implicitly acknowledging his own postmodern and poststructuralist intellectual genealogy, an intellectual origin that cannot be assumed among Native American and Indigenous studies (NAIS) scholars, Cabot's eco-participatory vision rests on a multiple ontological approach in which we all "are made up of participatory events," and "our lived worlds are ecologies," and lack any ontologically pure "starting points."[2] Like the Shawnee linguist Thomas Norton-Smith, Cabot acknowledges that "words make worlds" and elaborates that "participatory events are the best we can do to construct explanations."[3] For Indigenous peoples, these participatory events are often interactive storying of worlds, or *worlding*, whether told in social media or oral tradition, and I seek to shed light on particular filmic expressions of the worlding process, as this medium has received scant attention and, hence, has been undertheorized by scholars outside of NAIS despite the tremendous outpouring of work by Indigenous directors in recent years.[4]

Considering a range of case studies, specifically recent Mohawk- and Seneca-language films, I argue that these films *enact* ecologies of participation and *confirm* Cabot's observation that no ontologies are ultimately superior to others. Simultaneously, I argue for not relinquishing our capacity to make value-based judgments regarding those ontologies' ecological impacts, and I refuse to cede the sovereign assessment of these films within Indigenous metrics (as opposed to prevailing settler rubrics) based on eco-ethics. That is, these filmic expressions ultimately embody practices of "visual sovereignty" as defined by the Seneca scholar Michelle H. Raheja; this is intellectual territory I refuse to cede in employing Cabot's theory of ecologies, as its equalizing reflex does not retain an eco-ethical frame per se.[5] I also contend that Cabot's ecologies of participation bear more than a passing resemblance to *tribal theory*, that is, modalities of strategically engaging Indigenous languages and cultures and encoding tribal worldviews and worldmaking into Western genres. These practices define and revitalize Indigenous knowledges through settler genres while resting on Indigenous narrative and linguistic traditions.

As a particularly salient example, I consider Mohawk director Karahkwenhawi Zoe Hopkins's adaptation of George Lucas's blockbuster *Star Wars: A New Hope* in *Star Wars Tsyoriꞏwat IV—Yonhskáꞏneks* (2013) in this essay.[6] Karahkwenhawi's lively and humorous adaptation of the *Star Wars* saga enacts worldmaking and ultimately embodies ecologies of participation and tribal theory, thereby imagining how humanity might recover from our current planetary crisis or, at the very least, connect with ecological philosophies that would prevent its recurrence. As a key step in apprehending such ecologies of participation, Cabot petitions us to seek a "participatory raft" as a way to imagine other worlds; I argue that Karahkwenhawi, language instructor Karonhyawake Jeff Doreen, and students of Onkwawenna Kentyohkwa, a two-year adult Mohawk-language immersion school, have done just that through calling on multiple ontologies, narrative trajectories, and especially epistemological traditions in these film episodes.[7] Further, the trope of the raft resonates with the Hodínöhšö:ni:h creation story and Sky Woman's search for a place to land to begin the world that became Turtle Island. Thus we can consider the raft as constitutive of the basis from which all else is possible, much like Turtle's willingness to serve as the foundation for the earth that Beaver retrieves and that Sky Woman dances into a continent; this entire process reflects a participatory engagement of ecologies and ontologies and thus Hodínöhšö:ni:h philosophies. This symphony of ontologies, narratives, and epistemologies originates from numerous sources and embodies an interconnected storytelling methodology, one based in Kanien'keha language in conversation with settler ontologies, disarming pathological aspects of settler colonial narratives and advancing Indigenous ecocentric epistemes. In this regard I depart from Cabot, who ultimately argues for a value-free leveling of difference between Indigenous and settler ontologies; instead, I remain invested in identifying what we can learn from Indigenous strategies for invoking and reinflecting settler forms and genres, while incorporating Cabot's concept of ecologies of participation. Finally, in Karahkwenhawi's selective use of dialogue and events from Lucas's original, her Mohawk *Star Wars* sharply outlines indispensable and otherwise irretrievable concepts, rendering visible ontologies that viewers might otherwise be unable to see.

It is important to note that a Mohawk-language *Star Wars* film is possible only through Mohawk communities' historical relationships to technology, that is, through decisions made by individuals as part of a larger web of clans and nations, bands and social networks, and ultimately arising from and supported by a process of consensus that predates contact. In contrast, until recently it would have been nearly impossible to imagine a Seneca-language version of *Star Wars*, because each of the Iroquois nations has its own historical relationship to technology and its own widely varying policies about circulating their languages in electronic fora. While Mohawk people have allowed the recording and circulation of their language for roughly fifty years, Senecas—until quite recently—have had a uniform policy of not allowing the Seneca language to be recorded in any format. Facebook has been a space for criticism of Seneca-language recordings and use in social media, YouTube, and the Seneca Nation of Indians (SNI) website: specifically, some targets of critique have included SNI's Language Department practices, among them the creation of Seneca-language tools placed before the public eye in venues like senecalanguage.com, an SNI-language website and online repository. One key observation regarding these marked differences is that the policies of protection and exclusivity have been necessitated in Seneca communities and that different policies of language circulation and dissemination have emerged in Mohawk communities situated at the eastern door of the Iroquois Confederacy. Thus these communities face a more imminent threat of language assault; ergo, each situation has led to different outcomes. Owing to these differing histories and trajectories, each nation has made distinctive decisions and crafted language policies and practices based on the needs of its own communities. Invariably, Mohawk-language speakers and instructors have taken a much more public, more visible, and less protectionist role in their language use; a correlative would be allowing outsiders into the Kahnawake longhouse, which functions as both a public and a ceremonial space. For Senecas, the traditional teaching that the language is a living entity and should never be recorded has led to a more cautious relationship with media; in addition, violations of longhouse protocol by non-Native anthropologists who recorded ceremonies without permission midcentury punctuated this reticence.

Into this context for Mohawk language and media design enters Karahkwen-hawi Zoe Hopkins, a Kanien'keha-language instructor, writer, and filmmaker. On beginning and completing her two-year training at Onkwawenna Kentyohkwa in 2011 and 2013, Karahkwenhawi was interviewed by Owennatekha Brian Maracle, language instructor and founder of the school, in a YouTube video titled "Zoe Hopkins Before & After."[8] Impressively, after her two-year study Karahkwenhawi is fluent in the language. When asked what she wants to do now that her training is concluding, Karahkwenhawi is clear that her ultimate goal is to work at the school as a teacher and to create Mohawk-language films and books: "That's what I want; that's why I studied our language." Since the completion of this film in 2013, Karahkwenhawi's career trajectory has encompassed a steady stream of Mohawk-language films, such as *Sky World* and *Goldilocks*, in addition to online course design and instruction, and it is not surprising that her body of work provides ample material for understanding *ecologies of participation* and worldmaking (as in "words make worlds") in a contemporary Mohawk context.[9] Karahkwenhawi's *Star Wars Tsyori:wat IV—Yonhská:neks* (2013) functions on many levels as a précis or synopsis of *Star Wars: A New Hope* (1977), yet, in its elision of portions of dialogue and events from the Lucas original, the film elevates overlooked concepts—that is, brings to the surface subsumed ontologies that are otherwise invisibilized. In so doing, these exposed ontologies enact ecologies of participation, thus activating worldmaking and crafting new forms of existence not previously imagined (or identified) as Mohawk pop cultural in settler visual culture (fig. 1). The plot elements that Karahkwenhawi's film retains and subsequently highlights include the following: Leia's recorded message to Obi Wan Kenobi; Owen's purchase of the droids C3PO and R2D2; the recognition scene where Luke brings R2 to Ben Kenobi; the playing of Leia's message; Luke's Jedi training under Obi Wan; the burning of Uncle Owen and Aunt Beru's homestead; the cantina scene; the death of Obi Wan; Luke's destruction of the Death Star; and the closing celebration and presentation of medals.[10] The result is a shorthand, Morse-type transmission or remixing of Lucas's *Star Wars* universe into a Mohawk ontology—or, better yet, cosmology—that marks Earth, Alderaan, or any other planet as merely a stopping point on a much longer journey; this envisioning centralizes Hodínöhšö:ni:h philosophies and ontologies to such a degree that Lucas's original work is barely identifiable to the informed—that is, Mohawk—eye.[11]

What exactly do Mohawk-language *Star Wars* videos do for us, meaning both Mohawk and/or Indigenous, and settler and/or arrivant viewers? On the face of it, these films, most important, show contemporary Mohawk people engaging with and *generating* popular culture. In so doing, they refuse stereotypes of Indigenous

Figure 1. Karahkwenhawi Zoe Hopkins as Princess Leia Organa recording a message to R2D2 in *Star Wars Tsyorì:wat IV—Yonhská: neks*, 2013.

peoples as sealed in the past and separated from a common temporality. The existence of these films establishes for non-Natives that Indigenous peoples have an investment and vital presence in popular culture. The 2013 release of a Navajo-language dubbed version of *Star Wars* provides an important point of comparison. Manuelito Wheeler, director of the Navajo Nation Museum, explains his nation's own motivation for creating the film: "We needed a way to preserve our culture. Language is at the core of a culture. And I felt we needed a more contemporary way to reach not just young people but the population in general."[12] Wheeler notes that Navajo is "very descriptive, very descriptive." He says: "If you ask for an object in Navajo you will know you'll be getting a round object, you'll be getting a skinny, soft object, you'll be getting a flat rigid object. So, the trick was choosing from the variety of definitions that the group came up with." One example of a challenging word to translate is *robot*. Wheeler observes, "It's a thinking machine; a machine that thinks for itself." Manuelito's wife Jennifer Wheeler elaborates, "R2-D2 would be the short metal thing that's alive."[13] Thus there are important choices to be made about language, and the five Navajo translators who dubbed the film opted for neologisms. To begin, in interpreting the script for *Star Wars Tsyorì:wat IV—Yonhská:neks*, Karahkwenhawi chose to not translate proper nouns (and the worlds associated with them), like *Corellian ships* and *Corellia*, while translating the generic word for *ship* as "fast bird"; these choices suggest an investment in maintaining everyday Mohawk and ensuring its use while highlighting the untranslatability of commodified Western "technology" and perhaps embedding a critique in these highlighted differences. Moving beyond the realm of the commodifiable in the nexus of values created by Lucas (e.g., see Leia's dismissal of Solo for his sole focus on material reward), the word for "the Force" is provided in the Mohawk language and translated as "the great power."[14] This translation suggests that there is an overlap between the concept of the Force and Hodínöhšö:ni:h traditional spiritual belief, insofar as it *is* translatable.[15] At the same time, Karahkwenhawi incorporates Western technology in her Mohawk world-building process, but she underscores her engagement of multiple ontological sources by *not* translating branded Western products or the worlds from which they originate, most notably those related to transportation. A reading of *Star Wars Tsyorì:wat IV—Yonhská:neks* focused on its ecologies of participation reveals the constructed nature of Lucas's vision and normativizes Indigenous peoples who might otherwise be viewed as

Figure 2. Karahkwenhawi Zoe
Hopkins as Han Solo in the same
scene, 2013.

limited to a past (not future) existence; further, these Native peoples bear an ecological vision that emanates from an Indigenized force that ultimately guides them to save humanity even in the face of their own home's destruction.

Karahkwenhawi's *Star Wars Tsyorì:wat IV—Yonhská:neks* uses humor as a key storytelling method in portraying Indigenous existence and offering a "participatory raft," as Cabot terms it, to help viewers grasp its narrative and representations. The strategic use of humor takes on numerous forms that enact a particularly Mohawk ecology of participation, one that engages Western ontologies of the sci-fi genre and highlights the not-yet-internalized, or ambivalently embraced, nature of the technologies that are its givens. Perhaps the most immediately noticeable use of humor is the constant substitution of key actors (i.e., Karahkwenhawi, Karonhyawake) into new, sometimes gender-bending roles, changes that may occur multiple times in a scene. Karahkwenhawi alternately plays Owen, Obi Wan, and Han, and in the cantina scene Karahkwenhawi plays both Obi Wan and Han as they negotiate for Kenobi and Skywalker's passage to Alderaan (figs. 2–3). Karahkwenhawi enacts Solo's masculine bravado to a T, all while speaking across the table to herself in a very fake white beard as Kenobi; Solo's braggadocio is immediately deflated in the next scene, which cuts to Solo, Leia, Chewbacca, and C3PO running to a Toyota Millennium van to make their escape. Karahkwenhawi and her coproducers also deploy the ludicrous use of "special effects," which include hand puppets for droids, balloons for the Death Star, and hand-drawn sound effects ("Katonh!"); the similarly arch use of the Star Wars theme as hummed by Karahkwenhawi; the flippant use of

Figure 3. Karahkwenhawi Zoe
Hopkins as Obi Wan in the cantina
scene, 2013.

Figure 4. Karonhyawake Jeff Doreen as Luke Skywalker flying a go-kart as an X-wing snubfighter.

"tighty-whities" and white T-shirts as key elements in the stormtrooper costumes; similar use of children's four-wheeled toys as jet fighters by adult actors; a stuffed snake for the serpentine monster in the trash compactor scene; the continual use of everyday items as "technology" in the film, including a 1960s film projector for Leia's recorded message to Obi Wan, the use of a row of institutional water heaters to portray the computers on the Death Star, and the inside of a garage door for the wall of the trash compactor (figs. 4–5). Having key actors play multiple roles in the same scene and throughout the movie signifies on countless levels. I will briefly analyze one example for readers who are curious: the play of gender in having an Indigenous woman enact multiple white and masculine-coded characters in the same scene, from the masculine bravado of Solo to the aged and bearded wizard character of Kenobi, a scene in which they are power-brokering and negotiating for passage to Alderaan, hyperbolizing that masculinity while lampooning it, commenting on settler colonial patriarchy's futile efforts to disenfranchise Native women. Solo's character becomes even more comical than normal in its swaggering self-presumption, and Kenobi's fetishized, enshrined sagacity also collapses as we peer through a clearly glued-on beard at him or her. Further, Karahkwenhawi's role in both directorial and performative modes gestures to its own sutures in a self-aware critique of the constructed nature of settler masculinities it redeploys as part of its sovereign vision.

Karahkwenhai's self-reflexive use of technology points to the constructed nature of settler modernity and embeds in the films a critique of its ephemerality;

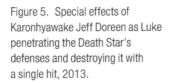

Figure 5. Special effects of Karonhyawake Jeff Doreen as Luke penetrating the Death Star's defenses and destroying it with a single hit, 2013.

further, its easy rupture and manipulation allow for expressions of Mohawk world building that exceed the late capitalistic moment of environmental collapse. Thus Karahkwenhawi's *Star Wars Tsyorì:wat IV—Yonhská:neks* actually highlights the presence of multiple, differing worlds, and the film's script punctuates it with the destruction of Leia's home planet Alderaan. If words make worlds, then the complex decisions made around translation in the film signal the nuanced means by which the world building in Karahkwenhawi's film is effected. An attentive viewing establishes that the director and actors lampoon the Lucas film and undercut its cultural capital even as they enact and affirm it. These ecologies of participation have many potentials: the clear reading that emerges is a built world that rearticulates and subsumes the futuristic vision of Lucas's saga, centralizing the Indigenous peoples who might be read as rebels, those guided by a force larger than themselves for the sake of "saving the planet," even as they watch their own planet, Alderaan, obliterated with few survivors.[16]

Further, the collective belief in the intrinsic values of resisting evil and refusing personal gain for the benefit of the greater good runs throughout both the original film by Lucas and the new episodes filmed by Karahkwenhawi; in fact, as has already been suggested, this value is a constant source of strife between Leia and Han Solo.[17] Simultaneously illustrating the complex positioning of Indigenous ontologies, Zoe's portrayal of Leia retains the Hopi-style circular braids adopted by Lucas, an aspect of her costume historically critiqued by Native American film scholars for a host of nuanced reasons. Thus Karahkwenhawi's rendition affirms that there are no pure ontologies, as per Cabot, crafting characters who embody both mimicry and performativity and engaging conversations about Native subjectivity and representation already in play. Karahkwenhawi's costume choice might also be read as an empowered claiming of this appropriation of Native women's hairstyles by an actor who, in this case, is actually Indigenous, though not Hopi: like many Indigenous cultures, Hodínöhšö:ni:h peoples also have traditions specific to young women "under the husk," as yet unwed, and Karahkwenhawi's choice might be interpreted as claiming this status in a way that is legible, or at least visible, to non-Native viewers.[18]

We can perhaps gain a greater understanding of Karahkwenhawi's *Star Wars Tsyorì:wat IV—Yonhská:neks* by placing it in dialogue with other Iroquois-language films. One distinctive example of Seneca creativity in film that reflects the Seneca Nation of Indians' recent embrace of recording technology is *Kohgeh and Tśih* (2017, 2018); *Kohgeh and Tśih* comprises four episodes to date and is produced by the Seneca Nation of Indians Allegany Language Department as part of their "Ruppets" series. These Seneca-language films use hand-rod puppets à la Sesame Street with Kohgeh playing a Burt-type bear character and Tśih (Tśihsedéjih) playing a humorous human neophyte whose name suggests that he literally was born this morning. Thus Kohgeh, a Seneca Nation of Indians employee, must continually explain "everything" to Tśih, including how to open the doors to the community center. In their first meeting Kohgeh must rescue Tśih from getting lost in the woods and drives out into the country to retrieve him. The directors of *Kohgeh and Tśih* at the Seneca Nation of Indians are clearly intervening in the childhood imaginary and appealing to Onödowá'ga:' children learning the language. The world building involved in *Kohgeh and Tših* resonates with past popular television shows like *Sesame Street* and attempts to render these ontologies in light of Seneca knowledges. In an NPR interview, Rosemarie Truglio, senior vice president of curriculum and content at Sesame Workshop, identifies the show's goals as diversity and inclusivity; further, *Sesame Street* is a place where the producers "want all children to see themselves."[19] Like *Sesame Street*, the Kohgeh and Tših videos send a message that "we're all different, but we're all the same," articulating inclusion as a goal tied to both *Sesame Street*'s legacy and to Hodínöhšö:ni:h community ideals. The efforts here seek to appeal to a younger audience and build a seamless experience of an all-Seneca-language environment; examples of individuals to whom this might appeal include students at the all-Seneca-language Faithkeepers School. In many cases, these students benefit from all-day Seneca-language instruction but return home to parents and siblings who are not fluent speakers. Thus these films represent an attempt to support the Seneca-language world building that they participate in throughout their day.

In Karahkwenhawi's world, however, there is a visible and audible expression of an ongoing and acute awareness of contact and colonialism: rather than blend seamlessly and create an impression of an always already Western technological presence, as the directors of *Kohgeh and Tših* do with technology like phones, cars, and security doors, Karahkwenhawi insists on foregrounding these supposed "advances" of Western technocratic capitalism. In some ways, these efforts in world building resonate with Karahkwenhawi's endeavor, which is an outgrowth of her work as a language instructor at a Mohawk immersion school for adults. By highlighting the constructed, fallible, and ephemeral nature of these technologies, Karahkwenhawi potentiates other technologies and ecologies based in Mohawk ontologies. There is an innocence that *Kohgeh and Tših* understandably turns on, given its intended audience; yet, while the scriptwriters do not foreground technology as artificial by situationally obviating the need to translate those terms, they do portray Tših as confused by a film camera in a self-referential way and injuring his eye on the SNI retinal scanner on his first day of work. Thus both *Kohgeh and Tših* and *Star Wars Tsyorì:wat* foreground colonialism and capitalism with different strategies and different chronotypes. *Kohgeh and Tših* enacts ecologies of participation that are multi-ontological and that blend Western and Seneca ontologies in pivotal ways, while *Star Wars Tsyorì:wat IV—Yonhská:neks* often sutures multiple ontologies together in telling (non)translations rather than synthesize them without a trace. For instance, the discourse surrounding the Force, an imagined "ancient religion" described by Lucas in the film series, is guided and inflected by Karahkwenhawi and students at Onkwawenna Kentyohkwa who directed and produced the film so as to lead viewers to read the Force potentially as an expression of traditional longhouse belief while refusing entry to knowledge of longhouse practices. Thus the Force, like the Good Mind, instructs in the necessity of living in balance, maintaining a connection to this power's origin, and embodying an ethos that moves beyond the individual.

Ultimately, despite their own situational differences, both *Star Wars Tsyorì:wat IV—Yonhská:neks* and *Kohgeh and Tših* embody aspects of world building contingent on the epistemologies inherent within Mohawk and Seneca languages. In *Talking Indian* Anna Lee Walters writes about the worlds made possible by Otoe- and Pawnee-language environments, lamenting the severing of her connection to Pawnee worlds when she is sent away to school. Walters defines the power of words in worlding and creation, invoking Otoe and Pawnee oral traditions simultaneously: "This is where everything began. This is where these words began. This is where creation began. This is where time began. This is where the people began."[20] Walters is clear that Otoe and Pawnee languages are distinct and unrelated, yet in her description both oral traditions create worlds in ways that can be reduced to a common process. The storyteller and audience are part of a shared world building and act as participants in multiple ecologies of participation; similarly, both *Star Wars Tsyorì:wat IV—Yonhská:neks* and *Kohgeh and Tših* perform Hodínöhšö:ni:h world building through their utterance of Iroquois languages and their fashioning of new visual representations of Mohawk and Seneca peoples. In discussing differences between Native and non-Native views of the world, the Native American philosopher Viola Cordova tells us that Indigenous worlding frustrates any desire for the "universal-absolute"; in fact, Indigenous worldviews and world building refuse to confirm any single, all-encompassing truth.[21] At the same time, *Star Wars Tsyorì:wat IV—Yonhská:neks* and *Kohgeh and Tših* both perform worlds based in Indigenous epistemes and borrow handy tools from settler society, confirming that these ecologies of participation encompass ways of being in the world that are porous and possessive of multiple origins. Ultimately, what we gain from these examples is multiple windows into Indigenous worlds where Indigenous actors and producers render themselves seen and visible, challenging the always already seen nature of rigid representations of Indigenous peoples. Like Sky Woman, the stories these films tell give us a place on which to stand, a "participatory raft" in Cabot's conception; from here, worlds unfold, worlds brought into being through the careful crafting of language and engagement of ontologies.

PENELOPE KELSEY (Seneca descent) is professor and founding director of the Center for Native American and Indigenous Studies at the University of Colorado Boulder. Her books include *Tribal Theory* (2008) and *Reading the Wampum* (2014), and her current work considers Indigenous languages and settler colonial weaponization of food.

Notes

1   Throughout this essay I want to acknowledge my own position as a person of Seneca descent and thank Terry Jones, who provided vital feedback during the drafting process. I highlight differences in language policies among Hodínöhšö:ni:h communities because they provide critical context for understanding the evolution of film technology in each nation and because they may provide helpful information to other communities facing similar decisions and challenges around language revitalization. Bringing our minds together as one is an English translation of part of the Thanksgiving or Opening Address, and it reflects the motives of the founders of this Facebook group, which makes it an appropriate designation.

2   Cabot, *Ecologies of Participation*, 3–8.

3   Cabot, *Ecologies of Participation*, 3–5.

4   I use *worlding* here as an innovation on prior work done by Sander Gilman and others in the field and more specifically by James Clifford, Christopher Leigh Connery, David Watson, Rob

Wilson, and other contributors to *The Worlding Project*. Growing out of the University of California, Santa Cruz's, World Literature and Cultural Studies group and its discussions of a "transnationalized cultural studies," *The Worlding Project* edited collection, Watson says, is "a creative and critical blend of art and politics that suggests a whole new way to globalize" (Wilson and Connery, *The Worlding Project*, x). Yet this project remains bound in one particular world, one particular planet, with the exception of sole contribution on Indigenous topics by Clifford, who in defining "articulated sites of indigeneity" discusses Indigenous histories' having "roots prior to and outside the world system" (17). Clifford's analysis, however, remains rooted in just one world, one planet, despite indigenous histories' recounting of migrations from other worlds and other planets/realms. Yet Clifford does anticipate the focus of this essay in observing how, despite the loss of their languages, Indigenous peoples continue to survive without what are perceived as "critical organs," akin to their "heart or lungs" (24). In fact, Indigenous peoples do survive and also use film as a vehicle to recover their languages and associated knowledges.

5   Raheja writes, "Native people have been engaging in 'visual sovereignty' since the beginning of time through the present as a means of understanding the world and representing varied experiences of life" ("Visual Sovereignty," 29).

6   In deference to Iroquois naming practices, after first giving individuals' Hodínöhšö:ni:h and Ga:nyö'öka:' names, I refer to them exclusively by their Indigenous names.

7   Students and instructors at Onkwawenna Kentyohkwa are credited with acting in and producing both extant episodes of *Star Wars Tsyori:wat IV—Yonhská:neks*.

8   Onkwawenna Kentyohkwa, "Zoe Hopkins Before & After."

9   Martell, "Immersion Key to Retaining Language, Says Zoe Hopkins."

10   It should also be noted that Hopkins and Okwawenna Kentyohkwa have created a briefer Mohawk-language adaptation of the trash compactor scene. While this is not the focus of my essay, I will discuss where its strategic use of humor overlaps with the longer film.

11   See Navas, Gallagher, and burrough, *Keywords in Remix Studies*, for further discussions of the significance of remixing in racial representations.

12   National Public Radio, "The Force Is with the Navajo."

13   Trudeau, "Translated into Navajo, *Star Wars* Will Be."

14   Karahkwenhawi Zoe Hopkins, email to author, June 18, 2019.

15   Even so, Karahkwenhawi shares that there was a genuine struggle to translate "light saber" into Mohawk ("it is his" vs. "it used to be his"), as first-language speakers of Mohawk were "confounded" by her initial choice to use the definite form of the verb: "I puzzled then about ownership and possession of things" (email to author, June 20, 2019).

16   The following query from Senator Leia Organa to another senator speaks directly to Indigenous themes and world building: "What act of terror could be more horrible than what happened to Alderaan? Have you forgotten that? I was there. I saw it happen, stood there watching while they destroyed my world, my home, everyone I had ever loved—"

17   This imperviousness to corruption and commitment to the common good are the metrics by which candidates for *royaner* (or Chiefs' offices) are evaluated before selection by Clan Mothers, who "stand up" the candidates.

18   Katsitsionni Fox's film *Oherok:on: Under the Husk* (2016) documents the movement led by Bear Clan Mother Louise MacDonald at Akwesasne Reserve to reclaim this tradition for young people in her community.

19   Cornish, "Fifty Years Young."

20   Walters, *Talking Indian*, 21.

21   Moore et al., *How It Is*, 69.

Works Cited

Cabot, Zayin. *Ecologies of Participation: Agents, Shamans, Mystics, and Diviners.* Boulder, CO: Lexington, 2018.

Cornish, Audie. "Fifty Years Young: How the Music of 'Sesame Street' Keeps Up with the Times." National Public Radio, June 10, 2019. www.npr.org/2019/06/10/731284296/50-years-young-how-the-music-of-sesame-street-keeps-up-with-the-times.

Martell, Creeden. "Immersion Key to Retaining Language, Says Zoe Hopkins." *Saskatoon Star Phoenix*, November 26, 2015. thestarphoenix.com/news/local-news/immersion-key-to-retaining-language-says-zoe-hopkins.

Moore, Kathleen Dean, Kurt Peters, Ted Jojola, and Amber Lacy. *How It Is: The Native American Philosophy of V. F. Cordova.* Tucson: University of Arizona Press, 1994.

National Public Radio. "The Force Is with the Navajo: *Star Wars* Gets a New Translation." *All Things Considered*, June 5, 2013. www.npr.org /sections/codeswitch/2013/07/03/188676416 /star-wars-in-navajo.

Navas, Eduardo, Owen Gallagher, and xtine burrough, eds. *Keywords in Remix Studies*. New York: Routledge, 2018.

Onkwawenna Kentyohkwa. "Zoe Hopkins Before & After." YouTube. Uploaded January 21, 2015. www.youtube.com/watch?v=ItpFw9opTJ4.

Raheja, Michelle H. "Visual Sovereignty." In *Native Studies Keywords*, edited by Stephanie Nohelani Teves, Andrea Smith, and Michelle H. Raheja, 25–34. Tucson: University of Arizona Press, 2015.

Trudeau, Christine. "Translated into Navajo, *Star Wars* Will Be." *National Public Radio's Morning Edition*, June 20, 2013. www.npr.org/2013/06 /20/193496493/translated-into-navajo-star -wars-will-be.

Walters, Anna Lee. *Talking Indian: Reflections on Survival and Writing*. Ithaca, NY: Firebrand, 1992.

Wilson, Rob, and Christopher Leigh Connery, eds. *The Worlding Project: Doing Cultural Studies in the Era of Globalization*. Santa Cruz, CA: New Pacific Press, 2007.

Keep up to date on new scholarship

Issue alerts are a great way to stay current on all the cutting-edge scholarship from your favorite Duke University Press journals. This free service delivers tables of contents directly to your inbox, informing you of the latest groundbreaking work as soon as it is published.

To sign up for issue alerts:

1. Visit **dukeu.press/register** and register for an account. You do not need to provide a customer number.

2. After registering, visit **dukeu.press/alerts**.

3. Go to "Latest Issue Alerts" and click on "Add Alerts."

4. Select as many publications as you would like from the pop-up window and click "Add Alerts."

read.dukeupress.edu/journals